ABRAHAM LINCOLN   *A History*

CLASSIC AMERICAN HISTORIANS

Paul M. Angle, GENERAL EDITOR

ABRAHAM

────────────────────────── *A HISTORY*

LINCOLN

by John G. Nicolay
and John Hay

abridged and edited by Paul M. Angle

THE UNIVERSITY OF CHICAGO PRESS   *Chicago & London*

Abraham Lincoln: A History was first published in book form in ten volumes by the Century Company, after having been serialized in the *Century* from November, 1886, through May, 1890.

Library of Congress Catalog Card Number: 66-20590
THE UNIVERSITY OF CHICAGO PRESS, CHICAGO & LONDON
The University of Toronto Press, Toronto 5, Canada
Published 1966. Printed in the United States of America

General Editor's Preface

FEW TODAY read the great American historians. Few can. If a reader limited himself to those chosen for inclusion in this series —Prescott, Parkman, Bancroft, McMaster, Moses Coit Tyler, Henry Adams, Nicolay and Hay, and Rhodes—he would find himself straining his eyes eight hours a day for at least a year. This, in the modern world, is an impossible requirement.

Yet that the works of these men should remain unknown is deplorable. Something is better than nothing. From that conviction this series was born. But what should that "something" be? A series of condensations? How can one condense the sixteen volumes of Parkman, or the nine volumes of Henry Adams, into one volume without doing inexcusable violence to the whole? On the other hand, representative selections, each of substantial length, can convey a good idea of point of view, breadth of treatment, narrative skill, and style. This was the method chosen.

After this choice was made, the general editor came across a relevant pronouncement which John Hay made during the serialization of *Abraham Lincoln: A History*. "The only question," Hay wrote to Richard Watson Gilder, editor of the *Century*, "is whether you want the Life to run three years or four. If the former, you must take heroic measures. Leaving out a chapter here and there, or retrenching an adjective, will do no good. . . . You must cut great chunks of topics out. . . . Neither

Nicolay nor I can write the work over again for the purpose of saving a half chapter here and there." Nor, we submit, can anyone else.

The books in this series were designed for reading, not research. All documentation has, therefore, been eliminated. Editors of individual volumes have used their discretion in retaining expository footnotes. Such footnotes as they have added are identified by their initials. The typographical style, punctuation, and spelling of the original texts have been followed.

PAUL M. ANGLE

Introduction

ON May 18, 1860, Abraham Lincoln was nominated as the Republican candidate for the presidency of the United States. He soon discovered that he would need help in answering the flood of mail that poured in upon him. His friend and political associate Ozias M. Hatch, Illinois Secretary of State, recommended a young man from his own office, John George Nicolay, for the position of private secretary. Lincoln agreed, and Nicolay was installed in the Illinois State House, in which Lincoln had been given quarters suited to his new dignity.

Before the summer was over, Nicolay saw the need for an assistant. The choice fell upon John Hay, then studying law in the office of his uncle, Milton Hay, in Springfield. In this informal manner, without benefit of political pressures, Nicolay and Hay became the secretaries, and intimates, of Abraham Lincoln.

When Lincoln left Springfield for Washington on February 11, 1861, both young men accompanied him. After the inauguration they took up quarters in the White House—the Executive Mansion, as it was then called—Nicolay as the President's private secretary, Hay as his assistant.

Neither had the political experience that their positions would call for today. Nicolay had been born in Bavaria in 1832, and had been brought to the United States by his parents when he was six years old. His formal education equaled Lincoln's—a year altogether—but he had the advantage of several years in the office of the *Free Press* of Pittsfield, Illinois, as printer's devil, typesetter, and, finally, editor and publisher. In 1856 he sold the paper to move to Springfield and enter the office of the newly elected Secretary of State, his fellow townsman.

John Hay, in 1860, was twenty-one years old. His education, however, was vastly superior to Nicolay's. Hay had attended an academy at Pittsfield and a jejune college at Springfield, but had entered Brown University as a sophomore and had graduated from that institution in 1858. After a few unhappy months in Warsaw, Illinois, which he considered typical of the "barbarous West," he undertook to study law, an occupation which had little interest for him, in Springfield.

In Washington, Nicolay and Hay, young as they were, soon saw that they occupied a unique position. The Civil War would certainly be a time of trial second to no other in the history of the country. The war, moreover, had its focus in the White House, where they were privy to all that went on. Both quickly recognized the elements of greatness in Lincoln. Together, when the time came, they would write the record of the nation's supreme agony. To this end, with Lincoln's approval, both men made preparations. Hay kept a diary, though only intermittently, and Nicolay made many memoranda of conversations and events.[1]

Toward the end of Lincoln's first term, Nicolay and Hay both sought escape from Washington. The war was drawing to a close, and with its end they saw that the White House would cease to be the place of high excitement they had known for four years. Besides, their relations with Mrs. Lincoln, never happy, were becoming increasingly difficult. In March, 1865,

---

[1] Tyler Dennett, ed., *Lincoln and the Civil War in the Diaries and Letters of John Hay* (New York: Dodd, Mead, 1939). Many of Nicolay's memoranda are referred to, sometimes without identification, in *Abraham Lincoln: A History;* some are quoted in Helen Nicolay, *Lincoln's Secretary: A Biography of John G. Nicolay* (New York: Longmans, Green, 1949).

Hay obtained an appointment as secretary to the American legation in Paris. Shortly before Lincoln's second inauguration the president appointed Nicolay United States consul in Paris. In an unusual tribute, the Senate confirmed the nomination the same day.

With the exception of several visits to the United States, Hay remained abroad until 1870, serving successively as United States chargé d'affaires at Vienna and as secretary of legation at Madrid. In the latter post he collected the impressions that he embodied in his engaging and durable book of travel *Castilian Days*. Nicolay, removed by the Grant administration, returned to the United States in 1869.

Both men were approaching middle age, yet neither had an occupation or a goal in life. Nicolay, in poor health, tried to regain his strength in Florida. In 1870 he spent three months in Chicago as editor of a new newspaper, the *Chicago Republican*—the proprietors doubted the orthodoxy of the *Chicago Tribune!*—but the venture faltered. Nicolay, still plagued by ill health, resigned. Again he tried to recuperate in Florida, then in New Hampshire, and finally on a small farm on the outskirts of Springfield, Illinois. In December, 1872, the United States Supreme Court rescued him from aimlessness and frustration by appointing him its marshal, a post which carried with it a comfortable office in the capitol, a modest but adequate salary, "and," as he put it, "not too much hard work."

When Hay returned to the United States he expected to take a position, under Nicolay, on the *Chicago Republican*, but the paper failed before he reached Chicago. Turning to New York, he became night editor and editorial writer on the *New York Tribune*, but a year after his marriage in 1874 to Clara L. Stone, a wealthy young woman of Cleveland, he gave up journalism for good. He was now free to pursue his literary interests and to undertake, with Nicolay, the Lincoln book.

As early as 1867 Nicolay and Hay had thought about embarking on the biography, but several New York publishers told Hay that the market was glutted. Soon afterward he talked with Robert Lincoln, who would go no further than to say that he hoped some day to have the help of the former secretaries in putting his father's papers in order. Robert Lincoln too seems to have felt that the time was not yet ripe for a full-length biography.[2]

Six years passed. In May, 1873, Nicolay wrote to Robert Lincoln asking whether he had as yet done anything toward examining and arranging his father's papers. Nicolay offered to help with the job. In writing the proposed history he and Hay "must of necessity begin with your father's papers."[3] A year later Nicolay learned that Robert Lincoln had had the Lincoln papers shipped from Bloomington, where they had been in the custody of David Davis, to Chicago. In a letter to Robert Lincoln, Nicolay pressed the point he had made before:

I think it in every way most desirable that I should be there at the first overhauling of the papers, as there may be many little things of which note should be taken at the moment, whose importance might not be so familiar to yourself, and would be entirely unknown to any clerk to whom you might confide any preliminary examination. I am also specially anxious—and I press this point particularly—that not a scrap of paper of any kind be destroyed. The merest memorandum, mark, signature or figure, may have a future historical value, which we cannot now arbitrarily determine, and the only good rule is to *save everything*.[4]

Robert Lincoln soon sent the papers to Nicolay, who put them in a basement room of the capitol which he said was safer than any bank vault in Chicago. In 1875 the two men began to write. Nicolay blocked out the chapters. After discussion, each chose those which he preferred. Each sent his first draft to his collaborator, asking for criticism, trimming, verification, and additions.[5] Hay expressed the spirit of their joint enter-

[2] Tyler Dennett, *John Hay: From Poetry to Politics* (New York: Dodd, Mead, 1933), pp. 133-34.
[3] Nicolay, *Lincoln's Secretary*, pp. 270-71.
[4] Nicolay, *Lincoln's Secretary*, pp. 271-72.
[5] William Roscoe Thayer, *Life and Letters of John Hay* (Boston and New York: Houghton Mifflin, 1915), Vol. II, p. 17.

prise when at its outset he asked Nicolay for frank comment on a chapter he had written. "As to style, arrangement, effect, am I, in your opinion, holding my own? I confess I cannot tell. I never could, when I get into a streak of working hard, whether it is pretty good or pretty bad"[6]—which was quite an admission for the author of *Pike County Ballads* and *Castilian Days*.

The work did not go smoothly. Both men struggled with ill health. Nicolay's eyes often failed him. For days at a time he had to remain in a darkened room; he gave up reading except for the biography; and he rarely went into society. Hay was no better off. On June 23, 1876, he wrote to Nicolay: "I went industriously to work last winter. Got a fine start on my material and commenced putting it in shape. I had even written a few pages when I was struck with partial blindness. I have had numerous doctors at me almost ever since, but the trouble is not yet over." A year later Hay wrote again: "My old foe, the headache, is lying in wait for me, but I hope to get free." As late as 1885, when serial publication loomed, Hay promised: "If I can keep well, and I am not very much encouraged about it, I can write a volume in a year."[7]

The authors had other troubles. The government was in the process of publishing the official records of the Civil War. Nicolay and Hay—and particularly Nicolay—encountered a curious reluctance on the part of officials to allow these indispensable records to be examined. One functionary wrote to Nicolay on December 26, 1876, that in view of the fact that the War Department was publishing its own records "they should be kept from the public until Congress orders their distribution." This official went further, touching on a subject still sensitive: "I am firm in the belief that such portions of the records of the Executive Mansion in your possession as are of a public nature are the property of the Government and should be filed in the Departments of the affairs to which they relate."[8]

[6] Nicolay, *Lincoln's Secretary*, p. 285.

[7] Nicolay, *Lincoln's Secretary*, p. 282; Thayer, *Life and Letters*, Vol. II, pp. 19-20, 28.

[8] Nicolay, *Lincoln's Secretary*, p. 283.

Rutherford B. Hayes, elected President—or was he?—in 1876, broke the impasse with an order that Nicolay should be given access to such records as he wished to examine. "Even then," Nicolay's daughter wrote, "permission was granted grudgingly and in an ungracious letter signed by a lesser official who implied that such favoritism was 'manifestly unfair' but that the privilege would be granted as an exception in his case, provided the books were speedily returned and that my father did not allow anybody else to use them."[9]

The collaborators had advantages as well as problems. Nicolay's official duties were not burdensome. Hay had no fixed occupation and no need of one. In 1886 he moved to Washington, and communication between the two men became easy. Messages and manuscripts shuttled constantly between the Hay mansion on Lafayette Square and Nicolay's house near the capitol. When a talk seemed desirable, it was Hay who made the effort, usually climbing aboard a horse car instead of using one of his carriages. Perhaps, Helen Nicolay speculated, Hay found "more of the spirit of the sixties" in Nicolay's modest dwelling than in his own luxurious establishment.

Soon after Nicolay and Hay set to work in earnest, the word spread in publishing circles. Offers came in. They turned down all until they were well along with the writing. In November, 1885, they accepted the offer of the Century Company for serial rights to be followed by publication in book form. The price for serialization was fifty thousand dollars, the largest sum an

[9] Nicolay, *Lincoln's Secretary*, pp. 283-84.

There are many citations to the *Official Records* in Nicolay and Hay, and many of them are incorrect. Vol. I of the *Official Records* was not published until 1881, when the authors were well along with their task. By 1886, when they were practically finished, only seventeen volumes, in twenty-four parts, had appeared. Ultimately, the series ran to seventy volumes in 128 books.

It is my theory, for which I can adduce no evidence, that Nicolay and Hay used the proof sheets of many volumes of the *Official Records* and that the final pagination turned out to be different from that indicated on the proofs.

Some Civil War historians have used Nicolay and Hay's inaccurate citations to the *Official Records*, implying that they themselves had consulted the sources. The shortcuts of research are sometimes amusing.

American magazine had ever paid. The first installment appeared in the *Century* for November, 1886, the last in May, 1890. Altogether, about a third of the total work was published serially.

On his farm near Springfield, William H. Herndon, Lincoln's law partner, read the early magazine installments and made a prediction: "I will bet you a chicken cock that Nicoly [*sic*] & Hay's book will tire out the public by its length and unimportant trash. You mark what I say unless a change is made by N & H."[10] Herndon was wrong. The *Century's* circulation rose, and correspondence from readers indicated lively public interest. Of course no such reception could be expected for the complete work, but the book sold five thousand copies in a short time.

Critical opinion was on the whole favorable, although some reviewers complained about length and bulk, and others deplored, though mildly, the authors' unceasing admiration of Lincoln and their Republican bias.[11] The case of these critics would have been much strengthened if they had been aware of letters, since published, that passed between Nicolay, Hay, and Robert Lincoln while the book was in the making.

Herndon, through the intuition that was so often wrong but occasionally right, sensed a truth when he wrote, early in the serial publication: "H & N, in my opinion, are afraid of Bob: he gives them materials and they in their turn play *hush*."[12] The old man would have chortled if he could have seen the letter John Hay wrote to Lincoln's son on January 27, 1884:

Dear Bob:—
Nicolay tells me he has laid before you or is about to do so, the first volumes of our history, containing the chapters in which I have described the first forty years of your father's life.

[10] To Jesse W. Weik, in Benjamin P. Thomas, *Portrait for Posterity: Lincoln and His Biographers* (New Brunswick: Rutgers University Press, 1947), p. 123.
[11] Contemporary appraisals are summarized in Thomas, *Portrait for Posterity*, pp. 125-29.
[12] Thomas, *Portrait for Posterity*, p. 124.

I need not tell you that every line has been written in a spirit of reverence and regard. Still you may find here and there words or sentences which do not suit you. I write now to request that you will read with a pencil in your hand and strike out everything to which you object. I will adopt your view in all cases, whether I agree with it or not, but I cannot help hoping you will find nothing objectionable. . . .[13]

And there were sequels. On February 4, 1885, Robert Lincoln, after reading the chapters on his father's early life, wrote to Hay:

I was delighted with the way you had done your work. As you say I noted some places but I left one thing to speak of when I might see you. It is this—It is beyond doubt that my departed grandfather Lincoln was not an enterprising man and it is likely that your graphic assaults upon him *passim* are not undeserved but I could not help feeling better if you "let up" on him a little on a final revision. He did not have much chance to prepare to pose in the reflection of his son's fame and I feel sorry for him.

A few weeks later Hay replied: "I will do what you suggest in final revision. It is better, even as a matter of taste and without regard to your wishes which would, of course, be conclusive." Hay wrote to Lincoln at least once more on the subject of Thomas Lincoln: "I have gone over the whole thing twice again. . . . But of course before final publication I shall give you another hack at it, with plenary blue pencil powers."[14]

Neither Hay nor Nicolay attempted to conceal his pro-Lincoln bias. Objectivity, Hay told his collaborator on August 10, 1885, must characterize their work:

We must not show ourselves to the public in the attitude of two old dotards fighting over again the politics of their youth. . . . We must not write a stump speech in eight vols., 8vo. We will not fall in with the present tone of blubbering sentiment, of course. But we ought to write the history of those times like

---

[13] Thayer, *Life and Letters*, Vol. II, pp. 24-25.
[14] The Hay-Robert Lincoln correspondence is quoted in Henry B. Van Hoesen, "Lincoln and Hay," in *Books at Brown* XVIII (Oct., 1960): 172-73. This excellent monograph deserves to be far better known.

two everlasting angels who know everything, judge everything, and don't care a twang of their harps about one side or the other.

But, Hay concluded: "there will be one exception. We are Lincoln men all through."[15]

In fact, there were other exceptions. Both men despised George B. McClellan. "I have toiled and labored through ten chapters over him," Hay informed Nicolay. "I think I have left the impression of his mutinous imbecility, and I have done it in a perfectly courteous manner. . . . It is of the utmost moment that we should *seem* fair to him, while we are destroying him." To Hay, "Stonewall" Jackson was a "howling crank," but it would be "the greatest folly" to say so.[16] In Nicolay's opinion, Robert E. Lee was a traitor, pure and simple. "I do not mean to say, even in conversation, that as a matter of policy the penalty he rendered himself legally liable to ought to have been inflicted. But I do mean to say that his adherents and admirers ought to be grateful to the people and the government of the United States for the Great Pardon with which they have covered all these offenses against law and humanity."[17] The remark horrified Gilder. "A simple truth of law and equity," Hay commented. Jefferson Davis was another of Nicolay's abominations. While *Abraham Lincoln* was appearing serially, Hay wrote to his collaborator: "If you can see your way to soften your *tone* toward old Jeff—though I don't suppose you can—it would be politic. Let the facts make him as despicable as he is—*we* do not want to appear to hate and despise him.—But we do, and I suppose we can't keep it from sticking out."[18]

Both men found it hard to realize the extent of their Republican partisanship. When Nicolay's *Outbreak of the Rebellion* was published in 1881, Hay, who had read the book in manuscript, could not understand why it was criticized for "aggressive Northernism." He had thought it eminently fair. To Nico-

[15] Thayer, *Life and Letters*, pp. 31-33.
[16] Thayer, *Life and Letters*, pp. 31-33.
[17] Nicolay, *Lincoln's Secretary*, pp. 296-97.
[18] Dennett, *John Hay*, p. 140.

lay, partisanship did not exist. Right and wrong were the verities. The North, and of course the Republican party, were right. "We deny that it is partizanship," he wrote, "to use the multiplication table, revere the Decalogue, or obey the Constitution of the United States. When logic, morals and law all unite to condemn the secession and rebellion of 1861, he will be a rash critic to pronounce censure upon anyone who helped put down that rebellion, or who ventures truthfully to record its incidents."[19]

In any appraisal of the enduring value of *Abraham Lincoln: A History*, these attitudes of the authors, unacceptable to present-day historians, demand notice.

First of all, how serious was the censorship exercised by Robert Lincoln?

David C. Mearns, thoroughly familiar with the Lincoln Papers, notes that most of the alterations in the first four chapters of Volume One of *Abraham Lincoln: A History*, which have survived in manuscript form, were made by John Hay in accordance with what he conceived to be Robert Lincoln's wishes.[20] Mearns notes only one exception: Robert Lincoln's insistence that the incident of sewing up the hogs' eyes, which his father had included in his autobiography, be deleted.[21] And, I ask: who, among the most dedicated of today's "scientific" historians, can be sure that he would not have taken the same position had his own father confessed to such an insensate act?

The truth seems to be that Robert Lincoln rarely availed himself of the "plenary blue pencil" privilege that the authors accorded him. On the other hand, the two men were keenly

[19] Nicolay, *Lincoln's Secretary*, pp. 296-97.

[20] The reader who is curious about these alterations will find them set forth in detail in Thomas, *Portrait for Posterity*, pp. 112-18. Thomas concluded, correctly: "The revised version was in better taste than the original; but to a modern historian such truckling to the whims of Robert Lincoln would seem intolerable. . . . Strangely enough, he was unconsciously doing history a service. For, even in its diluted form, John Hay's characterization of Thomas Lincoln was too severe in the light of modern discoveries."

[21] David C. Mearns, *The Lincoln Papers* (Garden City: Doubleday, 1948), Vol. I, p. 76.

aware that he would scrutinize whatever they wrote, and beyond question they held themselves in restraint. This, as Tyler Dennett has pointed out, caused them little soul-searching: they were conventional men and incapable, by temperament and experience, of any other than the conventional approach.

What of the pro-Lincoln, pro-Republican bias? If, in biographical or historical writing, an author achieves complete impartiality, his work is likely to be lifeless. Macaulay wrote as a Whig. Does that make his *History of England* worthless? Should James Ford Rhodes be discarded because he, like Nicolay and Hay, was a staunch Union man and Republican? Albert J. Beveridge called *Abraham Lincoln: A History* "atrocious" because of the prejudices of the authors, yet in his own *Abraham Lincoln: 1809-1858* Stephen A. Douglas is the hero.

When bias and partisanship are open and obvious enough to be clear to the reader, they do no harm. When bias and partisanship are expressed insidiously—by the use of disparaging or laudatory adjectives, unfair summaries of speeches and letters, one-sided sources—they lead, or should lead, to oblivion.[22]

Unfortunately, Nicolay and Hay had opened themselves to the suspicion that they might be guilty of the insidious approach, notably in the instances of McClellan, Davis, Lee, and Jackson. In fact, were they guilty?

With the exception of McClellan, one finds little evidence of more than ordinary bias in their treatment of these men. (They could hardly have been expected to accord Jefferson Davis the same degree of admiration they had for Lincoln.) And to this day, competent authorities divide on the question whether or not McClellan deserved what he got in their pages. James G. Randall and William S. Myers believed Nicolay and Hay maligned the general outrageously; T. Harry Williams and Kenneth P. Williams endorsed their verdict in essence if not perhaps the severe terms in which it was expressed.

[22] Cases in point are George Fort Milton, *The Eve of Conflict: Stephen A. Douglas and the Needless War* (Boston and New York: Houghton Mifflin, 1934), and Claude G. Bowers, *The Tragic Era* (Cambridge, Mass.: Houghton Mifflin, 1929).

Factually, the Nicolay and Hay book holds up well except for that part of the first volume which deals with Lincoln's youth and young manhood. Since they wrote, much research has been done on this period, and many of their statements and conclusions need correction. There are of course other weak spots. A. K. McClure, editor of the *Philadelphia Times*, attacked the authors violently for their account of the substitution of Andrew Johnson for Hannibal Hamlin as the vice-presidential nominee in 1864, but where truth lies no one knows even now. Horace White charged them with suppressing relevant facts in connection with the Fort Sumter crisis and the dismissal of Simon Cameron as minister of war.[23] But for ten octavo volumes, these are few lapses.

One of the reasons for this high degree of accuracy was the authors' distrust of memory as a source of history. Today's "professional historian" could find no fault with the statement John Hay made in a letter to Charles Francis Adams, written in 1903:

When Nicolay and I came to Washington we thought we should have great advantage in personal conversation with Lincoln's contemporaries in regard to the important events of his time, but we ascertained after a very short experience that no confidence whatever could be placed in the memories of even the most intelligent and most honorable men when it came to narrating their relations with Lincoln. . . . The example worked upon us so powerfully that in our *History* . . . we did not set down a single fact from our personal recollection, nor in the course of those ten volumes did we quote one word of Lincoln of which we had not a written memorandum made at the time.[24]

In spite of its defects, *Abraham Lincoln: A History* continues to merit the respectful attention of students of Lincoln and the Civil War. The authors had the advantage, too often belittled today, of having been on the scene. As they said in their preface, "we were the daily and nightly witnesses of the incidents, the anxieties, the fears, and the hopes which pervaded the Execu-

[23] Thomas, *Portrait for Posterity*, p. 127.
[24] Dennett, *John Hay*, p. 137.

tive Mansion and the National Capital. . . . We had personal acquaintance and daily official intercourse with Cabinet Officers, Members of Congress, Governors, and Military and Naval Officers of all grades, whose affairs brought them to the White House." Charles W. Eliot, president of Harvard University, gave the authors less than their due when he denied that their work was history, but he was correct in asserting that they had prepared "invaluable materials for the subsequent historian."[25]

Much of the archival and manuscript material which Nicolay and Hay used is now in print—but not all. Lincoln's own letters and speeches from the great collection to which Robert Lincoln gave them access have all been published, but this is not true of the letters to Lincoln, which they also used. For General Scott's daily reports to the President in April, 1861, many of Nicolay's memoranda, and other personal papers, one must still go to the *History*.

Moreover, this is one narrative that covers the whole great sweep of events—political developments, South as well as North; military campaigns, not only in the East but also in the often-neglected West and Southwest; the naval war; emancipation; military government and the problems it occasioned; foreign affairs; reconstruction; Lincoln's assassination and funeral.[26]

A concluding word about style. Hay had a natural bent for sprightly prose, as his diary proves. Nicolay was inclined to long and somewhat ponderous sentences. The collaborating process transmuted the distinctive characteristics of both writers into a style peculiar to neither—a style characterized by sobriety, clarity, coherence, and occasionally an eloquence that approaches the Churchillian.

PAUL M. ANGLE

[25] To Henry Adams, in Worthington C. Ford, ed., *Letters of Henry Adams* (Boston and New York: Houghton Mifflin, 1938), Vol. II, p. 8 *n*.

[26] I used this sentence in *A Shelf of Lincoln Books* (New Brunswick: Rutgers University Press, 1946), p. 37. In spite of the flood of books occasioned by the Civil War Centennial, the statement remains true.

Contents

THE BALANCE OF POWER	3
THE DRIFT OF POLITICS	18
FROM THE BALLOT TO THE BULLET	26
SOUTH CAROLINA SECESSION	32
THE NATIONAL UPRISING	44
THE OHIO LINE	63
CIVIL WAR	74
BULL RUN	85
MONITOR AND MERRIMAC	99
THE SHILOH CAMPAIGN	115
NEW ORLEANS	127
HARRISON'S LANDING	137
ANTIETAM	152
THE EDICT OF FREEDOM	163
CHANCELLORSVILLE	173
GETTYSBURG	190
VICKSBURG	203
CHATTANOOGA	217
GRANT GENERAL-IN-CHIEF	235
LINCOLN RENOMINATED	243
LINCOLN REËLECTED	264
PETERSBURG	290
THE MARCH TO THE SEA	309
FRANKLIN AND NASHVILLE	322
THE THIRTEENTH AMENDMENT	337
APPOMATTOX	352
THE END OF REBELLION	367
LINCOLN'S FAME	378
BIBLIOGRAPHICAL NOTE	387
INDEX	401

ABRAHAM LINCOLN   *A History*

Nicolay (seated) and Hay as Lincoln's secretaries. Photograph by Alexander Gardner, November 8, 1863. On the same day Hay recorded in his diary: "Nico & I immortalized ourselves by having ourselves done in a group with the Prest."

ABRAHAM LINCOLN *was born of obscure parents in central Kentucky on February 12, 1809. Seven years later his father and mother took him to southwestern Indiana. From there, in 1830, the family migrated to Illinois. A year later young Lincoln left home to become, successively, storekeeper, postmaster, surveyor, and lawyer. He entered politics, serving four terms in the General Assembly of Illinois and one term in Congress. In 1849 he returned to Springfield, determined to give up political activity and devote himself to his profession.*

This, in barest outline, is the story to which Nicolay and Hay devote two-thirds of their first volume. While Lincoln was attaining a reputation at the bar, the problems of the nation were growing in complexity and awesome import. At this point in their narrative Nicolay and Hay began to write on the scale that would earn for their work its subtitle, A History.

The Balance of Power

WE shall see in the course of the present work how the life of Abraham Lincoln divides itself into three principal periods, with corresponding stages of intellectual development: the first, of about forty years, ending with his term in Congress; the second, of about ten years, concluding with his final campaign of political speech-making in New York and in New England, shortly before the Presidential nominations of 1860; and the last, of about five years, terminating at his death. We have thus far traced his career through the first period of forty years. In the several stages of frontier experience through which he had passed, and which in the main but repeated the trials and vicissitudes of thousands of other boys and youths in the West, only so much individuality had been developed in him as brought him into the leading class of his contemporaries. He had risen from laborer to student, from clerk to lawyer, from politician to legislator. That he had lifted himself by healthy ambition and unaided industry out of the station of a farm-hand, whose routine life begins and ends in a backwoods log-cabin, to that representative character and authority which seated him in the national Capitol to aid in framing laws for his country, was already an achievement that may well be held to crown honorably a career of forty years.

Such achievement and such distinction, however, were not so uncommon as to appear phenomenal. Hundreds of other boys born in log-cabins had won similar elevation in the manly, practical school of Western public life. Even in ordinary times there still remained within the reach of average intellects several higher grades of public service. It is quite probable that the talents of Lincoln would have made him Governor of Illinois or given him a place in the United States Senate. But the story of his life would not have commanded, as it now does, the unflagging attention of the world, had there not fallen upon his generation the unusual conditions and opportunities brought about by a series of remarkable convulsions in national politics. If we would correctly understand how Lincoln became, first a conspicuous actor, and then a chosen leader, in a great strife of national parties for supremacy and power, we must briefly study the origin and development of the great slavery controversy in American legislation which found its highest activity and decisive culmination in the single decade from 1850 to 1860. But we should greatly err if we attributed the new events in Lincoln's career to the caprice of fortune. The conditions and opportunities of which we speak were broadly national, and open to all without restriction of rank or locality. Many of his contemporaries had seemingly overshadowing advantages, by prominence and training, to seize and appropriate them to their own advancement. It is precisely this careful study of the times which shows us by what inevitable process of selection honors and labors of which he did not dream fell upon him; how, indeed, it was not the individual who gained the prize, but the paramount duty which claimed the man.

It is now universally understood, if not conceded, that the

Rebellion of 1861 was begun for the sole purpose of defending and preserving to the seceding States the institution of African slavery and making them the nucleus of a great slave empire, which in their ambitious dreams they hoped would include Mexico, Central America, and the West India Islands, and perhaps even the tropical States of South America. Both a real and a pretended fear that slavery was in danger lay at the bottom of this design. The real fear arose from the palpable fact, impossible to conceal, that the slave system was a reactionary obstacle in the pathway of modern civilization, and its political, material, philosophical, and religious development. The pretended danger was the permanent loss of political power by the slave States of the Union, as shown in the election of Lincoln to the presidency, which they averred would necessarily throw all the forces of the national life against the "peculiar institution," and crush it under forms of law. It was by magnifying this danger from remote into immediate consequence that they excited the population of the cotton States to resistance and rebellion. Seizing this opportunity, it was their present purpose to establish a slave Confederacy, consisting of the cotton States, which should in due time draw to itself, by an irresistable gravitation of sympathy and interest, first, the border slave States, and, in the further progress of events, the tropical countries towards the equator.

The popular agitation, or war of words between the North and the South on the subject of slavery, which led to the armed insurrection was threefold: First, the economic efforts to prevent the destruction of the monetary value of four millions of human beings held in bondage, who were bought and sold as chattels, and whose aggregate valuation, under circumstances existing at the outbreak of the civil war, was variously computed at $400,000,000 to $1,600,000,000; second, a moral debate as to the abstract righteousness or iniquity of the system; and, third, a political struggle for the balance of power in government and public policy, by which the security and perpetuity of the institution might be guaranteed.

This sectional controversy over the institution of slavery in its threefold aspect had begun with the very birth of the nation, had continued with its growth, and become intensified with its strength. The year before the *Mayflower* brought the Pilgrims to Plymouth Rock, a Dutch ship landed a cargo of African slaves at Jamestown, in Virginia. During the long colonial period the English Government fostered and forced the importation of slaves to America equally with English goods. In the original draft of the Declaration of Independence, Thomas Jefferson invoked the reprobation of mankind upon the British King for his share in this inhuman traffic. On reflection, however, this was discovered to be but another case of Satan rebuking sin. The blood money which reddened the hands of English royalty stained equally those of many an American rebel. The public opinion of the colonies was already too much debauched to sit in unanimous moral judgment on this crime against humanity. The objections of South Carolina and Georgia sufficed to cause the erasure and suppression of the obnoxious paragraph. Nor were the Northern States guiltless: Newport was yet a great slave-mart, and the commerce of New England drew more advantage from the traffic than did the agriculture of the South.

All the elements of the later controversy already existed. Slave codes and fugitive-slave laws, abolition societies and emancipation bills, are older than our Constitution; and negro troops fought in the Revolutionary war for American independence. Liberal men could be found in South Carolina who hated slavery, and narrow men in Massachusetts who defended it. But these individual instances of prejudice or liberality were submerged and lost in the current of popular opinion springing from prevailing interests in the respective localities, and institutions molded principles, until in turn principles should become strong enough to reform institutions. In short, slavery was one of the many "relics of barbarism"—like the divine right of kings, religious persecution, torture of the accused, imprisonment and enslavement for debt, witch-burning, and kindred "institutions"—which were transmitted to that generation from former ages as so many burdens of humanity, for help in the removal of which the new nation was in the providence of God perhaps called into existence. The whole matter in its broader aspects is part of that persistent struggle of the centuries between despotism and individual freedom; between arbitrary wrong, consecrated by tradition and law, and the unfolding recognition of private rights; between the thraldom of public opinion and liberty of conscience; between the greed of gain and the Golden Rule of Christ. Whoever, therefore, chooses to trace the remote origin of the American Rebellion will find the germ of the Union armies of 1861-5 in the cabin of the *Mayflower*, and the inception of the Secession forces between the decks of that Dutch slaver which planted the fruits of her avarice and piracy in the James River colonies in 1619.

So elaborate and searching a study, however, is not necessary to the purposes of this work. A very brief mention of the principal landmarks of the long contest will serve to show the historical relation, and explain the phraseology, of its final issues.

The first of these great landmarks was the Ordinance of 1787. All the States tolerated slavery and permitted the slave-trade during the Revolution. But in most of them the morality of the system was strongly drawn in question, especially by the abolition societies, which embraced many of the most prominent patriots. A public opinion, not indeed unanimous, but largely in the majority, demanded that the "necessary evil" should cease. When the Continental Congress came to the practical work of providing a government for the "Western lands," which the financial pressure and the absolute need of union compelled New York and Virginia to cede to the general Government, Thomas Jefferson proposed, among other features in his plan and draft of 1784, to add a clause prohibiting slavery in all the North-west territory after the year 1800. A North Carolina member moved to strike out this clause. The form of the question put by the chairman was, "Shall the clause stand?" Sixteen members voted aye and seven members voted no; but under the clumsy legislative machinery of the Confederation these seven noes carried the question, since a majority of States had failed to vote in the affirmative.

Three years later, July 13, 1787, this first ordinance was repealed by a second, establishing our more modern form of territorial government. It is justly famed for many of its provisions; but its chief value is conceded to have been its sixth article, ordaining the immediate and perpetual prohibition of slavery. Upon this all the States present in Congress—three Northern and five Southern—voted in the affirmative; five States were absent, four Northern and one Southern. This piece of legislation is remarkable in that it was an entirely new bill, substituted for a former and altogether different scheme containing no prohibition whatever, and that it was passed through all the forms and stages of enactment in the short space of four days. History sheds little light on the official transaction, but contemporary evidence points to the influence of a powerful lobby.

Several plausible reasons are assigned why the three slave States of Maryland, Virginia, and North Carolina voted for this prohibition. First, the West was competing with the Territory of Maine for settlers; second, the whole scheme was in the interest of the "Ohio Company," a newly formed Massachusetts emigrant aid society which immediately made a large purchase of lands; third, the unsettled regions south of the Ohio River had not yet been ceded to the general Government, and were therefore open to slavery from the contiguous Southern States; fourth, little was known of the extent or character of the great West; and, therefore, fifth, the Ohio River was doubtless thought to be a fair and equitable dividing line. The ordinance itself provided for the formation of not less than three nor more than five States, and under its shielding provisions Ohio, Indiana, Illinois, Michigan, and Wisconsin were added to the Union with free constitutions.

It does not appear that sectional motives operated for or against the foregoing enactment; they were probably held in abeyance by other considerations. But it must not be inferred therefrom that the slavery question was absent or dormant in the country. There was already a North and a South. At that very time the constitutional convention was in session in Philadelphia. George Washington and his fellow-delegates were grappling with the novel problems of government which the happy issue of the Revolution and the lamentable failure of the Confederation forced upon the country. One of these problems was the presence of over half a million of slaves, nearly all in five Southern States. Should they be taxed? Should they be represented? Should the power to regulate commerce be allowed to control or terminate their importation? Vital questions these, which went not merely to the incidents but the fundamental powers of government. The slavery question seemed for months an element of irreconcilable discord in the convention. The slave-trade not only, but the domestic institution itself, was characterized in language which Southern politicians of later times would have denounced as "fanatical" and "incendiary." Pinckney wished the slaves to be represented equally with the whites, since they were the Southern peasantry. Gouverneur Morris declared that as they were only property they ought not to be represented at all. Both the present and the future balance of power in national legislation, as resulting from slaves already in, and hereafter to be imported into, old and new States, were debated under various possibilities and probabilities.

Out of these divergent views grew the compromises of the Constitution. 1. The slaves were to be included in the enumeration for representation, *five* blacks to be counted as *three* whites. 2. Congress should have the right to prohibit the slave-trade, but not till the lapse of twenty years. 3. Fugitive slaves should be delivered to their owners. Each State, large or small, was allowed two senators; and the apportionment of representatives gave to the North thirty-five members and fourteen senators, to the South thirty members and twelve senators. But since the North was not yet free from slavery, but only in process of becoming so, and as Virginia was the leading State of the Union, the real balance of power remained in the hands of the South.

The newly formed Constitution went into successful operation. Under legal provisions already made and the strong current of abolition sentiment then existing, all the Eastern and Middle States down to Delaware became free. This gain, however, was perhaps more than numerically counterbalanced by the active importation of captured Africans, especially into South Carolina and Georgia, up to the time the traffic ceased by law in 1808. Jefferson had meanwhile purchased of France the immense country west of the Mississippi known as the Louisiana Territory. The free navigation of that great river was assured, and the importance of the West immeasurably increased. The old French colonies at New Orleans and Kaskaskia were already strong outposts of civilization and the nuclei of spreading settlements. Attracted by the superior fertility of the soil, by the limitless opportunities for speculation, by the enticing spirit of adventure, and pushed by the restless energy inherent in the Anglo-Saxon character, the older States now began to pour a rising stream of emigration into the West and the South-west.

In this race the free States, by reason of their greater population, wealth, and commercial enterprise, would have outstripped the South but for the introduction of a new and powerful influence which operated exclusively in favor of the latter. This was the discovery of the peculiar adaptation of the soil and climate of portions of the Southern States, combined with cheap slave-labor, to the cultivation of cotton. Half a century of experiment and invention in England had brought about the concurrent improvement of machinery for spinning and weaving, and of the high-pressure engine to furnish motive power. The Revolutionary war was scarcely ended when there came from the mother-country a demand for the raw fiber, which promised to be almost without limit. A few trials sufficed to show Southern planters that with their soil and their slaves they could supply this demand with a quality of cotton which would defy competition, and at a profit to themselves far exceeding that of any other product of agriculture. But an insurmountable obstacle yet seemed to interpose itself between them and their golden harvest. The tedious work of cleaning the fiber from the seed apparently made impossible its cheap preparation for export in large quantities. A negro woman working the whole day could clean only a single pound.

It so happened that at this juncture, November, 1792, an ingenious Yankee student from Massachusetts was boarding in the house of friends in Savannah, Georgia, occupying his leisure in reading law. A party of Georgia gentlemen from the interior, making a visit to this family, fell into conversation on the prospects and difficulties of cotton-culture and the imperative need of a rapidly working cleaning-machine. Their hostess, an intelligent and quick-witted woman, at once suggested an expedient. "Gentlemen," said Mrs. Greene, "apply to my young friend, Mr. Eli Whitney; he can make anything." The Yankee student was sought, introduced, and had the mechanical problem laid before him. He modestly disclaimed his hostess's extravagant praises, and told his visitors that he had never seen either cotton or cotton-seed in his life. Nevertheless, he went to work with such earnestness and success, that in a few months Mrs. Greene had the satisfaction of being able to invite a gathering of gentlemen from different parts of the State to behold with their own eyes the working of the newly invented cotton-gin, with which a negro man turning a crank could clean fifty pounds of cotton per day.

This solution of the last problem in cheap cotton-culture made it at once the leading crop of the South. That favored region quickly drove all competitors out of the market; and the rise of English imports of raw cotton, from thirty million pounds in 1790 to over one thousand million pounds in 1860, shows the development and increase of this special industry, with all its related interests. It was not till fifteen years after the invention of the cotton-gin that the African slave-trade ceased by limitation of law. Within that period many thousands of negro captives had been added to the population of the South by direct importation, and nearly thirty thousand slave inhabitants added by the acquisition of Louisiana, hastening the formation of new slave States south of the Ohio River in due proportion.

It is a curious historical fact, that under the very remarkable material growth of the United States which now took place, the political influence remained so evenly balanced between the North and the South for more than a generation. Other grave issues indeed absorbed the public attention, but the abeyance of the slavery question is due rather to the fact that no considerable advantage as yet fell to either side. Eight new States were organized, four north and four south of the Ohio River, and admitted in nearly alternate order: Vermont in 1791, *free;* Kentucky in 1792, *slave;* Tennessee in 1796, *slave;* Ohio in 1802, *free;* Louisiana in 1812, *slave;* Indiana in 1816, *free;* Mississippi in 1817, *slave;* Illinois in 1818, *free.* Alabama was already authorized to be admitted with slavery, and this would make the number of free and slave States equal, giving eleven States to the North and eleven to the South.

The Territory of Missouri, containing the old French colonies at and near St. Louis, had attained a population of 60,000, and was eager to be admitted as a State. She had made application in 1817, and now in 1819 it was proposed to authorize her to form a constitution. Arkansas was also being nursed as an applicant, and the prospective loss by the North and gain by the South of the balance of power caused the slavery question suddenly to flare up as a national issue. There were hot debates in Congress, emphatic resolutions by State legislatures, deep agitation among the whole people, and open threats by the South to dissolve the Union. Extreme Northern men insisted upon a restriction of slavery to be applied to both Missouri and Arkansas; radical Southern members contended that Congress had no power to impose any conditions on new States. The North had control of the House, the South of the Senate. A middle party thereupon sprang up, proposing to divide the Louisiana purchase between freedom and slavery by the line of 36° 30′, and authorizing the admission of Missouri with slavery out of the northern half. Fastening this proposition upon the bill to admit Maine as a free State, the measure was, after a struggle, carried through Congress (in a separate act approved March 6, 1820), and became the famous Missouri Compromise. Maine and Missouri were both admitted. Each section thereby not only gained two votes in the Senate, but also asserted its right to spread its peculiar polity without question or hindrance within the prescribed limits; and the motto, "No extension of slavery," was postponed forty years, to the Republican campaign of 1860.

From this time forward, the maintenance of this balance of power,—the numerical equality of the slave States with the free,—though not announced in platforms as a party doctrine, was nevertheless steadily followed as a policy by the representatives of the South. In pursuance of this system, Michigan and Arkansas, the former a *free* and the latter a *slave* State, were, on the same day, June 15, 1836, authorized to be admitted. These tactics were again repeated in the year 1845, when, on the 3d of March, Iowa, a *free* State, and Florida, a *slave* State, were authorized to be admitted by one act of Congress, its approval being the last official act of President Tyler. This tacit compromise, however, was accompanied by another very important victory of the same policy. The Southern politicians saw clearly enough that with the admission of Florida the slave territory was exhausted, while an immense untouched portion of the Louisiana purchase still stretched away to the north-west towards the Pacific above the Missouri Compromise line, which consecrated it to freedom. The North, therefore, still had an imperial area from which to organize future free States, while the South had not a foot more territory from which to create slave States.

Sagaciously anticipating this contingency, the Southern States had been largely instrumental in setting up the independent State of Texas, and were now urgent in their demand for her annexation to the Union. Two days before the signing of the Iowa and Florida bill, Congress passed, and President Tyler signed, a joint resolution, authorizing the acquisition, annexation, and admission of Texas. But even this was not all. The joint resolution contained a guarantee that "new States, of convenient size, not exceeding four in number, in addition to the said State of Texas," and to be formed out of her territory, should hereafter be entitled to admission—the Missouri Compromise line to govern the slavery question in them. The State of Texas was, by a later resolution, formally admitted to the Union, December 29, 1845. At this date, therefore, the slave States gained an actual majority of one, there being fourteen free States and fifteen slave States, with at least equal territorial prospects through future annexation.

If the North was alarmed at being thus placed in a minority, there was ample reason for still further disquietude. The annexation of Texas had provoked the Mexican war, and President Polk, in anticipation of further important acquisition of territory to the South and West, asked of Congress an appropriation of two millions to be used in negotiations to that end. An attempt to impose a condition to these negotiations that slavery should never exist in any territory to be thus acquired was the famous Wilmot Proviso. This particular measure failed, but the war ended, and New Mexico and California were added to the Union as unorganized Territories. Meanwhile the admission of Wisconsin in 1848 had once more restored the equilibrium between the free and the slave States, there being now fifteen of each.

It must not be supposed that the important political measures and results thus far summarized were accomplished by quiet and harmonious legislation. Rising steadily after 1820, the controversy over slavery became deep and bitter, both in Congress and the country. Involving not merely a policy of government, but a question of abstract morals, statesmen, philanthropists, divines, the press, societies, churches, and legislative bodies joined in the discussion. Slavery was assailed and defended in behalf of the welfare of the state, and in the name of religion.

In Congress especially it had now been a subject of angry contention for a whole generation. It obtruded itself into all manner of questions, and clung obstinately to numberless resolutions and bills. Time and again it had brought members into excited discussion, and to the very verge of personal conflict in the legislative halls. It had occasioned numerous threats to dissolve the Union, and in one or more instances caused members actually to retire from the House of Representatives. It had given rise to resolutions of censure, to resignations, and had been the occasion of some of the greatest legislative debates of the nation. It had virtually created and annexed the largest State in the Union. In several States it had instigated abuse, intolerance, persecutions, trials, mobs, murders, destruction of property, imprisonment of freemen, retaliatory legislation, and one well-defined and formidable attempt at revolution. It originated party factions, political schools, and constitutional doctrines, and made and marred the fame of great statesmen.

New Mexico, when acquired, contained one of the oldest towns on the continent, and a considerable population of Spanish origin. California, almost simultaneously with her acquisition, was peopled in the course of a few months by the world-renowned gold discoveries. Very unexpectedly, therefore, to politicians of all grades and opinions, the slavery question was once more before the nation in the year 1850, over the proposition to admit both to the Union as States. As the result of the long conflict of opinion hitherto maintained, the beliefs and desires of the contending sections had by this time become formulated in distinct political doctrines. The North contended that Congress might and should prohibit slavery in all the territories of the Union, as had been done in the Northern half by the Ordinance of 1787 and by the Missouri Compromise. The South declared that any such exclusion would not only be unjust and impolitic, but absolutely unconstitutional, because property in slaves might enter and must be protected in the territories in common with all other property. To the theoretical dispute was added a practical contest. By the existing Mexican laws slavery was already prohibited in New Mexico, and California promptly formed a free State constitution. Under these circumstances the North sought to organize the former as a Territory, and admit the latter as a State, while the South resisted and endeavored to extend the Missouri Compromise line, which would place New Mexico and the southern half of California under the tutelage and influence of slavery.

These were the principal points of difference which caused the great slavery agitation of 1850. The whole country was convulsed in discussion; and again more open threats and more ominous movements towards disunion came from the South. The most popular statesman of that day, Henry Clay, of Kentucky, a slaveholder opposed to the extension of slavery, now, however, assumed the leadership of a party of compromise, and the quarrel was adjusted and quieted by a combined series of Congressional acts. 1. California was admitted as a free State. 2. The Territories of New Mexico and Utah were organized, leaving the Mexican prohibition of slavery in force. 3. The domestic slave-trade in the District of Columbia was abolished. 4. A more stringent fugitive-slave law was passed. 5. For the adjustment of her State boundaries Texas received ten millions of dollars.

These were the famous compromise measures of 1850. It has been gravely asserted that this indemnity of ten millions, suddenly trebling the value of the Texas debt, and thereby affording an unprecedented opportunity for speculation in the bonds of that State, was "the propelling force whereby these acts were pushed through Congress in defiance of the original convictions of a majority of its members." But it must also be admitted that the popular desire for tranquillity, concord, and union in all sections never exerted so much influence upon Congress as then. This compromise was not at first heartily accepted by the people; Southern opinion being offended by the abandonment of the "property" doctrine, and Northern sentiment irritated by certain harsh features of the fugitive-slave law. But the rising Union feeling quickly swept away all ebullitions of discontent, and during two or three years people and politicians fondly dreamed they had, in current phraseology, reached a "finality"* on this vexed quarrel. The nation settled itself for a period of quiet to repair the waste and utilize the conquests of the Mexican war. It became absorbed in the expansion of its commerce, the development of its manufactures, and the growth of its emigration, all quickened by the riches of its marvelous gold-fields; until unexpectedly and suddenly it found itself plunged once again into political controversies more distracting and more ominous than the worst it had yet experienced.

---

* Grave doubts, however, found occasional expression, and none perhaps more forcibly than in the following newspaper epigram describing "Finality":

> To kill twice dead a rattlesnake,
> And off his scaly skin to take,
> And through his head to drive a stake,
> And every bone within him break,
> And of his flesh mincemeat to make,
> To burn, to sear, to boil, and bake,
> Then in a heap the whole to rake,
> And over it the besom shake,
> And sink it fathoms in the lake—
> Whence after all, quite wide awake,
> Comes back that very same old snake!

FOUR YEARS *after the Compromise of 1850 Stephen A. Douglas, Chairman of the Senate Committee on Territories, introduced a bill to organize the territories of Kansas and Nebraska and to repeal, specifically, the Missouri Compromise of 1820. The Democratic administration threw all its power behind the measure, and in the spring of 1854 it became law.*
Nicolay and Hay assessed the effect.

The Drift of Politics

THE repeal of the Missouri Compromise made the slavery question paramount in every State of the Union. The boasted finality was a broken reed; the life-boat of compromise a hopeless wreck. If the agreement of a generation could be thus annulled in a breath, was there any safety even in the Constitution itself? This feeling communicated itself to the Northern States at the very first note of warning, and every man's party fealty was at once decided by his toleration of or opposition to slavery. While the fate of the Nebraska bill hung in a doubtful balance in the House, the feeling found expression in letters, speeches, meetings, petitions, and remonstrances. Men were for or against the bill—every other political subject was left in abeyance. The measure once passed, and the Compromise repealed, the first natural impulse was to combine, organize, and agitate for its restoration. This was the ready-made, common ground of coöperation.

It is probable that this merely defensive energy would have been overcome and dissipated, had it not at this juncture been inspirited and led by the faction known as the Free-soil party of the country, composed mainly of men of independent antislavery views, who had during four presidential campaigns been organized as a distinct political body, with no near hope of success, but animated mainly by the desire to give expression to their deep personal convictions. If there were demagogues here and there among them, seeking merely to create a balance of power for bargain and sale, they were unimportant in number, and only of local influence, and soon became deserters. There was no mistaking the earnestness of the body of this faction. A few fanatical men, who had made it the vehicle of violent expressions, had kept it under the ban of popular prejudice. It had long been held up to public odium as a revolutionary band of "abolitionists." Most of the abolitionists were doubtless in this party, but the party was not all composed of abolitionists. Despite objurgation and contempt, it had become since 1840 a constant and growing factor in politics. It had operated as a negative balance of power in the last three presidential elections, causing by its diversion of votes, and more especially by its relaxing influence upon parties, the success of the Democratic candidate, James K. Polk, in 1844, the Whig candidate, General Taylor, in 1848, and the Democratic nominee, Franklin Pierce, in 1852.

This small party of antislavery veterans, over 158,000 voters in the aggregate, and distributed in detachments of from 3000 to 30,000 in twelve of the free States, now came to the front, and with its newspapers and speakers trained in the discussion of the subject, and its committees and affiliations already in action and correspondence, bore the brunt of the fight against the repeal. Hitherto its aims had appeared Utopian, and its resolves had been denunciatory and exasperating. Now, combining wisdom with opportunity, it became conciliatory, and, abating something of its abstractions, made itself the exponent of a demand for a present and practical reform—a simple return to the ancient faith and landmarks. It labored specially to bring about the dissolution of the old party organizations and the formation of a new one, based upon the general policy of resisting the extension of slavery. Since, however, the repeal had shaken but not obliterated old party lines, this effort succeeded only in favorable localities.

For the present, party disintegration was slow; men were reluctant to abandon their old-time principles and associations. The united efforts of Douglas and the Administration held the body of the Northern Democrats to his fatal policy, though protests and defections became alarmingly frequent. On the other hand, the great mass of Northern Whigs promptly opposed the repeal, and formed the bulk of the opposition, nevertheless losing perhaps as many pro-slavery Whigs as they gained antislavery Democrats. The real and effective gain, therefore, was the more or less thorough alliance of the Whig party and the Free-soil party of the Northern States: wherever that was successful it gave immediate and available majorities to the opposition, which made their influence felt even in the very opening of the popular contest following the Congressional repeal.

It happened that this was a year for electing Congressmen. The Nebraska bill did not pass till the end of May, and the political excitement was at once transferred from Washington to every district of the whole country. It may be said with truth that the year 1854 formed one continuous and solid political campaign from January to November, rising in interest and earnestness from first to last, and engaging in the discussion more fully than had ever occurred in previous American history all the constituent elements of our population.

In the Southern States the great majority of people welcomed, supported, and defended the repeal of the Missouri Compromise, it being consonant with their pro-slavery feelings, and apparently favorable to their pro-slavery interests. The Democratic party in the South, controlling a majority of slave States, was of course a unit in its favor. The Whig party, however, having carried two slave States for Scott in 1852, and holding a strong minority in the remainder, was not so unanimous. Seven Southern Representatives and two Southern Senators had voted against the Nebraska bill, and many individual voters condemned it as an act of bad faith—as the abandonment of the accepted "finality," and as the provocation of a dangerous antislavery reaction. But public opinion in that part of the Union was fearfully tyrannical and intolerant; and opposition dared only to manifest itself to Democratic party organization—not to these Democratic party measures. The Whigs of the South were therefore driven precipitately to division. Those of extreme pro-slavery views, like Dixon, of Kentucky,—who, when he introduced his amendment, declared, "Upon the question of slavery I know no Whiggery and no Democracy,"—went boldly and at once over into the Democratic camp, while those who retained their traditional party name and flag were sundered from their ancient allies in the Northern States by the impossibility of taking up the latter's antislavery war-cry.

At this juncture the political situation was further complicated by the sudden rise of an additional factor in politics, the American party, popularly called the "Know-Nothings." Essentially, it was a revival of the extinct "Native-American" faction, based upon a jealousy of and discrimination against foreign-born voters, desiring an extension of their period of naturalization, and their exclusion from office; also based upon a certain hostility to the Roman Catholic religion. It had been reorganized as a secret order in the year 1853; and seizing upon the political disappointments following General Scott's overwhelming defeat for the presidency in 1852, and profiting by the disintegration caused by the Nebraska bill, it rapidly gained recruits both North and South. Operating in entire secrecy, the country was startled by the sudden appearance in one locality after another, on election day, of a potent and unsuspected political power, which in many instances pushed both the old organizations not only to disastrous but even to ridiculous defeat. Both North and South its forces were recruited mainly from the Whig party, though malcontents from all quarters rushed to group themselves upon its narrow platform, and to participate in the exciting but delusive triumphs of its temporary and local ascendency.

When, in the opening of the anti-Nebraska contest, the Free-soil leaders undertook the formation of a new party to supersede the old, they had, because of their generally democratic antecedents, with great unanimity proposed that it be called

the "Republican" party, thus reviving the distinctive appellation by which the followers of Jefferson were known in the early
days of the republic. Considering the fact that Jefferson had
originated the policy of slavery restriction in his draft of the
ordinance of 1784, the name became singularly appropriate, and
wherever the Free-soilers succeeded in forming a coalition it
was adopted without question. But the refusal of the Whigs in
many States to surrender their name and organization, and
more especially the abrupt appearance of the Know-Nothings
on the field of parties, retarded the general coalition between
the Whigs and the Free-soilers which so many influences favored. As it turned out, a great variety of party names were
retained or adopted in the Congressional and State campaigns
of 1854, the designation of "anti-Nebraska" being perhaps the
most common, and certainly for the moment the most serviceable, since denunciation of the Nebraska bill was the one all-
pervading bond of sympathy and agreement among men who
differed very widely on almost all other political topics. This
affiliation, however, was confined exclusively to the free States.
In the slave States, the opposition to the Administration dared
not raise the anti-Nebraska banner, nor could it have found
followers; and it was not only inclined but forced to make its
battle either under the old name of Whigs, or, as became more
popular, under the new appellation of "Americans," which grew
into a more dignified synonym for Know-Nothings.

Thus confronted, the Nebraska and anti-Nebraska factions,
or, more philosophically speaking, the pro-slavery and antislavery sentiment of the several American States, battled for political supremacy with a zeal and determination only manifested
on occasions of deep and vital concern to the welfare of the
republic. However languidly certain elements of American society may perform what they deem the drudgery of politics,
they do not shrink from it when they hear warning of real
danger. The alarm of the nation on the repeal of the Missouri
Compromise was serious and startling. All ranks and occupations therefore joined with a new energy in the contest it pro-

voked. Particularly was the religious sentiment of the North profoundly moved by the moral question involved. Perhaps for the first time in our modern politics, the pulpit vied with the press, and the Church with the campaign club, in the work of debate and propagandism.

The very inception of the struggle had provoked bitter words. Before the third Nebraska bill had yet been introduced into the Senate, the then little band of "Free-Soilers" in Congress— Chase, Sumner, Giddings, and three others—had issued a newspaper address calling the repeal "a gross violation of a sacred pledge"; "a criminal betrayal of precious rights"; "an atrocious plot," "designed to cover up from public reprehension meditated bad faith," etc. Douglas, seizing only too gladly the pretext to use denunciation instead of argument, replied in his opening speech, in turn stigmatizing them as "abolition confederates" "assembled in secret conclave" "on the holy Sabbath while other Senators were engaged in divine worship"—"plotting," "in the name of the holy religion"; "perverting," and "calumniating the committee"; "appealing with a smiling face to his courtesy to get time to circulate their document before its infamy could be exposed," etc.

The key-notes of the discussion thus given were well sustained on both sides, and crimination and recrimination increased with the heat and intensity of the campaign. The gradual disruption of parties, and the new and radical attitudes assumed by men of independent thought, gave ample occasion to indulge in such epithets as "apostates," "renegades," and "traitors." Unusual acrimony grew out of the zeal of the Church and its ministers. The clergymen of the Northern States not only spoke against the repeal from their pulpits, but forwarded energetic petitions against it to Congress, 3050 clergymen of New England of different denominations joining their signatures in one protest. "We protest against it," they said, "as a great moral wrong, as a breach of faith eminently unjust to the moral principles of the community, and subversive of all confidence in national engagements; as a measure full of danger to the peace and even the existence of our beloved Union, and exposing us to the righteous judgment of the Almighty." In return, Douglas made a most virulent onslaught on their political action. "Here we find," he retorted, "that a large body of preachers, perhaps three thousand, following the lead of a circular which was issued by the abolition confederates in this body, calculated to deceive and mislead the public, have here come forward with an atrocious falsehood, and an atrocious calumny against this Senate, desecrated the pulpit, and prostituted the sacred desk to the miserable and corrupting influence of party politics." All his newspapers and partisans throughout the country caught the style and spirit of his warfare, and boldly denied the moral right of the clergy to take part in politics otherwise than by a silent vote. But they, on the other hand, persisted all the more earnestly in justifying their interference in moral questions wherever they appeared, and were clearly sustained by the public opinion of the North.

Though the repeal was forced through Congress under party pressure, and by the sheer weight of a large Democratic majority in both branches, it met from the first a decided and unmistakable popular condemnation in the free States. While the measure was yet under discussion in the House in March, New Hampshire led off by an election completely obliterating the eighty-nine Democratic majority in her Legislature. Connecticut followed in her footsteps early in April. Long before November it was evident that the political revolution among the people of the North was thorough, and that election day was anxiously awaited merely to record the popular verdict already decided.

The influence of this result upon parties, old and new, is perhaps best illustrated in the organization of the Thirty-fourth Congress, chosen at these elections during the year 1854, which witnessed the repeal of the Missouri Compromise. Each Congress, in ordinary course, meets for the first time about one year after its members are elected by the people, and the influence of politics during the interim needs always to be taken into account. In this particular instance this effect had, if anything, been slightly reactionary, and the great contest for the Speakership during the winter of 1855-6 may therefore be taken as a fair manifestation of the spirit of politics in 1854.

The strength of the preceding House of Representatives, which met in December, 1853, had been: Whigs, 71; Free-soilers, 4; Democrats, 159—a clear Democratic majority of 84. In the new Congress there were in the House, as nearly as the classification could be made, about 108 anti-Nebraska members, nearly 40 Know-Nothings, and about 75 Democrats; the remaining members were undecided. The proud Democratic majority of the Pierce election was annihilated.

But as yet the new party was merely inchoate, its elements distrustful, jealous, and discordant; the feuds and battles of a quarter of a century were not easily forgotten or buried. The Democratic members, boldly nominating Mr. Richardson, the House leader on the Nebraska bill, as their candidate for Speaker, made a long and determined push for success. But his highest range of votes was about 74 to 76; while through 121 ballotings, continuing from December 3 to January 23, the opposition remained divided, Mr. Banks, the anti-Nebraska favorite, running at one time up to 106—within seven votes of an election. At this point, Richardson, finding it a hopeless struggle, withdrew his name as a candidate, and the Democratic strength was transferred to another, but with no better prospects. Finally, seeing no chance of otherwise terminating the contest, the House yielded to the inevitable domination of the slavery question, and resolved, on February 2, by a vote of 113 to 104, to elect under the plurality rule after the next three ballotings. Under this rule, notwithstanding the most strenuous efforts to rescind it, Nathaniel P. Banks, of Massachusetts, was chosen Speaker by 103 votes, against 100 votes for William Aiken, of South Carolina, with thirty scattering. The "ruthless" repeal of the Missouri Compromise had effectually broken the legislative power of the Democratic party.

THE REPEAL *of the Missouri Compromise aroused Lincoln, he wrote, as he had never been aroused before. He took the stump in Illinois to do what he could to reverse this new and, in his mind, eminently dangerous departure in national policy. In 1855 he failed of election to the United States Senate but did succeed in securing the office for Lyman Trumbull, then an anti-administration Democrat. The opponents of the new policy—Free Soilers, anti-slavery Democrats, and former Whigs—formed the Republican party, which Lincoln joined in 1856. Two years later he opposed Douglas for reelection to the Senate. Lincoln lost, but the debates of 1858 won him a national reputation. In 1860, as one who was "not the first choice of a very great many" but one who had fewer enemies than the leading contenders, he won the Republican presidential nomination and, subsequently, the election.*

Southern leaders had warned that the election of Lincoln, a "sectional" candidate, would precipitate secession. As early as October 5, 1860, Governor William H. Gist of South Carolina had written to the governors of the cotton states that in the event of Lincoln's election, which he considered certain, South Carolina would withdraw from the Union. What, Gist asked, would their states do?

A short chapter describes South Carolina's rush to carry out her governor's threat.

From the Ballot to the Bullet

THE secret circular of Governor Gist, of South Carolina, heretofore quoted, inaugurated the great American Rebellion a full month before a single ballot had been cast for Abraham Lincoln. This was but repeating in a bolder form the action taken by Governor Wise, of Virginia, during the Frémont campaign four years before. But, instead, as in that case, of confining himself to a proposed consultation among slave-State executives, Gov-

ernor Gist proceeded almost immediately to a public and official revolutionary act.

On the 12th of October, 1860, he issued his proclamation con-
vening the Legislature of South Carolina in extra session, "to
appoint electors of President and Vice-President . . . and also
that they may, if advisable, take action for the safety and protection of the State." There was no external peril menacing
either the commonwealth or its humblest citizen; but the significance of the phrase was soon apparent.

A caucus of prominent South Carolina leaders is said to
have been held on October 25, at the residence of Senator
Hammond. Their deliberations remained secret, but the determination arrived at appears clearly enough in the official
action of Governor Gist, who was present, and who doubtless
carried out the plans of the assemblage. When the Legislature
met on November 5 (the day before the Presidential election)
the Governor sent them his opening message, advocating both
secession and insurrection, in direct and undisguised language.
He recommended that in the event of Lincoln's election, a convention should be immediately called; that the State should
secede from the Federal Union; and "if in the exercise of arbitrary power and forgetful of the lessons of history, the Government of the United States should attempt coercion, it will be
our solemn duty to meet force by force." To this end he recommended a reorganization of the militia and the raising and
drilling an army of ten thousand volunteers. He placed the
prospects of such a revolution in a most hopeful and encouraging light. "The indications from many of the Southern
States," said he, "justify the conclusion that the secession of
South Carolina will be immediately followed, if not adopted
simultaneously, by them, and ultimately by the entire South.
The long-desired coöperation of the other States having similar
institutions, for which the State has been waiting, seems to be
near at hand; and, if we are true to ourselves, will soon be
realized."

Governor Gist's justification of this movement as attempted was (in his own language) "the strong probability of the election to the Presidency of a sectional candidate by a party committed to the support of measures, which if carried out will inevitably destroy our equality in the Union, and ultimately reduce the Southern States to mere provinces of a consolidated despotism to be governed by a fixed majority in Congress hostile to our institutions."

This campaign declamation, used throughout the whole South with great skill and success, to "fire the Southern heart," was wholly defective as a serious argument.

As to the alleged destruction of equality, the North proposed to deny to the slave States no single right claimed by the free States. The talk about "provinces of a consolidated despotism to be governed by a fixed majority" was, in itself an absurd contradiction in terms, which repudiated the fundamental idea of republican government. The acknowledgment that any danger from anti-slavery "measures" was only in the future, negatived its validity as a present grievance. Hostility to "our institutions" was expressly disavowed by full constitutional recognition of slavery under State authority. The charge of "sectionalism" came with a bad grace from a State whose newspapers boasted that none but the Breckinridge ticket was tolerated within her borders, and whose elsewhere obsolete "institution" of choosing Presidential electors by the Legislature instead of by the people, combined with such a dwarfed and crippled public sentiment, made it practically impossible for a single vote to be cast for either Lincoln or Douglas or Bell—a condition mathematically four times as "sectional" as that of any State of the North.

Finally, the avowed determination to secede because a Presidential election was about to be legally gained by one of the three opposing parties, after she had freely and fully joined in the contest, was an indulgence of caprice utterly incompatible with any form of government whatever.

There is no need here to enter upon a discussion of the many

causes which had given to the public opinion of South Carolina
so radical and determined a tone in favor of disunion. Maintaining persistence, and gradually gathering strength almost
continuously since the nullification furor of 1832, it had become something more than a sentiment among its devotees: it
had grown into a species of cult or party religion, for the existence of which no better reason can be assigned than that it
sprang from a blind hero-worship locally accorded to John C.
Calhoun, one of the prominent figures of American political
history. As representative in Congress, Secretary of War under
President Monroe, Vice-President of the United States under
President John Quincy Adams, for many years United States
Senator from South Carolina, and the radical champion of
States Rights, Nullification, and Slavery, his brilliant fame was
the pride, but his false theories became the ruin, of his State
and section.

Governor Gist and his secession coadjutors had evidently still
a lingering hope that the election might by some unforeseen
contingency result in the choice of Breckinridge. On no other
hypothesis can we account for the fact that on the 6th of November, when Northern ballots were falling in such an ample
shower for Lincoln, the South Carolina Legislature, with due
decorum and statute regularity, apointed Presidential electors
for the State, and formally instructed them to vote for Breckinridge and Lane. The dawn of November 7 dispelled these hopes.
The "strong probability" had become a stubborn fact.

When the certain news of Lincoln's election finally came, it
was hailed with joy and acclamation by both the leaders and
the people of South Carolina. They had at length their much
coveted pretext for disunion; and they now put into the enterprise a degree of earnestness, frankness, courage, and persist-
ency worthy of a better cause. Public opinion, so long prepared,
responded with enthusiasm to the plans and calls of the leaders.
Manifestations of disloyalty became universal. Political clubs
were transformed into military companies. Drill-rooms and
armories were alive with nightly meetings. Sermons, agricul-

tural addresses, and speeches at railroad banquets were only so many secession harangues. The State became filled with volunteer organizations of "minute men."

The Legislature, remaining in extra session, and cheered and urged on by repeated popular demonstrations and the inflamed speeches of the highest State officials, proceeded without delay to carry out the Governor's programme. In fact, the members needed no great incitement. They had been freshly chosen within the preceding month; many of them on the well-understood "resistance" issue. Their election took place on the 8th and 9th days of October, 1860. Since there was but one party in South Carolina, there could be no party drill; but a tyrannical and intolerant public sentiment usurped its place and functions. On the sixteen different tickets paraded in one of the Charleston newspapers, the names of the most pronounced disunionists were the most frequent and conspicuous. "Southern rights at all hazards," was the substance of many mottoes, and the palmetto and the rattlesnake were favorite emblems. There was neither mistaking nor avoiding the strong undercurrent of treason and rebellion here manifested, and the Governor's proclamation had doubtless been largely based upon it.

The first day's session of the Legislature (November 5) developed one of the important preparatory steps of the long-expected revolution. The Legislature of 1859 had appropriated a military contingent fund of one hundred thousand dollars, "to be drawn and accounted for as directed by the Legislature." The appropriation had been allowed to remain untouched. It was now proposed to place this sum at the control of the Governor to be expended in obtaining improved small arms, in purchasing a field battery of rifled cannon, in providing accouterments, and in furnishing an additional supply of tents; and a resolution to that effect was passed two days later. The chief measure of the session, however, was a bill to provide for calling the proposed State Convention, which it was well understood would adopt an ordinance of secession. There was scarcely a ripple of opposition to this measure. One or two members still pleaded for delay, to secure the cooperation of Georgia, but dared not record a vote against the prevailing mania. The chairman of the proper committee on November 10 reported an act calling a convention "for the purpose of taking into consideration the dangers incident to the position of the State in the Federal Union," which unanimously became a law November 13, and the extra session adjourned to meet again in regular annual session on the 26th.

Meanwhile public excitement had been kept at fever heat by all manner of popular demonstrations. The two United States Senators and the principal Federal officials resigned their offices with a public flourish of their insubordinate zeal. An enthusiastic ratification meeting was given to the returning members of the Legislature. To give still further emphasis to the general movement a grand mass meeting was held at Charleston on the 17th of November. The streets were filled with the excited multitude. Gaily dressed ladies crowded balconies and windows, and zealous mothers decorated their children with revolutionary badges. There was a brisk trade in firearms and gunpowder. The leading merchants and prominent men of the city came forth and seated themselves on platforms to witness and countenance a formal ceremony of insurrection. A white flag, bearing a palmetto tree and the legend *Animis opibusque parati* (one of the mottoes on the State seal), was, after solemn prayer, displayed from a pole of Carolina pine. Music, salutes, and huzzahs filled the air. Speeches were addressed to "citizens of the Southern Republic." Orations and processions completed the day, and illuminations and bonfires occupied the night. The preparations were without stint. The proceedings and ceremonies were conducted with spirit and abandon. The rejoicings were deep and earnest. And yet there was a skeleton at the feast; the Federal flag, invisible among the city banners, and absent from the gay bunting and decorations of the harbor shipping, still floated far down the bay over a faithful commander and loyal garrison in Fort Moultrie.

IN CHARLESTON HARBOR, *Major Robert Anderson, career officer from Kentucky, succeeded the aging commander of the Federal defenses. In Washington, on December 4, 1860, President Buchanan sent to Congress an annual message asserting in substance that secession was unconstitutional but that the Federal government could do nothing to prevent it or to compel the return of a state which should leave the Union. In Washington also, a Senate Committee of Thirteen and a House Committee of Thirty-Three tried to devise measures of conciliation. But South Carolina moved inexorably by calling a convention to take the state out of the Union.*

South Carolina Secession

THE delegates to the South Carolina Convention were elected on the 6th of December, and assembled and organized at Columbia, the capital of the State, on the 17th of the same month; on account of a local epidemic, however, both the convention and the Legislature adjourned to Charleston, where the former reassembled on the following day and the latter two days afterwards. Elected under the prevailing secession *furor* which tolerated no opposition, and embracing the leading conspirators in its membership, the convention was practically unanimous. "There is no honor," said the chairman on taking his seat, "I esteem more highly than to sign the ordinance of secession as a member of this body; but I will regard it as the greatest honor of my life to sign it as your presiding officer."

The Legislature of South Carolina had just elected a new governor, who was inaugurated on the same day on which the convention met. This was F. W. Pickens, a revolutionist of a yet more radical and energetic type than his predecessor Gist, and who, as we have seen, had been in close consultation with the Cabinet cabal at Washington, more than a month before. He was, of course, anxious to signalize his advent; and to this end immediately dispatched to Washington a special messenger, bearing the following letter to President Buchanan:

(Strictly confidential.)

COLUMBIA, December 17, 1860.

MY DEAR SIR: With a sincere desire to prevent a collision of force, I have thought proper to address you directly and truthfully on points of deep and immediate interest.

I am authentically informed that the forts in Charleston harbor are now being thoroughly prepared to turn, with effect, their guns upon the interior and the city. Jurisdiction was ceded by this State expressly for the purpose of external defense from foreign invasion, and not with any view that they should be turned upon the State.

In an ordinary case of mob rebellion, perhaps it might be proper to prepare them for sudden outbreak. But when the people of the State, in sovereign convention assembled, determine to resume their original powers of separate and independent sovereignty, the whole question is changed, and it is no longer an act of rebellion. I, therefore, most respectfully urge that all work on the forts be put a stop to for the present, and that no more force may be ordered there.

The regular convention of the people of the State of South Carolina, legally and properly called, under our Constitution, is now in session, deliberating upon the gravest and most momentous questions, and the excitement of the great masses of the people is great, under a sense of deep wrongs, and a profound necessity of doing something to preserve the peace and safety of the State.

To spare the effusion of blood, which no human power may be able to prevent, I earnestly beg your immediate consideration of all the points I call your attention to. It is not improbable that, under orders from the Commandant, or perhaps from the Commander-in-Chief of the Army, the alteration and defenses of those posts are progressing without the knowledge of yourself or the Secretary of War.

The arsenal, in the city of Charleston, with the public arms, I am informed, was turned over very properly to the keeping and defense of a State force, at the urgent request of the Governor of South Carolina. I would most respectfully, and from a sincere devotion to the public peace, request that you would allow me to send a small force, not exceeding twenty-five men and an officer, to take possession of Fort Sumter, immediately, in order to give a feeling of safety to the community. There are no United States troops in that fort whatever, or perhaps only four or five, at present; besides some additional workmen or laborers, lately employed to put the guns in order. If Fort Sumter could be given to me, as Governor, under a permission similar to that by which the Governor was permitted to keep the arsenal with the United States arms in the city of Charleston, then I think the public mind would be quieted under a feeling of safety; and as the convention is now in full authority, it strikes me that could be done with perfect propriety. I need not go into particulars, for urgent reasons will force themselves readily upon your consideration.

If something of the kind be not done, I cannot answer for the consequences.

I send this by a private and confidential gentleman, who is authorized to confer with Mr. Trescott fully, and to receive through him any answer you may think proper to give to this.

I have the honor to be, most respectfully,

Yours truly,   F. W. PICKENS.

To the President of the United States.

Arrived in Washington, the special messenger who bore this document sought the active agent of the central cabal, Mr. Trescott, Assistant Secretary of State, and was by him on Thursday morning, December 20, conducted to the White House and presented to Mr. Buchanan, to whom he personally delivered his communication. The President received the document and promised an answer to it on the following day. The temper and condition of his mind is plainly reflected in what he wrote. He seems to have realized no offense in this insult to the sovereignty and dignity of the United States whose Constitution he had sworn to "preserve, protect, and defend"; no patriotic resentment against the South Carolina conspirators who, as he knew by the telegraph, were assembling that same day in convention to inaugurate local rebellion;—his whole answer breathed a tone of apology that his oath and duties would not permit him to oblige the South Carolina Governor; and he feebly groped for relief from his perplexities in the suggestion that Congress might perhaps somehow arrange the trouble. This was the answer prepared:

WASHINGTON, December 20, 1860.

MY DEAR SIR: I have received your favor of the 17th inst.
by Mr. Hamilton. From it I deeply regret to observe that you
seem entirely to have misapprehended my position, which I
supposed had been clearly stated in my message. I have incurred, and shall incur, any reasonable risk within the clearly
prescribed line of my executive duties to prevent a collision
between the army and navy of the United States and the citizens of South Carolina in defense of the forts within the harbor
of Charleston. Hence I have declined for the present to reënforce these forts, relying upon the honor of South Carolinians
that they will not be assaulted whilst they remain in their present condition; but that commissioners will be sent by the convention to treat with Congress on the subject. I say with *Congress* because, as I state in my message, "Apart from the execution of the laws so far as this may be practicable, the Executive
has no authority to decide what shall be the relations between
the Federal Government and South Carolina. He has been invested with no such discretion. He possesses no power to change
the relations heretofore existing between them, much less to
acknowledge the independence of that State." This would be
to invest a mere executive officer with the power of recognizing
the dissolution of the confederacy among our thirty-three sovereign States. It bears no resemblance to the recognition of a foreign *de facto* government, involving no such responsibility. Any
attempt to do this would, on my part, be a naked act of usurpation.

As an executive officer of the Government, I have no power to
surrender, to any human authority, Fort Sumter or any of the
other forts or public property in South Carolina. To do this
would, on my part, as I have already said, be a naked act of
usurpation. It is for Congress to decide this question, and for
me to preserve the status of the public property as I found it
at the commencement of the troubles.

If South Carolina should attack any of these forts, she will
then become the assailant in a war against the United States.
It will not then be a question of coercing a State to remain in
the Union, to which I am utterly opposed, as my message
proves, but it will be a question of voluntarily precipitating a
conflict of arms on her part, without even consulting the only
authority which possesses the power to act upon the subject.
Between independent governments, if one possesses a fortress

within the limits of another, and the latter should seize it without calling upon the appropriate authorities of the power in possession to surrender it, this would not only be a just cause of war, but the actual commencement of hostilities.

No authority was given, as you suppose, from myself or from the War Department, to Governor Gist, to guard the United States Arsenal in Charleston by a company of South Carolina volunteers. In this respect you have been misinformed—I have, therefore, never been more astonished in my life, than to learn from you that unless Fort Sumter be delivered into your hands, you cannot be answerable for the consequences.

It is easy to infer from results, that while Mr. Buchanan was laboring over this document the central cabal was busy. They saw that the rash zeal of Governor Pickens was endangering the web of conspiracy they had wound around the President. He was committed to non-coercion; committed to non-reënforcement; committed to await the arrival of South Carolina commissioners. This new demand from a new authority not only indicated a division of sentiment and purpose in the insurrectionary councils in the Palmetto State, but created an opportunity through which Mr. Buchanan under a possible healthier impulse of patriotism might repudiate the whole obligation of non-resistance to their schemes into which they had beguiled him. They clearly saw, as they themselves explained, that though he would not deliver Sumter now, he might be willing to "approach such action" hereafter, "a possibility not at all improbable, and which ought to be kept open."

Mr. Trescott therefore hastened to take the advice of two of the South Carolina Congressmen,—McQueen and Bonham, —and it is not a violent presumption to assume, also of the chief Senatorial conspirators; for only six days had elapsed since the Congressional circular was signed and published, which called upon the Cotton States to proceed with the plot of secession and the formation of a Southern Confederacy. A telegram was at once sent to Charleston, mildly explaining to Governor Pickens the blunder he was making and asking his authority to withdraw his letter to Mr. Buchanan. Governor

Pickens must be credited with astuteness enough to comprehend the situation, for he gave the consent requested. On Friday morning Mr. Trescott waited upon Mr. Buchanan and informed him that he would not be required to answer as Governor Pickens had withdrawn his demand; and Mr. Trescott records, with an evident appreciation of the affair as a successful stroke of policy, that "the withdrawal of the letter was a great relief to the President." To understand more fully the whole scope and spirit of the incident, we must read the report of it which he then transmitted to Charleston:

WASHINGTON, December 21, 1860.
To HIS EXCELLENCY F. W. PICKENS,
    GOVERNOR OF SOUTH CAROLINA.

SIR: Your confidential letter to the President was duly delivered to him yesterday by D. H. Hamilton, Esq., according to your instructions. It was withdrawn (no copy having been taken) this morning by me, under the authority of your telegraphic dispatch. Its withdrawal was most opportune. It reached here under circumstances which you could not have anticipated, and it produced the —— effect upon the President.

He had removed Colonel Gardiner from command at Fort Moultrie, for carrying ammunition from the arsenal at Charleston; he had refused to send reënforcements to the garrison there; he had accepted the resignation of the oldest, most eminent, and highest member of his Cabinet, rather than consent to send additional force, and the night before your letter arrived, he, upon a telegraphic communication that arms had been removed from the arsenal to Fort Moultrie, the Department of War had issued prompt orders by telegraph to the officer removing them, to restore them immediately. He had done this upon his determination to avoid all risk of collision, and upon the written assurance of the majority of the Congressional Delegation from the State that they did not believe there was any danger of an attack upon the forts before the passage of the Ordinance, and an expression of their trust and hope that there would be none after, until the State had sent commissioners here. His course had been violently denounced by the Northern press, and an effort was being made to —— a Congressional investigation. At that moment he could not have gone to the extent of action you desired, and I felt confident that if forced to answer your letter then he would have taken such ground as would have prevented his ever approaching it hereafter, a possibility not at all improbable, and which ought to be kept open. I considered, also, that the chance of public investigation rendered the utmost caution necessary as to any communications from the State, and having presented the letter, and ascertained what the nature of the reply would be, you had all the advantage of knowing the truth, without the disadvantage of having it put on record. Besides this, the President seemed to think that your request was based upon the impossibility of your restraining the spirit of our people; an interpretation which did you injustice, and the possibility of which I deemed it due to you to avoid. He also appeared to labor under the impression that the representations of the Members of Congress and your own differed essentially, and this, I thought, on account of both, should not be stated in any reply to you. I was also perfectly satisfied that the status of the garrisons would not be disturbed.

Under these circumstances, if I had been acting under formal credentials from you, and the letter had been unsealed, I would have delayed its presentation for some hours, until I could have telegraphed you, but that was impossible. As Mr. Hamilton, therefore, had brought with him General McQueen and General Bonham, when he called on me and delivered the letter, and had even gone so far as to express the wish that they should be present when he delivered it to the President,—a proposition which they declined, however,—I deemed it not indiscreet, nor in violation of the discretionary confidence which your letter implied, to take their counsel. We agreed perfectly, and the result was the telegraphic dispatch of last night. The withdrawal of the letter was a great relief to the President, who is most earnestly anxious to avoid an issue with the State or its authorities, and, I think, has encouraged his disposition to go as far as he can in this matter, and to treat those who may represent the State with perfect frankness.

I have had this morning an interview with Governor Floyd, the Secretary of War. No order has been issued that will at all disturb the present condition of the garrisons, and while I cannot even here venture into details, which are too confidential to be risked in any way, I am prepared to say, with a full sense of the responsibility, that nothing will be done which will either do you injury or properly create alarm. Of course when your commissioners have succeeded or failed to effect their negotiations, the whole issue is fairly before you, to be met as courage, honor, and wisdom may direct.

My delay in answering your telegraph concerning Colonel Huger, was caused by his absence from this place. He came, in reply to my telegraph last night, and this morning I telegraphed upon his decision, which I presume he has explained by a letter of this same date. As Dr. Hamilton leaves this evening, I have only time to write this hurried letter, and am, sir,

Very respectfully,
WM. HENRY TRESCOTT.

I inclose your confidential letter in this.

We must now turn our attention from the executive rooms of the Presidential mansion in Washington to the executive rooms of South Carolina in Charleston, where on the same day a counterpart of the transaction we have described was going on. Since the beginning of these new troubles, especially since the discussion and issuing of his message, President Buchanan had been anxious and ill at ease. He could not shut his eyes to the fact that in South Carolina, at least, the tide of revolution was steadily rising. He appears to have dimly felt that his official responsibility and honor were somehow involved; and since he had reasoned the executive power into nothingness, the idea suggested itself to his mind that a little friendly expostulation at least was due from him. Under some such impulse he wrote the following letter to Governor Pickens, and with it dispatched Caleb Cushing to Charleston, to see if he might not exert a personal influence upon the malcontents, who paid no heed to any wishes or interests but their own:

WASHINGTON, December 18, 1860.

MY DEAR SIR: From common notoriety, I assume the fact that the State of South Carolina is now deliberating on the question of seceding from the Union. Whilst any hope remains that this may be prevented, or even retarded, so long as to allow the people of her sister States an opportunity to manifest their opinions upon the causes which have led to this proceeding, it is my duty to exert all the means in my power to avert so dread a catastrophe. I have, therefore, deemed it advisable to send to you the Hon. Caleb Cushing, in whose integrity, ability, and prudence I have full confidence, to hold communications with you on my behalf, for the purpose of changing or modifying the contemplated action of the State in the manner I have already suggested. Commending Mr. Cushing to your kind attention, for his own sake, as well as that of the cause, I remain,

Very respectfully, your friend,

JAMES BUCHANAN.

HIS EXCELLENCY FRANCIS W. PICKENS.

Mr. Cushing was a man of great affability, and of prominence in the Democratic party. He had been Attorney-General under President Pierce, and was called to preside over the Charleston Convention, until the dissension in that body between Northern and Southern Democrats caused its disruption and adjournment to Baltimore. In the second disruption at Baltimore, Mr. Cushing had followed the fortunes of the Southern leaders, and with them had seceded, and presided over that fraction of the original body which nominated Breckinridge. Though a Massachusetts man, he was thus affiliated in party principle, party organization, and party action with the South, and President Buchanan not unnaturally thought that he was personally an agreeable agent, and ought to be an influential party representative, capable, in behalf of the Administration, of dissuading the Charleston conspirators from their dangerous determination, or at least from their reckless precipitancy. But the sequel shows that Buchanan both misunderstood the men he had to deal with, and was unequal in purpose and will to cope with their superior daring and resolution.

Mr. Cushing arrived in Charleston on the day the South Carolina Convention passed its ordinance of secession. He obtained an interview with the Governor, and presented the President's letter. "I had but a short interview with him," said Governor Pickens in his message of November 5, 1861, "and told him I would return no reply to the President's letter, except to say very candidly that there was no hope for the Union, and that, so far as I was concerned, I intended to maintain the separate independence of South Carolina, and from this pur-

pose neither temptation nor danger should for a moment deter
me." There is a notable contrast in this haughty and defiant
reception by a South Carolina governor of the messenger of
the President of the United States, to the cringing and apolo-
getic spirit in which the President had on that same morning
received the messenger of the Governor and replied to his demand. Mr. Cushing's reply deserves special notice. "He said,"
continues Governor Pickens, "that he could not say what
changes circumstances might produce, but when he left Washington, there was then no intention whatever to change the
status of the forts in our harbor in any way." By this language
Mr. Cushing himself seems to have changed his errand from
a patriotic mission of protest and warning to one conveying
advantageous information to the conspirators.

It could hardly have been without a sense of personal mortification to Mr. Cushing that the drama which he had been
sent to avert, or at least to postpone, immediately unrolled itself
under his very eyes, and his mortification must have risen to
indignation when he was requested by his presence to grace
the pageant. The South Carolina Convention, during the two
days which had elapsed since its adjournment hither from
Columbia, had been deliberating in secret session. A little
after midday of December 20, the streets of Charleston were
filled with placards giving the public the first notice of its
action.

The usual jubilations immediately followed—ringing of bells,
salutes of cannon, and the noise and display of street parades.
The convention resolved to celebrate the event further by a public ceremonial to which it invited the Governor, the Legislature,
and other dignitaries; and both branches of the Legislature also
sent a committee to Caleb Cushing to give him an official invitation to attend. At half-past six that evening the members of
the convention marched in procession to Institute Hall, where
the public signing of the ordinance of secession was performed
with appropriate solemnities, and at its close the presiding
officer announced: "The ordinance of secession has been signed

and ratified, and I proclaim the State of South Carolina an Independent Commonwealth."

The city and the State joined in general exultation as if a great work had been accomplished, as if the efforts of a generation had been crowned with fulfillment, and nothing remained but to rest and enjoy the ripened fruit of independence. There seemed to be no dream amid all this rejoicing, that nothing definite had as yet been effected; that the reckless day's act was but the prelude to the most terrible tragedy of the age, the unchaining of a storm which should shake the continent with terror and devastation, leaving every Southern State a wreck, and sweeping from the face of the earth the institution in whose behalf the fatal work was done.

The secession ordinance having been passed, signed, and proclaimed, the convention busied itself for the next few days in making up a public statement of its reasons for the anomalous procedure. The discussion showed a wide divergence of opinion as to the causes which had produced the act. One ascribed it to the election of Lincoln, another to the failure of the Northern States to execute the fugitive-slave law, a third to the anti-slavery sentiment of the free States, a fourth to the tariff, a fifth to unconstitutional appropriations by Congress, and so on. On the 24th of December the convention adopted a "Declaration of Causes," and an "Address to the Slave-holding States," the two papers together embracing the above and other specifications. Since neither the Constitution of the United States nor the laws of Congress contained any section, clause, word, or reasonable implication that authorized an act of secession, the "Declaration of Causes" formulated the doctrine of States rights in justification. That doctrine in substance was, that the several States entered the Union as sovereignties; that in forming the Federal Government they delegated to it only specific powers for specific ends; that the Federal Government was not a sovereign over sovereignties, but was only an agent between them; that there existed no common arbiter to adjudge differences; that each State or sovereignty might judge for itself any violation of the common agreement and choose its own mode of redress; consequently that each State might adhere to or secede from the Union, at its own sovereign will and pleasure.

This doctrine, springing from early differences of constitutional interpretation, had not been promulgated in its ultra form until South Carolina's nullification movement in 1832. It had been accepted and sustained by only a small fraction of the American people. The whole current, action, and development of the government of the United States under the Constitution was based upon the opposite theory. Washington and the succeeding Presidents rejected it in their practical administration; Marshall and the Supreme Court condemned it in their judicial decisions; Webster refuted it in his highest constitutional arguments; Congress repudiated it in its legislation; Jackson denounced it in executive proclamation as treasonable and revolutionary; and the people of the Union at large regarded it as an absurd and dangerous political heresy.

After their account of the passage of the Ordinance of Secession, Nicolay and Hay devoted more than a full volume to the events which took place between December 20, 1860, and April 12, 1861. These included: Major Anderson's sudden transfer, on December 26, of his garrison from vulnerable Fort Moultrie to much stronger Fort Sumter; the maneuverings of South Carolina "commissioners," who attempted to secure the acquiescence of the Buchanan administration in that state's withdrawal from the Union; the disintegration and subsequent strengthening of Buchanan's cabinet; the secession of other cotton states and the organization of the provisional government of the Confederate States of America; the inauguration of Lincoln; and, finally, the fall of Fort Sumter.

War had come. North and South responded with equal fervor.

The National Uprising

THE guns of the Sumter bombardment woke the country from the political nightmare which had so long tormented and paralyzed it. The lion of the North was fully roused. Betrayed, insulted, outraged, the free States arose as with a cry of pain and vengeance. War sermons from pulpits; war speeches in every assemblage; tenders of troops; offers of money; military proclamations and orders in every newspaper; every city radiant with bunting; every village-green a mustering ground; war appropriations in every legislature and in every city or town council; war preparations in every public or private workshop; gun-casting in the great foundries; cartridge-making in the principal towns; camps and drills in the fields; parades, drums, flags, and bayonets in the streets; knitting, bandage-rolling, and lint-scraping in nearly every household. Before the lapse of forty-eight hours a Massachusetts regiment, armed and equipped, was on its way to Washington; within the space of a month the energy and intelligence of the country were almost completely turned from the industries of peace to the activities of war. The very children abandoned their old-time school-games, and played only at soldiering.

From every governor of every free State to whom the President's proclamation and the requisition of the Secretary of War were addressed, most gratifying and loyal answers were promptly returned. They not only promised to obey the call and furnish the regiments asked for, but in their replies reflected the unanimity with which their people rallied to the defense of the assaulted Union. "The Governor's call was published on yesterday, and he has already received the tender of forty companies," said Illinois. "Our citizens throughout the State will respond with great enthusiasm to any call for sustaining the Government against the designs of the conspirators," said Vermont. "Ten days ago we had two parties in this State; to-day we have but one, and that one is for the Constitution and Union unconditionally," said Iowa. The war spirit rose above all anticipation, and the offer of volunteers went far beyond the call. "We have 6000 men in camp here and will have 8000 men by to-morrow night. . . . I have also made a tender of six additional regiments to which I have received no answer. I shall put the six additional regiments in camp and under discipline, and hold them subject to the Government's order at least for a time." Such was the greeting from Indiana. A no less inspiring report was made by her sister State. "I find that I have already accepted and have in camp, or ready to march instantly to it, a larger force than the thirteen regiments named as the contingent of Ohio under the late requisition of the President. Indeed, without seriously repressing the ardor of the people, I can hardly stop short of twenty regiments." The telegrams and letters here quoted are fair samples of the language and spirit with which the people of the North answered the President's official summons. Special mention deserves to be made of the untiring zeal and labors of the various executives of the free States in organizing and equipping troops, which earned for them the popular and honorable title of the "war governors."

If we would catch a glimpse of the dramatic forms in which popular fervor manifested itself in the President's own State, we need but read how the town of Quincy, Illinois, sent away her first company:

Yesterday, Sunday, Captain Prentiss left with his command for Springfield. At 12 M. all the pastors of the city, with their congregations, met the gallant captain and his loyal company in Washington Square, to give them a parting benediction. Six or seven thousand persons were present. A banner was presented, a hymn was sung, prayer was made, and the soldiers addressed by one of the clergymen and myself. We then marched with them to the depot, where the "Star-Spangled Banner" was sung, many thousands joining in the chorus. The scene altogether was the most solemn and impressive I have ever witnessed, and showed unmistakably how intensely the fires of patriotism are burning in the hearts of our people.

In the Gulf States the revolutionary excitement rose to a similar height, but with contrary sentiment. All Union feeling and utterance vanished; and, overawed by a terrorism which now found its culmination, no one dared breathe a thought or scarcely entertain a hope for the old flag. The so-called Government of the Confederate States, convinced that it must at length confront actual war, made such haste as it could to put an army in the field, manifesting meanwhile an outward gayety at the prospect which its members could hardly have felt at heart. Montgomery telegrams stated that the Cabinet of the Confederate States read President Lincoln's proclamation "amid bursts of laughter." Alexander H. Stephens was reported as saying in an Atlanta speech that it would require seventy-five times 75,000 men to intimidate the South.

In addition to the 21,000 volunteers conditionally asked for on April 8, the rebel Secretary of War notified the Governors of the seven Cotton States that 32,000 more must be immediately got ready to take the field, and also asked that the forts and military posts within their limits be formally turned over to the control of the Montgomery authorities. Arkansas and Tennessee not yet being members of the Confederacy, permission was asked of their executives to plant batteries to blockade the Mississippi. Spare guns from the captured Charleston forts were sent south, and extraordinary efforts were made to concentrate an army at Pensacola for the reduction of Fort Pickens.

It was at this time (April 17) that Jefferson Davis issued a proclamation, inviting applications for letters of marque and reprisal, under which privateers were offered the opportunity to roam the high seas and ravage the commerce of the United States "under the seal of these Confederate States." The final hope of the rebel leaders was in cotton and free trade; and they believed that privateering was the easy stepping-stone to European intervention. The reasoning was plausible, and the time not ill-chosen; but the proclamation found itself confronted by the prompt precautionary act of the United States Government. Two days later (April 19) President Lincoln issued a counter-proclamation, setting on foot a blockade of the rebel ports "in pursuance of the laws of the United States and of the laws of nations," and declaring that offenders under pretended letters of marque would be held amenable to the laws against piracy.

Thus sixteen States in the North and seven in the South stood opposed in the attitude and preparation of war. Between these two extremes of sentiment lay the debatable land of the border slave States, the greater portion of their citizens tormented with anxiety, with doubt, with their affections evenly balanced between the Union on one hand and slavery on the other; with ties of consanguinity permeating alike the North and the South; with the horrible realization that in the impending conflict they were between the upper and the nether millstones. To a certain extent the Governors of these States had hitherto professed to share the irresolution of their people. Openly, they still expostulated with the Cotton States against precipitate disunion, and urged instead that all the slave States should join in a convention and demand constitutional guarantees from the North.

All this, however, was largely a mere pretext, because they very well knew that the extreme demands which they formulated would not be granted. Secretly, most of them were in the revolutionary plot; and when, by the assault on Sumter and President Lincoln's call for troops, they were compelled to take sides, all save two immediately gave their voice and help more or less actively in aid of the rebellion.

This course they began by refusing the regiments called for under the President's proclamation. "Kentucky will furnish no troops for the wicked purpose of subduing her sister Southern States," answered Governor Magoffin. "I can be no party to this wicked violation of the laws of the country, and to this war upon the liberties of a free people. You can get no troops from North Carolina." So ran the response from Governor Ellis. "The people of this commonwealth are freemen, not slaves, and will defend to the last extremity their honor, lives, and property against Northern mendacity and usurpation," was the reply from Governor Rector of Arkansas. "In such unholy crusade no gallant son of Tennessee will ever draw his sword," wrote Governor Harris. "Your requisition, in my judgment, is illegal, unconstitutional, and revolutionary in its object, inhuman and diabolical, and cannot be complied with," said Governor Jackson of Missouri.

Chief among the plotting border-State executives was Governor Letcher of Virginia. A former chapter has set forth the drift of that State towards rebellion under his leadership and instigation. The apparent Union majority in the Virginia Convention had somewhat restrained and baffled him and his coadjutors; but now they adroitly turned the fresh war excitement to their own advantage. Pretended Virginia Unionists had aided secession by clamoring for the unconditional evacuation of Sumter and other forts. Now that the Government and the North resolved to repel force by force, the ground necessarily sank from under them. They were overwhelmed with arguments and reproaches. One or two vainly essayed to stem the tide. But when Anderson's flag went down even their measured and conditional patriotism withered like Jonah's gourd. There was nothing more but brass-bands, meetings, war speeches, and torchlight processions. The Virginia commissioners reported Lincoln's answer to the convention without comment, and shrinking Unionists admitted that "if the President means sub-jugation of the South, Virginia has but one course to pursue." Governor Letcher did not need any stronger hint. With a dra-matic affectation of incredulity and deliberation, to impress not only public opinion, but especially the wavering, dissolving majority of the convention, he waited a day before telegraphing his refusal to furnish troops—repeating the staple phrase about "subjugation." Then, in the face of his own avowed project to capture Fort Monroe, and with the assaulting guns of Beau-regard still ringing in his ears, he replied to Cameron, "You have chosen to inaugurate civil war."

Meanwhile, the fever heat of the populace communicated itself to the convention. An outside "States-Rights" assemblage of prominent Virginia politicians, which thronged into Rich-mond at this juncture, added its not inconsiderable tribute of pressure to the sweeping tide of treason. Under such impulses the convention went into secret session on Wednesday, April 17, and by a vote of 88 to 55 passed an ordinance of secession—or, as they softly phrased it, "An ordinance to repeal the rati-fication of the Constitution of the United States." On the same day Governor Letcher signed a proclamation announcing the dissolution of the Union and the existence of the rebel Provi-sional Government, and calling on all the armed regiments and companies of volunteers in the State to hold themselves in readiness for orders. Nor did his zeal confine itself to paper edicts. Under his instructions, doubtless matured and prepared in advance, seizures of the custom-house and government build-ings in Richmond, of a private powder depot in Lynchburg, and of a number of steamers in the James River were hurriedly made, and military movements were begun to capture the United States arsenal at Harper's Ferry and the United States navy yard at Norfolk.

Of the two remaining border slave States, Delaware lay in such an isolated geographical position, and had withal so few slaves, that she was practically a part of the North, though still dominated in her local politics by pro-slavery influence. Allied to the South rather by tradition than by present interest, her executive took refuge in a course of inaction. He replied by saying that the laws of Delaware gave him no authority to comply with the requisition of the Secretary of War, and that the organized volunteer companies of the State might at their option tender their services to the United States; and to this effect he issued his official proclamation. The people took him at his word, and by their own action bore a patriotic and honorable part in the dangers and achievements of the Union army.

Of more immediate and vital importance, however, than that of any other border slave State, was the course of Maryland in this crisis. Between that State and Virginia lay the District of Columbia, originally ten miles square of Federal territory, containing the capital, the Government, and the public archives. In Baltimore, the chief city of Maryland, centered three of the great railroad routes by which loyal troops must approach Washington. It was a piece of exceptional good fortune that the Governor of Maryland was a friend of the Union, though hardly of that unflinching fearlessness needed in revolutionary emergencies. Whatever of hesitancy or vacillation he sometimes gave way to, resulted from a constitutional timidity rather than from a want of patriotism; and with brief exceptions to be more fully narrated, he was active and energetic in behalf of the Government. The population of the State was divided by a sharp antagonism, the Unionists having the larger numbers, the secessionists the greater persistence and daring. The city of Baltimore was so far corrupted by treasonable influences that Wigfall had established a successful recruiting office there for the rebel armies. As yet, disunion was working secretly; but this increased rather than diminished its effectiveness.

Like the other border-State executives, Governor Hicks had urged concession, compromise, peace, and joint border-State action to maintain the Union. In this, while his colleagues for the greater part used such talk to cover their meditated treachery, he was entirely sincere and patriotic. When Lincoln's call for troops reached him, he had no thought of refusing or resisting, but nevertheless hurried to Washington to deprecate civil war, and to ask that Maryland soldiers might not be sent to subjugate the South. Since the President had never entertained any purpose of "subjugation," Hicks was assured that the Maryland regiments should be employed to defend Maryland itself and the Federal District and capital. The Governor thereupon wrote to the Secretary of War: "The condition of affairs in this State at this time requires that arms shall be placed in the hands of true men and loyal to the United States Government alone," and requested arms "for arming four regiments of militia for the service of the United States and the Federal Government."

Other prominent Marylanders were already combining for demonstrative action to sustain the Government. A Congressional election in the State was near at hand. On the day of the President's proclamation Henry Winter Davis announced himself, in a Baltimore evening paper, as a candidate for Congress "upon the basis of the unconditional maintenance of the Union." But the official announcements and the exciting rumors with which the newspapers were filled had also stirred the disunion elements of Maryland into unwonted activity, and the pressure of sentiment hostile to Federal authority was quickly brought to bear on Governor Hicks, and developed the timid and hesitating qualities of his character. He issued his proclamation April 18, containing, among many sage counsels in behalf of quiet and peace, two paragraphs doubtless meant by him for good, but which were well calculated to furnish the disunionists hope and encouragement:

I assure the people that no troops will be sent from Maryland, unless it may be for the defense of the national capital. . . . The people of the State will in a short time have the opportunity afforded them, in a special election for Members of the Congress of the United States, to express their devotion to the Union, or their desire to see it broken up.

With this outline view of the political condition of the country at large, and especially of the border States of Virginia and Maryland, let us follow events at the Federal capital as recorded in the daily reports of General Scott to the President. On April 15, the day on which Lincoln issued his first call for 75,000 troops, the general says, in his report:

I have but little of special interest to report to-day, except that Colonel Smith, the commander of the Department of Washington, like myself, thinks our means of defense, with vigilance, are sufficient to hold this city till reënforcements arrive. I have telegraphed the commander at Harper's Ferry armory to say whether he can station, to advantage, for the defense of that establishment, additional recruits from Carlisle. The ground about the armory is very contracted and rocky.

General Scott's daily report, April 16, then proceeds:

For the President. He has no doubt been informally made acquainted with the reply of the officer commanding at Harper's Ferry, yesterday, viz.: that he wants no reënforcement. Nevertheless, as soon as the capital, the railroad to the Delaware at Wilmington, and Fort Monroe are made secure, my next object of attention will be the security of Harper's Ferry—proposing, in the mean time, or rather suggesting that the spare marines from the navy yards of Philadelphia, Brooklyn, and Boston be promptly sent to the Gosport navy yard. This relief may serve, by compelling the secessionists to enlarge their preparations, to give us time to send a regiment of volunteers to that important point, in advance of any formidable attack upon it. With the authority of the Secretary of War we are engaged in mustering into the service eight additional companies of District volunteers. These, I think, place the capital a little ahead of impending dangers, and we will maintain, at least, that advantage, till by the arrival (in a week) of regulars and abundant volunteers our relative advantage will, I trust, be more than doubled.

General Scott's daily report, April 17:

I repeat in writing some details which I had the honor to submit verbally to the President this forenoon. Three or four regiments from Massachusetts (believed to be the first ready under the recent call) may be expected (three of them) to arrive here, and (one of them) at Fort Monroe, in two or three days. One of the three may, I think, be safely spared for Harper's Ferry, if the danger there (and I shall know to-morrow) shall seem imminent. Captain Kingsbury, a most capable officer of the Ordnance Department, goes up this afternoon for that purpose, and to act a few days as superintendent; that is, till a new appointment (of a civilian) can be made. Two of the Massachusetts regiments are needed here; one of them I shall endeavor to intercept at Baltimore and direct it to Harper's Ferry. As soon as one of the four reaches Fort Monroe, it perhaps may be safe to detach thence for the Gosport navy yard two or three companies of regulars to assist in the defense of that establishment. By to-morrow, or certainly the next day, we shall have Colonel Delafield here, an excellent engineer, to send to Gosport (with a letter from the Secretary of the Navy giving the necessary authority) to devise, in conjunction with the naval commander there, a plan of defense. Colonel Delafield will take instructions to call for the two or three companies of regulars as mentioned above. Excepting the reënforcement of marines (suggested yesterday), and until the arrival of more volunteers, I know not what else can be done for the security of the Gosport navy yard. To-night all the important avenues leading into Washington shall be well guarded.

The current demoralization of politics in the country had infected the army and the navy; and striking high as well as low, misdirected the zeal of Captain Adams, caused the dishonor of Major-General Twiggs, commanding the Department of Texas, and carried into rebellion Brigadier-General Joseph E. Johnston, the Quartermaster-General, and Samuel Cooper, the Adjutant-General of the Army. Among these victims of the States-Rights heresy was yet another man destined to become prominent in the rebellion, who undertook the maintenance of a principle and a policy, by him recognized and acknowledged to be false and monstrous. This was Robert E. Lee, a West Point graduate, an accomplished and experienced soldier, frequently recognized and promoted, the captor of John Brown at Harper's Ferry, and recently (March 16, 1861) made colonel of the First Cavalry by the Lincoln Administration; he was about two years older than President Lincoln, of fine presence, ripe judgment, and mature manhood. Lee was a favorite of Scott: under the call for troops the General-in-Chief at once selected him in his own mind as the most capable and promising officer in the service to become the principal commander in the field; and of this intention he spoke to many without reserve, having no misgiving as to his loyalty.

Scott's confidence proved to be sadly misplaced. Repeated resignations and defections had very naturally engendered in the minds of the President and the Cabinet a distrust of every officer of Southern birth. Lincoln therefore requested F. P. Blair, senior, an intimate friend, to ascertain Lee's feelings and intentions. On the 18th of April, the third day after the President's call for troops, the day after Virginia's secret secession ordinance, and the day before the Baltimore riot, Mr. Blair invited Lee to an interview, informed him of the promotion and duties to which he was soon likely to be called, and thus unofficially offered him the command of the Union army. A flat contradiction exists as to the character of Lee's answer. Cameron, then Secretary of War, says he accepted the offer.* Montgomery Blair, then Postmaster-General, says he was undecided what he would do.† Both these gentlemen apparently

---

* "General Lee called on a gentleman who had my entire confidence, and intimated that he would like to have the command of the army. He assured that gentleman, who was a man in the confidence of the Administration, of his entire loyalty, and his devotion to the interests of the Administration and of the country. I consulted with General Scott, and General Scott approved of placing him at the head of the army. The place was offered to him unofficially with my approbation, and with the approbation of General Scott. It was accepted by him verbally, with the promise that he would go into Virginia and settle his business, and then come back to take command."—Hon. Simon Cameron, debate in the U. S. Senate, Feb. 19, 1868 ("Globe," p. 1270).

† "General Lee said to my father when he was sounded by him, at the request of President Lincoln, about taking command of our army against the rebellion, then hanging upon the decision of the Virginia Convention, 'Mr. Blair, I look upon secession as anarchy. If I owned the four millions of slaves at the South, I would sacrifice them all to the Union; but how can I draw my sword upon Virginia, my native State?' He could not determine then; said he would consult with his friend General Scott, and went on the same day to Richmond, probably to arbitrate difficulties; and we see the result."—Hon. Montgomery Blair to Bryant, "National Intelligencer," August 9, 1866.

derived their information from the elder Blair. On the other hand, Lee himself asserts that he declined the proposition, because, "though opposed to secession and deprecating war, I could take no part in an invasion of the Southern States."* He further explains his motive to have been an unwillingness to "take part against my native State," or to "raise my hand against my relatives, my children, my home." But in his interview with Blair he also affirmed that secession was anarchy; that if he owned the whole four million slaves of the South he would sacrifice them all for the Union; and he appears to have substantially repeated the sentiment written to his son a few weeks before, as follows:

Secession is nothing but revolution. The framers of our Constitution never exhausted so much labor, wisdom, and forbearance in its formation, and surrounded it with so many guards and securities, if it was intended to be broken by every member of the Confederacy at will. It was intended for "Perpetual Union," so expressed in the preamble, and for the establishment of a government, not a compact, which can only be dissolved by revolution, or the consent of all the people in convention assembled. It is idle to talk of secession. Anarchy would have been established, and not a government, by Washington, Hamilton, Jefferson, Madison, and the other patriots of the Revolution.

Under a liberal interpretation, Lee's personal denial must be accepted; but the times, the circumstances, his qualifying declarations, and the strong statements of Cameron and Blair clearly reveal his hesitation and indecision. After his interview with Blair, Lee sought an interview with Scott, where the topics which filled men's hearts and occupied men's lips—

---

* "I never intimated to any one that I desired the command of the United States army, nor did I ever have a conversation but with one gentleman, Mr. Francis Preston Blair, on the subject, which was at his invitation, and, as I understood, at the instance of President Lincoln. After listening to his remarks, I declined the offer he made me, to take command of the army that was to be brought into the field, stating, as candidly and as courteously as I could, that, though opposed to secession and deprecating war, I could take no part in an invasion of the Southern States."— Lee to Reverdy Johnson, February 25, 1868. J. W. Jones, "Life of Lee," p. 141.

Union, secession, Virginia, subjugation, duty and honor, defection and treason—were once more, we may be quite sure, thoroughly discussed. It is morally certain that Scott, also a Virginian, gave Lee a lesson in patriotism; but he caught no generous emulation from the voice and example of his great chief.

From Scott's presence Lee seems to have retired to his home and family at Arlington, to wrestle with the haunting shadows of duty. Pregnant news came to him, thick and fast. The secession of Virginia was verified in Washington that same evening. The next evening the Sixth Massachusetts marched in mingled pride and sorrow to the Capitol, having made an immortal record of service to their country. Here were new and important elements to influence his decision. Virginia seceded, Maryland in revolt, Washington threatened, Sumter lost, the border States defiant, the Confederate States arming, and uttering a half-official threat that the rebel flag should float over the Capitol by the 1st of May. If the walls of Arlington heard secret or open conferences with conspirators from Washington, or conspirators from Richmond, no record of them has come to light; but Saturday, April 20, Lee wrote to his old commander:

GENERAL: Since my interview with you on the 18th instant, I have felt that I ought not longer to retain my commission in the army. I therefore tender my resignation, which I request you will recommend for acceptance. It would have been presented at once, but for the struggle it has cost me to separate myself from a service to which I have devoted all the best years of my life and all the ability I possessed. . . . Save in defense of my native State, I never desire again to draw my sword.

Lee was at the time, in military phrase, "on leave of absence"; and without waiting to hear whether his resignation had been accepted, or even recommended for acceptance, as he himself had urged—without awaiting further orders, or permission, or discharge, or dismissal from service, on the 22d of April he was, by the Governor and the Convention of Virginia, appointed to, and on the 23d, in Richmond, publicly invested with, chief

command of the Virginia State forces under the secret secession ordinance and Letcher's revolutionary proclamation, with
all his military obligations to the United States intact and un-
canceled; thus rendering himself guilty of desertion and treason.* No danger whatever menaced his "native State"—the
President had positively disclaimed all intention to invade it.
In the course of events we find him not alone defending his
native State, to which he owed nothing, but seeking to destroy
the Union, which had done everything for him; opposing war
by promoting "revolution," and redressing grievances by endeavoring to establish "anarchy."

In instructive contrast with the weakness and defects of Lee,
we have the honorable conduct and example of General Scott.
He, too, was a Virginian who loved his native State. He, too,
was opposed to secession and deprecated war. He, too, as officer, commander, diplomatist, and statesman, had learned from
books and from men the principles and practice of loyalty, and
perhaps better than any American exemplar was competent to
interpret a soldier's oath, a soldier's duty, a soldier's honor. To
avoid bloodshed he had declared his individual willingness to
say to the seceded States, "Wayward sisters, depart in peace."
But underneath pride of home, affection of kindred, and horror

* The Army Regulations of 1857, having the authority and force of law,
contained the following provisions:

"24. No officer will be considered out of service on the tender of his
resignation, until it shall have been duly accepted by the proper authority.

.   .   .   .

"28. In time of war, or with an army in the field, resignations shall take
effect within thirty days from the date of the order of acceptance."

For the offense thus defined by the Regulations of 1857, the Act of
August 5, 1861, provided specific punishment, as follows:

"Sec. 2. And be it further enacted, That any commissioned officer of the
army, navy, or marine corps, who, having tendered his resignation, shall,
prior to due notice of the acceptance of the same by the proper authority,
and, without leave, quit his post or proper duties with the intent to remain
permanently absent therefrom, shall be registered as a deserter, and punished as such."

If it be contended that Lee's offense was committed prior to this last
statute, the answer is that his transgression was a much graver one, for he
not only absented himself with intent to remain, but immediately entered
into hostile service, an act punishable under the broad principles of general military law.

of war, on the solid substratum of consistency and character, lay his recognition of the principle of government, his real, not simulated, veneration for the Constitution, his acceptance of the binding force of law, his unswerving fidelity to his oath, his undying devotion to his flag. The conspirators had long hoped for the assistance of his great name and authority. They filled the air with rumors of his disaffection. Since its abrupt secession ordinance, the Virginian Convention had sat with closed doors; but through a responsible witness, we know that on the day on which Lee wrote his resignation (April 20) a committee of that convention called on General Scott to tempt him with the offer of the command of the Virginia forces. Senator Stephen A. Douglas, on his way home to arouse the great West in aid of Lincoln's proclamation, told the circumstance in graphic language to excited listeners:

I have been asked whether there is any truth in the rumor that General Scott was about to retire from the American army. It is almost profanity to ask that question. I saw him only last Saturday. He was at his desk, pen in hand, writing his orders for the defense and safety of the American capital. Walking down the street I met a distinguished gentleman, a member of the Virginia Convention, whom I knew personally, and had a few minutes' conversation with him. He told me that he had just had an interview with Lieutenant-General Scott; that he was chairman of the committee appointed by the Virginia Convention to wait upon General Scott and tender him the command of the forces of Virginia in this struggle. General Scott received him kindly, listened to him patiently, and said to him, "I have served my country under the flag of the Union for more than fifty years, and as long as God permits me to live I will defend that flag with my sword, even if my own native State assails it."

An eye-witness reports that the rebuke contained an additional feature of unusual impressiveness. When the spokesman of the committee, a man of venerable years and presence, had vaguely and cautiously so far unfolded the glittering lure of wealth and honor which Virginia held out that the general could catch the drift of the humiliating proposal, Scott held up his hand and said emphatically, "Friend Robertson, go no farther. It is best that we part here before you compel me to resent a mortal insult." That same afternoon Scott also telegraphed to Senator Crittenden, in response to an anxious inquiry based on the false rumors set afloat about him, "I have not changed. I have not thought of changing. Always a Union man." And in that unshaken mood of patriotism he lived and died, beloved of his country, and honored by the world.

The Virginia secession ordinance, though secretly adopted on the 17th, became quickly known to the people of Richmond. It was immediately announced to the States-Rights Convention in session in another hall, and Governor Letcher, Senator Mason, ex-President Tyler, and ex-Governor Wise, from the convention, soon appeared there and glorified the event with speeches—the latter lamenting the "blindness which had prevented Virginia from seizing Washington before the Republican hordes got possession of it." Nevertheless, an effort was still made to prevent the news from going North. But that evening some of the unconditional Union delegates from western Virginia—then a part of the Old Dominion—deemed it prudent to shake the Richmond dust from their feet and secure their personal safety by prompt departure.

Delegates Carlisle and Dent were in Washington on the 18th, and in all probability informed Mr. Seward and the President how irretrievably eastern Virginia was committed to rebellion, even if Governor Letcher's reply and proclamation had left any doubt on that point. Ominous rumors came from Harper's Ferry, and also a premature report of the burning of the railroad bridges beyond Baltimore. On that day, too, a detachment of 460 Pennsylvania volunteers, "almost entirely without arms," and a company of regulars from Minnesota had been hurriedly forwarded from Harrisburg to Washington. The unruly elements of Baltimore were already in commotion, the cars containing these men being in their passage through that city cheered by the crowd at some points and hooted and stoned at others, though no casualties occurred. Noting all these rumors and acts of hostility, Secretary Cameron telegraphed to Governor Hicks that "the President is informed that threats are made and measures taken by unlawful combinations of misguided citizens of Maryland to prevent by force the transit of United States troops across Maryland on their way, pursuant to orders, to the defense of this capital"—and strongly intimated to the Governor that the loyal authorities of Maryland ought to put them down.

The events of the week—the daily mustering of volunteers, the preparations for defense, the telegrams from the various State capitals—had thrown Washington into a military fever. The social sympathies of the permanent population of Washington, and especially of its suburbs, Georgetown and Alexandria, were strongly Southern; but the personal interests of its inhabitants and property holders were necessarily bound up with the course and fate of the existing Government.

The Union manifestations were for the moment dominant, and volunteers came forward readily, even with some enthusiasm, to fill up the District quota. The city was also yet full of office-seekers from various States north and west. Cassius M. Clay of Kentucky, and Senator-elect James H. Lane of Kansas, both men of mark and courage, after an evening or two of flaming speech-making, organized them respectively into the "Clay Battalion" and the "Frontier Guards." These companies, of from thirty to sixty men each, were what might be called irregular volunteers—recruits from East and West, of all ranks in the great army of politics, who came forward to shoulder a musket without enlistment, commission, paymaster, or commissariat.

By this time the danger had become so threatening that every scrap and show of military force was welcome and really useful. The Government furnished them arms, and gave them in charge of Major (afterwards Major-General) David Hunter, who, on the evening of the 18th, stationed Clay's company in Willard's Hall, with orders to patrol the streets, and took Lane's Frontier Guards to the post of honor at the Executive Mansion.

At dusk they filed into the famous East Room, clad in citizens'
dress, but carrying very new, untarnished muskets, and following Lane, brandishing a sword of irreproachable brightness.
Here ammunition-boxes were opened and cartridges dealt out;
and after spending the evening in an exceedingly rudimentary
squad drill, under the light of the gorgeous gas chandeliers, they
disposed themselves in picturesque bivouac on the brilliant-pat-
terned velvet carpet—perhaps the most luxurious cantonment
which American soldiers have ever enjoyed. Their motley composition, their anomalous surroundings, the extraordinary emergency, their mingled awkwardness and earnestness, rendered
the scene a medley of bizarre contradictions,—a blending of
masquerade and tragedy, of grim humor and realistic serious-
ness,—a combination of Don Quixote and Daniel Boone altogether impossible to describe. However, their special guardian-
ship of the East Room lasted only for a night or two, until more
suitable quarters could be extemporized; and for many days
they lent an important moral influence in repressing and over-
awing the lurking treason still present in a considerable fraction
among the Washington inhabitants.

The graphic pen of Bayard Taylor, who happened to be in
Washington on this same afternoon of April 18, has left us a
sharp and strong historical picture of the city at the time:

Everywhere around me the flag of the Union was waving;
troops were patrolling the streets, and yonder the watchful Marshal Lamon was galloping on the second horse he had tired
out since morning. Everybody seemed to be wide awake, alert,
and active. On reaching Willard's Hotel, the scene changed.
The passages were so crammed that I had some difficulty in
reaching the office. To my surprise, half the faces were Southern
—especially Virginian—and the conversation was carried on in
whispers. Presently I was hailed by several Northern friends,
and heard their loud, outspoken expressions of attachment to
the Union. The whisperers near us became silent and listened
attentively. I was earnestly questioned as to whether the delay
of the mails was occasioned by rails being torn up or bridges
destroyed. Every one seemed to suspect that a treasonable
demonstration had taken place in or near Baltimore. The most

exciting rumors were afloat. Harper's Ferry was taken—Virginia had secretly seceded—Wise was marching on Washington—always winding up with the impatient question, "Why don't the troops come on?"

From Willard's Hotel Bayard Taylor went to the State Department, and afterwards to make a call on Lincoln. He continues:

I need not describe the President's personal appearance, for nearly everybody has seen him. Honesty, firmness, and sound common-sense were the characteristics with which personally he impressed me. I was very glad to notice the tough, enduring vitality of his temperament—he needs it all. He does not appear to be worn or ill, as I have heard, but, on the contrary, very fresh and vigorous. His demeanor was thoroughly calm and collected, and he spoke of the present crisis with that solemn, earnest composure which is the sign of a soul not easily perturbed. I came away from his presence cheered and encouraged.

ON APRIL 19, 1861, *Massachusetts and Pennsylvania troops, hurrying to Washington, were attacked by a mob in Baltimore. Several were killed, and for six days no armed force could get through to a jittery capital. Federal commanders found a way around the disaffected city, while in Maryland at large latent Union sentiment came into the open and thwarted the advocates of secession.*

Throughout the North, governors moved with alacrity to raise troops and form lines of defense. Nicolay and Hay explain why the line of the Ohio was of supreme importance.

The Ohio Line

THE American rebellion cannot be studied without constantly bearing in mind the immense geographical area of the United States. From the Alleghany mountains to the Mississippi River, across a territorial breadth of nine degrees of longitude, runs the Ohio River in a south-westerly course; beginning at Pittsburgh among the western spurs of the Alleghanies and ending at Cairo, where it empties itself into the Mississippi. The Ohio is both a great political and commercial factor; for almost a thousand miles it was then the dividing line between free and slave States and on its banks at intervals the cities of Pittsburgh in Pennsylvania, Wheeling in Virginia, Cincinnati in Ohio, Louisville in Kentucky, Evansville in Indiana, and Cairo in Illinois, gathered for it, notwithstanding the competition of railroads, a heavy tribute of commerce from six of the principal Western States. At Cairo, the thousand miles of navigation of the Ohio are joined to another thousand miles of navigation southward to New Orleans, and an additional thousand northward on the Mississippi to St. Paul, not to mention the Missouri River and various other tributaries.

Cairo, therefore, where the Ohio joins the Mississippi, is the military key of the Mississippi Valley, so far as that may be said of any interior point. In relation to the civil war it was doubly so, not merely because it controlled such a vast network of navigation, but because it lay on the extreme southern point of the free State of Illinois, running like a dividing wedge deep between the slave States of Kentucky and Missouri. Cairo was also the terminus of the Illinois Central Railroad, giving it a direct northern connection with Chicago. Being in addition the point nearest of any in the free States to New Orleans, it had unequaled advantages as a base for military operations against the South.

That the people of the Mississippi Valley shared the prevailing excitement over the rebellion, needs hardly to be repeated; it is sufficiently indicated in the insulting replies of the slave State Governors, and the patriotic responses of the "War Governors" from the free States in that section to the President's proclamation. With Virginia in secession, and Kentucky setting up the pretense of armed neutrality, the Ohio line became at once a quasi-military frontier, and the river commerce, with its advantages and risks, was instantly an object of paramount solicitude to the great cities of Pittsburgh, Cincinnati, and Louisville, and in relative measure to all the border States on both sides.

Illinois, holding the extreme right flank of the Ohio line, was neither unmindful of the importance of Cairo, nor forgetful of her patriotic pride as Lincoln's home State. Lincoln on his part did not lose sight of the loyalty of Illinois and the free West, nor the military value of its great river system. No sooner had disloyalty in the border slave States shown itself in the contumacious answers of their Governors than a dispatch went from the Secretary of War to the Governor of Illinois: "As soon as enough of your troops are mustered into service, send a brigadier-general with four regiments to or near Cairo."

Governor Yates had no organized and equipped regiments of State militia. There were in the principal cities and towns of Illinois some scattering and slender volunteer companies of young men organized for holiday parades; perhaps five hundred stands of miscellaneous arms in the State arsenal, and one man holding an antiquated commission of brigadier-general. But he lived in Chicago, and had practical Western ideas and habits. Governor Yates immediately telegraphed General Swift: "As quick as possible have as strong a force as you can raise, armed and equipped with ammunition and accouterments, and a company of artillery ready to march at a moment's warning. A messenger will start to Chicago to-night."

The official report shows that at eleven o'clock on the 21st, only forty hours after the Governor's summons, General Swift started from Chicago with a force of 595 men and four six-pounder pieces of artillery. "This expedition," continues the report, "indifferently armed with rifles, shotguns, muskets, and carbines, hastily gathered from stores and shops in Chicago, arrived at Big Muddy Bridge on the Illinois Central Railroad at five o'clock A.M., April 22, and detaching Captain Harding's company at that point, arrived at Cairo at eight o'clock the following morning. The batteries were unprovided with shot, shell, or canister, but slugs hurriedly prepared—and some of which were used at a critical time and with terrible effect by one of these batteries at Fort Donelson—answered the purpose of all." Next day, April 24, three other batteries from northern Illinois were added to the expedition; and seven newly organized companies from Springfield also reached Cairo, under Colonel Benjamin M. Prentiss, a gallant volunteer officer, who had served in Mexico, and who assumed command.

These troops found a field for immediate usefulness at Cairo. At the very beginning the rebels were forced to lament and endeavor to repair their want of foresight and preparation for war. "Consult with merchants in Alexandria as to the feasibility of obtaining bacon from Ohio or Kentucky," wrote General Lee from Richmond, April 24. On the same day Governor Pickens telegraphed from Charleston to the rebel Secretary of War, "I desire to send an agent to St. Louis and Louisville to make large purchases of provisions." Walker responded that "an agent has been sent to St. Louis and Louisville to make purchases for the army." Other purchasers, it seems, were also in the field, for that day Governor Yates telegraphed from Springfield to Colonel Prentiss at Cairo: "The steamers *C. E. Hillman* and *John D. Perry* are about to leave St. Louis with arms and munitions. Stop said boats and seize all the arms and munitions."

The orders were duly executed, and Governor Yates, who had given them on his own responsibility as Commander-in-Chief for Illinois, reported his action to Washington. "We have directed the officer in command at Cairo," he wrote, "to seize munitions of war passing that point, but have not yet assumed the responsibility of preventing commercial intercourse." Under date of April 29 there came to the President a letter from Governor Harris of Tennessee complaining of the seizure, and asking whether it was by authority, to which Mr. Lincoln prepared the following reply:

SIR: Yours of the 29th ultimo calling my attention to the supposed seizure near Cairo, Illinois, of the steamboat *C. E. Hillman*, and claiming that the said boat and its cargo are the property of the State of Tennessee and her citizens, and demanding to know whether the seizure was made by the authority of this Government or is approved by it, is duly received. In answer, I have to say this Government has no official information of such seizure; but assuming that the seizure was made, and that the cargo consisted chiefly of munitions of war owned by the State of Tennessee, and passing into the control of its Governor, this Government avows the seizure for the following reasons:

A legal call was recently made upon the said Governor of Tennessee to furnish a quota of militia to suppress an insurrection against the United States, which call said Governor responded to by a refusal couched in disrespectful and malicious language. This Government therefore infers that munitions of war passing into the hands of said Governor are intended to be used against the United States; and the Government will not indulge the weakness of allowing it, so long as it is in its power to prevent. This Government will not at present question, but that the State of Tennessee by a majority of its citizens is loyal to the Federal Union, and the Government holds itself respon-

sible in damages for all injuries it may do to any one who may
prove to be such.

This letter by Lincoln, owing to more pressing occupations,
was never signed or sent; but it shows us his feeling and intention, and it is specially characteristic for the ready discernment
with which it draws the distinction between the insurrectionary
course of Governor Harris, the legal attitude of the State of
Tennessee, and the rights of loyal Tennesseeans.

The occupation of Cairo created great excitement in the adjacent South and indignation among the rebels whose schemes
it interrupted; hasty telegrams went from them to Montgomery
announcing the event and suggesting remedies, defense, and re-
taliation. An incautious Kentucky State Senator, resident at
Paducah, forgetting that Paducah was in the State of Kentucky
and Cairo in the State of Illinois, wrote a letter of protest to
Lincoln on the subject, and to this disciple of States Rights
and armed neutrality the President returned a reply of good-
natured irony. Under his direction one of his secretaries wrote:
"The President directs me to acknowledge the receipt of your
letter of the 26th ultimo, protesting against the stationing of
United States troops at Cairo. He directs me to say that the
views so ably stated by you shall have due consideration, and
to assure you that he would never have ordered the movement
of troops complained of had he known that Cairo was in your
Senatorial district."

Of scarcely less immediate interest to the authorities and
people of Illinois than the occupation of Cairo, was the safety
of the United States arsenal at St. Louis, Missouri. It had been
and was then more than ever in jeopardy from the secession
intrigues for its capture, which will be more fully related in another chapter. Governor Richard Yates needed arms for the
volunteers that were gathering at his call. He made application
for them to General William S. Harney at St. Louis, who, probably from habit of routine and over-caution, refused them. Captain Nathaniel Lyon, his subordinate, readier to act in revolutionary emergencies, recommended a large transfer to Illinois.

Governor Yates hurried off a messenger with Lyon's official recommendation and his own requisition for 10,000 stands of arms, who arrived in Washington on Saturday, April 20, the day following the Baltimore riot. He brought letters which sustained and confirmed Lyon's recommendation. The President, with the concurrence of Secretary Cameron and General Scott, directed that Governor Yates should have the arms; that Harney should be relieved, and that three Illinois regiments should be sent to reënforce the arsenal.

The messenger who had come through Baltimore that Saturday morning went back through the turbulent city the same evening, bearing on his person papers which had they been discovered would have insured him short shrift at the first lamppost. In two days more the order was in Governor Yates's hands; but then came the dilemma how to transport the arms without exciting a secession riot to capture the arsenal. There is not room here to relate the well-planned devices to lull the suspicion and elude the attention of the St. Louis rebels. On April 25, at midnight, 10,000 stands of arms in boxes were loaded on a river steamer; and as the time seemed favorable, and the remaining arms were in evident danger, Captain James H. Stokes of Chicago, who was managing the removal, asked permission "to empty the arsenal." Captain Lyon bravely took the responsibility, and 11,000 additional stands of arms, together with quantities of ammunition and equipments, were transferred to the boat, and a company of Missouri volunteers went aboard as a guard. There was a moment of consternation when the steamer was found to be aground with overweight, and the night hours were rapidly slipping away; but the moving of some two hundred boxes to the stern lightened the bow so that the steamer could back off into deep water. Then followed a laconic dialogue between the captain of the boat and the officer in charge. "Which way?" "Straight to Alton in the regular channel." "What if we are attacked?" "Then we will fight." "What if we are overpowered?" "Run her to the deepest part of the river and sink her."

But the precautions had been well taken, and so heroic a sacrifice did not become necessary.

By early dawn of April 26 the steamer touched the wharf at Alton, Illinois, twenty-five miles above St. Louis, where a railroad train stood waiting. The city fire-bell was rung, and as the startled citizens assembled, volunteer working-parties were formed to carry the heavy boxes to the cars; in a couple of hours "the train moved off, amid their enthusiastic cheers, for Springfield." Governor Yates's report of the transaction was brief and business-like. "We this day received from the St. Louis arsenal 21,000 stands of arms, and 110,000 musket cartridges, and two field-pieces all complete. There are left there 8000 stands of arms."

The transition from peace to war along the Ohio line did not fail to produce numberless inconveniences and embarrassments which were greatly complicated by the uncertain sentiment and hesitating attitude of Kentucky. Desiring to treat this State with all tenderness and consideration, General Scott telegraphed on May 2, "It is deemed inexpedient, because irritating to Kentucky and other States bordering on the Ohio, to detain cargoes of provisions descending the rivers from those States." To this the officer at Cairo replied, "No boats have been searched unless I had been previously and reliably informed that they had on board munitions of war destined to the enemies of the Government"; while Governor Oliver P. Morton explained that citizens of Indiana were also anxious to take advantage of the brisk demand for their surplus products; but that such a commerce was simply a channel by which rebel armies in the South would be supplied. He suggested that trade should be cut off with all the States which had refused to furnish volunteers under the President's call. The urgent necessity of some such prohibition very soon became apparent; and on the 8th of May the positive orders of the Secretary of War were telegraphed that provisions must be stopped at Cairo.

Meanwhile the military frontier, shaping itself much more

slowly than east of the Alleghanies, yet so far took definite form that the Department of the Ohio (created on May 3), consisting of the States of Ohio, Indiana, and Illinois, was now formally organized by General George B. McClellan, who assumed command about the middle of May, and who recommended a system of defense, for observation rather than for immediate action. He thought Cairo ought to be occupied with a heavy battery, two or three regiments, and three gun-boats. "Governor Morton is anxious to establish batteries against Louisville. I cannot permit this at present; it would only serve to irritate. . . . The moral effect of the presence of troops at Cairo, Evansville, and Camp Dennison [near Cincinnati] ought to be sufficient to reassure the Union men in Kentucky, although I confess that I think all our calculations should be based on the supposition that Kentucky will secede."

Before any suggestion came of the need of gun-boats on the Western rivers the Government had taken measures to have them supplied. On the 16th of May Secretary Welles issued to Commander John Rodgers the following order: "You will proceed to Cincinnati, Ohio, or the headquarters of General McClellan, wherever they may be, and report to that officer in regard to the expediency of establishing a naval armament on the Mississippi and Ohio rivers, or either of them, with a view of blockading or interdicting communication and interchanges with the States that are in insurrection." Nor did the Government hesitate to set in action whatever agency or resource offered itself, which gave reasonable promise of success. Captain James B. Eads, then little known, but afterwards famous as a civil engineer, came from St. Louis to Washington, and being introduced by Attorney-General Bates to the President and Cabinet, laid before them his plans of war vessels for the Western rivers. He carried back with him the direction of Secretary Cameron, that the subject was referred "to General McClellan, who will consult with Mr. Eads and with such naval officers as the Navy Department may send out for that purpose, and then, as he shall find best, take order for the proper preparation of the boats."

The fact that the efforts of many leading Kentuckians committed that State to the doctrine of "armed neutrality," and the hollow pretense of maintaining this abnormal status, retarded the definition of the true military frontier and the development of military operations. General Simon B. Buckner, then in command of the militia of Kentucky and in the confidence and plans of her Governor, held two interviews with McClellan, one on the 8th and the second on the 13th of June, in which the subject was discussed at length. McClellan reports:

We differed entirely as to the position that Kentucky should assume in the present controversy. He regarded the State as the most loyal one in the Union. I considered his view of the status of Kentucky as inconsistent with true loyalty. In the course of the conversation Buckner voluntarily proffered me his word of honor that he would use all his influence to have Kentucky troops drive out any Confederate forces that might invade the State, and that if he did not possess the necessary power, he would take steps to have me called upon for assistance. To this I replied that the State authorities must be prompt in their call else they would find me there before it, as I would not stand on ceremony in such a case. This, General, is substantially the gist of the interview. I made no stipulations with Buckner, neither did I, directly nor by implication, recognize the neutrality of Kentucky.

So long as the disposition to carry out this promise in good faith continued, the duties of McClellan and succeeding Union commanders along that part of the Ohio line bordering on Kentucky were mainly advisory and administrative, and the local intercourse of that State with the North remained unbroken. Towards the close of the month of May McClellan's attention and active service were required on and beyond that part of the Ohio River bordering the then State of Virginia, now the State of West Virginia. At the western end of the Ohio line little took place except holding and strengthening Cairo and some adjacent points in order to make it a military depot and a principal base of supplies, while armies were being gathered and gun-boats built for the expected fall and winter campaigns. This comparative military idleness on the lower Ohio and the equivocal and uncertain attitude of Kentucky which sustained it were not destined to be of long continuance. The "neutrality" of that State was something to be respected by the rebellion only so long as it might hope to secure her adhesion. As early as July 4 the Richmond authorities created a military department embracing substantially the river counties of the lower Mississippi north of Red River and below Kentucky. To this command General Leonidas Polk, late a bishop, was assigned, with headquarters at Memphis, and to him was confided the duty of watching and opposing the progress of the Union armies from Cairo southward.

All these preparations moved forward under incidental characteristics of confusion and delay that were extremely vexatious to both the Government and the public. To mobilize a hundred thousand soldiers is a task of magnitude even for nations working under military government and provided with standing armies. To expect that such a feat should be accomplished with system and order in a few weeks, by a nation having the merest skeleton of a regular army, where military traditions had nearly faded out, where the people were deeply absorbed in peaceful industries, would be to suppose impossibilities. Yet the stupendous undertaking found a practical if not an ideal accomplishment. Under the inspiring calls issued by the War Governors, volunteers were thronging to the great military camps, improvised not only by the States of Ohio, Indiana, and Illinois, but also by each of their North-western sisters. The great Pittsburgh foundries began to cast mortars and heavy guns; and though regiments were often sent to post or garrison in advance of arms and equipments, these were supplied at the earliest moment they could be obtained.

The military martinet, reviewing these incipient stages of the war of the rebellion, finds on every hand shortcomings to point out and irregularities to censure. We shall hear him frequently, prating of political generals, and building a sagacious after-criticism on the texts of Big Bethel and Bull Run. But the historian will see in these beginnings the sign of a prodigious popular movement, in whose spontaneous energy and persistent continuance early defects and missteps are but as bubbles on the surface of a mighty river. Of all the conflicting calls for arms, for equipments, for siege-guns and field-batteries, for gunboats and transports, for officers to muster-in regiments and perform staff duty, for supplies, for credit, for cash, only a fraction could be immediately supplied. Promises by the Government and the exercise of patience by the applicants were the only alternatives.

THE AUTHORS *describe the frantic efforts of the two sections of an unarmed nation to prepare for full-scale war.*

Civil War

THE Administration was not slow to learn the lesson of the hour. Only half of the twenty days' notice to disperse, given the rebels by Lincoln's first proclamation, had elapsed—the troops under the first call had not been mustered in—and Washington could not be considered permanently safe, when the formation of a new army for more thorough and prolonged work was announced—not publicly as yet, but to the Governors of the States who would be required to furnish the new levy. The several events detailed in the last few chapters dictated the step as one of such unmistakable necessity that it can hardly be said to have been discussed. It needed no demonstration to show that the South was in revolt, and that the North was determined to suppress it.

The actual boundaries, the time and course and the probable phases of the conflict, could not be mapped out; but the substantial fact of a serious military struggle of considerable proportions was self-evident. Preparations for it were therefore at once begun, with cautious deliberation. Ten days after the first proclamation the Secretary of War wrote in response to the overwhelming tenders of three-months' volunteers from several Governors: "No further troops beyond the quota of your State can be received at present, unless they will agree to volunteer for the period of three years, if not sooner discharged. In that event, and upon such terms, one or two regiments more would be accepted from your State and mustered into service." This was written to the Governor of New Jersey, April 26, and similar replies went to Connecticut, Indiana, and Michigan. From day to day the same general answer and notification were sent out to other States, and a week later (May 3) appeared the President's proclamation, calling into service 42,034 three-years' volunteers, 22,714 enlisted men to add ten regiments to the regular army, and 18,000 seamen for blockade service—a total immediate increase of 82,748; swelling the entire military establishment of the nation, including the regular army and navy and the troops under the first call, to an army of 156,861 and a navy of 25,600.

It was easy enough for the President to insert numbers in a proclamation; but there is not room here to describe the task of deciding constitutional powers and responsibilities, examining laws, devising organization and arranging details, all of which had to be done in a single week, and in the midst of dangers. President, Cabinet, and military and naval officers were busy day and night. It is scarcely possible to enumerate the elements of perplexity and unavoidable confusion suddenly thrown together. The abrupt revolutionary uprising; the tumult of enthusiasm in the North; the interruption of mail and telegraph by the Baltimore riot; the succession of military resignations and changes; the orders of the Government at Washington; the extraordinary powers given to the New York Committee and acts performed by it; military orders by General Scott at the capital, and independent distribution of arms and munitions directed in the emergency by General Wool at New York; conflicting questions and requisitions from sixteen different State executives; four different grades of military service, regulars, three months' volunteers, State militia, and three-years' volunteers, still further complicated by independent organizations in border States whose Governors refused coöperation; and all amid a quasi-field campaign about Washington—it was a bedlam compared to the dignified and deliberate red tape and pigeon-hole methods of quiet times.

What with the added necessity for urgency and secrecy, the principal departments of the Government, greatly disorganized by resignation, for a short time staggered under the sudden burdens of routine work which could not wait, and which there were neither sufficient chiefs of bureaus nor clerks to expedite.

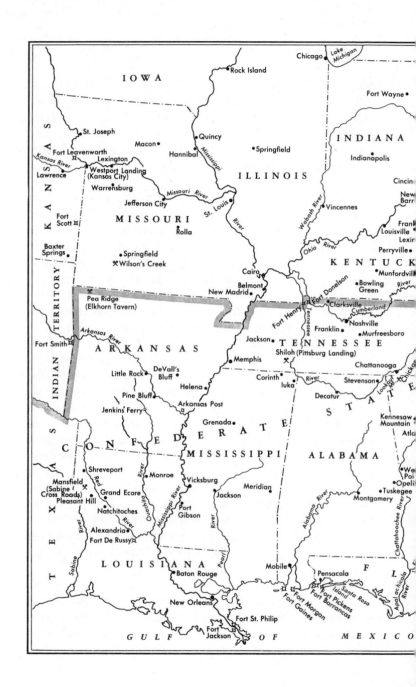

THE CIVIL WAR
1861–1865

0   50   100   150
SCALE OF MILES

Confusion even grew out of good-natured willingness to coöperate and zeal to assist. Impatient governors and State agents, and irrepressible colonels and captains, went to whatever fountainhead of authority they could reach—to Seward for a battery of guns, or to Chase for a horse-contract to mount a regiment. There is no counting the knotty tangles of red tape which as a last resort were brought for the President to cut by his superior authority.

Had Lincoln been a careless or a reckless man, it is difficult to imagine the damage he might have done, or the risk and excess he might have suffered the Government to run into under such conditions. The enthusiasm of the North was already changing to impatience. He was beset by appeals to show energy; by clamors to accept more troops. Suggestions of every shade and merit were pressed upon him, to consider or embark in showy and startling projects. One would have him seize and hang traitors; another, burn Baltimore; a third, destroy Charleston; a fourth, liberate and arm the slaves; a fifth, raise an army of 300,000. Whatever might be other differences, everybody was for promptness, vigor, action, advance. Delay was denounced, muttered accusations of incompetency were heard, and the "New-York Times," echoed by journals of less importance, boldly advised the immediate resignation of the Cabinet and, as already mentioned, warned the President that he might be superseded.

In such a whirl, Lincoln's steady common sense and caution were a rock of safety to the nation. Whatever was essential, involving no matter how much responsibility, he did as soon as the necessity became apparent. But, with equal purpose, he refrained from doing what was not essential; and often—generally indeed—refrained even from explaining or defending his nonaction; or if he did explain, it was only by a casual and general allusion. Thus, on the 1st of May, during an interview with half a dozen members of the Seventh New York, the President, in the course of friendly conversation, spoke in a tone of amusement rather than harshness of the "Times's" proposition to de-

pose him; and said that just now the Government had three
things to do: defend Washington, blockade the ports, and retake Government property. All possible dispatch was to be
used in these matters, and it would be well if the people would
cordially assist in this work before clamoring for more. The
proclamation for calling out the troops, he said, was only two
weeks old; no other people on earth could have surpassed what
we had done in that time. But while he was thus patient and
hopeful about the proximate form and issue of the contest, his
discernment of its ultimate and underlying principle was clearer
and deeper than that of any of his critics:

For my own part, I consider the first necessity that is upon
us, is of proving that popular government is not an absurdity.
We must settle this question now,—whether in a free government the minority have the right to break it up whenever they
choose. If we fail, it will go far to prove the incapability of the
people to govern themselves. There may be one consideration
used in stay of such final judgment, but that is not for us to use
in advance. That is, that there exists in our case an instance of
a vast and far-reaching disturbing element which the history of
no other free nation will probably ever present. That, however,
is not for us to say at present. Taking the government as we
found it, we will see if the majority can preserve it.

The increase of the army once determined upon, and the
proclamation issued, the chief care of the Administration was
bestowed upon the organization of the new force. The best officers were promoted out of the old into the new "regular" regiments; the best arms were reserved for them and the three-
years' volunteers. No little complaint grew out of this discrimination; every regiment, no matter of what service or term of
enlistment, protested it would receive only arms of the latest
invention and most perfect pattern. The Northern arsenals
were very scantily supplied, except with indifferent arms of
antiquated manufacture. Commanders gave notice of danger
that the term of service of some of the regiments would expire
before they could be equipped. The national armories were
driven to their utmost capacity; the President authorized the

erection of a new and extensive establishment at Rock Island, Illinois, to supply the West; all available private factories and workshops were brought into service; purchases in Europe were authorized. But military supplies cannot be extemporized, and the nation had no adequate preparation for such a vast army, so soon to be further augmented to colossal proportions. From all quarters came requisitions and demands for rifles, for cannon, for ammunition, for equipments, for tents, for transportation, for subsistence.

Many places in the country, hitherto unconscious of danger, suddenly felt alarm at the possibility of exposure. The New England seaboard wanted garrisons in the Government forts, and heavy guns to guard against possible privateers. A feeling of insecurity spread along the river towns of the Ohio. The Western frontier asked for arms, to prepare in time for the Indian outbreaks likely to follow hostile conflict. And to provide these resources, the Administration had a nearly extinguished revenue and a paltry ten-million loan! Fortunately, at this point, the enthusiastic patriotism of the hour touched everything with its miraculous wand. In the fervor of these early weeks, considerations of money faded from the popular thought. The men who were willing to die for the Union, tendered it their wealth with unstinted liberality. For the three weeks ending May 8, the indirect donations for war purposes were estimated at twenty-three millions. Government credit was unbounded; and a man might as well have insulted the national flag as to have questioned the national solvency or honesty. There was no more talk of compromise and conciliation, of conventions and constitutional amendments. The universal determination of the North was well summarized by Mr. Seward in a diplomatic dispatch under date of May 4:

The United States waited patiently while their authority was defied in turbulent assemblies and in seditious preparations, willing to hope that mediation, offered on all sides, would conciliate and induce the disaffected parties to return to a better mind. But the case is now altogether changed. The insurgents have instituted revolution with open, flagrant, deadly war to compel the United States to acquiesce in the dismemberment of the Union. The United States have accepted this civil war as an inevitable necessity. The constitutional remedies for all the complaints of the insurgents are still open to them and will remain so. But on the other hand, the land and naval forces of the Union have been put into activity to restore the Federal authority and to save the Union from danger.

Meanwhile the rebellion was not idle. The hotspurs of the South were eager for a sufficient "blood-sprinkling" to arouse a crusade against the Yankees, and to cover the false pretense under which they had lured the States into secession; but the leader dreaded the test of prolonged war, and clung to the hope that the North would not fight. On March 4, the rebel War Department submitted estimates for a modest peace establishment, and on the 14th an additional army of five thousand men to reduce Fort Pickens was the only project for an active campaign. Even after Sumter, Howell Cobb declared there would be no war and advised the people that "they could go on cultivating their crops." Letcher, as late as April 24, by proclamation counseled his gathering Virginians, not in the military service of the State, "to return to their usual avocations, in connection with the trade and commerce of the country."

Out of this long-cherished dream of "peaceable secession," the South was for the first time fully awakened when regiment after regiment came pouring into Washington, when treason was choked in Maryland, when the Western capitals became great camps, when the blockade began to close the seaports of the South. More alarming was that increasing activity of the Northern uprising, the earnestness of which could no longer be denied nor mistaken. Justice John A. Campbell, who had by this time resigned his seat on the Supreme bench, sent Jefferson Davis an impressive warning on this point, under date of April 28, from Washington.

The Northern States are in the wildest condition of excitement. Some of the truest friends of the South have given in their adhesion to the policy of "defending the capital." General

Pierce, General Cushing, and Mr. Dickinson will occur to you at once as men not likely to yield to a slight storm. . . . It seems to me that the importance of peace was never greater than for the next sixty days. . . . We cannot get along at all by looking only at our own side of the question, or to the emanations of our own people. . . . The seven Confederate States have not more than double the number of male population capable of bearing arms which has been offered to this Government as volunteers since the 15th of this month. New York, Boston, and Philadelphia will pour out its capital even for subjugation. The impression that we had firm, stanch friends North who would fight for us was a delusion. Oh! I pray you do not rest upon it.

Though not anticipating this result, Davis had probably long since counted it among the chances of the rebellion in which he was embarked. Always possessed of great self-confidence he made a show of composure at the unwelcome prospect. For him the crisis had its encouragements as well as dangers. Half of Virginia had joined him. He yet had hopes of Maryland, and two thousand extra muskets were at Harper's Ferry to strengthen the next *émeute*. The last vestige of Union defense was gone from Texas, where Van Dorn had just compelled the surrender of the remnants of the United States forces, and also captured the famous steamship, *Star of the West*. North Carolina (though she did not formally secede till May 20) was already to all intents and purposes a member of the rebel Confederacy, and at that moment sending Jefferson Davis captured arms from the Fayetteville arsenal, and marching regiments organized under State authority. In the other four border slave States, the conspiracy was so active and strong, and so thoroughly assured was he of their adhesion, that he had made formal requisitions on them (April 22 and 26) for regiments which should rendezvous at Lynchburg and Harper's Ferry, to help "sustain Baltimore," and make sure of Maryland. His faith was not entirely misplaced; directly and indirectly, Tennessee sent three regiments, Kentucky one, and Arkansas one, in response to his summons; Missouri replied with promises of future help. In spite of the conspiracy of their Governors and other State officers, both Kentucky and Missouri were saved to the Union; but for the moment Jefferson Davis was perhaps justified in believing that the whole South would soon be solid for the rebellion.

Under his call the rebel Congress met at Montgomery in special session, April 29, and deliberated till May 21, enacting, by the advice of himself and his Cabinet, such laws as the crisis seemed to demand. An act recognizing war and regulating privateering; acts admitting Virginia, North Carolina, Tennessee, and Arkansas to the "Confederate States"; an act authorizing a fifty-million loan, for twenty years, at eight per cent.; and an act regulating the export of cotton, require no special comment. More noteworthy was the act practically confiscating for the use of the rebellion all debts due from Southern to Northern citizens. Warily also they laid the foundation for that unsparing military despotism which their desperate enterprise demanded. In mockery of their States Rights theory, the central principle and very pivot of secession, they authorized Davis to accept and organize "companies" into regiments, regardless of any call on the States; to accept "outside" regiments; and to assign Confederate officers to command State troops without displacement or loss of rank. Perhaps their most important action was a joint resolution removing the seat of government to Richmond, where on the 1st of June the rebel capital was duly established. Davis had been warned that a Union reaction was at work in Virginia; and it was doubtless intended that both the sentiment of pride and the rigor of his personal discipline should hold her steadily to the fortunes of the rebellion.

Since the organization of the Montgomery Government in February, some four different calls for Southern volunteers had been made, which would yield in the aggregate 82,000 men. In his message of April 29 to the rebel Congress, Jefferson Davis proposed to organize and hold in readiness for instant action an army of 100,000; making the total equal to the total of both army and navy summoned by Lincoln. The work of fortification was going on in all directions; on the sea-coast, on the Potomac,

on the Mississippi. The captured forts and the Norfolk and
Pensacola navy-yards had furnished them an abundance of
heavy guns; the six or eight captured arsenals supplied them
with 18,650 rifles and 145,154 muskets—the latter inferior
arms, it is true, but yet effective if well used. In addition several
States had made separate purchases. The martial spirit was up,
and paper regiments were becoming real ones. There was an
occasional ebullition of impatience and insubordination from
Southern Governors; but the farcical republics of South Carolina and other Cotton commonwealths were things of the past,
and the "Confederate States of America" pretended to an
empire of territory, and no mean nation of inhabitants. Jefferson Davis had been orator, statesman, soldier, and Secretary
of War; had practiced the art of government, and seen something of the operation of armies. He was cold, cynical, ambitious; but had talent, experience, energy, and an indomitable
will. He was now virtual dictator of the South, and understood
the crushing, fusing, welding power of military rule. We must
assume that under these favoring conditions he believed in the
success he predicted—that since he had matured his conspiracy
he would establish his Government.

By THE EARLY SUMMER *of 1861 the cry, "Forward to Richmond!" swelled in the North. End the war with one sudden blow. In camps around Washington the Federal commander Irvin McDowell had thirty-four thousand men. The Confederate forces, concentrated in the vicinity of Centreville, Virginia, twenty-five miles west of the capital, numbered slightly more than twenty thousand, with reinforcements not far away.*

The advance began on July 16. On the 18th, when General Daniel Tyler reached Centreville, he found that the Confederates had retired behind Bull Run, a sluggish stream flowing in a southeasterly direction. At Blackburn's Ford, Tyler became engaged prematurely and suffered some sixty casualties—a setback which cooled the ardor of his green troops.

At this point we resort to the narrative of Nicolay and Hay.

Bull Run

McDowell began his campaign with the purpose of turning the right flank of the enemy at Union Mills; but the examinations made on the 18th satisfied him that the narrow roads and rough country in that direction made such a movement impracticable. When, in addition, he heard Tyler's cannonade on the same day, he hurried forward his divisions to Centreville; but the report of that day's engagement also seemed to prove it inexpedient to make a direct attack. That night McDowell assembled his division commanders at Centreville and confidentially informed them that he had changed his original plan, and resolved to march westward and turn Beauregard's left flank. All of Friday, the 19th, and Saturday, the 20th, were spent in an effort of the engineers to find an unfortified ford over Bull Run in that direction; and thus the main battle was postponed till Sunday, July 21. During those two days, while McDowell's army was supplied with rations, the strength of the enemy in his front was greatly increased.

McDowell's movement was based upon the understanding and promise that Patterson should hold Johnston in the Shenandoah Valley, and General Scott made every exertion to redeem this promise. On the 13th he directed Patterson to detain Johnston "in the valley of Winchester"; and as the critical time approached, and hearing no official report from him for three whole days, he sent him a sharp admonition: "Do not let the enemy amuse and delay you with a small force in front, whilst he reënforces the [Manassas] Junction with his main body." And still more emphatically on the 18th, while the engagement of Blackburn's Ford was being fought by McDowell's troops: "I have certainly been expecting you to beat the enemy. If not, to hear that you had felt him strongly, or at least had occupied him by threats and demonstrations. You have been at least his equal, and, I suppose, superior in numbers. Has he not stolen a march and sent reënforcements toward Manassas Junction? A week is enough to win victories."

Patterson was touched by the implied censure, and answered restively: "The enemy has stolen no march upon me. I have kept him actively employed, and by threats and reconnaissances in force caused him to be reënforced." But the facts did not bear out the assertion. The enemy was at that moment making the stolen march which Scott feared, and of which Patterson remained in profound ignorance till two days later.

Since the 9th of July his readiness to "offer battle," or to "strike" when the proper moment should arrive, had oozed away. He became clamorous for reënforcements, and profuse of complaints. Making no energetic reconnaissance to learn the truth, and crediting every exaggerated rumor, he became impressed that he was "in face of an enemy far superior in numbers." Understanding perfectly the nature and importance of his assigned task, and admitting in his dispatches that "this force is the key-stone of the combined movements"; ambitious to perform a brilliant act, and commanding abundant means to execute his plan, his energy failed in the trying moment. "Tomorrow I advance to Bunker Hill," he reported on July 14, "preparatory to the other movement. If an opportunity offers, I shall attack." Reaching Bunker Hill on the 15th, he was within nine miles of the enemy. His opportunity was at hand. Johnston had only 12,000 men all told; Patterson, from 18,000 to 22,000. All that and the following day he must have been torn by conflicting emotions. He was both seeking and avoiding a battle. He had his orders written out for an attack. But it would appear that his chief-of-staff, Fitz-John Porter, together with Colonels J. J. Abercrombie and George H. Thomas, at the last moment persuaded him to change his mind.

Making only a slight reconnaissance on the 16th, he late that night countermanded his orders, and on July 17 marched to Charlestown—nominally as a flank movement, but practically in retreat. Johnston, the Confederate commander, was at Winchester, in daily anticipation of Patterson's attack, when at midnight of July 17 he received orders to go at once to the help of Beauregard at Manassas. By nine o'clock on the morning of the 18th his scouts brought him information that Patterson's army was at Charlestown. Relieved thus unexpectedly from a menace of danger which otherwise he could neither have resisted nor escaped, he lost no time. At noon of the same day he had his whole effective force of nine thousand men on the march; by noon of Saturday, July 20, six thousand of them, with twenty guns, were in Beauregard's camp at Bull Run, ready to resist McDowell's attack.

The Union army lay encamped about Centreville; from there the Warrenton turnpike ran westward over a stone bridge, crossing Bull Run to Gainesville, several miles beyond. Unaware that Johnston had joined Beauregard, McDowell desired to seize Gainesville, a station on the railroad, to prevent such a junction. The stone bridge was thought to be defended in force, besides being mined, ready to be blown up. The engineers, however, late on Saturday, obtained information that Sudley Ford, two or three miles above, could be readily carried and crossed by an attacking column.

On Saturday night, therefore, McDowell called his officers

together and announced his plan of battle for the following day. Tyler's division was ordered to advance on the Warrenton turnpike and threaten the stone bridge; while Hunter and Heintzelman, with their divisions, should make a circuitous and secret night march, seize and cross Sudley Ford, and descending on the enemy's side of Bull Run should carry the batteries at the stone bridge by a rear attack, whereby Tyler would be able to cross and join in the main battle.

Beauregard, on his part, also planned an aggressive movement for that same Sunday morning. No sooner had Johnston arrived than he proposed that the Confederates should sally from their intrenchments, cross the five. fords of Bull Run they were guarding, march by the various converging roads to Centreville, and surprise and crush the Union army in its camps. The orders for such an advance and attack were duly written out, and Johnston, as ranking officer, signed his approval of them in the gray twilight of Sunday morning. But it proved wasted labor. At sunrise Tyler's signal guns announced the Union advance and attack. The original plan was thereupon abandoned, and Beauregard proposed a modification—to stand on the defensive with their left flank at the stone bridge, and attack with their right from the region of Blackburn's Ford. This suggestion again Johnston adopted and ordered to be carried out.

There had been confusion and delay in the outset of McDowell's march, and the flanking route around by Sudley Ford had proved unexpectedly long. Tyler's feigned attack at the stone bridge was so feeble and inefficient that it betrayed its object; the real attack by Hunter and Heintzelman, designed to begin at daylight, could not be made until near eleven o'clock. The first sharp encounter took place about two-thirds of a mile north of the Warrenton turnpike; some five regiments on each side being engaged. The rebels tenaciously held their line for an hour. But the Union column was constantly swelling with arriving batteries and regiments. Tyler's division found a ford, and crossing Bull Run a short distance above the stone bridge, three of its brigades joined Hunter and Heintzelman. About twelve o'clock the Confederate line, composed mainly of Johnston's troops, wavered and broke, and was swept back across and out of the valley of the Warrenton turnpike, and down the road running southward from Sudley Ford to Manassas Junction.

The commanders and other officers on both sides were impressed with the conviction that this conflict of the forenoon had decided the fortunes of the day. Beauregard's plan to make a counterattack from his right flank against Centreville had failed through a miscarriage of orders; and leaving Johnston at headquarters to watch the entire field, he hastened personally to endeavor to check the tide of defeat. Brigadier-General T. J. Jackson, who on this field gained his sobriquet of "Stonewall," had already formed his fresh brigade, also of Johnston's army, on the crest of a ridge known as the Henry Hill, half a mile south of the Warrenton turnpike. Other regiments and batteries were hurried up, until they constituted a semicircular line of twelve regiments, twenty-two guns, and two companies of cavalry, strongly posted and well hidden in the edge of a piece of woods behind the screen of a thick growth of young pines.

At half-past two o'clock in the afternoon, McDowell attacked this second position of the enemy with an immediately available force of about fourteen regiments, twenty-four guns, and a single battalion of cavalry. Here the advantages of position were all strongly against him. The enemy was posted, concealed, and his artillery concentrated; while McDowell's brigades were at the foot of the hill, not only where the ascent must be made in open view, but where the nature of the ground rendered a united advance impossible. A series of successive and detached assaults followed. Two batteries that had been posted near the crest of the hill in advance of the main body of infantry were lost by mistaking a rebel for a Union regiment; and, because of the lax organization and want of discipline in the raw volunteer regiments, the strength of McDowell's command melted away in a rapid demoralization. The scales of victory, however, yet vibrated in uncertainty, until at four in the afternoon the remainder of Johnston's army arrived, and seven fresh rebel regiments were thrown against the extreme right and partly in rear of the Union line.

This heavy numerical overweight at a decisive time and place terminated the battle very suddenly. The abundant rumors that Johnston was coming to the help of Beauregard seemed verified; and the Union regiments, ignorant of the fact that they had been successfully fighting part of his force all day, were seized with a panic, and began by a common impulse to move in retreat. The suddenness of their victory was as unexpected to the rebel as to the Union commanders. Jefferson Davis, who had come from Richmond, arriving at Manassas at four o'clock, was informed that the battle was lost, and was implored by his companions not to endanger his personal safety by riding to the front. Nevertheless he persisted, and was overjoyed to find that the Union army had, by a sudden and unexplained impulse, half run, half marched from the field.

The rebel detachments of cavalry hung about the line of retreat, but they dared not venture a serious attack; and so unconvinced were they as yet of the final result, that that night the rebel commanders set a strong and vigilant guard in all directions against the expected return, and offensive operations by McDowell next morning. The precaution was needless, for the Union army was so much demoralized that the commanders deemed it unsafe to make a stand at Centreville, where the reserves were posted; and a rapid though orderly retreat was continued through the night, and until all organized regiments or fragments reached their old camps within the fortifications on the Potomac, and the scattered fugitives made their way across the river into the city of Washington.

Patterson had been charged with the duty of defeating or holding Johnston in the Shenandoah Valley; he had a double force with which to perform his task. Had he done so, McDowell, who in that case would have been superior in numbers to Beauregard, and whose plans were in the main judicious, could easily have conquered. It was Johnston's army, which Patterson had permitted to escape, that principally fought the battle of Bull Run and defeated McDowell. Nor is there good sense in that criticism which lays the blame upon General Scott and the Administration for not having first united the two Federal armies. The administration furnished a superior force against Beauregard at Bull Run, and an overwhelming force against Johnston at Winchester, and assured victory in each locality by the only reliable condition—other things being equal —an excess of numbers. Had Patterson held his foe, as he might, and McDowell defeated Beauregard, as he should have done, the capture of Johnston's force between the two Federal armies was practically certain, as General Scott intended.

Scott was aware of the danger which Patterson's negligence had created. "It is known that a strong reënforcement left Winchester on the afternoon of the 18th, which you will also have to beat," he telegraphed McDowell on the day of the battle, when it was too late to countermand the attack. He also promised him immediate reënforcements. The confidence of the General-in-Chief remained unshaken, and he telegraphed McClellan: "McDowell is this forenoon forcing the passage of Bull Run. In two hours he will turn the Manassas Junction and storm it to-day with superior force."

It may well be supposed that President Lincoln suffered great anxiety during that eventful Sunday; but General Scott talked confidently of success, and Lincoln bore his impatience without any visible sign, and quietly went to church at eleven o'clock. Soon after noon copies of telegrams began to come to him at the Executive Mansion from the War Department and from army headquarters. They brought, however, no certain information, as they came only from the nearest station to the battlefield, and simply gave what the operator saw and heard. Towards three o'clock they became more frequent, and reported considerable fluctuation in the apparent course and progress of the cannonade. The President went to the office of General Scott, where he found the general asleep, and woke him to talk over the news. Scott said such reports were worth nothing as indications either way—that the changes in the currents of wind and the variation of the echoes made it impossible for a distant listener to determine the course of a battle. He still expressed his confidence in a successful result, and composed himself for another nap when the President left.

Dispatches continued to come about every ten or fifteen minutes, still based on hearing and hearsay; the rumors growing more cheering and definite. They reported that the battle had extended along nearly the whole line; that there had been considerable loss; but that the secession lines had been driven back two or three miles, some of the dispatches said, to the Junction. One of General Scott's aides also brought the telegram of an engineer, repeating that McDowell had driven the enemy before him, that he had ordered the reserves to cross Bull Run, and wanted reënforcements without delay.

The aide further stated substantially that the general was satisfied of the truth of this report, and that McDowell would immediately attack and capture the Junction, perhaps to-night, but certainly by to-morrow noon. Deeming all doubt at an end, President Lincoln ordered his carriage and went out to take his usual evening drive.

He had not returned when, at six o'clock, Secretary Seward came to the Executive Mansion, pale and haggard. "Where is the President?" he asked hoarsely of the private secretaries. "Gone to drive," they answered. "Have you any late news?" he continued. They read him the telegrams which announced victory. "Tell no one," said he. "That is not true. The battle is lost. The telegraph says that McDowell is in full retreat, and calls on General Scott to save the capital. Find the President and tell him to come immediately to General Scott's."

Half an hour later the President returned from his drive, and his private secretaries gave him Seward's message, the first intimation he received of the trying news. He listened in silence, without the slightest change of feature or expression, and walked away to army headquarters. There he read the unwelcome report in a telegram from a captain of engineers: "General Mc-Dowell's army in full retreat through Centreville. The day is lost. Save Washington and the remnants of this army. . . . The routed troops will not re-form." This information was such an irreconcilable contradiction of the former telegram that General Scott utterly refused to believe it. That one officer should report the army beyond Bull Run, driving the enemy and ordering up reserves, and another immediately report it three miles this side of Bull Run, in hopeless retreat and demoralization, seemed an impossibility. Yet the impossible had indeed come to pass; and the apparent change of fortune had been nearly as sudden on the battlefield as in Washington.

The President and the Cabinet met at General Scott's office, and awaited further news in feverish suspense, until a telegram from McDowell confirmed the disaster. Discussion was now necessarily turned to preparation for the future. All available troops were hurried forward to McDowell's support; Baltimore was put on the alert; telegrams were sent to the recruiting stations of the nearest Northern States to lose no time in sending all their organized regiments to Washington; McClellan was ordered to "come down to the Shenandoah Valley with such troops as can be spared from Western Virginia."

A great number of civilians, newspaper correspondents, and several Senators and Representatives had followed McDowell's army to Centreville; Representative Alfred Ely of New York, went to the battlefield itself, and was captured and sent for a long sojourn in Libby Prison at Richmond. Such of these non-combatants as had been fortunate enough to keep their horses and vehicles were the first to reach Washington, arriving about midnight. President Lincoln had returned to the Executive Mansion, and reclining on a lounge in the Cabinet room he heard from several of these eye-witnesses their excited and exaggerated narratives, in which the rush and terror and unseemly stampede of lookers-on and army teamsters were altogether disproportionate and almost exclusive features. The President did not go to his bed that night; morning found him still on his

lounge in the executive office, hearing repetitions of these recitals and making memoranda of his own conclusions.

As the night elapsed, the news seemed to grow worse. Mc-
Dowell's first dispatch stated that he would hold Centreville.
His second, that "the larger part of the men are a confused mob,
entirely demoralized"; but he said that he would attempt to
make a stand at Fairfax Court House. His third reported from
that point that "many of the volunteers did not wait for
authority to proceed to the Potomac, but left on their own
decision. They are now pouring through this place in a state of
utter disorganization. . . . I think now, as all of my commanders
thought at Centreville, there is no alternative but to fall back to
the Potomac." Reports from other points generally confirmed
the prevalence of confusion and disorganization. Monday morning the scattered fugitives reached the bridges over the
Potomac, and began rushing across them into Washington. It
was a gloomy and dismal day. A drizzling rain set in which
lasted thirty-six hours. Many a panic-stricken volunteer remembered afterwards with gratitude, that when he was wandering
footsore, exhausted, and hungry through the streets of the
capital, her loyal families opened their cheerful doors to give
him food, rest, and encouragement.

One of the principal reasons which prevented McDowell's
making a stand at Centreville or Fairfax Court House was the
important fact that the term of service of the three months'
militia, organized under President Lincoln's first proclamation,
was about to expire. "In the next few days," says McDowell
in his report, "day by day I should have lost ten thousand of
the best armed, drilled, officered, and disciplined troops in the
army." This vital consideration equally affected the armies at
other points; and bearing it, as well as the local exigency, in
mind, the President and the Cabinet determined on several
changes of army leadership. McDowell was continued in command on the Virginia side of the Potomac, with fifteen regiments to defend and hold the forts. McClellan was called to
Washington to take local command, and more especially to

organize a new army out of the three-years' regiments which
were just beginning to come in from the various States. Patterson was only a three months' general, appointed by the Governor of Pennsylvania; his time expired, and he was mustered
out of service. Banks was sent to Harper's Ferry to succeed
him. Dix was put in command at Baltimore, and Rosecrans in
Western Virginia.

By noon of Monday the worst aspects of the late defeat were
known; and especially the reassuring fact that the enemy was
making no pursuit; and so far as possible immediate dangers
were provided against. The War Department was soon able to
reply to anxious inquiries from New York: "Our loss is much
less than was at first represented, and the troops have reached
the forts in much better condition than we expected." "We are
making most vigorous efforts to concentrate a large and irresistible army at this point. Regiments are arriving. . . . Our works
on the south bank of the Potomac are impregnable, being well
manned with reënforcements. The capital is safe." On the following day Lincoln in person visited some of the forts and
camps about Arlington Heights, and addressed the regiments
with words of cheer and confidence.

Compared with the later battles of the civil war, the battle
of Bull Run involved but a very moderate loss in men and
material. Its political and moral results, however, were wide-
spread and enduring. The fact that the rebel army suffered
about equal damage in numbers of killed and wounded, and
that it was crippled so as to be unable for months to resume the
offensive, could not be immediately known. The flushed hope of
the South magnified the achievement as a demonstration of
Southern invincibility. The event of a pitched battle won gave
the rebellion and the Confederate Government a standing and
a sudden respectability before foreign powers it had hardly
dared hope for. With the then personal Government of France,
and with the commercial classes whose influence always rules
the Government of England, it gained at once a scarcely dis-
guised active sympathy.

Upon the irritated susceptibilities, the wounded loyalty, the sanguine confidence of the North, the Bull Run defeat fell with cruel bitterness. The eager hopes built on the victories in Western Virginia were dashed to the ground. Here was a fresher and deeper humiliation than Sumter or Baltimore. But though her nerves winced, her will never faltered. She was both chastened and strengthened in the trial. For the moment, however, irritation and disappointment found vent in loud complaint and blind recrimination. One or two curious incidents in this ordeal of criticism may perhaps be cited.

A few days after the battle, in a conversation at the White House with several Illinois Members of Congress, in the presence of the President and the Secretary of War, General Scott himself was so far nettled by the universal chagrin and fault-finding that he lost his temper and sought an entirely uncalled-for self-justification. "Sir, I am the greatest coward in America," said he. "I will prove it. I have fought this battle, sir, against my judgment; I think the President of the United States ought to remove me to-day for doing it. As God is my judge, after my superiors had determined to fight it, I did all in my power to make the army efficient. I deserve removal because I did not stand up, when my army was not in a condition for fighting, and resist it to the last." The President said, "Your conversation seems to imply that I forced you to fight this battle." General Scott then said, "I have never served a President who has been kinder to me than you have been." Representative William A. Richardson, who in a complaining speech in Congress related the scene, then drew the inference that Scott intended to pay a personal compliment to Mr. Lincoln, but that he did not mean to exonerate the Cabinet; and when pressed by questions, further explained: "Let us have no misunderstanding about this matter. My colleagues understood that I gave the language as near as I could. Whether I have been correctly reported or not I do not know. If I did not then make the correct statement, let me do it now. I did not understand General Scott, nor did I mean so to be understood, as implying that the President had forced him to fight that battle."

The incident illustrates how easily history may be perverted by hot-blooded criticism. Scott's irritation drove him to an inaccurate statement of events; Richardson's partisanship warped Scott's error to a still more unjustifiable deduction, and both reasoned from a changed condition of things. Two weeks before, Scott was confident of victory, and Richardson chafing at military inaction.

Historical judgment of war is subject to an inflexible law, either very imperfectly understood or very constantly lost sight of. Military writers love to fight over the campaigns of history exclusively by the rules of the professional chess-board, always subordinating, often totally ignoring, the element of politics. This is a radical error. Every war is begun, dominated, and ended by political considerations; without a nation, without a Government, without money or credit, without popular enthusiasm which furnishes volunteers, or public support which endures conscription, there could be no army and no war—neither beginning nor end of methodical hostilities. War and politics, campaign and statecraft, are Siamese twins, inseparable and interdependent; and to talk of military operations without the direction and interference of an Administration is as absurd as to plan a campaign without recruits, pay, or rations.

Applied to the Bull Run campaign, this law of historical criticism analyzes and fixes the responsibilities of government and commanders with easy precision. When Lincoln, on June 29, assembled his council of war, the commanders, as military experts, correctly decided that the existing armies—properly handled—could win a victory at Manassas and a victory at Winchester, at or near the same time. General Scott correctly objected that these victories, if won, would not be decisive; and that in a military point of view it would be wiser to defer any offensive campaign until the following autumn. Here the President and the Cabinet, as political experts, intervened, and on their part decided, correctly, that the public temper would not admit of such a delay. Thus the Administration was responsible for the forward movement, Scott for the combined strategy of the two armies, McDowell for the conduct of the Bull Run battle, Patterson for the escape of Johnston, and Fate for the panic; for the opposing forces were equally raw, equally undisciplined, and as a whole fought the battle with equal courage and gallantry.

THE WAR *grew in intensity. In the West, Henry W. Halleck supplanted John C. Frémont, who had worked himself into an impossible situation in Missouri. In February, 1862, Commodore Foote's gunboats took Fort Henry, and U. S. Grant won a notable victory at Fort Donelson. In the East, the administration became increasingly restive at the inactivity of George B. McClellan, who had succeeded to the command of the Army of the Potomac after Bull Run, and had been made general-in-chief upon the retirement of the old and feeble Winfield Scott in November.*

By March, 1862, McClellan had been prodded into planning an advance upon Richmond. Contrary to Lincoln's wishes, the general insisted upon transporting his troops by water to Fort Monroe and advancing from that point to the Confederate capital by land. Early in the month a Confederate warship, embodying an innovation in naval design, threatened to thwart McClellan's plans.

Monitor and Merrimac

IN a great war such as that of the rebellion an inventive people like the Americans could not fail to originate novelties and develop progress in methods of fighting. The most critical point of the contest on both sides was the possibility of foreign intervention. This compelled the North to find effective means to enforce the long and difficult sea-coast blockade; while for the South it constituted a prime object to break it. Both sides therefore turned eagerly to experiments in the new system of iron-clad ships. In the destruction of the Gosport navy yard at the outbreak of the war, the United States steam-frigate *Merrimac* was burned to the water's edge and sunk. The rebels soon raised her, and finding her hull undamaged, and the engines yet serviceable, they proceeded by help of the Tredegar iron-works, at Richmond, to convert her into an ironclad. A wedge-shaped prow of cast-iron, weighing 1500 pounds, was fastened to the stem two feet under water, and projecting about two feet in front. A roof of wood two feet thick, with its sides inclining at thirty-six degrees to the water's edge, was made to cover about two-thirds of the hull, being the central part; this was plated with iron armor composed of two plates, each two inches thick. Within this protection was placed a battery of ten guns, four on each broadside, and one each at the stem and stern.

The Navy Department at Washington was no less prompt to study the question of ironclads. The special session of Congress appropriated one and a half million of dollars for the work. A public advertisement invited plans and offers of construction. A competent board of naval officers examined the devices presented, and recommended three of the most promising, which by way of trial were put under contract. "Our immediate demands," said the report, "seem to require, first, so far as practicable, vessels invulnerable to shot, of light draft of water, to penetrate our shoal harbors, rivers, and bayous." Of the three plans adopted the one presented by John Ericsson of New York, a Swede by birth but an American citizen by adoption, a man of original genius, of great scientific acquirements, and of long experience in engineering service, proved in the end to conform best to these requirements. The board had doubts of its sea-going qualities, but at once recognized it as "a plan which will render the battery shot and shell proof." The hull, 127 feet long, 36 feet wide, and 12 feet deep, was covered by a flat, over-hanging deck, slightly wider but much longer, pointed at both ends, closed and made water-tight, and rising only one or two feet above the water-line. On this stood a revolving turret, twenty feet in diameter and nine feet high, composed of wrought-iron plates bolted together to a total thickness of eight inches. Inside this were two 11-inch Dahlgren guns, trained side by side and revolving with the turret. Ericsson named his novel ship the *Monitor*. When public humor afterwards christened his invention by calling it a "cheese-box on a raft," the designation expressed the exact intention of his model. In observing the movements of timber-rafts down the Norwegian coast, he had noticed that they suffered no danger from the waves, which simply rolled over them. So the closed platform of the *Monitor,* which would permit the waves to roll freely over its surface, required only its comparatively thin edge above and below the water-line to be protected with heavy iron armor. By this clever device, weight, which is the main difficulty in armored ships, was reduced to a minimum, and enabled him to combine great thickness of mail with the utmost lightness of draft.

Information concerning the progress of the work on these first American ironclads reached both belligerents. The officers at Fort Monroe reported in October, 1861, that the *Merrimac* (she was named the *Virginia* by the rebels) would probably make an effort to get to sea.* This proved a premature rumor. Late in the following February the Navy Department had more trustworthy information, through a Union mechanic then at work upon her, that she was nearly finished. The rebels doubtless had similar information concerning the ironclads building at the North. But in each case such clandestine knowledge was necessarily vague and fragmentary. Enough, however, was known in Washington to make it probable that the *Merrimac* would prove formidable in a naval contest. Delay had occurred in the work on the Union ironclads, the time of their possible presence there could not be fixed with certainty, and their ability to meet such an antagonist was purely a matter of speculation. When the *Monitor* was recommended by the Naval Board, and put under contract, even the most experienced and most sanguine officers had no expectation of the remarkable fighting powers she afterwards demonstrated.

On Thursday night, the 6th of March, 1862, the Assistant Secretary of the Navy was called to a council of war then being held at the Executive Mansion, at which the President, Cabinet, and various military officers were present. The Peninsular

* Before her capture by the Confederates the ship was listed in the U. S. Navy Register as the *Merrimack.* Nearly all writers on the Civil War have dropped the "k."—P.M.A.

Campaign had been substantially agreed upon, but its details were yet under discussion. President Lincoln once more explained that taking the whole army first to Annapolis, to be embarked in transports, would appear to the extremely sensitive and impatient public opinion very much like a retreat from Washington. It would be impolitic to explain that it was merely a first step by way of the Chesapeake Bay and Fort Monroe towards Richmond. Could not, he asked, 50,000 or even 10,000 men be moved in transports directly down the Potomac? This would be a self-evident forward movement, which the public would comprehend without explanation. The objection was that transports could not safely pass existing rebel batteries on the Potomac. Could not the navy destroy those batteries? Assistant Secretary Fox replied that the navy could silence the batteries, but that unless held by our army, they would immediately be reoccupied, rebuilt, and again armed and manned by the rebels, and we needed a prolonged not a temporary respite.

The army officers objected that to occupy, hold, and defend those batteries from land attacks would produce a local and partial movement and diversion only to cripple and delay the main and distant expedition. Lincoln finally decided that the navy should in any event engage and silence the Potomac batteries, even if only for a temporary and moral effect. There being as yet no telegraph to Fort Monroe, orders were transmitted by sea directing that certain ships of war, and the *Monitor* which that day sailed from New York, should ascend the Potomac for this duty. The *Merrimac* was for the moment forgotten, but being remembered next day, supplementary orders were sent directing a suspension of action till Assistant Secretary Fox could visit Fort Monroe and consult the naval officers in command. When he arrived there on Sunday morning, an important naval engagement had occurred, the renewal and conclusion of which he witnessed.

Three Union frigates lay at anchor under the guns of Fort Monroe, and two others under the guns of the Union earthworks near Newport News, six miles to the southwest, when on

Saturday, March 8, about noon, the *Merrimac* appeared in the
mouth of the Elizabeth River channel, which enters Hampton
Roads about midway between the points named above, and
headed directly for Newport News. She was accompanied by
two small tugs armed with one gun each, while three other side-
wheel steamers out of the James River, respectively of one, two,
and twelve guns, also joined the *Merrimac* after the attack.
The ships at Fort Monroe immediately slipped their cables and
started for the encounter, following the *Merrimac* towards the
southwest—the *Minnesota* (twin-ship to the original *Merrimac*) under steam, the *St. Lawrence,* sailing frigate, in tow of a
gunboat, and the *Roanoke,* with a broken shaft, towed by tugs.
But owing to a recent northwest gale, water was low in the
channel, and all of the vessels, being of deep draft, soon
grounded—the *Minnesota* north of the middle ground, one and
a half miles from Newport News, the *St. Lawrence* near her, and
the *Roanoke* still farther behind. Beyond an occasional exchange of fire at long distances they were therefore unable to
join in the main fight. The sailing frigate *Congress,* and the
razeed frigate *Cumberland,* anchored at Newport News, saw the
Merrimac coming, and prepared for action. Plowing up the bay,
with her sloping roof and her low prow, she looked to them
"like a huge half-submerged crocodile." Her warning shot was
given when yet a mile away. Exchanging a broadside with the
Congress as she passed her at the distance of three hundred
yards, she rushed full speed at the *Cumberland,* which had
opened on her with her pivot guns, and now greeted her with
broadsides as she neared. But neither the broadsides of the
wooden ships, nor the fire of the shore batteries, had any apparent effect. The showering iron hail glanced and bounded
from the sloping, tortoise-shaped back of the leviathan like
india-rubber balls. On and on she came with accelerated mo-
mentum, till within fifteen minutes after the first shot was fired
she struck the *Cumberland* forward of the starboard fore-chains.
The crash of her iron prow through the timbers and hull "was
distinctly heard above the din of battle." The attacked vessel

was forced back upon her anchors with great violence, and a hole the size of a hogshead was opened in the hull, into which the water rushed in a deluge. Pumps were of no avail against such a flood, and the good ship was doomed. And, besides this, the shells of her iron-cased destroyer were spreading death on her decks. As she backed away but yet hovered over her victim at convenient nearness, her guns continued to belch forth irresistible havoc.

History records no more determined bravery than was displayed by the officers and crew of the *Cumberland*. Neither present disaster nor impending danger checked their devoted heroism. With men cut down at their guns, and the ship settling to her fate under their feet, they answered broadside with broadside, shot with shot. When the water in the hold rose and drowned the forward magazine, they still passed up powder from the one aft. The last gun was fired when the sea was already running into the muzzle of the gun beside it. After three-quarters of an hour of such fighting the gallant ship, with the dead and wounded of her crew, and some even of her heroic defenders who clung doggedly to their posts after orders had been given to save themselves, went to the bottom in fifty feet of water with the stars and stripes still flying from her masthead. Her antagonist did not come from the encounter entirely unharmed. The blow which sunk the *Cumberland* wrenched off her iron prow and slightly twisted her stem. The *Cumberland's* solid shot broke the muzzles of two of her guns and killed two of her men, wounding nineteen others.

Ebb tide having begun, the *Merrimac* steamed a short distance up stream to turn, and then attacked the *Congress* which lay several hundred yards east of the *Cumberland*. The *Congress*, seeing the fate of her companion, slipped her cable, and by using her sails, and with the help of a tug, ran ashore and grounded where the iron monster could not follow. But the precaution was futile. The *Merrimac*, returning, took up a raking position off her quarter at two cables' length, soon silenced the few guns that bore upon her, and after an hour's fight, cre-

ating frightful carnage, the commander having been killed and
the ship set on fire in several places, the *Congress* struck her
colors. Confederate officers charge that fire was again opened
from the *Congress* after surrender, which Union officers deny.
The conflict of assertion is probably explained by the circumstance that fire was opened upon the rebel boats from the shore
with both cannon and musketry, a proceeding perfectly justi-
fiable by the laws of war. The event caused the *Merrimac* to
open once more on the *Congress* with hot shot and incendiary
shells, and whether from these or other causes she burned till
midnight, when the explosion of her magazine ended the conflagration. The *Merrimac*, with her consorts, withdrew from the
field of conflict, firing at both the *Minnesota* and *St. Lawrence*
as they passed down the channel at the distance of a mile, but
the *Merrimac* offered no serious attack, probably expecting to
capture them the following day. At nightfall the rebel flotilla
anchored under the guns of their shore batteries on Sewall's
Point at the entrance of the channel to Norfolk, whence they
had come. Among the Union commanders the gloomy disasters
of the afternoon were heightened by the seemingly hopeless apprehension for the morrow. With great difficulty the tugs had
hauled the *Roanoke* and *St. Lawrence* back to Fort Monroe;
the *Minnesota* was hard aground. But what ship, ashore or
afloat, could stand before this new and terrible marine engine,
that moved unharmed through the repeated broadsides of the
most powerful naval armaments?

Telegraphic news of these events reached Washington the
next morning, Sunday, and the hasty meeting of the Cabinet
and other officials who immediately gathered at the White
House was perhaps the most excited and impressive of the
whole war. Stanton, unable to control his strong emotion,
walked up and down the room like a caged lion. McClellan was
dumfounded and silent. Lincoln was, as usual in trying moments, composed but eagerly inquisitive, critically scanning
the dispatches, interrogating the officers, joining scrap to scrap
of information, applying his searching analysis and clear logic

to read the danger and find the remedy; Chase impatient and ready to utter blame; Seward and Welles hopeful, yet without encouraging reasons to justify their hope. The possibilities of the hour were indeed sufficiently portentous to create consternation. What might not this new and irresistible leviathan of the deep accomplish? A fleet destroyed; Fort Monroe besieged; the blockade broken; the Richmond campaign thwarted; New York laid under contribution; Washington City and the public buildings burned and the Government in flight;* foreign intervention would surely follow a succession of events like these, which heated imagination easily called up. Even at the risk of creating a momentary panic it seemed necessary to warn the authorities of the seaboard cities to prepare all possible resources of their own for defense. The best available provision to make Washington City secure, that could be suggested, was to prepare and load barges and canal-boats to be sunk in the channel of the Potomac at Kettlebottom Shoals and other points. Quartermaster-General Meigs and Captain Dahlgren were charged by the Secretary of War with this duty. Since guns were of no avail against the *Merrimac,* it was decided to have recourse to her own process of ramming. For this purpose the strongest and swiftest merchant steamer in New York, the *Vanderbilt,* was chartered, strengthened by filling her bow with timbers and plating it outside with iron, and sent to Fort Monroe under orders to try to run down her antagonist, at the first opportunity, and at whatever risk. But more effective help had arrived, and even while these counsels were in progress, was bringing the question to a practical solution. By the light of the burning *Congress,* on Saturday night a rebel pilot saw a strange craft glide into the waters of Hampton Roads; it was the *Monitor,* which, safely towed from New York, arrived between nine and ten o'clock. So little was the new system and model in favor, that the older officers of the navy had generally con-

* Mr. Welles, who was in the habit of coldly noting in his deadly diary all the indiscretions of his colleagues, says that Mr. Stanton closed his list of sinister prophecies by predicting that a shell or a cannon-shot from the *Merrimac* would probably land in the Cabinet-room before they separated.

demned it in advance and manifested no ambition to command her. Lieutenant John L. Worden, however, had accepted the duty, and was immediately informed that a critical trial was at hand. A little after midnight he moved to a station near the *Minnesota,* which was still aground.

On Sunday morning, March 9, the *Merrimac* once more came out and steamed towards the *Minnesota,* with the expectation of easily capturing or destroying her, but as she approached the *Monitor* went out to meet her. "The contrast was that of a pigmy to a giant." The *Merrimac* was twice her length and breadth, had more than four times her displacement, and five times as many guns. But her great draft, twenty-two feet, confined her manœuvres to deep water, while the *Monitor* drawing only ten feet could run where she pleased. The huge tortoise-back of the *Merrimac* was an easy target, while her broadsides passed harmlessly over the low, flat deck of the *Monitor,* only one or two feet above water. The shore spectators now witnessed a prolonged and exciting naval duel. The small rebel gunboats withdrew. The *Merrimac* occasionally exchanged fire with the *Minnesota,* but her principal fight was with the *Monitor.* The two ironclads moved fearlessly towards each other, firing as favorable opportunity offered. But the nine-inch and eleven-inch shells glanced without effect alike from the sloping roof of the *Merrimac* and the round side of the *Monitor's* tower. The superior mobility of the latter proved a great advantage.

She and her turret [says the rebel commander] appeared to be under perfect control. Her light draft enabled her to move about us at pleasure. She once took position for a short time where we could not bring a gun to bear on her. Another of her movements caused us great anxiety; she made for our rudder and propeller, both of which could have been easily disabled. We could only see her guns when they were discharged; immediately afterwards the turret revolved rapidly, and the guns were not again seen until they were again fired. . . . When we saw that our fire made no impression on the *Monitor* we determined to run into her, if possible. We found it a very difficult feat to do. Our great length and draft, in a comparatively narrow channel with but little water to spare, made us sluggish in our movements and hard to steer and turn. When the opportunity presented all steam was put on; there was not, however, sufficient time to gather full headway before striking. The blow was given with the broad wooden stem, the iron prow having been lost the day before. The *Monitor* received the blow in such a manner as to weaken its effect, and the damage was to her trifling.

Three hours passed in this singular contest. The *Monitor* had fired forty-one shots. She inflicted no direct damage, neither did she receive any. On both sides the shells only made slight indentations in the thick iron armor. Yet it was apparent to the rebel officers that the little "cheese-box on a raft" was gradually wearing out her bulky antagonist. It became evident that if the *Merrimac* were by accident struck twice in the same place, her shield would be penetrated. She was already leaking badly. Her loss of prow, anchor, and consumption of coal was raising her so as dangerously to expose her water-line, where the iron plating was only one inch thick; a chance shot here would send her to the bottom. But at this time the *Monitor* met with a serious accident. Her pilot-house was constructed of great iron logs, nine by twelve inches thick, laid up after the manner of a log-cabin, leaving spaces of half an inch between them, through which to observe the enemy and steer the ship. Lieutenant Worden, the commander, was standing in this pilot-house giving orders, when one of the *Merrimac's* shells struck the outside of the logs between which he was looking. The concussion drove the smoke and iron-dust through with such force as temporarily to blind him, disabling him from command, and causing a short suspension of all guidance of the *Monitor* until he could be properly cared for. When, however, after the lapse of some twenty minutes, Lieutenant Greene, the second officer, who had by Worden's direction assumed command, turned his vessel again to face his antagonist, he saw that the *Merrimac* had already started in the direction of Elizabeth River. He fired a few shots after her, but she continued her retreat, refusing further combat.

If, as the rebel commander states, the *Merrimac* was yet willing to have continued the fight, she was equally ready to consent to its cessation. Making no further effort to shell the *Minnesota,* which still lay aground within easy reach of her guns, she quit the waters of Hampton Roads at noon, three hours before high water, and steamed back to Norfolk whence she had come. In reality the contest had been decided by the evident prospective superiority of the *Monitor* rather than by any present necessity of either combatant. Counted merely by blows received and given it was a drawn battle. But, practically, a victory, which seemed providential in its sudden relief and immense results, remained with the *Monitor*. The whole event was even still broader in its effect. That three hours' battle in Hampton Roads changed the naval warfare of the civilized world. A quarter of a century has elapsed and still the great powers of Europe are testing the yet unsolved problem of the largest gun to destroy, and the strongest armor to protect, a ship-of-war.

The welcome news reached the Washington authorities that same night by the newly laid telegraph, changing deep anxiety into lively exultation. Lincoln, always prudent, at once saw clearly the immense value of the *Monitor's* victory, and resolved it should not be placed in jeopardy. He therefore sent orders that she should not be unduly exposed, and that on no account should she attempt to go to Norfolk alone. The preparations for blocking the Potomac channel were completed and held in constant readiness, and several additional swift merchant vessels were soon after stationed at Fort Monroe to make the destruction of the *Merrimac* reasonably sure by running her down. It turned out that she was never in a condition to go to sea, and that her great draft prevented her ascending the Potomac. After the Peninsular Campaign was begun, there was always an immense number of Union transports in the adjacent waters, to which she could have done incalculable damage. For about two months she thus remained a vague terror, though the menace was effectually "neutralized" by the *Monitor* and the merchant war vessels assembled in triple and quadruple force to oppose and annihilate her. On her part the *Merrimac* profited by the blockade to which she was subjected, by being repaired and much strengthened, by a new steel and wrought-iron prow, by iron plating on her hull, and improved ammunition. On the 11th of April she descended again to Hampton Roads, in company with three rebel gunboats and nine small tugs. But beyond getting the various unarmed vessels out of the way the Union fleet made no movement; for its orders provided that the *Monitor* and other vessels should not be separated, but that if the *Merrimac* came out into favorable waters they should all go at her. "The position is one of defiance on both sides," wrote a newspaper correspondent; "the rebels are challenging us to come up to their field of battle, and we are daring them to come down." The Union fleet understood too well its primary duty of keeping the *Merrimac* from any possibility of reaching the army transports in York River, while on their part the rebel officers were also restrained by orders to remain for the protection of Norfolk. No battle grew out of this game of strategy, and at night the rebel vessels withdrew.

We must anticipate somewhat the chronological order of events to bring within the present chapter the final fate of both the *Monitor* and *Merrimac*. In the progress of the Peninsular Campaign, when the Confederates found McClellan's army advancing against Richmond in such powerful numbers, it became necessary to draw in all available detachments for the defense of their capital, and on the 1st of May the evacuation of Norfolk was determined upon. On the 4th of May the *Merrimac* was ordered to take station where she could prevent the Union forces from ascending the James River. Huger, the rebel military commander, however, obtained a postponement of this duty till his preparations for evacuation should be further advanced.

It happened by a curious coincidence that President Lincoln,

Secretary Chase, and Secretary Stanton started in the evening
of the 5th of May for a visit to Fort Monroe. So far as is known
it had only a general object: to ascertain by personal observation whether some further vigilance and vigor might not be
infused into the operations of the army and navy at that point.
Delayed by bad weather on the Potomac, they arrived at their
destination on Tuesday night, May 6. Late as it was they immediately proceeded to the steamship *Minnesota,* and held
a conference with Commodore L. M. Goldsborough, the flag-
officer, "about the condition of things" and "military and naval
movements in connection with the dreaded *Merrimac.*" Next
day, May 7, the party visited the various places of interest—
the *Vanderbilt,* the *Monitor,* the ruined village of Hampton, the
Rip Raps and Fort Monroe, with doubtless a running council
of war among themselves and the naval and military commanders; for two important orders appear to have been given
by the President that same Wednesday evening, preparations
for executing which were made during the night. In pursuance
of these orders, on the morning of Thursday, May 8, the new
ironclad *Galena* with two other gunboats were sent up the
James River; and a considerable section of the remaining fleet
moved across the waters of the bay to an attack on the Confederate Sewall's Point batteries. This was a reconnaissance in
force; troops were already embarked in transports to push
across and effect a landing if it appeared practicable, with a
view to advance on Norfolk. But the cannonade from the ships
called forth a spirited reply from the rebel batteries on Sewall's
Point, and after a while the *Merrimac* appeared to take part in
the fray. "All the big wooden vessels," writes Chase, who with
Lincoln and Stanton witnessed the bombardment from the Rip
Raps, "began to haul off. The *Monitor* and *Stevens,* however,
held their ground. The *Merrimac* still came on slowly, and in
a little while there was a clear sheet of water between her and
the *Monitor.* Then the great rebel terror paused, then turned
back, and having finally attained what she considered a safe
position, became stationary again."

"That was thought to have shown the inability of an attempt to land at Sewall's Point while the *Merrimac* lay watching it," says Chase, in another letter, and the troops were disembarked from the transports. But all this commotion had stirred up inquiry and elicited information; and a pilot suggested that a landing might be found to the eastward beyond Willoughby Point. Against the general incredulity of the officers, Chase on Friday morning, May 9, took the revenue cutter *Miami*, on which the party had come from Washington, and a tug, and went on a reconnaissance to the shore indicated. Here, some five or six miles from Fort Monroe, soundings disclosed a feasible landing, undefended by batteries or even pickets, and a boat sent ashore obtained valuable information of passable roads leading to Norfolk. "When I got back to Fort Monroe," continues Chase, "I found the President had been listening to a pilot and studying a chart, and had become impressed with a conviction that there was a nearer landing and wished to go and see about it on the spot. So we started again and soon reached the shore, taking with us a large boat and some twenty armed soldiers from the Rip Raps. The President and Mr. Stanton were on the tug and I on the *Miami*. The tug was of course nearest shore, and as soon as she found the water too shoal for her to go farther safely, the Rip Raps boat was manned and sent in. . . . We had again found a good landing, which at the time I supposed to be between two and three miles nearer Fort Monroe, but which proved to be only one-half or three-quarters of a mile nearer."

It is probable that these opportune discoveries were supplemented by other important information. On the previous evening (of Thursday) a Norfolk tug-boat seized the favorable opportunity to desert from the rebel service and run into Newport News. Its officers reported that Norfolk was being evacuated by the Confederates, and that the two or three thousand troops yet there would probably soon be gone. When therefore the officials and officers were once more assembled at Fort Monroe, an immediate advance to Norfolk was agreed upon,

and troops were again embarked on transports and other preparations hurried forward on Friday night.

On Saturday morning, May 10, a successful landing and de-
barkation was effected at the point examined by the President,
and General Wool marched to Norfolk with a force of nearly
six thousand men. It is easy to glean from the various accounts
that there was great want of foresight and confusion in all the
military arrangements, and the Secretary of the Treasury, who
accompanied the advance, was probably gratified by the entirely unexpected rôle of being for once in his life the gener-
alissimo of a military campaign. They met only the merest show
of resistance and delay at a burning bridge, which was overcome by an easy detour. By evening they passed through the
strong but abandoned intrenchments and received from the
Mayor of Norfolk the official surrender of the city. The navy
yard at Gosport was in flames, but the heavy guns which armed
the earthworks remained as trophies. A military governor was
appointed, and protection promised to peaceful inhabitants,
and from that time forward Norfolk remained under the authority of the Union flag. The most substantial fruit of the
movement soon followed. The officers of the *Merrimac* observed
on Saturday morning, from their moorings in the mouth of
Elizabeth River, that the Confederate flag was no longer flying over the Sewall's Point batteries; and investigation during the day proved the landing and march of the Union
forces, the precipitate retreat of the rebel troops from all points,
and the final surrender and occupation of Norfolk. The un-
wieldy crocodile-back ironclad was thus caught between two
fires. "The ship," reports her commander, "was accordingly
put on shore, as near the mainland in the vicinity of Craney
Island as possible, and the crew landed. She was then fired, and
after burning fiercely, fore and áft, for upward of an hour,
blew up a little before five on the morning of the 11th."

The President receiving the welcome news at the moment
of departure for Washington, prolonged his stay to accompany
the delighted dignitaries and officers on a flying trip up Eliza-

beth River to the newly captured town, and then the prow of the *Miami,* on Sunday evening, plowed past Fort Monroe and up the Potomac. "So," writes Chase in conclusion, "has ended a brilliant week's campaign of the President; for I think it quite certain that if he had not come down Norfolk would still have been in possession of the enemy, and the *Merrimac* as grim and defiant and as much a terror as ever. The whole coast is now virtually ours."

Like the *Merrimac* the *Monitor* also had a dramatic end. After various services she was, in the following December, sent to sea under sealed orders, and foundered in a gale off Cape Hatteras, nearly all the officers and crew, however, being saved by boats from the *Rhode Island,* which was towing her. Thus the pioneer ships of the new system of iron armor did not long survive their first famous exploit that so astounded the nations of the earth. Other Union ironclads of a different model had joined the Hampton Roads squadron before the destruction of the *Merrimac;* and before the *Monitor* went down she had given her name as a generic term to a whole fleet built after her model, her first successor, the monitor *Passaic,* having already reached the seat of war for active service.

AFTER FORT DONELSON *the Union command in the West decided to move south in Tennessee and destroy enemy railroad centers at Jackson, Tennessee, and Corinth, Mississippi. In mid-March, 1862, Grant was given command of the field force. With his troops at and around Pittsburg Landing on the Tennessee River a few miles north of the Mississippi border, he awaited the arrival of Buell's Army of the Ohio. In this quiet setting one of the bloodiest battles of the war took place.*

The Shiloh Campaign

IT has been already stated that after the fall of Fort Donelson the rebel commanders fled southward in confusion and dismay. We have the high authority and calm judgment of General Grant, in the mature experience and reflection of after years, that "if one general who would have taken the responsibility had been in command of all the troops west of the Alleghanies, he could have marched to Chattanooga, Corinth, Memphis, and Vicksburg with the troops we then had"; but the secessionists of the Southwest recovered rapidly from the stupefaction of unexpected disaster. In the delay of four or five weeks that the divided ambition and over-cautious hesitation of the Union generals afforded them, they had renewed their courage, and united and reënforced their scattered armies. The separation of the armies of Johnston from those of Beauregard, which seemed irreparable when the Tennessee River was opened, had not been maintained by the prompt advance that everybody pointed out, but which nobody executed. By the 23d of March the two Confederate generals had, without opposition, effected a junction of their forces at and about Corinth, and thus reversed the pending military problem. In the last weeks of February it could have been the united Unionists pursuing the divided Confederates. In the last weeks of March it was the

Vol. V, Chap. XVIII, pp. 320-35. In *Abraham Lincoln: A History* this chapter follows "New Orleans." Here I have reversed the original order.— P.M.A.

united Confederates preparing to attack the divided armies of Halleck and Buell. The whole situation and plan is summed up in the dispatch of General Albert Sidney Johnston to Jefferson Davis, dated April 3, 1862: "General Buell is in motion, 30,000 strong, rapidly from Columbia by Clifton to Savannah; Mitchel behind him with 10,000. Confederate forces, 40,000, ordered forward to offer battle near Pittsburg. Division from Bethel, main body from Corinth, reserve from Burnsville converge to-morrow near Monterey on Pittsburg. Beauregard second in command; Polk, left; Hardee, center; Bragg, right wing; Breckinridge, reserve. Hope engagement before Buell can form junction."

The Confederate march took place as projected, and on the evening of April 5 their joint forces went into bivouac two miles from the Union camps. That evening the Confederate commanders held an informal conference. Beauregard became impressed with impending defeat; their march had been slow, the rations they carried were exhausted, and their extra rations and ammunition were not yet at hand. They could no longer hope to effect the complete surprise that was an essential feature of their plan. Beauregard advised a change of programme —to abandon the projected attack and convert the movement into a "reconnaissance in force." General Johnston listened, but refused his assent, and orders were given to begin the battle next morning. No suspicion of such a march or attack entered the mind of any Union officer; and that same day Grant reported to Halleck, "The main force of the enemy is at Corinth."

The natural position occupied by the Union forces is admitted to have been unusually strong. The Tennessee River here runs nearly north. North of the camps, Snake Creek with an affluent, Owl Creek, formed a barrier stretching from the river bank in general direction towards the southwest. South of the camps, Lick Creek and river sloughs also formed an impassable obstruction for a considerable distance next to the Tennessee. The river on the east, and Snake and Owl creeks on the west, thus inclosed a high triangular plateau with sides three or four miles in length, crossed and intersected to some extent by smaller streams and ravines, though generally open towards the south. The roads from Pittsburg Landing towards Corinth followed the main ridge, also towards the southwest. A network of other roads, very irregular in direction, ran from the Corinth roads to various points in the neighborhood. Alternate patches of timber, thick undergrowth, and open fields covered the locality. Over two miles in a straight line, or nearly three by the roads, southwest from Pittsburg Landing, stood a log meeting-house, called Shiloh Church, which was destined to give its name to the conflict.

Five of Grant's divisions were camped on this triangular plateau, not with any view of defense against an attack, but mainly with reference to convenience while there, and for a later movement upon Corinth. An advance line about three miles long between Lick Creek and Owl Creek, if by courtesy we call it a line, was only partly occupied, and none of the regiments on this front had ever been under fire. Three brigades of Brigadier-General W. T. Sherman's division filled, in a desultory way, the space from Owl Creek bridge to a point some distance beyond Shiloh Church. South and eastward near half a mile rested the right of Brigadier-General B. M. Prentiss's division of seven regiments, entirely raw, only recently arrived, more recently armed, and one without ammunition. To the left and rear of this embryo division there was another large interval of nearly a mile where was Colonel David Stuart's brigade of three regiments. It belonged to Sherman's division, but had at the time of landing been thus located upon the Hamburg road, two miles away from its division commander, to watch the fords in that quarter; at the time of the battle it formed the extreme left of the army. Between this front line and Pittsburg Landing were camped two other divisions: Major-General John A. McClernand's from a half to three-quarters of a mile in the rear of the right center, and that of Brigadier-General S. A. Hurlbut about one mile in rear of the left center. In the rear of all these, and north of the road which ran due west from the Landing, was Smith's division, then commanded by Brigadier-General W. H. L. Wallace. In these divisions were many of the veterans of Belmont and Donelson, and they were the only ones upon the field who had stood the test of battle. Still another division, under General Lew. Wallace, had been left at Crump's Landing, six miles to the north, as a guard against rebel raids, which threatened to gain possession of the banks of the Tennessee at that point to destroy the river communications. Grant had apprehensions of a raid of this character and cautioned his officers against it, causing such vigilance as had existed for several days.

Most of the particulars of the battle that followed will probably always form a subject of dispute. There were no combined or dramatic movements of masses that can be analyzed and located. The Union army had no prepared line of defense; three lines in which the rebel army had been arranged for the attack became quickly broken and mingled with one another. On the Union side the wide gaps between the camps, their irregular alignment, and the rapidity of the attack compelled the formation of whatever line of battle could be most hurriedly improvised by each separate corps or detachment. General Force says: "A combat made up of numberless separate encounters of detached portions of broken lines, continually shifting position and changing direction in the forest and across ravines, filling an entire day, is almost incapable of a connected narrative."

At five o'clock in the morning of Sunday, April 6, 1862, the rebel lines moved forward to the attack. The time required to pass the intervening two miles, and the preliminary skirmishes with Union pickets and a reconnoitering Union regiment that began the fight, gradually put the whole Union front on the alert; and when the main lines closed with each other, the divisions of Prentiss and Sherman were sufficiently in position to offer a stubborn resistance, and thus enabled reënforcements to come to their support from the other divisions. The Confederates found themselves foiled in the easy surprise and confusion that they had counted upon. It would be a tedious waste of time to attempt to follow the details of the fight, which, begun before sunrise, continued till near sunset.

Along the labyrinth of the local roads, over the mixed patchwork of woods, open fields, and almost impenetrable thickets, across stretches of level, broken by miry hollows and abrupt ravines, the swinging lines of conflict moved intermittently throughout the entire day. There was onset and repulse, yell of assault and cheer of defiance, screeching of shells and sputtering of volleys, advance and retreat. But steadily through the fluctuating changes the general progress was northward, the rebels gaining and pushing their advance, the Unionists stubbornly resisting, but little by little losing ground. It was like the flux and reflux of ocean breakers, dashing themselves with tireless repetition against a yielding, crumbling shore. Beauregard, to whom the Confederate commander on going to the front had committed the duties of general headquarters, advanced with the general staff to Shiloh Church, near which stood General Sherman's headquarters' tent. The time consumed and the lists of dead and wounded are sufficient evidence of the brave conduct of officers and the gallant courage of men on both sides. On the Union side the divisions of Hurlbut and W. H. L. Wallace had early been brought forward to sustain those of Sherman, McClernand, and Prentiss. It was, to a degree seldom witnessed in a battle, the slow and sustained struggle, through an entire day, of one whole army against another whole army. The five Union divisions engaged in the battle of Sunday numbered 33,000. The total force of the Confederates attacking them was 40,000.

It was in the afternoon that the more noteworthy incidents of the contest took place. The first of these was the death of the Confederate commander, General Albert Sidney Johnston, who fell in front of Hurlbut between two and three o'clock, while personally leading the charge of a brigade. The knowledge of the loss was carefully kept from the Confederate army, and the headquarters management on their side of the conflict was not therefore impaired, because Beauregard had been mainly intrusted with it from the beginning. It has been mentioned that Stuart's brigade of three regiments was posted at the extreme left of the Union front; and although its right regiment quickly became demoralized and disappeared, the remaining two, not being as yet hard pressed, had, with some change of position towards the rear, held their place till about noon. From that time until two o'clock they bravely maintained their ground against sharp attacks from superior forces. After severe loss they were also driven back, but their gallant resistance materially retarded the enemy's advance next to the Tennessee River. About five o'clock in the afternoon a serious loss fell upon the Unionists. General Prentiss, commanding the Sixth Division, and General W. H. L. Wallace, commanding the Second Division, whose united lines had held one of the key-points of the Federal left center against numerous and well-concentrated assaults of the enemy, found that the withdrawal of troops both on the right and the left produced gaps that offered openings to the enemy. Prentiss had been instructed by General Grant to hold his position at all hazards, and consulting with Wallace they determined to obey the order notwithstanding the now dangerous exposure; but the enemy seizing the advantage, they quickly found themselves enveloped and surrounded; only portions of their command succeeded in cutting their way out; Wallace was mortally wounded, and Prentiss and fragments of the two divisions, numbering 2200 men, were taken prisoner.

This wholesale capture left a wide opening in the left of the Federal lines, and probably would have given the victory to the rebels but for another circumstance which somewhat compensated for so abrupt a diminution of the Union forces. The Union lines had now been swept back more than a mile and a half, and the rebel attack was approaching the main road, running from Pittsburg Landing along the principal ridge, which here lay nearly at a right angle to the river. Colonel J. D. Webster of General Grant's staff, noting the steady retreat of the Union lines and foreseeing that the advancing attack of the enemy would eventually reach this ridge, busied himself to post a line of artillery—from thirty-five to fifty guns—along the crest, gathering whatever was available, among which were several siege pieces. To man and support this extemporized battery he organized and posted, in conjunction with Hurlbut's division, such fragments of troops as had become useless at the front. To reach the crest of this ridge and this line of hastily planted cannon the enemy was obliged to cross a deep, broad hollow, extending to the river and partly filled with back-water. The topography of the place was such that the gunboats *Tyler* and *Lexington* were also stationed in the Tennessee, abreast the valley and sheet of back-water, and their guns were thus enabled to assist the line of cannon on the ridge by a cross-fire of shells.

General Grant had passed the night of April 5 at Savannah, where he had become aware of the arrival of the advance brigades of Nelson's division of Buell's army on the same day. He started by boat to Pittsburg Landing early Sunday morning, April 6, having heard the firing but not regarding it as an attack in force. Arrived there he became a witness of the serious nature of the attack, and remained on the battlefield, visiting the various division commanders and giving such orders as the broken and fluctuating course of the conflict suggested. But the defense, begun in uncertainty and haste before his arrival, could not thereafter be reduced to any order or system; it necessarily, all day long, merely followed the changes and the violence of the rebel attack. The blind and intricate battle-field offered little chance for careful planning; the haste and tumult of combat left no time for tactics. On neither side could the guidance of general command render the usual service; it was the division, brigade, and regimental commanders who fought the battle. About noon of Sunday, General Grant began to have misgivings of the result, and dispatched a letter for help to Buell's forces at Savannah, saying, "If you will get upon the field, leaving all your baggage on the east bank of the river, it will be a move to our advantage, and possibly save the day to us." He also sent an order to General Lew. Wallace, at Crump's Landing, to hasten his division to the right of the army.

So far as the Confederates had any distinct plan of battle, it was merely the simple one of forcing the Federals away from the river to gain possession of Pittsburg Landing, cut off their means of retreat by seizing or destroying the transports, and compel Grant to capitulate. But the execution of this leading design was completely frustrated by the difficult nature of the ground and the gallant resistance of the Federal left. The principal advance made by the rebels was not next to the river, where they desired it, but on the Union right next to Owl Creek, where it was of least value. Even after they had captured the whole residue of Prentiss's and Wallace's divisions, and had cleared out that terrible center of the Union fire which they had ineffectually assaulted a dozen times, and which by bitter experience they themselves learned to know and designate as the "Hornets' nest," and near which their commander had fallen in death, they were not yet within reach of the coveted banks of Pittsburg Landing. Before them was still a line of steep hills, separated from them by the broad valley, the back-water, the mire, across which screeched the shells from the gunboats and from the long death-threatening line of Webster's reserve artillery, behind which the bayonets of Hurlbut's division, yet solid in organization and strong in numbers, glinted in the evening sun. From Hurlbut's right the shattered but courageous remnants of the divisions of McClernand and Sherman stretched away in an unbroken line towards Owl Creek. Ground had been lost and ground had been won; the line of fire had moved a mile and a half to the north; the lines of combatants had been shortened from three miles in the morning to one mile in the evening; but now, after the day's conflict, when the sun approached his setting, the relations and the prospects of the bloody fight were but little changed. The Confederates held the field of battle, but the Unionists held their central position, their supplies, and their communications. The front of attack had

become as weak as the front of defense. On each side from eight
to ten thousand men had been lost, by death, wounds, and capture. From ten to fifteen thousand panic-stricken Union stragglers cowered under the shelter of the high river bank at
Pittsburg Landing. From ten to fifteen thousand Confederate
stragglers, some equally panic-stricken, others demoralized by
the irresistible temptations of camp-pillage, encumbered the
rear of Beauregard's army. The day was nearly gone and the
battle was undecided.

A controversy has recently arisen as to the personal impressions and intentions of General Grant at this crisis. His "Memoirs" declare in substance that he was still so confident of victory that he gave orders that evening for a renewal of the fight
on the following morning by a general attack. General Buell, on
the other hand, makes a strong argument that the evidence is
against this assumption. It is possible, as in so many other cases,
that the truth lies midway between the two statements. A
famous newspaper correspondent, who was on the battlefield,
made the following record of the affair long before this controversy arose: "The tremendous roar to the left, momentarily
nearer and nearer, told of an effort to cut him off from the
river and from retreat. Grant sat his horse, quiet, thoughtful,
almost stolid. Said one to him, 'Does not the prospect begin to
look gloomy?' 'Not at all,' was the quiet reply. 'They can't
force our lines around these batteries to-night—it is too late.
Delay counts everything with us. To-morrow we shall attack
them with fresh troops and drive them, of course.'" The correspondent adds, in a note: "I was myself a listener to this
conversation, and from it I date, in my own case at least, the
beginning of any belief in Grant's greatness." As this writer was
one of Grant's most candid critics, his testimony on this point
is all the more valuable.

The turning-point was at length reached. Whatever may
have been the much-disputed intentions and hopes of commanders at that critical juncture that were not expressed and
recorded, or what might have been the possibilities and con-

sequence of acts that were not attempted, it is worse than useless to discuss upon hypothesis. Each reader for himself must
interpret the significance of the three closing incidents of that
momentous Sunday, which occurred almost simultaneously.
Some of the rebel division commanders, believing that victory
would be insured by one more desperate assault against the
Union left to gain possession of Pittsburg Landing, made arrangements and gave orders for that object. It seems uncertain,
however, whether the force could have been gathered and the
movement made in any event. Only a single brigade made the
attempt, and it was driven back in confusion. The officer of
another detachment refused the desperate service. Still others
were overtaken in their preparation by orders from General
Beauregard to withdraw the whole Confederate army from the
fight, and to go into bivouac until the following day. Eager as
was that commander for victory, the conclusion had been forced
on his mind, that, for that day at least, it was not within the
power of his army to complete their undertaking; and accordingly he directed that the fight should cease. He reached this
determination not knowing that Buell had arrived, and still
hoping that he would not arrive even on the morrow.

In this hope Beauregard was disappointed. While yet his
orders to retire from the combat were being executed, and before the last desperate charge of the rebels towards Webster's
reserve artillery was beaten back, the vanguard of Nelson's division, which had marched from Savannah and had been ferried
across the river by transports, was mounting the bank at Pittsburg Landing and deploying in line of battle under the enemy's
fire, Colonel Jacob Ammen's fresh brigade first coming to the
support of the line of Union guns. A few men out of the brigade
fell by the rebel bullets, and then came twilight, and soon after
the darkness of night. The tide of victory was effectually turned.
Whatever the single army of Grant might or might not have
accomplished on the following day against the army of Beauregard is only speculation. Beauregard's attack had been ordered discontinued before the actual presence of Buell's troops

on the battlefield. Had the attack been continued, however, that opportune arrival would have rendered its success impossible.

After sunset of Sunday all chances of a rebel victory vanished. The remainder of Nelson's division immediately crossed the river and followed Ammen's brigade to the field. Brigadier-General T. L. Crittenden's division was next placed in position during the night. Finally Brigadier-General A. McD. McCook's division reached Pittsburg Landing early Monday morning and promptly advanced to the front. General Buell, who had come before the vanguard on Sunday, in person directed the placing and preparation of these three superb divisions of his army—a total of about twenty thousand fresh, well-equipped, and well-drilled troops—to renew an offensive conflict along the left of the Federal line. On the Federal right was stationed the fresh division of General Lew. Wallace, numbering 5000, which had arrived from Crump's Landing a little after nightfall, and which took position soon after midnight of Sunday. Along the Federal right center, Grant's reduced divisions which had fought the battle of Sunday were gathered and reorganized, McClernand and Sherman in front, Hurlbut and remnants of W. H. L. Wallace's division, with some new detachments, in reserve.

Grant and Buell met on Sunday evening and agreed to take the offensive jointly on Monday morning; Buell to command his three divisions on the left, Grant to direct his own forces on the right. No special plan was adopted other than simultaneously to drive the enemy from the field. The plan was carried out in harmony and with entire success. With only temporary checks, brought about by the too great impetuosity of the newly arrived reënforcements, the two wings of the Union army advanced steadily, and by three o'clock in the afternoon were in possession of all the ground from which they had been driven on the previous day; while the rebel army was in full retreat upon Corinth—foiled of its victory, dejected in spirit, and in a broken and almost hopeless state of disorganization. A little more genius and daring on the part of the Union commanders would have enabled them by vigorous pursuit to demolish or capture it; but they chose the more prudent alternative, and remained satisfied with only sufficient advance to assure themselves that the enemy had disappeared.

The statement of the Union losses at the battle of Shiloh, which has been compiled from official reports, is as follows: In the army of Grant, 1513 killed; 6601 wounded; and 2830 captured or missing. In the army of Buell, 241 killed; 1807 wounded; and 55 captured or missing.

The Confederate loss is stated to have been 1728 killed; 8012 wounded; and 959 missing.

AS EARLY *as the fall of 1861 the Union high command begin to study the possibilities of an expedition against New Orleans, the metropolis of the South. Experience, at Cape Hatteras in August and at Port Royal in November, demonstrated that even wooden ships could run past powerful shore batteries without much damage. New Orleans, one hundred miles by river from the gulf, was protected by two formidable forts, St. Philip and Jackson, but naval officers were confident that they would not be insuperable obstacles.*

The Navy Department designated Captain David G. Farragut, sixty years old with nearly fifty years of service behind him, to command the expedition. By the middle of April, Farragut stood before the forts with seventeen men-of-war; Commander David D. Porter had a mortar flotilla; General Benjamin F. Butler commanded an army contingent of 6,000 on transports.

The main bombardment of the forts began on April 18 and continued for six days. Early on the 24th, Farragut gave the final signal to pass the forts. A violent battle ensued, but the Union forces lost only one ship. The next day Farragut's ships moved to New Orleans, where the flag of the Union was raised on the 29th.

Nicolay and Hay describe an occupation which soon became a sensation.

New Orleans

THE way was now clear to New Orleans; and as soon as General Butler could get his transports from the Gulf side round into the river again, he proceeded, after occupying the forts, as rapidly as possible up the river with his troops. On the 1st of May the naval forces under Farragut turned over to him the formal possession of the city, and he continued in command of the Department of the Gulf until the following December. The withdrawal of General Lovell, and the abandonment of Forts Pike and McComb at the entrances to Lake Pontchartrain, left him with no serious campaign immediately on his hands; but the task of governing the city of New Orleans was one which put all his energy and shrewdness into requisition. The supply of provisions had been interrupted by the military operations of the rebels themselves before the coming of Farragut's fleet; a portion of these again were carried away with Lovell's retiring army. When Butler came, starvation was close upon 150,000 people of New Orleans. To avert this danger was the general's first urgent effort, and he made it successful over all difficulties. His second care was to quell and to control the dangerous disloyalty of the population. An order to his own soldiers forbade, under the severest penalties, the stealing of public or private property; a proclamation to the citizens established martial law and made minute regulations for the preservation of order. He gave to neutral aliens and to loyalists assurance of full protection to persons and property; and to non-combatant Confederates also, so far as the exigencies of the public service would permit. In their most favorable phases, war and martial law are full of necessary sacrifice and harshness, and it may be said that General Butler's military government, firm and vigilant throughout, was tolerant and even liberal to the well-disposed and orderly, but severe against transgressors and the malicious plottings of certain individuals, corporations, and classes in aid of rebellion.

These pages do not afford room for an extended review of General Butler's administration. In all the war no man was so severely criticized by his enemies or more warmly defended by his friends. Confederate newspapers, orators, and writers have exhausted the vocabulary of abuse for epithets to heap upon his name, from "Yankee" to "Beast" and "Butcher." Secession sympathizers in England approvingly echoed this defamation; Palmerston in the House of Commons went out of his way to swell the unthinking British clamor by repeating the unjust censure. The whole subject might profitably be buried as part of the "animosities and passions of the war," were it not that Jefferson Davis sought to turn the circumstance to the advantage of the rebellion by a sensational official proclamation declaring Butler "an outlaw and common enemy of mankind, . . . to be immediately executed by hanging" in case of capture, also adding that "all commissioned officers in the command of said Benjamin F. Butler be declared not entitled to be considered as soldiers engaged in honorable warfare, but as robbers and criminals deserving death; and that they and each of them be, wherever captured, reserved for execution."

Since the rebel chief thus prominently inscribed Butler and his officers on the historical record, the recitals of his proclamation deserve a passing notice. In the list of reasons assigned to support his declaration of outlawry the allegations of imprisonment or expulsion from the city may be at once dismissed as the ordinary incidents of war, which the Confederates themselves were daily practising in different parts of the country. So also of the complaint of military fines and assessments; manifestly they are a harsh and arbitrary mode of reprisal for treason and hostility, but international law recognizes them and all civilized nations practise them. The charge that Butler armed African slaves for a servile war first disappears technically under Butler's showing that he armed no slaves, but only free citizens of color, many of whom the rebels themselves had enlisted and drilled before his coming; while the whole charge disappears generally under President Lincoln's proclamation and policy of emancipation, begun before Davis's edict of outlawry was issued. There remain therefore but two further points to be examined, the execution of Mumford and the so-called "woman order."

Mumford, it will be remembered, tore down the United States flag, which by Farragut's order was raised over the Mint on the morning of April 27. He remained in the city, openly boasted of his crime, and courted applause for his recklessness. When Butler came, he had him arrested and tried by a military commission which, on June 5, convicted him "of treason and an overt act thereof"; and Butler ordered the sentence to be executed on June 7, on which day Mumford was hanged. Jefferson Davis's proclamation calls this "deliberate murder," "when said Mumford was an unresisting and non-combatant captive, and for no offense even alleged to have been committed by him subsequent to the date of the capture of the said city." Such a recital is the merest quibbling. The rebel President well knew that the flag torn down by Mumford had been raised by Farragut, after the demand of unqualified surrender on April 26; after the reply by the Mayor on the same day, that the city was evacuated by Confederate troops, its administration restored back to him, that it was without means of defense, and promising a "religious compliance" of the people to yield obedience to the conqueror. Mumford's crime was against the sovereignty of the United States, duly claimed and enforced by the commissioned officer and the naval power of the Government, to which the municipal authority had formally submitted. The offender thus violated not only military law but also the sanctity of the Mayor's promise. To declare that Mumford was executed for pulling down the flag at New Orleans before its occupation by the United States forces is willfully to ignore history, law, and evidence. There is no flaw in the chain of legal and technical justice. But if on merely humane considerations we question the severity of the punishment, Jefferson Davis's extravagant fulmination is rebuked by the acts of his own Government and his distinct approval of them. Six months before the hanging of Mumford, the rebel Secretary of War instructed his officer at Knoxville in regard to the "traitors" in East Tennessee: "All such as can be identified as having been engaged in bridge-burning are to be tried summarily by drumhead court martial, and if found guilty executed on the spot by hanging. It would be well to leave their bodies hanging in the vicinity of the burned bridges."

The consideration of the "woman order" requires a preliminary word. Nobody at the North could properly find fault with the women of the South for reflecting the political bias of Southern communities, or because the natural instincts of their sex led them to sympathize with, and warmly espouse, the secession

and rebellion in which their fathers, brothers, husbands, and
sons embarked. It was to be expected that their prayers would
go with them to the battlefield, and their labors, charities, and
sacrifices forward them cheer and comfort to camp and hospital. But the records and traditions of the war make it painfully
evident that in every rebel State the expression of hatred for
"Yankees" was intentionally practised and cultivated among
portions of the female population of towns and cities; and in
this members of the upper classes were frequently the most conspicuous transgressors. Not content with merely entertaining
feelings hostile to Union officers and soldiers, they indulged in
obtrusive manifestations of them, relying on the respect and
privilege accorded their sex for immunity from retort or re-
taliation. They turned their backs to avoid looking at them.
They stepped from sidewalks into the streets to avoid meeting
them. They held aside their skirts to indicate a dread of con-
tamination. They turned up their noses as if they smelt foul
odors. They feigned nausea as if their presence were insupport-
able. They retired from street cars or church pews when they
entered. They flaunted miniature secession flags and sang secession songs in their presence or thumped secession melodies
when they passed their open windows. They uttered uncompli-
mentary remarks in their hearing, and in some extreme cases
deliberately spat on the Federal uniform. Behavior of this nature was not isolated and local, but prevailed widely throughout
the South in multiplied forms during the war. Probably only
a minority of the women of the South indulged in these antics;
but it was a minority so considerable and so diffused that such
exhibitions uniformly attended the presence and progress of
Federal armies in rebel communities.

As a rule such behavior was only a rankling annoyance which
soldiers and officers endured in silence. But in New Orleans,
where a mere handful of troops had to govern a great population and prevent violence, it became a serious danger to discipline and authority. Such open and hourly disrespect was a constant incitement to disorder and mobs. "We were 2500 men,"

wrote Butler, "in a city seven miles long by two to four wide, of 150,000 inhabitants, all hostile, bitter, defiant, explosive; standing literally on a magazine, a spark only needed for destruction." But how abate the evil? The ordinary punishments of arrest, fine, and imprisonment were inapplicable. The offenses were too vague, the cases too numerous; he could not bring even a fraction of these female malignants into a police court. The only remedy was to stamp their public rudeness with the seal of public disgrace. In his own language: "No order could be made save one which would execute itself." He remembered an old ordinance of the City of London, which he had read in some law-book, and copying its phraseology he, on May 15, published his "Order No. 28," which announced that "As the officers and soldiers of the United States have been subject to repeated insults from the women (calling themselves ladies) of New Orleans in return for the most scrupulous non-interference and courtesy on our part, it is ordered that hereafter when any female shall, by word, gesture, or movement, insult or show contempt for any officer or soldier of the United States, she shall be regarded and held liable to be treated as a woman of the town plying her avocation."

General Butler's simple and plain intention was to abate a nuisance in public demeanor which could be reached in no other way, and he so explained it to the Mayor on the following day. "There can be, there has been," he wrote, "no room for the misunderstanding of General Order No. 28. No lady will take any notice of a strange gentleman, and *a fortiori* of a stranger, in such form as to attract attention. . . . If obeyed, it will protect the true and modest woman from all possible insult." We have the published testimony of a member of General Butler's staff as to the result. "Can I say anything stronger," he wrote, "in vindication of the propriety of this order, or of the general's sagacity in issuing it, than that the first twenty-four hours after its promulgation witnessed a complete, and it seemed to us who were there almost miraculous, change in the deportment of the ladies of the Crescent City? If success is the test of merit, then was it one of the most meritorious acts of the war."

One tremendous outcry, however, of denunciation and misconstruction of its language and intent arose from every rebel in the South and every rebel sympathizer in Europe. British blockade-runners were just beginning to reap their enormous profits from contraband trade with the rebellion; and Lord Palmerston, prime minister of England, grew eloquent, and the London "Times" and "Punch" indignant, over the "infamous" doings of the Yankee Haynau and Nana Sahib. General Butler's nature is combative, and he had a ready retort to such high criticism, which, in due time, he embodied in his farewell address. With a single additional comment the "woman order" may be dismissed from consideration. In his proclamation of outlawry against Butler, Jefferson Davis says of it: "The soldiers of the United States have been invited and encouraged by general orders to insult and outrage the wives, the mothers, and the sisters of our citizens." Unconsciously, the rebel President's language proved more than he intended. Like the testimony of many another prejudiced witness, his accusation answered itself. He wrote this assertion more than six full months after Butler's order was issued, and during the whole of which period it had remained in force. In the same proclamation Davis recited, in as pathetic and harrowing language as he could command, the wrongs and sufferings which he alleged Butler's administration had heaped upon the people of New Orleans—fine, imprisonment, exile, chains, labor, confiscation, starvation, murder—but not one single instance of insult, much less outrage, under the "woman order," is mentioned in the long sensational catalogue. The simple truth is, Order No. 28 sprang from no evil design of the commander, and was neither misunderstood by, nor provoked the least evil act from, his officers or soldiers. But for the prominence given it by Confederates to "fire the Southern heart" and stimulate the intervention of France and England, it would have merited no discussion except as a question of taste. In that respect it

can no more be defended than can the unseemly parade of it
as a Southern grievance; at the same time its salutary influence
in checking the public misbehavior at which it was aimed will
scarcely be denied.

However loud was the outcry against Butler's methods, there
is a cheerful and universal admission of his energy and efficiency. Never in its long history was New Orleans so quiet,
orderly, clean, and healthy. Though he rigorously exacted obedience to his police orders, and abstinence from public and
private hostility to the flag and laws of his Government, he re-
paid the people a thousand-fold by keeping the wolf of starvation from their doors and the dreadful scourge of yellow fever
out of their homes. The city was without provisions and without
occupation; with trade stagnant, with supplies cut off, with industry paralyzed, with a worthless currency, with credit destroyed, with confidence gone, with poverty wide-spread and
irremediable, with demoralization in every part of the social
structure. These combined evils he grappled with intelligent
resolution and the confidence born of an indomitable will. He
distributed among the poor the captured Confederate rations.
He allowed provisions already purchased by the city to be freely
brought from Mobile and Red River; he organized relief associations. Finding certain lists of wealthy citizens who had sub-
scribed a million and a quarter to the rebel war fund, he assessed
them one-fourth their subscription and applied it to feeding the
poor. This relief fund was augmented by contributions levied on
another list of merchants who had published a newspaper card
advising planters not to send their produce to New Orleans. But
he also made this relief fund serve a wider purpose than mere
charity. He used it to employ from one to two thousand laborers every day "in cleaning the streets and building up the levees,
and putting the city to rights, generally. All the drainage of
the city is done by means of canals, and we cleaned out between
ten and eleven miles of canal, some of which had not been
cleaned for twelve or fifteen years. The consequence was that
we had comparatively no sickness in the city of New Orleans.

I had a regiment, a thousand strong, in the city during the months of July and August, and it buried but one man." This was one essential step, maintaining public health; but he did not neglect the other. "I established a very strict quarantine," continues his testimony. "I would not allow any vessel that came from an infected port to come up to the city under thirty days. If she had anything like a perishable cargo it was taken out and thoroughly overhauled and fumigated. . . . I did allow a small steamer from New York to come up, the captain stating that he touched at Nassau merely to take in coal, and was there but a short time. It turned out, however, that he did take passengers on board, one of whom had the yellow fever after he arrived at New Orleans. I immediately had the square shut up completely, allowed no one to enter or leave it, whitewashed everything, cleaned the square up, fumigated it, and when the man died buried him and pretty much everything he had ever looked at. This ended the matter; we did not have another case of yellow fever in New Orleans. That, however, demonstrated the fact that yellow fever is not indigenous there, but requires to be imported, and that it may be quarantined even after it has been brought into the river. It perhaps can be fully done only by military measures, but it was effectually done there, although they had it everywhere on the coast,—at Matamoras, Galveston, Sabine Pass, and at Pensacola,—and I had five or six cases down at quarantine."

It must not be inferred that the rebels threw no obstacles in Butler's way. The persistent effort of the Mayor to recant his surrender of the city has been noted; and following out this policy, which was prompted from Richmond, secret machinations by prominent Confederates perplexed the commanding general at almost every step of his administration. They abused his permits to bring food, by secret mails and contraband supplies. The city authorities neglected efficient coöperation. The rebel Governor refused to allow provisions to be brought. Banks and corporations connived with foreign consuls to hide rebel funds. It was a running fight between loyal government and all the subterfuges which treason could invent, and Butler used his power of detection and punishment unsparingly upon willful offenders. But a fair balancing of motives and acts would show that in his hands military despotism, instead of bringing oppression and inflicting suffering, compelled the community to submit to peace and protection, to charity and bounty, to health and life. Under the teachings of its leaders, and its blind political rage, New Orleans had done its full share to create war; Butler, with autocratic will, forced upon it quiet and order. With suicidal folly it had created destitution and want and raised the gaunt specter of famine; with imperious authority Butler filled its hungry mouths and obliged it to reorganize industry and reëstablish trade. Through misrule and indolent neglect it had invited pestilence; Butler relentlessly constrained it to a cleanliness and health it had never experienced. One might almost transpose the Scripture parable to contrast their contumacious opposition and his beneficent compulsion. They asked a scorpion, and he gave them an egg; they asked a serpent, and he gave them a fish; they asked a stone, and he gave them bread.

TWO WEEKS *before Farragut faced Fort St. Philip and Fort Jackson, McClellan arrived at Fort Monroe to take charge of his campaign up the peninsula to Richmond. For a month he allowed his advance to be held up by a Confederate force at Yorktown and Williamsburg which he could have scattered by one sharp attack. Not until the end of May did the two armies lock in battle near Richmond. Hard fighting culminated in the Seven Days' Battles which began on June 25 and ended on July 1. Robert E. Lee, commanding the Confederate forces after June 1, saved Richmond but failed to destroy the Federal army. McClellan shifted his base to Harrison's Landing on the James River, there to restore his badly mauled troops and to indulge in recriminations for which Nicolay and Hay never forgave him.*

Harrison's Landing

GENERAL McClellan was greatly agitated by the battle of Gaines's Mill,* and by the emotions incident to his forced departure for the James. Under the influence of this feeling he sent to the Secretary of War, from Savage's Station, on the 28th of June, an extraordinary dispatch, which we here insert in full, as it seems necessary to the comprehension of his attitude towards, and his relations with, the Government.

Vol. V, Chap. XXIV.

* Lieutenant-Colonel B. S. Alexander, of the Corps of Engineers, gave the following sworn evidence before the Committee on the Conduct of the War [p. 592]. He said he saw, on the evening of the 28th, at General Mc-Clellan's headquarters at Savage's Station, an order directing the destruction of the baggage of the officers and men, and he thought also the camp equipage; appealing to the officers and men to submit to this privation because it would be only for a few days, he thought the order stated. He went to the general at once, and remonstrated with him against allowing any such order to be issued, telling him he thought it would have a bad effect upon the army—would demoralize the officers and men; that it would tell them more plainly than in any other way that they were a defeated army running for their lives. This led to some discussion among the officers at headquarters, and Colonel Alexander heard afterward that the order was never promulgated, but suppressed. Brevet Brigadier-General James F. Rusling informs us that he saw and read this order, and that it was issued and acted upon to a certain extent.

I now know the full history of the day. On this side of the
river (the right bank) we repulsed several strong attacks. On
the left bank our men did all that men could do, all that soldiers
could accomplish; but they were overwhelmed by vastly superior numbers, even after I brought my last reserves into action.
The loss on both sides is terrible. I believe it will prove to be
the most desperate battle of the war. The sad remnants of my
men behave as men. Those battalions who fought most bravely,
and suffered most, are still in the best order. My regulars were
superb, and I count upon what are left to turn another battle,
in company with their gallant comrades of the volunteers. Had
I 20,000 or even 10,000 fresh troops to use to-morrow, I could
take Richmond, but I have not a man in reserve, and shall be
glad to cover my retreat, and save the material and personnel
of the army. If we have lost the day, we have yet preserved our
honor, and no one need blush for the Army of the Potomac. I
have lost this battle because my force was too small. I again
repeat that I am not responsible for this, and I say it with the
earnestness of a general who feels in his heart the loss of every
brave man who has been needlessly sacrificed to-day. I still
hope to retrieve our fortunes, but to do this the Government
must view the matter in the same earnest light that I do. You
must send me very large reënforcements, and send them at once.
I shall draw back to this side of Chickahominy, and think I can
withdraw all our material. Please understand that in this battle
we have lost nothing but men, and those the best we have. In
addition to what I have already said, I only wish to say to the
President that I think he is wrong in regarding me as ungenerous when I said that my force was too weak. I merely intimated
a truth which to-day has been too plainly proved. If, at this instant, I could dispose of ten thousand fresh men, I could gain
a victory to-morrow. I know that a few thousand more men
would have changed this battle from a defeat to a victory. As
it is, the Government must not and can not hold me responsible
for the result. I feel too earnestly to-night; I have seen too many
dead and wounded comrades to feel otherwise than that the
Government has not sustained this army. If you do not do so
now, the game is lost. If I save this army now, I tell you plainly
that I owe no thanks to you or to any other persons in Washington. You have done your best to sacrifice this army.

It is probable that no other general would have retained his
commission for twenty-four hours after the receipt of such a

communication by his superiors; but it is easy to see the reason why he was never called to account for it. The evident panic and mental perturbation which pierced through its incoherence filled the President with such dismay that its mutinous insolence was entirely overlooked. He could only wonder what terrible catastrophe, already accomplished or to come, could have wrung such an outcry as this from the general commanding. Even the surrender of the army was not an impossible disaster to expect from a general capable of writing such a dispatch. Secretary Chase has left a memorandum showing that some such action was regarded as indicated by General McClellan's telegrams, and that even after his arrival at Harrison's Landing, General Marcy, his father-in-law and chief-of-staff, in a visit to Washington, spoke of it as a possibility. Not knowing the extent of the mischance which had fallen upon the army, the President hastened at once to send a kind and encouraging answer to McClellan's dispatches:

Save your army at all events. Will send reënforcements as fast as we can. Of course they cannot reach you to-day, to-morrow, or next day. I have not said you were ungenerous for saying you needed reënforcements. I thought you were ungenerous in assuming that I did not send them as fast as I could. I feel any misfortune to you and your army quite as keenly as you feel it yourself. If you have had a drawn battle, or a repulse, it is the price we pay for the enemy not being in Washington. We protected Washington, and the enemy concentrated on you. Had we stripped Washington, he would have been upon us before the troops could have gotten to you. Less than a week ago you notified us that reënforcements were leaving Richmond to come in front of us. It is the nature of the case, and neither you nor the Government are to blame. Please tell at once the present condition and aspect of things.

The President also, with the greatest diligence, sent dispatches on the same day to General Dix, at Fort Monroe, to Admiral Goldsborough, commanding the naval forces in the James, and to General Burnside, in North Carolina, directing all three of them to strain every nerve in order to go to McClel-

lan's assistance. At the same time he ordered Halleck to send
a large portion of his forces to the rescue.

As the 29th and 30th of June passed without news of any
further catastrophe, the President and the Secretary of War
began to think better of the situation, and concluded that it
might possibly be improved by a change of base to the James.
Mr. Stanton telegraphed to General Wool that it looked "more
like taking Richmond than at any time before." But on the 1st
of July a dispatch, dated at Turkey Bridge, arrived from General McClellan, who was still under the influence of great
agitation, announcing that he is "hard pressed by superior numbers," and fearing that he shall be forced to abandon his material and save his men under cover of the gunboats. "If none
of us escape, we shall at least have done honor to the country.
I shall do my best to save the army. Send more gunboats."
While waiting for his troops to come to the new position he
had chosen for them, he continued asking for reënforcements.
"I need," he says, "50,000 more men, and with them I will retrieve our fortunes." The Secretary of War at once answered
that reënforcements were on the way, 5000 from McDowell and
25,000 from Halleck. "Hold your ground," he says encourag-
ingly, "and you will be in Richmond before the month is over."
On the morning of the battle of Malvern, McClellan writes
again, "I dread the result if we are attacked to-day by fresh
troops. . . . I now pray for time." It has been seen that his dread
was uncalled for. Meanwhile, before hearing of the battle, the
President had telegraphed:

It is impossible to reënforce you for your present emergency.
If we had a million of men we could not get them to you in
time. We have not the men to send. If you are not strong enough
to face the enemy you must find a place of security, and wait,
rest, and repair. Maintain your ground if you can, but save the
army at all events, even if you fall back to Fort Monroe. We
still have strength enough in the country, and will bring it out.

On the 2d, the flurry of the week having somewhat subsided,
the President sent him the following.

Your dispatch of Tuesday morning induces me to hope your army is having some rest. In this hope allow me to reason with you a moment. When you ask for 50,000 men to be promptly sent you, you surely labor under some gross mistake of fact. Recently you sent papers showing your disposal of forces made last spring for the defense of Washington, and advising a return to that plan. I find it included in and about Washington 75,000 men. Now, please be assured I have not men enough to fill that very plan by 15,000. All of Frémont's in the Valley, all of Banks's, all of McDowell's not with you, and all in Washington, taken together, do not exceed, if they reach, 60,000. With Wool and Dix added to those mentioned I have not, outside of your army, 75,000 men east of the mountains. Thus the idea of sending you 50,000, or any other considerable force, promptly is simply absurd. If in your frequent mention of responsibility you have the impression that I blame you for not doing more than you can, please be relieved of such impression. I only beg that, in like manner, you will not ask impossibilities of me. If you think you are not strong enough to take Richmond just now, I do not ask you to try just now. Save the army, material, and personnel, and I will strengthen it for the offensive again as fast as I can. The Governors of eighteen States offer me a new levy of 300,000, which I accept.

This quiet and reasonable statement produced no effect upon the general. On the 3d he wrote again in a strain of wilder exaggeration than ever. He says:

It is of course impossible to estimate, as yet, our losses; but I doubt whether there are to-day more than 50,000 men with their colors. To accomplish the great task of capturing Richmond and putting an end to this rebellion reënforcements should be sent to me, rather much over than much less than 100,000 men. I beg that you will be fully impressed by the magnitude of the crisis in which we are placed.

The didactic, not to say magisterial, tone of this dispatch formed a not unnatural introduction to the general's next important communication to the President, laying before him an entire body of administrative and political doctrine, in which alone, he intimated, the salvation of the country could be found.

HEADQUARTERS ARMY OF THE POTOMAC,
CAMP NEAR HARRISON'S LANDING,
VIRGINIA, JULY 7, 1862.

MR. PRESIDENT: You have been fully informed that the rebel army is in our front, with the purpose of overwhelming us by attacking our positions, or reducing us by blocking our river communications. I cannot but regard our condition as critical, and I earnestly desire, in view of possible contingencies, to lay before your Excellency, for your private consideration, my general views concerning the existing state of the rebellion, although they do not strictly relate to the situation of this army, or strictly come within the scope of my official duties. These views amount to convictions, and are deeply impressed upon my mind and heart. Our cause must never be abandoned; it is the cause of free institutions and self-government. The Constitution and the Union must be preserved, whatever may be the cost in time, treasure, and blood. If secession is successful, other dissolutions are clearly to be seen in the future. Let neither military disaster, political faction, nor foreign war shake your settled purpose to enforce the equal operation of the laws of the United States upon the people of every State. The time has come when the Government must determine upon a civil and military policy covering the whole ground of our national trouble. The responsibility of determining, declaring, and supporting such civil and military policy, and of directing the whole course of national affairs in regard to the rebellion, must now be assumed and exercised by you, or our cause will be lost. The Constitution gives you power sufficient even for the present terrible exigency.

This rebellion has assumed the character of a war. As such it should be regarded, and it should be conducted upon the highest principles known to Christian civilization. It should not be a war looking to the subjugation of the people of any State in any event. It should not be at all a war upon population, but against armed forces and political organizations. Neither confiscation of property, political executions of persons, territorial organization of States, or forcible abolition of slavery should be contemplated for a moment.

In prosecuting the war all private property and unarmed persons should be strictly protected, subject only to the necessities of military operations; all private property taken for military use should be paid or receipted for; pillage and waste should

be treated as high crimes, all unnecessary trespass sternly prohibited, and offensive demeanor by the military towards citizens
promptly rebuked. Military arrests should not be tolerated,
except in places where active hostilities exist; and oaths not
required by enactments—constitutionally made—should be
neither demanded nor received. Military government should
be confined to the preservation of public order and the protection of political rights. Military power should not be allowed
to interfere with the relations of servitude, either by supporting
or impairing the authority of the master, except for repressing
disorder, as in other cases. Slaves, contraband under the act of
Congress, seeking military protection, should receive it. The
right of the Government to appropriate permanently to its own
service claims to slave labor should be asserted, and the right of
the owner to compensation therefor should be recognized. This
principle might be extended upon grounds of military necessity
and security to all the slaves within a particular State, thus
working manumission in such State; and in Missouri, perhaps
in Western Virginia also, and possibly even in Maryland, the
expediency of such a military measure is only a question of
time. A system of policy thus constitutional and conservative,
and pervaded by the influences of Christianity and freedom,
would receive the support of almost all truly loyal men, would
deeply impress the rebel masses and all foreign nations, and it
might be humbly hoped that it would commend itself to the
favor of the Almighty.

Unless the principles governing the further conduct of our
struggle shall be made known and approved, the effort to obtain requisite forces will be almost hopeless. A declaration of
radical views, especially upon slavery, will rapidly disintegrate
our present armies. The policy of the Government must be supported by concentrations of military power. The national
forces should not be dispersed in expeditions, posts of occupation, and numerous armies; but should be mainly collected
into masses and brought to bear upon the armies of the Confederate States. Those armies thoroughly defeated, the political structure which they support would soon cease to exist.

In carrying out any system of policy which you may form,
you will require a commander-in-chief of the army; one who
possesses your confidence, understands your views, and who is
competent to execute your orders by directing the military
forces of the nation to the accomplishment of the objects by you
proposed. I do not ask that place for myself. I am willing to

serve you in such position as you may assign me, and I will do so as faithfully as ever subordinate served superior.

I may be on the brink of eternity, and as I hope foregiveness from my Maker, I have written this letter with sincerity towards you and from love for my country.

Very respectfully, your obedient servant,

G. B. McClellan,

Major-General Commanding.

His Excellency Abraham Lincoln, President.

This letter marks the beginning of General McClellan's distinctively political career. He had always been more or less in sympathy with the Democratic party, and consequently in an attitude of dormant opposition to the Administration; although, after the manner of officers of the regular service, he had taken no pronounced political attitude. In fact, on his first assuming command of the Army of the Potomac, he had seemed to be in full sympathy with the President and Cabinet, in the proceedings they thought proper to adopt for the suppression of the rebellion. He had even entered heartily into some of the more extreme measures of the Government. His orders to General Banks directing the arrest of the secessionist members of the Maryland Legislature might have been written by a zealous Republican. "When they meet on the 17th," he says, "you will please have everything prepared to arrest the whole party, and be sure that none escape." He urges upon him the "absolute necessity of secrecy and success"; speaks of the exceeding importance of the affair—"If it is successfully carried out it will go far towards breaking the backbone of the rebellion." This was in September, 1861. Later in that year he was repeatedly urged by prominent Democratic politicians to declare himself openly as a member of their party. They thought it would be to his advantage and to theirs to have the General-in-Chief of the Army of the Potomac decidedly with them. At this time he declined their overtures, but they were pressingly repeated at Yorktown and afterwards; and he appears finally to have yielded to their solicitations, and the foregoing letter was the result.

It is not at all probable that this document was prepared during the flight from the Chickahominy, or during the first days of doubt and anxiety at Harrison's Landing. It had probably been prepared long before, and is doubtless referred to in the general's dispatch of the 20th of June, in which he says, "I would be glad to have permission to lay before your Excellency, by letter or telegraph, my views as to the present state of military affairs throughout the whole country." He had at that time some indefinite hope of taking Richmond; and such a manifesto as this, coming from a general crowned with a great victory, would have had a far different importance and influence from that which it enjoyed issuing from his refuge at Harrison's Bar, after a discrediting retreat. But the choice of occasion was not left to him; the letter could not be delayed forever, and such as it was, it went forth to the country as the political platform of General McClellan, and to the President as a note of defiance and opposition from the general in command of the principal army of the United States. Though more moderate in form, this letter was as mutinous in substance as the dispatch from Savage's Station. He assumes to instruct the President as to his duties and the limits of his constitutional power. He takes it for granted that the President has no definite policy, and proceeds to give him one. Unless his advice is followed "our cause will be lost." He postures as the protector of the people against threatened arbitrary outrage. He warns the President against any forcible interference with slavery. He lets him know he can have no more troops, except on conditions known and approved. He tells him plainly that "a declaration of radical views, especially upon slavery, will rapidly disintegrate our present armies." Finally, he directs him to appoint a commander-in-chief of the army, and thinks it necessary to inform him that he does not ask the place for himself.

The President, engrossed with more important affairs, paid no attention, then or afterwards, to this letter. He simply passed it by in good-natured silence. General McClellan continued his dispatches, constantly announcing an impending attack upon his position, and constantly asking for reënforcements. He continued this until General Lee withdrew his army to Richmond, a movement which General McClellan at once characterized as "a retreat."

During all the time McClellan remained at Harrison's Landing his correspondence with the Government was full of recrimination and querulousness; and his private letters which have been published since his death show an almost indecent hostility to his superiors. He writes: "I have no faith in the Administration. . . . I am tired of serving fools. . . . Marcy and I have just been discussing people in Washington, and conclude they are a 'mighty trifling set.' . . . I begin to believe they wish this army to be destroyed. When you contrast the policy I urge in my letter to the President with that of Congress and of Mr. Pope, you can readily agree with me that there can be little natural confidence between the Government and myself. We are the antipodes of each other. I am satisfied that the dolts in Washington are bent on my destruction. . . . My communication with Halleck was unsatisfactory in the extreme. He did not even behave with common politeness; he is a *bien mauvais sujet*—he is not a gentleman."

We need not multiply these utterances. They have already been judged by the highest authority. General Sherman says, referring to this period, "The temper of his correspondence, official and private, was indicative of a spirit not consistent with the duty of the commanding general of a great army."

The President had been much disturbed by the conflicting reports that reached him as to the condition of the Army of the Potomac, and he therefore resolved by a personal visit to satisfy himself of the state of affairs. He reached Harrison's Landing on the 8th of July, and while there conferred freely, not only with General McClellan himself, but with many of the more prominent officers in command. With the exception of General McClellan, not one believed the enemy was then threatening his position. Sumner thought they had retired, much damaged;

Keyes that they had withdrawn to go towards Washington; Porter that they dared not attack; Heintzelman and Franklin thought they had retired; Franklin and Keyes favored the withdrawal of the army from the James; the rest opposed it. Mr. Lincoln came back bearing a still heavier weight of care. One thing that gave him great trouble was the enormous number of absentees from the army. On returning to Washington he wrote this note to General McClellan, which, like most of his notes, it is impossible to abridge:

I am told that over 160,000 men have gone into your army on the Peninsula. When I was with you the other day we made out 86,500 remaining, leaving 73,500 to be accounted for. I believe 23,500 will cover all the killed, wounded, and missing in all your battles and skirmishes, leaving 50,000 who have left otherwise. Not more than 5000 of these have died; leaving 45,000 of your army still alive and not with it. I believe half or two-thirds of them are fit for duty to-day. Have you any more perfect knowledge of this than I have? If I am right, and you had these men with you, you could go into Richmond in the next three days. How can they be got to you, and how can they be prevented from getting away in such numbers for the future?

To this note the general replied in a letter which can hardly be regarded as a satisfactory answer to the President's searching questions. He says, in general terms, that there is always a difference between the returns and the effective force of armies. He thinks, but is not certain, that the force given to him is not so much as 160,000, but admits that he has at that moment, present for duty, 88,665; absent by authority, 34,472; without authority, 3778. This is very far from the "fifty thousand with their colors" which he reported a few days before; and he gives no adequate reason for the vast aggregate of those absent by authority.

But another question, far more important and more grevious, was, what was to be done with the Army of the Potomac? General McClellan would listen to nothing but an enormous reënforcement of his army, and another chance to take Richmond.

Many of his prominent officers, on the contrary, thought that an advance on Richmond under existing conditions would be ill-advised, and that for the army to remain in its present position during the months of August and September would be more disastrous than an unsuccessful battle. The President had already placed General John Pope at the head of the Army of Virginia, in front of Washington, and he now took the resolution of sending to Corinth for General Halleck, whom he placed in chief command of the armies of the United States. This was done by an order of the 11th of July, and General Halleck was requested to start at once for Washington. As soon as he could place his command in the hands of General Grant, the next officer in rank in his department, he came on to Washington, assumed command of the army on the 23d, and the next day was sent to the camp of General McClellan, where he arrived on the 25th.

He asked the general his wishes and views in regard to future operations. McClellan answered that he proposed to cross the James River and attack Petersburg. Halleck stated his impression of the danger and impracticability of the plan, to which McClellan finally agreed. The General-in-Chief then told him that he regarded it as a military necessity to concentrate Pope's army and his on some point where they could at the same time cover Washington and operate against Richmond; unless it should be that McClellan felt strong enough to take the latter place himself with such reënforcements as would be given him. McClellan thought he would require thirty thousand more than he had. Halleck told him that the President could only promise twenty thousand, and that if McClellan could not take Richmond with that number, some plan must be devised for withdrawing his troops from their present position to some point where they could unite with General Pope without exposing Washington. McClellan thought there would be no serious difficulty in withdrawing his forces for that purpose; but he feared the demoralizing influence of such a movement on his troops, and preferred they should stay where they were until sufficient reënforcements could be sent him. Halleck had no authority to consider that proposition, and told him that he must decide between advising the withdrawal of his forces to meet those of Pope, or an advance upon Richmond with such forces as the President could give him. Halleck gained the impression that McClellan's preference would be to withdraw and unite with General Pope; but after consultation with his officers he informed Halleck the next morning that he would prefer to take Richmond. He would not say that he thought the probabilities of success were in his favor, but that there was "a chance," and that he was "willing to try it." His officers were divided on the subject of withdrawing or making an attack upon Richmond. McClellan's delusion as to the number of the enemy had infected many of the most intelligent generals in his command. General Keyes, in a letter to Quartermaster-General Meigs, assured him that the enemy had two hundred thousand, more than double our number. At the same time General Meigs himself, simply from reading the Richmond newspapers and controlling their accounts with his own common-sense, had formed an estimate of the rebel force very much nearer the truth than that made by the generals at the front. He found it to consist of 152 regiments, which, at an average of 700 men— too high an average—would give a total force of 105,000. By General McClellan's returns for the 10th of August he himself had an aggregate present of 113,000 men.

Halleck's return to Washington was followed by a shower of telegrams from McClellan urging the reënforcement of his army. "Should it be determined to withdraw it," he says on the 30th of July, "I shall look upon our cause as lost, and the demoralization of the army certain"—a statement which certainly was lacking in reserve. The weight of opinion, however, among the generals of highest rank, was on the other side. General Keyes wrote in the strongest terms urging the withdrawal of the army. General Barnard, McClellan's chief of engineers, and General Franklin counseled the immediate withdrawal from the James to reunite with the forces covering the capital.

Upon General Halleck's return to Washington, this course was resolved upon. General Halleck's first order in that direction was dated the 30th of July, requesting McClellan to send away his sick as quickly as possible. Four days afterwards, without having taken in the meanwhile any steps to obey the order, McClellan sent General Hooker to Malvern Hill. He drove away the Confederates from there after a sharp cavalry skirmish. This so brightened McClellan's spirits that he telegraphed to Halleck on the 5th that with reënforcements he could march his army to Richmond in five days; a suggestion to which Halleck made the curt rejoinder, "I have no reënforcements to send you."

The order to dispose of the sick was not promptly obeyed, because General McClellan insisted upon knowing the intentions of the Government in regard to his army, and after being informed that it was to be withdrawn from the James several days more were wasted in wearisome interchange of dispatches between himself and Halleck; McClellan protesting with the greatest energy and feeling against this movement, and Halleck replying with perfect logic and temper in defense of it. In a long and elaborate dispatch, in which Halleck considered the whole subject, he referred to the representation made to him by McClellan and some of his officers that the enemy's forces around Richmond amounted to 200,000, and that McClellan had reported that they had since received large reënforcements.

General Pope's army covering Washington [he adds] is only about 40,000. Your effective force is only about 90,000. You are thirty miles from Richmond, and General Pope eighty or ninety, with the enemy directly between you, ready to fall with his superior numbers upon one or the other as he may elect. . . . If General Pope's army be diminished to reënforce you, Washington, Maryland, and Pennsylvania would be left uncovered and exposed. If your force be reduced to strengthen Pope you would be too weak to even hold the position you now occupy. . . . You say that the withdrawal from the present position will cause the certain demoralization of the army. . . . I cannot understand why, . . . unless the officers themselves assist in that demoralization, which I am satisfied they will not. . . . But you will reply, Why not reënforce me here so that I can strike Richmond from my present position? To do this you said at our interview that you required 30,000 additional troops. . . . You finally thought that you would have "some chance" of success with 20,000. But you afterward telegraphed me that you would require 35,000. . . . To keep your army in its present position until it could be so reënforced would almost destroy it in that climate. . . . In the mean time General Pope's forces would be exposed to the heavy blows of the enemy without the slightest hope of assistance from you.

He tells McClellan in conclusion that a large number of his highest officers are decidedly in favor of the movement.

Weary at last of arguments, Halleck became more and more peremptory in his orders; and this failing to infuse any activity into the movements of McClellan, he had recourse to sharp dispatches of censure which provoked only excuses and recriminations. In some of his replies to Halleck's urgent dispatches, enjoining the greatest haste and representing the grave aspect of affairs in Northern Virginia, McClellan replied in terms that indicated as little respect for Halleck as he had shown for the President and Secretary of War. On the 6th of August, in answer to an order insisting on the immediate dispatch of a battery of artillery to Burnside, he calmly replies, "I will obey the order as soon as circumstances permit. My artillery is none too numerous now." On the 12th, little or no progress having yet been made, he says, "There shall be no unnecessary delay, but I cannot manufacture vessels. . . . It is not possible for any one to place this army where you wish it, ready to move, in less than a month. If Washington is in danger now, this army can scarcely arrive in time to save it. It is in much better position to do so from here than from Aquia." At the same time the Quartermaster-General reported that nearly every available steam vessel in the country was then under the control of General McClellan. Only on the 17th of August was McClellan able to telegraph that he had left his camp at Harrison's Bar, and only on the 27th of the month, when Pope's campaign had reached a critical and perilous stage, did he report himself for orders at Alexandria, near Washington.

LINCOLN, *having lost confidence in McClellan, resorted to a wily expedient. He did not relieve the general, but organized a new force, the Army of Virginia, at the head of which he appointed a Western general, John Pope. Pope quickly proved that he had more skill in bombast than in strategy and tactics. In the Second Battle of Bull Run, August 29-30, 1862, he was disastrously defeated. Reluctantly, Lincoln restored McClellan to full command.*

Antietam

As soon as General McClellan was replaced in command of the Army of the Potomac he began to put the forces in order; and the ease and rapidity with which this was accomplished show that both he and General Pope, with very different intentions, had equally exaggerated the state of their demoralization. The troops were not in so bad a condition at Centreville as Pope imagined, and the army that Mr. Lincoln handed over to McClellan at Washington was, both in numbers and morale, a formidable host. Its morning returns show an aggregate of over 100,000 men, and General McClellan himself reports that he had at Antietam 87,000. But the vast discrepancy between the force on paper and the effectives in battle gives a margin of which writers are apt to avail themselves according to their prejudices or prepossessions. General Palfrey, who took part in the campaign and who afterwards examined the reports on both sides with scrupulous care, says that in this single instance McClellan overstated the number of his troops in action, and that 70,000 would be nearer the mark. It is true he could afford it, as in the same estimate he very nearly doubled the number of the enemy. The Confederate rosters show some forty-five brigades of infantry, exclusive of cavalry and artillery. Lee says in his report that the battle of Antietam was fought by less than 40,000 troops, on his side.

McClellan's time for training and drilling his recovered

army was brief; for within a few days the news came that Lee had crossed the Potomac into Maryland. There was no time now for indecision, and Lincoln's stern and constantly repeated injunction, "You must find and hurt this enemy now," had to be obeyed.

General Lee has given in his own report a sufficiently clear statement of what he hoped to accomplish by his invasion of Maryland. The supplies of rich and productive districts were thus made accessible to his army, and he wished to prolong this "state of affairs in every way desirable, and not to permit the season for active operations to pass without endeavoring to inflict further injury upon the enemy." He also makes an acknowledgment which shows that he, in common with others at Richmond, had been grossly deceived by the accounts which rebel refugees from Maryland, and their sympathizing correspondents at home, had given of the oppressive tyranny of Lincoln, and the resentment it had caused in that commonwealth. He says:

The condition of Maryland encouraged the belief that the presence of our army, however inferior to that of the enemy, would induce the Washington Government to retain all its available force to provide against contingencies which its course towards the people of that State gave it reason to apprehend. At the same time it was hoped that military success might afford us an opportunity to aid the citizens of Maryland in any efforts they might be disposed to make to recover their liberties. The difficulties that surrounded them were fully appreciated, and we expected to derive more assistance in the attainment of our object from the just fears of the Washington Government than from any active demonstration on the part of the people, unless success should enable us to give them assurance of continued protection.

In a hasty note he informed the Richmond Government of his purpose, and took the initial steps to execute it with great promptness. He crossed his entire army between the 4th and 7th of September near Leesburg, and camped in the vicinity of Frederick. He took it for granted that our force at Harper's

Ferry would be at once withdrawn; thereafter he intended to move the army into Western Maryland, establish his communications with Richmond through the Shenandoah Valley, and then move into Pennsylvania and draw McClellan from his base to fight in a field of his own selection. If all his surmises had been correct, if Miles had been withdrawn from Harper's Ferry, if Maryland had risen in revolt, if McClellan had allowed him to range through Western Maryland at his leisure, the plan would have been an admirable one and the results of it most fruitful; but all these expectations failed. After two days at Frederick he found that Maryland was contented with the oppressor's yoke, and that Miles remained at Harper's Ferry. He therefore considered it necessary to detach a large portion of his force, under Jackson, McLaws, and Walker, to surround and capture the garrison at that place; the rest of the army withdrew from Frederick to Boonsboro'.

Meantime McClellan was slowly approaching. He felt, of course, the need of more troops. With an army and trains about him so enormous that, as he says in his report, they would occupy fifty miles of road in marching order, he still paused on the 10th to write to General Halleck, begging for reënforcements. He first assures him that the capital is in no danger and that all the troops there may safely be sent to him; but in order to guard against any possible rejoinder he adds, "Even if Washington should be taken while these armies are confronting each other, this would not, in my judgment, bear comparison with the ruin and disaster which would follow a signal defeat of this army," an opinion which has no especial value except as showing what General McClellan's judgment was worth in such a matter. Except when he was in Washington, he always regarded its possible capture as a trifling affair. But his demand was complied with: Porter's corps was ordered to join him with a kind message from the President, which he acknowledged courteously, and then—asked for the remainder of Keyes's corps! He was in no haste; he ordered his officers beforehand to avoid collisions. He attempted in his report to account for his tardy marching on the ground that the authorities at Washington wished him not to go too far from the capital. General Halleck says that no order capable of bearing this construction was ever given. He says: "I telegraphed him that he was going too far, not from Washington, but from the Potomac. . . . I thought he should keep more upon the Potomac and press forward his left rather than his right, so as more readily to relieve Harper's Ferry, which was the point then in most immediate danger."

But two days after the above-mentioned letter asking for reënforcements, McClellan received information which was enough to put a soul of enterprise into the veriest laggard that ever breathed. There never was a general so fruitlessly favored by fortune as McClellan, and never was such a piece of good luck offered, even to him, as that which fell into his hands on the 13th of September. He had been advancing in his leisurely manner from Washington on parallel roads, making only about six miles a day, when on the 13th he arrived at Frederick and one of his officers brought to him Lee's special order of the 9th, that a private soldier had found, containing his entire plan of campaign. By this he learned that his enemy was before him, a day's march away; that Lee's whole force was inferior to his own; and that it was divided into two portions, one in camp near Boonsboro' and the other besieging Miles at Harper's Ferry. It is not too much to say that his enemy had been delivered into his hands. After he had read this order an immediate contest between him and Lee, other things being equal, would have been like a fight between a man blindfolded and one having use of his eyes. He not only knew of the division of his enemy's army in half, but he knew where his trains, his rearguard, his cavalry, were to march and to halt, and where the detached commands were to join the main body.

He seemed to appreciate the importance of his discovery, but it was not in his nature to act promptly enough. Franklin was at Buckeystown, about twelve miles east of South Mountain, a prolongation northward of the Blue Ridge, beyond which Lee's army lay. Instead of giving him immediate orders to march with all possible speed to Harper's Ferry, he wrote at his leisure a long and judicious instruction directing him to march to that point the next day. The weather was perfect; the roads were in good order. McClellan knew there was no enemy between him and Crampton's Gap. Every possible consideration urged him to make use of every instant of time. The precious opportunity was neglected, and it was noon the next day, the 14th of September, when Franklin stormed the crest of the mountain after a brilliant and easy victory over General Cobb's detachment of McLaws's division, which had been left to guard the pass. The Union right wing spent the whole of the same day in a stubborn fight for the possession of Fox's and Turner's Gaps, some six miles farther north. After sharp fighting, in which General Jesse L. Reno, an officer of the highest merit, was killed, and Colonel Hayes, afterwards President of the United States, was wounded, advanced positions were secured. At neither Crampton's nor Turner's was the victory pushed to advantage. Franklin did nothing to relieve the beleaguered garrison at Harper's Ferry, and the force at Turner's Gap rested on the ground that they had won until, when the mists of the morning cleared away on the 15th, they saw the enemy had retreated from their front. Much valuable time had been lost, and more than time; for early on the morning of the 15th the blundering and bewildered defense of Harper's Ferry had ceased by the surrender of the garrison, its unhappy commander having been killed after he had displayed the white flag.

But McClellan had not yet lost all his advantage; and the sacrifice of Harper's Ferry would have been amply compensated if he had moved at once with all possible speed upon Lee, who, with only Longstreet's and D. H. Hill's troops, had taken up his position at Sharpsburg. Jackson was still south of the Potomac. He had no fear of night marches, and was making all possible speed to join Lee through the day and night of the 15th. The force of McLaws got away from in front of Franklin, and, though making a long détour and crossing the Potomac twice, still joined the main army at Sharpsburg on the 17th. All this time, while the scattered detachments of Lee were moving with the utmost expedition to join their main body, making two or three times the distance which separated Lee from McClellan, the latter made his preparations for an attack, as if, to quote Johnston again, time was of no especial value to him. On the 15th he marched down to Antietam Creek and placed his soldiers in position. He rode from end to end of his line, enjoying one of the grandest greetings ever given by an army to its commander. The thunder of cheers which met him at every point showed that there was no lack of morale in that mighty army, and that they were equal to any service their beloved commander might choose to require of them.

It seems almost incredible, as we write it, and it will appear inexplicable to such readers as may come after us, that McClellan made no movement during the afternoon of Monday, the 15th, and did nothing during the entire day of the 16th but to advance a portion of his right wing across Antietam Creek, and this while the ragged legions of Lee were streaming in from across the Potomac to take up their positions for the impending conflict. Every minute which he thus let slip was paid for in the blood of Union soldiers next day. Never had McClellan's habit of procrastination served him so ill a turn as during the whole day of the 16th. Lee's error of dividing his army would have been fatal to him if even on the morning of the 16th McClellan had advanced upon him in force. The loss of the afternoon of the 15th in that case would scarcely have been felt. The reduction of Harper's Ferry had taken a day longer than Lee expected, and when night fell the divisions of McLaws, Anderson, A. P. Hill, and Walker were still beyond the Potomac. He would have been compelled to withstand the attack of McClellan's whole army with nothing but the divisions of D. R. Jones and D. H. Hill on the right and center, and of Hood, Ewell, and J. R. Jones on the left. But before noon of the 17th most of Lee's forces were on the ground, and the rest arrived during the battle. McClellan had rejected the proffered favors of fortune. His delay had given back to Lee all the advantages afforded McClellan by the separation of Lee's army and the discovery of his plan of campaign. Lee had had unbroken leisure for forty-eight hours to study his ground and the dispositions of his antagonist, which had been made in plain view under his eyes. Lee's advantage of position was fully equal to McClellan's advantage of numbers; and it was therefore on even terms between the two armies that the battle of Antietam began.

The ground was highly favorable to Lee. In front of him was Antietam Creek, the high ground, some of it wooded, affording an advantageous position and cover for his batteries. There was little field for manœuvering, and little was attempted. From daylight till dark of the 17th the battle went on. There was nothing of it but sheer, persistent, brutal slaughter. McClellan's plan was to throw forward his right wing, the corps of Hooker leading, supported by that of Mansfield, and by those of Sumner and Franklin if necessary; when the battle became well engaged on the right, the left wing, under Burnside, was to cross the lower bridge to try to turn the enemy's right. On this simple plan the battle was contested. Hooker advanced early in the morning, and fought until his corps, giving and receiving about equal injuries, was shattered to pieces, and himself borne from the field, severely wounded. General Meade succeeded to the command, and Mansfield came to his assistance. The latter's corps also did heroic service, and its veteran commander was killed in the front of his foremost line. His corps was led during the rest of the day by General A. S. Williams. As the Union left remained entirely inactive, Lee was able to use most of his force on our right, and his resistance was so obstinate that Sumner's corps was drawn into the conflict, where it met with heavy losses; Richardson, one of the best division commanders in the army, received a mortal hurt, and Sedgwick was twice wounded. Before the battle ended on the right, even Franklin's corps, which McClellan had intended to hold in reserve, was drawn into the whirlpool of blood and fire. Corps by corps, division by division, one might almost say brigade by brigade, those brave and devoted troops were hurled in succession, without intelligent plan, without any special concert of action, against Lee's left. The carnage was frightful, the result in no proportion to the terrible expense.

It was afternoon before the left wing, under Burnside, began its part of the work. The lower bridge was crossed about one o'clock and the west bank gained, but no further advance was made by Burnside until after three o'clock. He then moved forward his forces, under General Cox's command, upon the enemy's right, making good progress, until, late in the afternoon, as if Fortune, weary of having her favors rejected by General McClellan, had turned to the other side, the division of A. P. Hill, which had marched seventeen miles in seven hours, arrived on the field from Harper's Ferry and made a vigorous attack upon our extreme left, killed General Isaac P. Rodman, and threw his division into some disorder. This unlooked-for demonstration checked the advance of the Federal column, and it fell back a little distance to the hills near the Antietam. Night came on, and the long, desperate battle was at an end. The tactical advantage was with General McClellan. On his left, his center, and his right, he had gained a little ground. Both armies had suffered losses which it shocks the sense to contemplate. They were almost equal—over 12,000 killed and wounded on the Union side, over 11,000 on the Confederate; but Lee's loss was more than one-fourth of his army, while McClellan's was only one-sixth of his. In his report General McClellan says:

The . . . night brought with it grave responsibilities. Whether to renew the attack on the 18th or to defer it, even with the risk of the enemy's retirement, was the question before me.

There could be little doubt of his decision of the question. He was keenly alive to the sufferings of his army. He loved them, and was loved by them in return. The piled heaps of the slain, the thousands of wounded and dying, the wreck and havoc of the conquered field, all impressed his imagination so powerfully that he was unable to conceive the worse condition of the enemy. There rose before his mind also an appalling picture of the consequences that would ensue if he risked another battle and lost it. He saw Lee's army marching in triumph on Washington, Baltimore, Philadelphia, and New York, the country ravaged, the cause lost. Every impulse of his heart and conscience forbade him to assume so enormous a responsibility. He would not absolutely decide which course to adopt, but, after his habit, concluded to wait until the 19th before making a final decision.

The occasion, however, would not wait for him. Lee knew, if McClellan did not, that the Confederate army was in no condition to risk another battle. The straggling of McClellan's force was one of the reasons that induced him to delay. No doubt there was a great deal of it in his command. One day Mr. Lincoln, exasperated at the discrepancy between the aggregate of troops he had sent to McClellan and the number McClellan reported as having received, exclaimed in a grotesque simile, "Sending men to that army is like shoveling fleas across a barnyard; not half of them get there." But the case on the other side was worse still. Lee reported to Jefferson Davis on the 21st of September that the efficiency of his army was "paralyzed by the loss to its ranks of the numerous stragglers." "On the morning after the battle," he said, "General Evans reported to me on the field, where he was holding the front position, that he had but 120 of his brigade present, and that the next brigade to his, that of General Garnett, consisted of but 100 men. General Pendleton reported that the brigades of Generals Lawton and Armistead, left to guard the ford at Shepherdstown, together contained but 600 men. This," he added feelingly, "is a woful condition of affairs." But of course General McClellan had no personal knowledge of this; and, as we have seen in the course of this narrative, he was utterly destitute of those intuitions of the situation and the intention of his enemy which we find in all great commanders. The fight of the day before had been so terrible in the struggle and carnage, he had made his personal influence so little felt on the field, he had gained so little advantage in comparison with his frightful losses, that it would be unjust to expect to find in him on the morning of the 18th that alacrity and elation of victory which would have impelled him in pursuit of his shattered enemy. Beaten as Lee was, his promising campaign brought to a disastrous failure by his own error, he was still less affected by it than was McClellan by his victory. He even thought for the moment, before twilight had settled on the battle of the 17th, of executing with his usual instrument his usual movement, of sending Stonewall Jackson by the left to attack the right flank of McClellan's army. He opposed a bold front to his ill fortune, and closed his description of the battle by saying that he deemed it injudicious to push his advantage further.

McClellan was almost alone in his decision not to continue the battle on the 18th. General Burnside, who commanded on the left, testified that he thought the attack should be renewed at early dawn, and gave this opinion to McClellan the night of the battle. General McClellan said he would think the matter over and make up his mind before morning, and a staff-officer of Burnside's was kept in waiting through the night at McClellan's headquarters to learn his decision.

General Franklin, in command of the center, also testified that he showed McClellan a position on our right of great importance, and advised an attack on that place in the morning. He said there was no doubt that we could carry it, as we had plenty of artillery bearing on it. He thought that by this means the whole left flank of the enemy would have been uncovered. When asked what reasons were given for rejecting this plan, he repeated McClellan's customary fatal excuse for delay, that he would prefer to wait for reënforcements. Hooker, who had commanded the right wing, was also of the opinion that the attack should be resumed, although his wounds would have prevented his taking part in it.

But it was too much to expect of General McClellan that he would follow such advice. He had, it is true, a moment of elation on the morning of the 15th after the engagement at South Mountain. To attack an enemy in position, and drive him, was to McClellan so new a sensation that he was evidently greatly exhilarated by his success at Turner's Gap. He reported Lee as admitting "they had been shockingly whipped," and as "making for Shepherdstown in a perfect panic." But after the terrible conflict at Antietam the cold fit came on, and his only dispatches to Washington were of his heavy losses and of holding what he had gained. He evidently thought more of being attacked on that day than of attacking. "The battle," he says, "will probably be renewed to-day. Send all the troops you can, by the most expeditious route." It was therefore with feelings of the greatest relief that he saw Lee's rear-guard disappear across the Potomac, and in the forenoon of the 19th he joyfully telegraphed to Washington, "Our victory was complete. The enemy is driven back into Virginia. Maryland and Pennsylvania are now safe."

The President received this news, as was natural, with mingled gratitude and disappointment. He was glad and thankful for the measure of success which had been achieved, but the high hope he had entertained of destroying Lee's army before it recrossed the Potomac was baffled. His constant entreaty to McClellan, from the time he put him in command of the army up to the day of the battle, was, "Please do not let him get off without being hurt." It was with this hope and purpose that he had given McClellan everything he asked for, infusing his own indomitable spirit into all the details of work at the War Department and the headquarters of the army. It was by his order that McClellan had been pushed forward, that Porter had been detached from the defense of Washington, that the militia of Pennsylvania had been hurried down to the border. He did not share General McClellan's illusion as to the monstrous number of the enemy opposed to him; and when he looked at the vast aggregate of the Army of the Potomac by the morning report on the 20th of September, which shows 93,149 present for duty, he could not but feel that the result was not commensurate with the efforts made and the resources employed.

As EARLY AS *July, 1862, Lincoln had decided that if the North were to win the war he must strike at slavery, the economic prop of the South and its vast reserve of manpower. On July 22 he read to his Cabinet a proclamation of emancipation. Seward, Secretary of State, had no objection to the measure but argued that the time was not propitious. The military situation was such that the proclamation would be considered the "last shriek on the retreat." Lincoln, impressed, put his draft aside and waited for a Union victory.*

Antietam was no victory; neither was it a defeat. Lincoln decided that it would serve his purpose. On September 22, five days after the battle, he called the Cabinet together and read to its members the proclamation he had determined to issue. On the central matter, he said, he had made up his mind, but he would entertain suggestions as to phraseology. A few were offered and accepted. The proclamation was then engrossed and signed that afternoon and published the following morning. It promised "that on the first day of January, in the year of our Lord one thousand eight hundred and sixty-three, all persons held as slaves within any State, or designated part of a State, the people whereof shall then be in rebellion against the United States, shall be then thenceforward, and forever free."

Nicolay and Hay describe the signing of the definitive proclamation and discuss its validity.

The Edict of Freedom

IT is a custom in the Executive Mansion to hold on New Year's Day an official and public reception, beginning at eleven o'clock in the morning, which keeps the President at his post in the Blue Room until two in the afternoon. The hour for this reception came before Mr. Lincoln had entirely finished revising the engrossed copy of the proclamation, and he was compelled to hurry away from his office to friendly handshaking and festal greeting with the rapidly arriving official and diplomatic guests. The rigid laws of etiquette held him to this duty for the space of three hours. Had actual necessity required it, he could of course have left such mere social occupation at any moment; but the President saw no occasion for precipitancy. On the other hand, he probably deemed it wise that the completion of this momentous executive act should be attended by every circumstance of deliberation.

Vast as were its consequences, the act itself was only the simplest and briefest formality. It could in no wise be made sensational or dramatic. Those characteristics attached, if at all, only to the long-past decisions and announcements of July 22 and September 22 of the previous year. Those dates had witnessed the mental conflict and the moral victory. No ceremony was made or attempted of this final official signing. The afternoon was well advanced when Mr. Lincoln went back from his New Year's greetings, with his right hand so fatigued that it was an effort to hold the pen. There was no special convocation of the Cabinet or of prominent officials. Those who were in the house came to the executive office merely from the personal impulse of curiosity joined to momentary convenience. His signature was attached to one of the greatest and most beneficent military decrees of history in the presence of less than a dozen persons; after which it was carried to the Department of State to be attested by the great seal and deposited among the archives of the Government.

Since several eminent lawyers have publicly questioned the legal validity of Mr. Lincoln's Edict of Freedom,—as his final Emancipation Proclamation may be properly styled,—it is worth while to gather, if possible, Mr. Lincoln's own conception and explanation of the constitutional and legal bearings of his act. There is little difficulty in arriving at this. His language, embodied in a number of letters and documents, contains such a distinct and logical exposition of the whole process of his thought and action, from the somewhat extreme conservatism of his first inaugural to his great edict of January 1,

1863, and the subsequent policy of its practical enforcement, that we need but arrange them in their obvious sequence. The proper beginning is to be found in a letter of April 4, 1864, to A. G. Hodges, of Frankfort, Kentucky. In this he says:

I am naturally antislavery. If slavery is not wrong, nothing is wrong. I cannot remember when I did not so think and feel, and yet I have never understood that the Presidency conferred upon me an unrestricted right to act officially upon this judgment and feeling. It was in the oath I took that I would, to the best of my ability, preserve, protect, and defend the Constitution of the United States. I could not take the office without taking the oath. Nor was it my view that I might take an oath to get power, and break the oath in using the power. I understood, too, that in ordinary civil administration this oath even forbade me to practically indulge my primary abstract judgment on the moral question of slavery. I had publicly declared this many times, and in many ways. And I aver that, to this day, I have done no official act in mere deference to my abstract judgment and feeling on slavery. I did understand, however, that my oath to preserve the Constitution to the best of my ability imposed upon me the duty of preserving, by every indispensable means, that Government—that nation, of which that Constitution was the organic law. Was it possible to lose the nation and yet preserve the Constitution? By general law, life and limb must be protected, yet often a limb must be amputated to save a life; but a life is never wisely given to save a limb. I felt that measures otherwise unconstitutional might become lawful by becoming indispensable to the preservation of the Constitution through the preservation of the nation. Right or wrong, I assumed this ground, and now avow it. I could not feel that, to the best of my ability, I had even tried to preserve the Constitution, if, to save slavery or any minor matter, I should permit the wreck of Government, country, and Constitution all together. When, early in the war, General Frémont attempted military emancipation, I forbade it, because I did not then think it an indispensable necessity. When, a little later, General Cameron, then Secretary of War, suggested the arming of the blacks, I objected because I did not yet think it an indispensable necessity. When, still later, General Hunter attempted military emancipation, I again forbade it, because I did not yet think the indispensable necessity had come. When in March and May and July, 1862, I made earnest and successive appeals to the border States to favor compensated emancipation, I believed the indispensable necessity for military emancipation and arming the blacks would come unless averted by that measure. They declined the proposition, and I was, in my best judgment, driven to the alternative of either surrendering the Union, and with it the Constitution, or laying strong hand upon the colored element. I chose the latter.

The question of legal and constitutional validity he discusses briefly, but conclusively, in his letter of August 26, 1863, to James C. Conkling of Springfield, Illinois. In this, addressing himself to his critics, he says: "You say it is unconstitutional. I think differently. I think the Constitution invests its Commander-in-Chief with the law of war in time of war. The most that can be said, if so much, is, that slaves are property. Is there, has there ever been, any question that, by the law of war, property, both of enemies and friends, may be taken when needed? And is it not needed whenever taking it helps us or hurts the enemy? Armies the world over destroy enemies' property when they cannot use it; and even destroy their own to keep it from the enemy. Civilized belligerents do all in their power to help themselves or hurt the enemy."

Admitting the general principle of international law, of the right of a belligerent to appropriate or destroy enemies' property, and applying it to the constitutional domestic war to suppress rebellion which he was then prosecuting, there came next the question of how his military decree of enfranchisement was practically to be applied. This point, though not fully discussed, is sufficiently indicated in several extracts. In the draft of a letter to Charles D. Robinson he wrote, August 17, 1864: "The way these measures were to help the cause was not to be by magic or miracles, but by inducing the colored people to come bodily over from the rebel side to ours." And in his letter to James C. Conkling of August 26, 1863, he says: "But negroes, like other people, act upon motives. Why should they do anything for us if we will do nothing for them? If they stake their lives for us, they must be prompted by the strongest motive, even the promise of freedom. And the promise, being made, must be kept."

The actual tangible military result which he declares was his constitutional and legal warrant for his edict of military emancipation is set forth in the following extracts. Whether we judge it by the narrow technical rules of applied jurisprudence, or by the broader principles of the legal philosophy of Christian nations, it forms equally his complete vindication. In the draft of a letter to Isaac M. Schermerhorn he wrote, September 12, 1864: "Any different policy in regard to the colored man deprives us of his help, and this is more than we can bear. We cannot spare the hundred and forty or fifty thousand now serving us as soldiers, seamen, and laborers. This is not a question of sentiment or taste, but one of physical force, which may be measured and estimated as horse power and steam power are measured and estimated. Keep it, and you can save the Union. Throw it away, and the Union goes with it."

And in the one already quoted, to Robinson, August 17, 1864: "Drive back to the support of the rebellion the physical force which the colored people now give and promise us, and neither the present nor any coming Administration can save the Union. Take from us and give to the enemy the hundred and thirty, forty, or fifty thousand colored persons now serving us as soldiers, seamen, and laborers and we cannot longer maintain the contest."

So also in an interview with John T. Mills he said: "But no human power can subdue this rebellion without the use of the emancipation policy and every other policy calculated to weaken the moral and physical forces of the rebellion. Freedom has given us 200,000 men, raised on Southern soil. It will give us more yet. Just so much it has subtracted from the enemy. . . . Let my enemies prove to the country that the destruction of slavery is not necessary to a restoration of the Union; I will abide the issue."

We might stop here and assume that President Lincoln's argument is complete. But he was by nature so singularly frank and conscientious, and by mental constitution so unavoidably logical, that he could not, if he had desired, do things or even seem to do them by indirection or subterfuge. This, the most weighty of his responsibilities and the most difficult of his trials, he could not permit to rest upon doubt or misconstruction. In addition to what we have already quoted he has left us a naked and final restatement of the main question, with the unequivocal answer of his motive and conviction. It has been shown above how Mr. Chase, in the discussions of the final phraseology of the January proclamation, urged him to omit his former exemptions of certain fractional parts of insurrectionary States. Despite the President's adverse decision, Mr. Chase continued from time to time to urge this measure during the year 1863. To these requests the President finally replied as follows on the 2d of September:

Knowing your great anxiety that the Emancipation Proclamation shall now be applied to certain parts of Virginia and Louisiana which were exempted from it last January, I state briefly what appear to me to be difficulties in the way of such a step. The original proclamation has no constitutional or legal justification, except as a military measure. The exemptions were made because the military necessity did not apply to the exempted localities. Nor does that necessity apply to them now any more than it did then. If I take the step must I not do so without the argument of military necessity, and so without any argument except the one that I think the measure politically expedient and morally right? Would I not thus give up all footing upon Constitution or law? Would I not thus be in the boundless field of absolutism? Could this pass unnoticed or unresisted? Could it fail to be perceived, that without any further stretch I might do the same in Delaware, Maryland, Kentucky, Tennessee, and Missouri, and even change any law in any State?

In these extracts we have the President's outline explanation of the legal validity of the proclamation. Like all his reasoning, it is simple and strong, resting its authority on the war powers of the Government and its justification upon military necessity. As to the minor subtleties of interpretation or comment which it might provoke from lawyers or judges after the war should be ended, we may infer that he had his opinions, but that they did not enter into his motives of action. On subsequent occasions, while continuing to declare his belief that the proclamation was valid in law, he nevertheless frankly admitted that what the courts might ultimately decide was beyond his knowledge as well as beyond his control.

For the moment he was dealing with two mighty forces of national destiny, civil war and public opinion; forces which paid little heed to theories of public, constitutional, or international law where they contravened their will and power. In fact it was the impotence of legislative machinery, and the insufficiency of legal dicta to govern or terminate the conflicts of public opinion on this identical question of slavery, which brought on civil strife. In the South slavery had taken up arms to assert its nationality and perpetuity; in the North freedom had risen first in mere defensive resistance; then the varying fortunes of war had rendered the combat implacable and mortal. It was not from the moldering volumes of ancient precedents, but from the issues of the present wager of battle, that future judges of courts would draw their doctrines to interpret to posterity whether the Edict of Freedom was void or valid.

When, in the preceding June, the crisis of the McClellan campaign had come upon the President, he had written his well-considered resolve: "I expect to maintain this contest until successful, or till I die, or am conquered, or my term expires, or Congress or the country forsakes me." Grand as was the historical act of signing his decree of liberation, it was but an incident in the grander contest he was commissioned and resolved to maintain. That was an issue, not alone of the bondage of a race, but of the life of a nation, a principle of government, a question of primary human right.

Was this act, this step, this incident in the contest, wise or unwise? Would it bring success or failure? Would it fill the army, weaken the enemy, inspirit the country, unite public opinion? These, we may assume, and not a lawyer's criticisms of phrase or text, dictum or precedent, were the queries which filled his mind when he wrote his name at the bottom of the famous document. If the rebellion should triumph, establishing a government founded on slavery as its corner-stone, manifestly his proclamation would be but waste paper, though every court in Christendom outside the Confederate States should assert its official authority. If, on the other hand, the Union arms were victorious, every step of that victory would become clothed with the mantle of law. But if, in addition, it should turn out that the Union arms had been rendered victorious through the help of the negro soldiers, called to the field by the promise of freedom contained in the proclamation, then the decree and its promise might rest secure in the certainty of legal execution and fulfillment. To restore the Union by the help of black soldiers under pledge of liberty, and then for the Union, under whatever legal doctrine or construction, to attempt to reënslave them, would be a wrong at which morality would revolt. "You cannot," said Mr. Lincoln in one of his early speeches, "repeal human nature."

The problem of statesmanship therefore was not one of theory, but of practice. Fame is due Mr. Lincoln, not alone because he decreed emancipation, but because events so shaped themselves under his guidance as to render the conception practical and the decree successful. Among the agencies he employed none proved more admirable or more powerful than this two-edged sword of the final proclamation, blending sentiment with force, leaguing liberty with Union, filling the voting armies at home and the fighting armies in the field. In the light of history we can see that by this edict Mr. Lincoln gave slavery its vital thrust, its mortal wound. It was the word of decision, the judgment without appeal, the sentence of doom.

But for the execution of the sentence, for the accomplishment of this result, he had yet many weary months to hope and to wait. Of its slow and tantalizing fruition, of the gradual dawning of that full day of promise, we cannot get a better description than that given in his own words in his annual message to Congress, nearly a year after the proclamation was signed:

When Congress assembled a year ago the war had already lasted nearly twenty months, and there had been many conflicts on both land and sea, with varying results. The rebellion had been pressed back into reduced limits; yet the tone of public feeling and opinion, at home and abroad, was not satisfactory. With other signs, the popular elections, then just past, indicated uneasiness among ourselves; while, amid much that was cold and menacing, the kindest words coming from Europe were uttered in accents of pity that we were too blind to surrender a hopeless cause. Our commerce was suffering greatly by a few armed vessels built upon and furnished from foreign shores, and we were threatened with such additions from the same quarter as would sweep our trade from the sea and raise our blockade. We had failed to elicit from European governments anything hopeful upon this subject. The preliminary emancipation proclamation, issued in September, was running its assigned period to the beginning of the new year. A month later, the final proclamation came, including the announcement that colored men of suitable condition would be received into the war service. The policy of emancipation and of employing black soldiers gave to the future a new aspect, about which hope and fear and doubt contended in uncertain conflict. According to our political system, as a matter of civil administration, the General Government had no lawful power to effect emancipation in any State, and for a long time it had been hoped that the rebellion could be suppressed without resorting to it as a military measure. It was all the while deemed possible that the necessity for it might come, and that if it should the crisis of the contest would then be presented. It came, and, as was anticipated, it was followed by dark and doubtful days. Eleven months having now passed, we are permitted to take another review. The rebel borders are pressed still further back, and by the complete opening of the Mississippi the country dominated by the rebellion is divided into distinct parts, with no practical communication between them. Tennessee and Arkansas have been substantially cleared of insurgent control, and influential citizens in each, owners of slaves and advocates of slavery at the beginning of the rebellion, now declare openly for emancipation in their respective States. Of those States not included in the Emancipation Proclamation, Maryland and Missouri, neither of which three years ago would tolerate any restraint upon the extension of slavery into new Territories, only dispute now as to the best mode of removing it within their own limits.

Of those who were slaves at the beginning of the rebellion, full one hundred thousand are now in the United States military service, about one-half of which number actually bear arms in the ranks; thus giving the double advantage of taking so much labor from the insurgent cause and supplying the places which otherwise must be filled with so many white men. So far as tested it is difficult to say they are not as good soldiers as any. No servile insurrection or tendency to violence or cruelty has marked the measures of emancipation and arming the blacks. These measures have been much discussed in foreign countries, and contemporary with such discussion the tone of public sentiment there is much improved. At home the same measures have been fully discussed, supported, criticized, and denounced, and the annual elections following are highly encouraging to those whose official duty it is to bear the country through this great trial. Thus we have the new reckoning. The crisis which threatened to divide the friends of the Union is past.

AFTER ANTIETAM, *McClellan found one reason after another for not taking the offensive. In early November, Lincoln lost patience, relieved McClellan, and put Ambrose E. Burnside in command of the Army of the Potomac.*

Burnside accepted reluctantly. He did not consider himself equal to the position, and said so. But having accepted the command he decided to give the administration what it wanted: action. On December 13, 1862, he threw his troops against the Army of Northern Virginia, occupying an almost impregnable position in the vicinity of Fredericksburg, Virginia. The Army of the Potomac suffered a shocking defeat.

A month later Burnside tried again, only to be hit by a two-day rainstorm that made any movement impossible. By this time it was evident that he had lost the confidence of the entire army. In his place, on January 25, 1863, Lincoln put Joseph Hooker.

Chancellorsville

THE President did not leave General Hooker in ignorance of any of his sentiments towards him. On the day that he appointed him Commander of the Army of the Potomac he wrote him the following letter, which is equally remarkable for its frankness and its magnanimity: "I have placed you at the head of the Army of the Potomac. Of course I have done this upon what appears to me to be sufficient reasons, and yet I think it best for you to know that there are some things in regard to which I am not quite satisfied with you. I believe you to be a brave and skillful soldier, which, of course, I like. I also believe you do not mix politics with your profession, in which you are right. You have confidence in yourself, which is a valuable, if not an indispensable, quality. You are ambitious, which, within reasonable bounds, does good rather than harm; but I think that during General Burnside's command of the army, you have taken counsel of your ambition, and thwarted him as much as you could, in which you did a great wrong to the country and to a most meritorious and honorable brother officer. I have heard, in such a way as to believe it, of your recently saying that both the army and the Government needed a dictator. Of course, it was not for this, but in spite of it, that I have given you the command. Only those generals who gain successes can set up dictators. What I now ask of you is military success, and I will risk the dictatorship. The Government will support you to the utmost of its ability, which is neither more nor less than it has done and will do for all commanders. I much fear that the spirit, which you have aided to infuse into the army, of criticizing their commander and withholding confidence from him, will now turn upon you. I shall assist you as far as I can to put it down. Neither you nor Napoleon, if he were alive again, could get any good out of an army while such a spirit prevails in it. And now beware of rashness. Beware of rashness, but with energy and sleepless vigilance go forward and give us victories." A friend, to whom Hooker showed this letter immediately upon its reception, says it made a deep impression upon the general. While he was somewhat chagrined by its severe chiding he was touched by its tone of mingled authority and kindness. "He talks to me like a father," the general said. "I shall not answer this letter until I have won him a great victory."

He immediately went about his work in the most faithful and efficient manner. The spirit of gloom and demoralization which other observers had noticed in the Army of the Potomac became more evident to him, now that he had command of the whole army, than it had been while he commanded one of the Grand Divisions. "Desertions," he says, "were at the rate of about two hundred a day." A large number of the officers were openly hostile to the policy of the Government; there was a spirit of dormant revolt which began to show itself after the Proclamation of Emancipation. General Hooker felt that the first thing to be done was to check desertion and to renew, as far as possible, the morale of the army. He found absent from their commands some 3000 officers, and 80,000 privates. By a judicious system of punishment and of furloughs he corrected this evil to a great extent. He reorganized his staff departments. To occupy the troops who were rusting in idleness, he greatly increased the amount of drill and field exercise. He consolidated the cavalry and improved its efficiency; by frequent small expeditions and skirmishes he brought up the spirit and discipline of this arm to a higher point than it had before reached. In the early part of April he was able to say that he had under his command "a living army, and one well worthy of the republic." On one occasion he called it "the finest army on the planet."

This necessary and valuable work occupied him during three months of the late winter and early spring. About the middle of April he felt that an active movement was required. The troops were ready for it and public opinion demanded it. He had an army of about 130,000 men effective for service; that of General Lee on the opposite side of the river had been reduced by Longstreet's departure for the South to not less than 60,000.

Hooker was confident of success—perhaps too confident. He wrote to the President on the 11th announcing his intended movement, and saying: "I am apprehensive that he [the enemy] will retire from before me the moment I should succeed in crossing the river, and over the shortest line to Richmond, and thus escape being seriously crippled." He hoped, however, to delay and check him with cavalry, and thus get a fight out of him. The President, on the same day, made the following memorandum showing his clear perception of the immediate work in hand:

My opinion is that, just now, with the enemy directly ahead of us, there is *no* eligible route for us into Richmond; and consequently a question of preference between the Rappahannock route and the James River route is a contest about nothing. Hence our prime object is the enemy's army in front of us, and is not with or about Richmond at all, unless it be incidental to the main object.

What then? The two armies are face to face with a narrow river between them. Our communications are shorter and safer than are those of the enemy. For this reason we can, with equal powers, fret him more than he can us. I do not think that by raids towards Washington he can derange the Army of the Potomac at all. He has no distant operations which can call any of the Army of the Potomac away; we have such operations which may call him away, at least in part. While he remains intact, I do not think we should take the disadvantage of attacking him in his intrenchments; but we should continually harass and menace him, so that he shall have no leisure nor safety in sending away detachments. If he weakens himself, then pitch into him.

The plan of campaign which Hooker adopted was simple, bold, and perfectly practicable. The failure of Burnside had eliminated several elements from the problem. There were no practicable fords below Fredericksburg and none above Fredericksburg as far as the mouth of the Rapidan. Hooker, writing to a friend about this time, said: "You must be patient with me. . . . Remember that my army is at the bottom of a well and the enemy holds the top." There were many points where crossing of the river was possible, but it was almost hopeless to think of gaining a footing on the hills beyond, exposed as the troops would be for a long distance to a concentrated artillery fire. The first place above the city where favorable conditions of approach were to be found was Banks's Ford, about six miles by the road. This was heavily fortified; two of the enemy's lines were so close to each other that both could bring their fire at once upon troops crossing the river. About seven miles further there was another practicable approach to the stream, the United States Mine Ford, also strongly fortified with long lines of infantry parapets. The enemy had not thought it worth while to expend much labor on the Rappahannock above the mouth of the Rapidan; an attack involving so great a detour and the crossing of two difficult rivers seemed to him so improbable that he took no measures to prevent it. It was this route, therefore, that Hooker wisely chose. He resolved to threaten the enemy's right wing by a heavy demonstration under General John Sedgwick, with three corps, a few miles below Fredericksburg, while he threw a strong force across the Rappahannock at Kelly's Ford and essayed, by a rapid march down the Rappahannock, to "knock away" the enemy's force holding the United States and Banks's Fords by attacking them in rear, and as soon as these fords were re-opened to reënforce the marching columns sufficiently for them to attack and rout the rebel army wherever they should meet it outside of its works.

He had intended to anticipate this movement of his infantry by a great cavalry raid through Virginia. He gave orders to General Stoneman on the 12th of April to take his entire cavalry force to turn the enemy's position on his left, to throw a force between him and Richmond, cutting off his supplies, intercepting his retreat, and injuring him in every way possible; and enjoined upon him the utmost vigilance and energy. "Let your watch-word be fight, and let all your orders be fight, fight, fight." In pursuance of these orders the cavalry left their camps the next day; but on the second day out a great rain-storm came on. The river became impassable and every ravine turned to a foaming torrent. The expedition was therefore compelled to wait. A start was made on the 28th, and on the 29th the cavalry corps crossed the Rappahannock.

The infantry movement was executed with astonishing celerity and success. The general had kept secret from his corps commanders the details of his plan. Three corps were put in motion on the 27th of April; by a rapid march on the 28th they crossed the Rappahannock on a canvas pontoon bridge, finding nothing but a small picket to oppose them. They crossed the Rapidan on the morning of the 30th. Lee, whose attention had been diverted by the noisy demonstration which Sedgwick was making below the river, knew nothing of the more formidable enemy approaching on his left. The army coming down the right bank of the Rappahannock uncovered the United States Ford, as Hooker had anticipated, and the engineers rapidly bridged the Rappahannock at that point. So far the march of Hooker had been one of the most successful made in the war. The rebel general was completely deceived. When he heard of the turning column on the Rappahannock, he imagined it was on the way to Gordonsville, and he sent his cavalry upon that track and therefore lost the use of it for twenty-four hours. If Hooker had continued his march with the same success and swiftness with which it was begun, it is hard to see how Lee could have escaped a crushing defeat. On the evening of the 30th Hooker had four corps at Chancellorsville; three roads run from there to Fredericksburg; on the right a plank road, on the left a road skirting the river, and between them a road called the old turnpike. Here he wasted the greater part of an afternoon and a morning—hours of inestimable importance.

It was eleven o'clock on the 1st of May when General Hooker began his direct movement upon the enemy's rear. Slocum's corps, followed by that of Howard, had the extreme right, Sykes and Hancock took the turnpike, Griffin and Humphreys of Meade's corps went by the river road, each column preceded by a detachment of Pleasonton's cavalry. Sickles's corps, which had just arrived, was held in reserve. Any criticism of the operations of armies in this country would be unjust if we did not keep constantly in mind the nature of the ground. Except for rare clearings, the whole country in which Hooker now found himself was a dense and tangled forest, in every part of which the axman had to be employed before the artillerist could be made available; cavalry were for the most part of no use; the troops could not be seen by their officers; a regiment deployed as skirmishers disappeared from the sight of their colonel as if the earth had swallowed them. After half an hour's march through the thicket the best equipped troops would reappear in rags and tatters. General Doubleday says, "It was worse than fighting in a dense fog." The frightful reverberation of battle among the trees was enough to appal the stoutest heart, yet a few hundred yards away nothing would be heard. The generals on either side, shut out from sight or from hearing, had to trust to the unyielding bravery of their men till couriers brought word which way the conflict was tending, before they could send the needed support.

It was through such a wilderness as this that Hooker advanced his army on the 1st of May. The enemy had of course to contend with the same difficulties, with this advantage on their side that they knew the by-roads of the whole region. But having advanced there could be no question that Hooker should have continued as far as possible. Instead of doing this, he acted with unusual prudence and with something like hesitation. Sykes in the center met with some opposition from McLaws. Slocum was not abreast of him on his right, while Meade was too far away on the river road to connect with him; he therefore fell back upon Hancock, who pushed forward and checked the enemy. Now, if ever, was the need and justification for a great effort. Hooker was almost through the worst of the woods; Meade was nearly in sight of the important position of Banks's ford which was feebly defended; by pushing his forces resolutely forward on all three roads, General Hooker could have gained an advantageous position on open ground beyond. "The troops were in fine spirits," says Humphreys, "and we wanted to fight." "We ought to have held our advanced positions," says Hancock, "and still kept pushing on." General Warren, Chief of Engineers, was of the same opinion; he urged Couch not to abandon his position without further orders. Couch asked for permission to remain, which was flatly refused, and the army fell back to the position near Chancellorsville which they had left in the morning. This movement did not improve the spirits of the troops, and when Humphreys came back from the river road with his division, his keen, soldierly eye recognized clearly the fault of the position. The army was drawn in too closely in every direction; it had not the look of an army ready for battle; "they were in no confusion," he says, "but they seemed to be unoccupied."

The 1st of May thus passed without any progress having been made; the brilliant beginning of Hooker's campaign had not borne the fruit that was fairly to have been expected. Still the position was a strong one, and with a few hours of work, where it was most needed, the Army of the Potomac would have been safe from any attack the enemy was able to make. But unfortunately the work was not done; the extreme right, under General Howard, commanding the Eleventh Corps, was absolutely unprotected. All his defensive works were in his immediate front; his right wing was in the air. This point of weakness in the Union line was discovered by General Stuart and made known to General Lee on the evening of the 1st. A flank attack upon the Federal right wing had always been his favorite manœuvre, and the true and tried weapon with which he had so often succeeded was ready to his hand. He proposed to Stonewall Jackson that he should take his entire corps round to the right and rear of Hooker's army. Jackson entered into the plan with the greatest enthusiasm, and at early dawn on the morning of the 2d he started upon this bold and perilous enterprise with 26,000 troops. He moved by a zig-zag route, southwest, and then northwest across the Federal front, which in general faced south, leaving General Lee with a mere curtain of soldiers to occupy during his absence the attention of Hooker and his army.

Jackson's movement, though hazardous, was not so desperate as it has been sometimes represented. Lee had been convinced the night before that it was impossible for him to carry Hooker's line by a direct attack in front; he had therefore resolved upon this flanking attempt as the only resource left him. In case of the repulse of Jackson, Lee considered that he still had his chance of retreat by the Richmond Railroad, and Jackson could with little difficulty have made his way back to Gordonsville, and with their rapid movements they could have reunited their columns by the Central Railroad. The flanking movement did not pass undetected. Jackson's column was seen in the early morning passing a hill in front of General Birney of Sickles's corps, who had been detached to fill the gap between Howard and Slocum. He immediately reported his discovery to General Hooker, who was unable at the moment to make up his mind

whether it indicated an attack upon his right flank or a movement in retreat of the enemy. In fact, every act of his during those three days indicated a singular indecision entirely
at variance with what was previously known of his character. Yet he does not deserve all the blame for the disaster
of the 2d of May, for, immediately on receiving Birney's report,
he sent an urgent order to Slocum and to Howard to examine
their ground carefully and to take all possible measures against
an attack in flank. He told them that the right of their line did
not appear to be strong enough; no artificial defenses worth
naming had been thrown up; they had not troops enough on
their flank; and he thought they were not so favorably posted as
might be. He had good reason to suppose that the enemy was
moving to our right, and he concluded with an order to "advance your pickets for purposes of observation, as far as may
be safe, in order to obtain timely information of their approach."

With these urgent orders in his hands, supplemented by his
own observation of the movement of a column of Confederate
infantry westward, which he reported to Hooker about eleven
o'clock, General Howard did little to guard against the coming
danger. In view of the warnings he had received, he faced, it is
true, two regiments to the west, but this amounted to the same
as doing nothing; his pickets consisted of only two companies
and he had no grand guards to support them. Generals Devens
and Schurz thought our right flank too much in the air, but
Howard appeared to have a fixed idea that the attack of the
enemy, if made at all, would be in his front, and he was confident of his ability to repulse any force that could come against
him from that quarter. He waited, therefore, in perfect security,
until about six o'clock. At this hour his command, thinking
the day was to go by without their participating in the battle,
the noise of which they had heard fitfully rising and falling in
the distance on their left, were quite at their ease: the soldiers
were cooking their suppers; most of the regiments had stacked
their arms; many were scattered under the trees playing cards;

when all at once they were startled by a strange invasion—deer, rabbits, and birds came leaping and flying in a panic through the thick brush towards them, and behind these came their scanty pickets and outposts, with Stonewall Jackson's army corps, three lines deep, at their heels.

As soon as Birney had discovered the march of Jackson across his front, Sickles took Whipple's division to reënforce his left, and proceeded, cutting and slashing his way through the hilly wilderness, to attack the flank of the force he saw moving before him; but by the time he reached Jackson's line of march, the greater part of his corps had passed on. There was some sharp and successful skirmishing with the rear-guard; Jackson's trains were driven off to the road further south, and a considerable number of prisoners were taken by Sickles. He continually reported progress, and finding himself in such a favorable position to operate on either hand, he begged for orders to strike McLaws and Anderson on his left flank, or to proceed with reënforcements against Jackson's rear on his right; but as Lee had begun at this time a noisy demonstration upon Hooker's left to aid the attack of Jackson on the right, Hooker suffered, for the second time that day, from an attack of indecision, which had deplorable results. Before he had clearly made up his mind what to do, the Eleventh Corps was flying in panic in upon his center. The victorious troops of Jackson, inspired by a great success, which had instantly cured all fatigue of the forced march of fifteen miles, had taken in reverse the entire right flank of the army, and twilight was coming down on a scene of confusion and ruin.

Then, as often before and since, in the history of our war, it became the duty of subordinates, without orders, to rectify the errors of their superiors and to save the army from destruction. In the midst of the wreck and havoc created by Jackson's charge, several of the generals on the right, including General Howard, did their best to stay the incoming flood of the enemy; and the prominent officers who held the center of the field also kept their senses about them, and with admirable coolness and conduct executed what orders they were able to get. General Alfred Pleasonton, of the cavalry, had been sent to operate with Sickles in front, but when he reached him, finding the woods in that part of the field absolutely impassable, he started back, and at Hazel Grove a part of the Eleventh Corps passed him in full retreat. He had only two regiments of cavalry with him, but these and twenty-two guns of different batteries were very efficient. A gallant charge by the Eighth Pennsylvania Cavalry, under command of Major Pennock Huey, in which Major Peter Keenan and other officers were killed, checked for several minutes the advance of Jackson's corps; the twenty-two guns at Hazel Grove were brought into position, and held their place with wonderful steadiness amid the confused rush of fugitives from the right; and as the right of Jackson's advancing lines emerged from the woods, they were received with a fire so intense and so well sustained that they made no further progress until nightfall. Sickles had been left in a critical position, far in front of the rest of the Union line, with Jackson's corps on his right and rear; guided only by the sound and the flash of Pleasonton's guns, he made his way back through the wilderness, and afterwards by a gallant bayonet attack cleared the space to the turnpike.

In this twilight fighting the Confederates met with a personal loss equal to that of an army corps. In the impetuosity with which Jackson's corps attacked, their first line, commanded by Rodes, became mixed and mingled with their second, commanded by Colston. The nature of the ground, broken up by dense thickets, still further disordered the line, and Jackson's own fury and ardor perhaps contributed to the confusion. He kept right up with his own advance, mingling his frequent cries of "press forward" with short prayers of praise and thanksgiving, which he uttered with hand and face uplifted to the starlit sky. At last, perceiving that his lines were for the moment in hopeless disorder, he directed General A. P. Hill to divide his command, filing to the right and left of the highway to replace those of Rodes and Colston, who were to be withdrawn to the second line. While this was being done he rode forward, in his unrestrainable impatience, one hundred yards beyond his line of battle. All at once he found himself under the fire of the Union guns. Turning to regain his lines he was shot by his own men and mortally wounded. He died a few days later at Guiney's Station.

General Hooker, somewhat shaken by the untoward course of things for the last twenty-four hours, and not appreciating fully the value of the position held by his troops at Hazel Grove, the center and key of the field, on the evening of the 2d, had ordered his entire line to be withdrawn to a position nearer Chancellorsville.

The damage incurred in the rout of the Eleventh Corps, great as it was, had been almost repaired before the morning of the 3d by the readiness and energy of Pleasonton, Sickles, and Hiram G. Berry who was killed in the afternoon of that day. The lines which they formed during the night, if held, would have insured the safety of the army during the next day, especially as J. E. B. Stuart, who succeeded Jackson in command of his corps, abandoned Jackson's plan of turning the Federal right and occupying the fords, and devoted himself to desperate assaults directly in his front against the Union lines near the Chancellor House, and to establishing communication of his right with the left of Lee's army. All the morning of the 3d the officers in command suffered from great embarrassment, on account of an unfortunate accident to General Hooker. As he was standing by his headquarters at Chancellor's house, a column of the portico was struck by a cannon-shot and thrown violently against him; he fell senseless, and for some time was thought to have been fatally injured; he did not become conscious for half an hour, and for more than an hour longer he was incapable of giving any intelligent direction to the battle. General Couch was second in command, but, under the circumstances, naturally assumed as little responsibility as possible; and in the course of an hour or so General Hooker again resumed control; but valuable time had been lost, and he did not during the day fully recover from the effects of the shock he had received. The battle therefore lacked unity and energy from beginning to end, and although his troops fought well, with steady and dogged courage, they could do nothing more, under the circumstances, than punish the enemy severely whenever they were attacked, and then fall back in pursuance of orders. By their last withdrawal they gave up their valuable position commanding the three roads to Fredericksburg, simply retaining an intrenched front towards the enemy with both wings resting upon the river and covering their fords.

General Hooker always severely blamed General Sedgwick for his part in the failure at Chancellorsville, and the Committee on the Conduct of the War adopted his opinion, visiting General Sedgwick in their report with severe and undeserved censure. At nine o'clock at night, on the 2d of May, Hooker sent a peremptory order to Sedgwick, directing him to march with the greatest expedition upon Chancellorsville, and to attack and destroy any force he might fall in with upon the road; another order of the same purport was sent to him from General Butterfield, Chief of Staff, dated at midnight. It seems altogether unreasonable that Hooker should have expected Sedgwick to attack and defeat the force left at Fredericksburg, and then to march eleven miles and attack Lee's rear, and to do all this between midnight and daybreak; yet this he claims to have expected, and this the committee of Congress censured Sedgwick for not having done. It is true they induced several witnesses to say that if Sedgwick had accomplished this feat the result would have been the destruction of Lee's army, a proposition which need not be discussed. But it is difficult to see how Sedgwick could have proceeded with more expedition than he really used. Getting his orders at midnight, he began operations against Fredericksburg as early as he could. He moved by the flank, fighting all the way. The head of his column, at daylight, forced its way into the town and to the front of the intrenchments at the heights beyond; he assaulted with four regiments, which were repulsed from the enemy's rifle-pits. He attempted to turn the right of the enemy's position with a force under General Howe; he sent Gibbon's division to try to turn the enemy's left, and these efforts failing, he organized a strong storming party, which at last carried the enemy's center at the formidable point of Marye's Heights, which had proved so fatal to the army under Burnside. He did this at eleven o'clock in the morning; he seems to have delayed as little time as was possible to bring his troops into order again after the confusion of their assault and their victory. He then immediately put them in motion for Chancellorsville, meeting with some opposition all the way, until at Salem Church, little more than a third of the way to Hooker, the Confederates made a strong stand against him, having been heavily reënforced from Lee's main army. It is hard to see what more he could have done. He had taken Fredericksburg, had marched to Salem Church, fighting almost constantly, from daylight until dark. If all the generals of the army had done their duty equally well on that and the previous day, we should have no further disaster to chronicle. He had also nearly all the fighting on the next day, the 4th of May. He gave and received about equal injury. The enemy had, of course, reoccupied Fredericksburg, and came upon him from the East, West, and South. He applied to General Hooker for leave to cross the river, and received it. This permission was afterwards countermanded, but these later orders were only received by him after his command had gained the north bank of the Rappahannock.

Little was done by Hooker's army on the 4th. The disappointments of the three preceding days had greatly depressed him, and the physical injury which he had received on the 3d left him still faint and feeble. So vacillating and purposeless was his action on the 4th that the usual calumnious report obtained credence that he was under the influence of liquor that day. Had he been in possession of all his faculties he never could have left, as he did, 37,000 fresh troops out of the battle, who were waiting and willing to take part in it. The First and most of the Fifth Corps stood idle on Hooker's right, forbidden to go in. So anxious was General Reynolds to bear his part that, in spite of his orders, he sent forward a brigade to make a reconnaissance, hoping that in this way an engagement might be brought on; but to his disappointment the officers detailed to that service came back with only an excellent report and a lot of prisoners. Lee's army was left perfectly free to hammer Sedgwick at its will.

On the night of the 4th a council of war was called. Hooker, stating his views of the situation to his generals, retired and left them free to deliberate among themselves. Reynolds threw himself on a bed and went to sleep, saying he would vote with Meade. Meade, thinking the crossing would be too hazardous, voted to remain; so did Howard, who wished to give his corps a chance to redeem their reputation. Couch voted in favor of crossing the river. Sickles voted in the same sense. He afterwards gave as his justification for this vote, that their rations had given out, that the rain-storm of Tuesday had turned the Rappahannock into a rapid and swollen torrent, and had carried away one of the bridges and threatened the rest; besides they had only supplies enough for one day more of fighting, and defeat would entail a great disaster. These were the views of General Hooker himself, and, notwithstanding the majority of his corps commanders wished to stay and fight it out on the south side, he resolved to recross the river, and the movement was executed without further incident.

His confusion and bewilderment lasted long after the battle. He said himself to the committee of Congress, "When I returned from Chancellorsville I felt that I had fought no battle; in fact, I had more men than I could use, and I fought no general battle for the reason that I could not get my men in position to do so; probably not more than three or three and a half corps on the right were engaged in that fight."

We need not recapitulate the fatal errors to which we have alluded to show that Hooker's reputation as a great commander could not possibly survive his defeat at Chancellorsville.

Stonewall Jackson's bold and successful stroke on the Union
right would not have prevented a great victory if a man of even
ordinary capacity in great emergencies had been at the head
of the army. He threw away his chances one by one. On the
night of the 30th, and on the morning of the 1st, a swift movement forward would have brought him clear of the forest with
his left on Banks's Ford, and given him an enormous tactical
advantage in the attack which Lee was forced to deliver. And
even on the morning of the 3d, by simply holding the position
which Pleasonton, Sickles, and Berry had gained, with the
help of the fresh First and Fifth Corps on the right, and the
indomitable Hancock on the left, the enemy could, probably,
have been repulsed. The successive withdrawals of Hooker's
lines were a bitter mortification to his own troops and the subject of wonder and amazement to the enemy.

The attempt to throw the blame of his failure upon Sedgwick was as futile as Burnside's effort to saddle his upon Franklin. The distrust and criticisms which had darkened the latter
days of General Burnside's command of the army now gathered
about his luckless successor. He had been the most outspoken
and the most merciless of Burnside's critics, and the words
of the President's severe admonition must have often come
back to him when he felt himself exposed to the same measure
which he had meted out to Burnside. The opinion which General Warren expressed to the committee of Congress was that
of most of the officers of high rank of the Army of the Potomac:
"A great many of the generals lost confidence in him. . . . I must
confess that notwithstanding the friendly terms I was on with
General Hooker, I somewhat lost confidence in him from that
battle."

Stoneman's expedition, although he started with the largest
and most perfectly equipped cavalry corps which had ever been
brought together upon the continent, accomplished very little.
Instead of marching directly in a solid body upon Lee's line
of communications, he divided his force into several parties of

raiders, which spread wide alarm throughout the State, but did little serious and permanent damage.

The losses at Chancellorsville were large on both sides. The Union loss was 1606 killed, 9762 wounded, and 5919 missing, a total of 17,287. The rebel losses were 1649 killed, 9106 wounded, and 1708 captured: in all 12,463. The proportion of loss to the troops engaged was thus about the same on the Confederate and on the Union side.

LEE SPENT *the month after Chancellorsville in restoring his army, not badly hurt, to fighting trim. In that period of inactivity he decided on a bold move. He would carry the war into the North by invading Maryland and Pennsylvania. As he saw it, a victory on Northern soil would strengthen the sentiment for peace, already formidable; it might encourage England to recognize the Confederacy; at the very least it would open Pennsylvania's abundant food and supplies to his underfed and poorly equipped men.*

On June 3 Lee started the Army of Northern Virginia north from its camps around Fredericksburg. Hooker, alert, followed, keeping his troops to the east of Lee's advancing columns so as to shield Washington, Baltimore, and Philadelphia. Near the end of June, Hooker, involved in disputes with Halleck and hurt by the refusal of the War Department to send him reinforcements, resigned. Lincoln immediately put George Gordon Meade in Hooker's place.

On July 1 elements of the two armies stumbled into each other at Gettysburg, in southern Pennsylvania. Neither commander knew the whereabouts of the enemy; each began to pull his own forces together. Initial skirmishes grew into heavy fighting. By the end of the day the Confederates had driven the Union troops through the town, but Meade's army found a strong defensive position on high ground. On July 2 Lee attacked repeatedly, but the Union lines held. The climax came on the next day.

Gettysburg

ALTHOUGH General Lee has been much criticized for continuing the battle on the third day, it is not easy to see how he could have done otherwise. It is true, he had not accomplished all he hoped for in the operations of the 2d of July; but his partial successes were such as to render it impossible for him to withdraw. At the cost of terrible bloodshed he had gained the Emmitsburg road on his right and had established himself in the Federal intrenchments on his left; his center had hardly been engaged, and Pickett's strong division was to reënforce him during the day. His army was in fine spirits; he could not, even if he had been inclined, resist the martial impulse which was sweeping them on to what they expected would prove the great and crowning victory of the war. The only thing which was there to trouble hope and joy was the grave countenance and the disapproving words of his ablest general; but he put aside the remonstrances of Longstreet with his lofty good humor, and ordered him to make ready to assault the Federal left center.

The morning of the 3d of July brought a heavy responsibility to General Meade, which he accepted, if not with the high hope and buoyancy of his opponent, with equal coolness and resolution. It was not in his power to await the enemy's attack; the force which had lodged itself upon his right flank could not be permitted to remain there; it was dangerously near the Baltimore road and must be dislodged at any risk or cost; he ordered it assaulted therefore at the earliest dawn. He was not at all certain of the issue of the day, but he prepared for either fate with prudence and courage. In the midst of the roar of the guns which were opening upon Johnson's intruders in the intrenchments on Culp's Hill, he telegraphed to General Wm. H. French at Frederick that, in case the enemy should be beaten that day and fall back towards the Potomac, he wished him to reoccupy Harper's Ferry and to do all he could to annoy and harass the retreat. "If the result of to-day's operations," he said, "should be our discomfiture and withdrawal, you are to look to Washington and throw your force there for its protection." The ground of Culp's Hill was exceedingly broken and difficult, and an obstinate and desultory fight raged there for several hours. But Johnson was at last driven from his position, and Geary's men marched once more into their intrenchments, which had been in possession of the enemy overnight.

The little battle of Culp's Hill, although it lasted a good while, occupied but a small portion of either army, and after

it was finished a singular silence fell upon the field. The day
was clear and hot; the lassitude of midsummer seemed for several hours to have succeeded the furious activity of the last two
days. There was something disquieting to General Meade in the
intense stillness which at noon prevailed in the enemy's camp.
There were constant indications, however, of a movement to the
Confederate right, masked as far as possible by the woods and
by the crest of Seminary Ridge. General Lee had been employing the entire forenoon in preparations for his attack; and, after
a thorough consultation and careful survey of the entire field,
he again resolved to try to carry the crest of Cemetery Hill, and
intrusted the work once more to the able though unwilling hands
of Longstreet. There was a striking analogy between Burnside's
assault of Fredericksburg and the one which Lee was to deliver
on this 3d of July. In both cases a strong position, powerfully
defended, was to be attacked by brave and disciplined troops
under corps commanders who did not believe the attack could
succeed. The troops chosen for this final onslaught upon the
Union line, were on the right, the division of General Pickett,
composed of the Virginia chivalry, the flower of the Confederate
army, supported by Wilcox's division; and, on the left, Pettigrew's and Trimble's divisions that, like Wilcox's, belonged to
the command of A. P. Hill.

While the Union troops were waiting with intense expectation, the midday silence was broken by the report of two
guns fired at a short interval, and then, all at once, from every
point on the heights opposite, the simultaneous discharge of
130 pieces of artillery filled the air with smoke and flame and
the wide circuit of the surrounding hills with continuous volley-
ing thunders. Never in the experience of any of those seasoned
soldiers on either height was heard anything comparable. Hancock and Gibbon, Webb and Warren, to whom the thunder of
the captains and the shouting had become every-day experi-
ences, all agree in saying that they never heard or imagined
anything so terrific. But the Union artillery was not slow in
responding; there was not enough room in the Union lines to

bring so great a number of guns into action as those with which the Confederates had crowned the wide sweep of the opposing hills; but General Hunt had managed to get some seventy guns into position and they replied with great spirit to the furious cannonade from Seminary Ridge and the Emmitsburg road. This titanic artillery duel, in which two hundred guns were engaged, lasted about an hour. At the end of that time, General Hunt ordered his batteries gradually to cease firing; he desired to give his guns time to cool, and to reserve his ammunition for the infantry attack which it was now evident was coming.

General Lee, who expected important results from this extraordinary cannonade, thought he had silenced the Federal artillery, and the explosion of several caissons confirmed him in this belief. It is remarkable that so little damage was done by this prodigious fire. The shifty veterans of the Army of the Potomac had taken advantage of every hillock and every boulder to protect themselves; the artillery suffered somewhat, but whenever a battery was disabled its place was immediately supplied from the reserve. A certain number of faint hearts melted away from the line into the Baltimore road; but at the end of an hour of such a fire as the world has rarely seen, the Union lines were as strong as at the beginning. It may be said that they were even stronger, for, while they were not in the least shaken, they had drunk of the delight of battle and waited with firm nerves and eager eyes for the coming assault.

The fury of his own bombardment had not inspired Longstreet with any new confidence; he still believed the plan of his general-in-chief to be rash and well-nigh hopeless. He gave an order to Colonel E. P. Alexander, his chief of artillery, to watch the effect of the cannonading and give, on his own judgment, the signal of attack when the Federal line should appear to be broken. Alexander did not relish the responsibility; before and during the artillery duel he sent messages to Longstreet, which opened the door for a change in the orders. At last, as his ammunition got short, and the Union fire slackened, he let Pickett know that if the charge was to be made, then was the time to advance. Pickett sought Longstreet personally, and demanded his orders. Longstreet, drawn one way by the commands of his chief and the other by his own convictions, seemed unable, in his anguish of mind, to utter the fatal words required of him. Pickett at last said, "Very well, I shall go forward," to which Longstreet answered only with an affirmative nod.

The Union soldiers on Cemetery Ridge now had the opportunity to enjoy a wonderful spectacle. No sight so beautiful in a soldier's eyes, so full of the pomp and circumstance of glorious war, had ever before been seen upon this continent, as when Pickett led forth his troops from behind the ridge, where they had lain concealed, and formed them in column for attack. There was nothing like it possible in the swamps of the Chickahominy, or the tangled thickets of the Rappahannock, or on the wooded shores of the Rapidan. There no enemy was visible half a musket-shot away; but here, at a distance of nearly a mile across a cultivated valley, part of which was covered with waving grain and part smooth in stubble fields, the whole irradiated with the unclouded beams of the July sun, an army formed itself in line of battle under the eyes of an appreciative adversary. It came on across the valley in the form of a wedge, of which Pickett's own division about 5000 strong formed the finely tempered point; on the left was Heth's division, commanded by Pettigrew, swelled by a part of Trimble's division; on the right the column of Wilcox moved forward in support; altogether some 17,000 men. They came forward with the steadiness of troops on parade; the direction they took at first, if retained, would have brought them upon the First Corps; but, before they had advanced half-way across the valley, they began to bear off to the left and directly upon Hancock's front.

The Federal artillery, which they had supposed to be silenced, now opened upon them from right and left with terrible effect. George J. Stannard's Vermont brigade, occupying a little grove in advance of the Union line, poured a destructive fire into Pickett's right flank, causing it to double in somewhat upon the center. Alexander Hays, on Hancock's right, met the advancing column of Pettigrew with such fury and vigor of attack that a large part of it was captured, a still greater number gave way and fled to the rear, and those that were left alive moved to their right and joined the assaulting force of Pickett. Diminishing at every step, this devoted column moved on, and at last struck a point where Webb's slender brigade held the Union line. A short and terrible contest here took place. Two small regiments of Webb's held a stone fence a few rods in advance of the main line. As the Confederates leaped over this slight barrier, these regiments moved to the rear; the enemy, encouraged by this seeming success, came on with yells of triumph, imagining that the Union line was broken; but the apparent fugitives stopped among their guns, and encouraged by the example of their young general, fought with desperate energy, while from right and left, in a confused mass of unorganized valor, regiments and brigades rushed from their own places to join Webb and Hays in their heroic defense of the crest. If properly drawn up in line of battle, the mass of troops that gathered to the rescue at this point would have been four lines deep. But control was for an instant lost; the men could not be restrained, the colonels could not make their voices heard in the roar and tumult of battle; men fought as individuals. Such a chaos could only last for a few moments. The extreme point reached by the assaulting column was a little clump of woods where Lieutenant Alonzo H. Cushing, a young artillery officer (brother of Commander Cushing, who destroyed the *Albemarle*), stood by his gun; though desperately hurt, with his last strength he fired a final shot, and in the instant of death saluted his general with a gay farewell. General Lewis A. Armistead, who was foremost in the assault, rushed forward waving his hat upon his sword-point, and fell mortally wounded near Cushing's battery. This was the last leap of the advancing tide; from this moment it ebbed away. Pickett, with the few officers left him, gave the superfluous order to retire; for the fight was over, and already the plain was covered with fugitives flowing back, not so much over the track of their advance, as towards the Confederate center. The Union soldiers springing forward captured a great many prisoners and gathered in a wide harvest of battle-flags.

Meanwhile Wilcox had advanced his supporting column obliquely upon Pickett's right, until he found himself making an isolated attack between Little Round Top and the main battlefield. Stannard, who had wrought such havoc upon Pickett's right flank, now wheeled and tried the same tactics, with equal effect, upon Wilcox's left; the batteries on the spur of Little Round Top also rained death upon him, and the troops in his front received him with a sharp musketry fire; there was nothing to do but to turn and save himself with what speed he could. The briefest and proportionately the bloodiest of the three days of battle at Gettysburg was at an end.

Two cavalry fights had taken place during the day; Kilpatrick at eight o'clock received orders to move to the right and rear of Longstreet and attack with his division and the Regular brigade. His advance served to occupy the attention of Longstreet's forces in front of the Round Tops, during the assault on Cemetery Ridge. At half-past five Kilpatrick with more bravery than judgment ordered a charge which resulted in the death of the gallant and promising young general, Elon J. Farnsworth, and the loss of many of his men. J. E. B. Stuart, on Lee's extreme left, took up a position which menaced Meade's line of retreat on the Baltimore road, and was there attacked by the force of D. McM. Gregg and George A. Custer. A general cavalry battle ensued, in which charges and counter-charges were made, but with little advantage to either side; Stuart at last gave way, and the Federal cavalry held the field.

It is clear that General Meade did not immediately comprehend the magnitude of his victory. In the dispatch which he wrote in the evening to General Halleck he greatly understated the extent of his success, speaking of the victory merely as a "handsome repulse" of the enemy. So desperate had been the contest, so intense the strain of anxiety for three days, that there was not left enough of energetic impulse to press his great advantage. General Crawford, it is true, was sent forward on the left to reconnoiter the battlefield of the 2d of July; he came upon a brigade of Hood's division, capturing several hundred prisoners and many thousand stands of arms. The enemy fled across a little brook, an affluent of Plum Run, and was not further pursued. Hancock, while he was borne severely wounded from the field, dictated from his stretcher a note to Meade, begging him to pursue the broken enemy; but, in the deep fatigue and lassitude of a great deliverance, the general-in-chief preferred not to risk the important results already gained by any perilous enterprise. He had as yet no adequate idea of the injury he had inflicted upon the enemy, and his own losses had been enormous. Of the men upon whom he most leaned, his trusted comrades through two years of battle, Reynolds was dead, Sickles disabled, Hancock, Gibbon, Doubleday, Warren, Webb, and many others were wounded, and incapable of holding up his hands in the battles which a keen pursuit would have brought upon him.

General Lee had one moment of supreme exultation and triumph on this memorable afternoon; it was when he saw the blue flag of Virginia, borne by Pickett's troops, waving on the crest of Cemetery Ridge among the Union guns. His gratification lasted only an instant, for, a moment later, he saw the Virginia battle-flags dropping thickly to the ground and his most trusted troops flowing back towards him like a broken wave. He hastened at his utmost speed to meet this returning column, and did all in his power to calm and encourage his beaten soldiers. Again, like Burnside at Fredericksburg, he took all the blame and all the responsibility upon himself. He rode towards the Peach Orchard, where Colonel Alexander still commanded the artillery, and there, with Longstreet, concerted what hasty means of defense were in their power to meet the attack which they thought, of course, would follow; but as the hours passed by, and the long summer day faded into twilight, and no attack was made, General Lee concluded to mass his entire army on Seminary Ridge and prepare for defense or retreat in the morning.

The next day was the Fourth of July, to be made memorable for the second time to all generations of Americans, mingling the associations of Gettysburg and Vicksburg with those of Philadelphia in the last century. The reconnaissances sent out by General Meade, to his left and to his right, found the enemy still in position in front of the Round Tops; but from Benner's Hill and from the town of Gettysburg everything had disappeared; most of the enemy's wounded and the unburied dead were lying on the deserted field of battle. In the course of the day a request for a truce and exchange of prisoners was received from General Lee, which General Meade, under the circumstances, very properly declined. The day passed away in the Union army in the care of the wounded and the last offices to the dead: even yet General Meade was not aware of the magnitude of his victory. He issued, it is true, a brave and inspiriting order of the day, announcing that the enemy was "utterly baffled and defeated," and saying, "Our task is not yet accomplished, and the commanding general looks to the army for greater efforts to drive from our soil every vestige of the presence of the invader"; but at noon he telegraphed General Halleck, saying merely that the enemy had thrown back his left, that we had occupied Gettysburg, and that he should require some time to get up supplies and rest his army. A violent rain-storm came on during the day, which formed another reason for delay. At night he called together his corps commanders in council of war; he put to them the question whether to remain at Gettysburg or to take immediate measures to attack the enemy or cut off his retreat; the majority were in favor of remaining where they were, keeping a close watch upon the movements of the enemy.

On the morning of the 5th, the Confederates were discovered to be in full retreat. General Lee, as we have seen, gave as a reason for attacking the Federal army in position the difficulty of moving his trains through the mountains; but after his defeat he found no difficulty in moving those trains encumbered still further by thousands of wounded and prisoners. Through the night and the storm he retired by the Fairfield and Cashtown roads. Meade acted with sufficient promptness on receiving this news; he resolved to put his army in march on the enemy's flank by way of Middletown and the South Mountain passes, while he sent General Sedgwick with a considerable force in direct pursuit. Sedgwick came upon Lee's rear-guard at Fairfield Pass, and found him in a position so strong that it was unadvisable to attack him; he reported this to Meade, and joined the rest of the army in its march southward.

The news of this victory was received at Washington with great rejoicing, and the Government ordered every man whom it could reach to reënforce General Meade at Frederick. The President accompanied his generous words of praise and congratulation to the general with strict injunctions to give Lee no rest or respite. On the 7th he sent the inspiring news of the surrender of Vicksburg, and told Meade if he could "complete his work so gloriously prosecuted thus far, by the literal or substantial destruction of Lee's army," the rebellion would be over; on the same day he informed him that he had been appointed a brigadier-general in the regular army of the United States. Almost every hour Meade received from the War Department some words of stimulus or encouragement. Halleck wrote: "You have given the enemy a stunning blow at Gettysburg; follow it up and give him another before he can reach the Potomac." All through the 7th and 8th of July these pressing dispatches continued; General Meade seemed to grow weary of them at last, and began on the afternoon of the 8th to insist upon the difficulties of the enterprise so pressingly commended to him. "I expect," he says, "to find the enemy in a strong position well covered with artillery, and I do not desire to imitate his example at Gettysburg and assault a position where the chances were so greatly against success. I wish in advance to moderate the expectations of those who in igno-

rance of the difficulties to be encountered may expect too much."
In this strain the correspondence continued for the next three
days, the Government urging General Meade forward with as
much pressure as was consistent with proper courtesy and
consideration for a meritorious officer who had just rendered
an inestimable service, and the general expressing his intention
to do all he could, and his sense of the difficulties in the way.

In the mean time General Lee had arrived at the Potomac
and taken up his position on the line from Williamsport to
Falling Waters; he found his pontoon bridge partly destroyed
by General French and the river so swollen by the rains as to
be unfordable. In this critical condition he did all that was in
his power; he set to work to reconstruct his bridge, and while
waiting for the river to fall, he strongly intrenched himself
against attack. General Meade arrived in his front on the 10th,
and for two days, with the utmost caution, advanced inch by
inch until the two armies were less than a mile apart. On the
12th he announced his intention to attack the enemy the next
day "unless something intervenes to prevent it, for the reason
that delay will strengthen the enemy and will not increase my
force." Unfortunately something did intervene; it was a council of war. On the night of the 12th he called his corps commanders together, and a large majority unqualifiedly opposed
the projected attack. Meade himself favored it, but he was
supported only by General Wadsworth who, as a civilian general, did not impose his opinion with much authority upon the
council, and by General Howard, whose bad luck at Chancellorsville and Gettysburg had deprived him of much of his influence. In the face of this opposition Meade felt himself too
new in command of the army to disregard it entirely; he therefore resolved to pass the next day in a thorough series of reconnaissances, and if he could find a weak place in the enemy's
line to assault it; he announced this decision in a dispatch to
the War Department and received in reply a vehement message
signed by Halleck but evidently inspired by the President himself. "You are strong enough to attack and defeat the enemy

before he can effect a crossing. Act upon your own judgment
and make your generals execute your orders. Call no council
of war.* It is proverbial that councils of war never fight. . . .
Do not let the enemy escape."

The next morning, July 14, Meade's earliest reconnaissances
proved how just had been the fears of the Government. Lee's
lines were found deserted; he had crossed, in the night, a part
of his force by the bridge which he had repaired at Falling
Waters and a part at Williamsport, where the river had fallen
enough during the last twenty-four hours to be fordable. The
President, on receipt of this news, sent General Meade a dispatch expressing his great dissatisfaction at the result, which
General Meade felt so keenly that he immediately requested
to be relieved from command of the army. The President replied through Halleck that the dispatch was not intended as a
censure but as a stimulus to action, and declined to accept his
resignation. The cavalry started at once in pursuit and succeeded in capturing a brigade of infantry and some guns and
flags at Falling Waters.

The 12th and 13th had been passed by the President in intense anxiety, and when, on the 14th, he heard of Lee's escape

---

* This council of war should never have been called. Of the corps commanders and the men of brain and temperament who fought the battle of
Gettysburg, Reynolds was dead, Hancock and Sickles were wounded, Warren, Pleasonton, Hunt, and Humphreys, who were all in favor of the attack,
had no votes in the council, so that Meade was overborne by mere numbers. The true opinion of the leading officers of the army would be represented as follows: in favor of attack, Meade, Hancock, Sickles, Howard,
Wadsworth, Warren, Pleasonton, Humphreys, Hunt; against, Sedgwick,
Sykes, Hays, French, and Slocum. The matter was unfortunately decided
by the votes of the last five. General Wadsworth in conversation soon after
said, "The weight of authority in the council of war was decidedly against
fighting. French, Sedgwick, and Slocum strenuously opposed a fight, Meade
was in favor of it, Pleasonton was very eager for it, I said what I could.
Those opposed seemed to think that if we did not attack the enemy would,
and even Meade thought he was not ready for action; he had no idea that
the enemy intended to get away at once. Howard had little to say on the
subject. Meade was in favor of attacking in three columns, each of 20,000
men." Wadsworth further said in the same conversation that he thought
there were a good many officers of the regular army who had not yet entirely lost their West Point idea of Southern superiority.—J. H., Diary. See
also Report Committee on Conduct of the War.

he suffered one of the deepest and bitterest disappointments of the war. "We had them within our grasp," he said; "we had only to stretch forth our hands and they were ours, and nothing I could say or do could make the army move." He had been most unfavorably impressed by a phrase in Meade's general order after the victory in which he spoke of "driving the invader from our soil." He said upon reading it, "This is a dreadful reminiscence of McClellan; it is the same spirit that moved him to claim a great victory because 'Pennsylvania and Maryland were safe.' Will our generals never get that idea out of their heads? The whole country is our soil." He regretted that he had not himself gone to the army and personally issued the order for an attack.

The President's disappointment lasted through the week. He said at one time, "Our army held the war in the hollow of their hand and they would not close it"; and again, "We had gone through all the labor of tilling and planting an enormous crop, and when it was ripe we did not harvest it. Still," he added with his habitual instinctive justice, "I am very grateful to Meade for the great service he did at Gettysburg"; and, at the end of the week, having received a letter from General Howard justifying Meade's entire action at Williamsport, the President answered him expressing his deep mortification at the escape of Lee, rendered deeper by the high hopes inspired by the brilliant conduct of our troops at Gettysburg; he referred to his own long-cherished and often expressed conviction that if the enemy ever crossed the Potomac he might be destroyed; he said that Meade and his army had expended their skill and toil and blood up to the ripe harvest and then allowed it to go to waste; but he added that, after the lapse of several days, he now felt profoundly grateful to Meade and his army for what they had done without indulging in any criticisms for what they had not done, and General Meade had his full confidence as a brave and skillful officer and a true man.

ONE DAY *after Gettysburg, Vicksburg fell.*

The surrender was the culmination of a campaign which Grant had begun in December, 1862. He had first started south along the line of the Mississippi Central Railroad, only to be thwarted when Van Dorn burned the great Union supply depot at Holly Springs, Mississippi. Then Grant tried to evade the Vicksburg fortifications by cutting canals and using bayou waterways. All these expedients failed. The Union commander finally devised the strategy that would succeed: Admiral Porter's transports would run the batteries, and Grant would march his troops down the west bank of the Mississippi to a point below Vicksburg. Porter would take the army across the river; then it would sweep northeast, give battle to any Confederate forces in its way, and, if successful, march west and invest Vicksburg.

On May 14, 1863, the XVII Corps under McPherson and the XV Corps under Sherman struck a force of six thousand Confederates at Jackson, the state capital, and drove them from the town. Two days later the Federal troops attacked the main Confederate force at Champion's Hill, halfway between Jackson and Vicksburg, and inflicted a sharp defeat. On the 17th Pemberton made a stand at Big Black River, was defeated, and withdrew to Vicksburg.

Vicksburg

THE town of Vicksburg stands on a plateau some two hundred feet above the river level, which has been cut and carved by the rains of centuries so as to present a chaos of ravines and ridges running in every direction. The hills are composed of a peculiarly tough and fine-grained clay, and the ravines, cut out of them by the running streams, retain their form for many years, only gradually widening under the climate and weather. Except where the streams that form them are very large, the ravines are extremely narrow at the bottom. They are so steep that it is impossible for a full-armed soldier to climb them.

Vol. VII, Chap. X, pp. 282-92, 299-309.

The only way in which this net-work of hills and chasms can be traversed is by roads running along the crests of the ridges. All these crests were fully commanded by the Confederate works; and it was this which made the siege of Vicksburg so tedious and toilsome an enterprise.

When Grant arrived before the intrenchments, on the evening of May 18th, he thought it possible that the defeats of the last week had so demoralized and discouraged the defenders of the place that a quick rush of his victorious troops might carry the works by a *coup-de-main*. He therefore ordered a general attack on the afternoon of the 19th. Sherman's corps got up to the works, but, as McClernand's and McPherson's were at a greater distance, they were unable to afford Sherman the necessary support, and the attack failed, with no advantage to the Union forces except a nearer approach to the enemy's works, and the gaining of better ground for a future attempt.

General Grant did not wait long for his second trial. The reasons which he gave in his report for the second assault have been generally accepted by military critics as sound, in spite of the failure of the enterprise. He believed the assault could be made successful; secondly, he knew that Johnston was at Canton, and was being rapidly reënforced; he was anxious, therefore, to take the place before Johnston could fall upon his rear, and, having done this, he would himself have been able to turn upon Johnston and drive him from the State before the season was too late for campaigning; and, finally, he says: "The troops themselves were impatient to possess Vicksburg, and would not have worked in the trenches with the same zeal, believing it unnecessary, that they did after their failure to carry the enemy's works." He therefore ordered, on the evening of the 21st, an assault all along the line at ten o'clock the next morning, and caused all the corps commanders to set their watches by his so that the assault might be made at the same instant. This was done according to orders, and with equal bravery and energy in all three of the corps, and with equal lack of success. Sherman's, McPherson's, and McClernand's soldiers all rushed with the same valor for the narrow roads through which, alone, the assault could be made; each planted their flags upon the outer walls of the enemy's works; all were met with an energetic defense and repulsed with heavy loss.

A bitter controversy arose after the battle between General McClernand on the one side and General Grant and his friends on the other, in regard to an unfortunate incident by which the Union losses were greatly increased. Grant watched the attack from a hill on the Jackson road, which commanded a view of all the roads on which the assault was made. He saw the forward rush; the blaze of fire from the enemy's parapet; the planting of the Union colors on the outward slope; the check of his soldiers and their pause in the ditches. He was satisfied that the attacks had failed, and, starting to communicate with Sherman, in regard to the next step to be taken, he received a dispatch from General McClernand saying he was hard pressed, and asking for reënforcements. He continued his ride to Sherman's position, and on reaching there received a second dispatch from McClernand, saying that he had part possession of two forts, and that the Stars and Stripes were floating over them. Neither Grant nor Sherman placed full credence in this enthusiastic dispatch, but both agreed that it was impossible to neglect so important a message at such a time. Sherman said the note was official and must be credited, and offered to renew the assault with new troops. At McPherson's headquarters, whither he instantly hastened, General Grant received a third dispatch from McClernand of the same import, and at last ordered the attack to be renewed. The devoted soldiers sprang once more to the assault with the finest courage and energy, but it was useless; they were everywhere repulsed again, and the renewed attempt only added heavily to the list of the day's casualties. General McClernand always insisted that his dispatches were correct, and that he would have taken the town if he had been properly supported, but the facts seem to be that only Sergeant Joseph E. Griffith of the Twenty-second Iowa, with a squad of men, got into the enemy's works, and they were all killed but the valorous sergeant himself, who came out safely, bringing some prisoners with him.

This was General McClernand's last feat of arms. Unwilling to trust his exploits of the 22d of May to any less intelligent or friendly chronicler than himself, he wrote, on the 30th of May, and published to his troops, and not to his troops alone but to his fellow-citizens in the North, a congratulatory order, in which he recounted, in the style of Napoleon in Italy, the labors and the triumphs of the Thirteenth Army Corps, giving especial prominence to the affair of the 22d. If he had confined himself to the doughty deeds of his own soldiers, it might have passed unnoticed, but he unfortunately sought to gild his own achievements by slighting those of his comrades; and to place his own desert in a brighter light he even insinuated that the general-in-chief had not properly supported him. When this order, published in a St. Louis paper, came back to the camp it occasioned such effervescence as may easily be imagined in the corps of Sherman and McPherson. Both these generals joined immediately in a protest to General Grant against their censorious colleague, and Grant, fully sympathizing in their resentment, immediately relieved General McClernand from the command of the Thirteenth Army Corps, assigning in his place, subject to the President's approval, that able and modest soldier, E. O. C. Ord. In announcing this action to General Halleck, Grant said that he had tolerated General McClernand long after he thought the good of the service demanded his removal, which, he added, now that it had taken place, had "given general satisfaction; the Thirteenth Army Corps sharing, perhaps, equally in the feeling with other corps of the army."

After this severe repulse, which cost the Union army more than three thousand men with no compensating advantages whatever, Grant gave up all thought of taking the place by storm, and resolved upon a regular siege. In the peculiarities of topography to which we have already referred, this siege differs from any other in history. Vicksburg was, properly speaking, not a fortress, but an intrenched camp stretching for miles along the heights of the Mississippi and defended by innumerable gullies and ravines almost impassable to troops. Grant's forces at the beginning were altogether insufficient for the complete investment of such a camp; at the outset of the campaign his forces numbered about 43,000, though at the close his army had been increased to 75,000 men. In his official report Pemberton says that when he moved into the defenses he had 28,000 effectives. The parole lists after the surrender accounted for 29,491 men, which included the non-effectives. Not being able to garnish the entire semicircle of investment with troops Grant contented himself, at the beginning, with holding and strongly occupying the northern half of it; Sherman's corps holding the bank of the Mississippi and the heights to the east of it; McPherson coming next, and McClernand upon his left. General Jacob G. Lauman arrived two days after the assault, and was placed in position on McClernand's left to guard the Hall's Ferry and the Warrenton roads which enter Vicksburg from the south. Brigadier-General John McArthur, with three brigades, had already joined McPherson's corps and strengthened his line, and on the 11th of June, the division of General Herron arrived from the other side of the river, and completed the investment by taking up a strong position on the river south of the town. Lauman, moving to the right, formed a close connection with Hovey, thus hermetically closing all the avenues of approach to Vicksburg. Now, for the first time in his career, Grant, wishing by an overwhelming force to insure the capture of the town and to defend himself against the threatened attack of Johnston, asked for reënforcements which, even before his request was received, were promptly and ungrudgingly sent him as fast as they were needed or could be used; so that he was able, on the 8th of June, to say in a dispatch to Washington, "Vicksburg is closely invested. I have a spare force of about thirty thousand men with which to repel anything from the rear."

The troops, having been satisfied by the slaughter of the 22d of the impossibility of storming the works in their front and of

the absolute necessity of hard work to capture them, labored
for six weeks with cheerful and uncomplaining fortitude in the
drudgery of the siege. The army was most imperfectly provided
with all the material considered essential for the prosecution of
a work of this sort, and the ingenuity of the American soldier
found constant exercise in the invention of devices to supply
these deficiencies. They wattled their gabions with crushed cane
which abounded in the ravines and hollows; they took empty
barrels from the commissary department which, bound about
with fascines of cane, made excellent sap-rollers. They had no
cohorn mortars, and so improvised them by shrinking iron
bands on cylinders of hard wood and boring them for shells.
The negro refugees from the surrounding counties came in and
worked with cheerful and efficient industry under the novel
stimulus of regular wages. The peculiar nature of the ground
was the occasion of all sorts of eccentric siege inventions. When
it became necessary to cross one of the gullies commanded by
the enemy's fire, they would build in the night strong parapets
of logs, manning them with picked riflemen under which the
working parties were perfectly protected the next day; for the
first shot from the rebel works would be answered by a deadly
reply from the log parapets. The engineer's report refers in one
instance to a reconnaissance of a rebel ditch obtained by mounting a mirror upon a sap-roller. As the siege went on from day
to day, and the hostile armies came nearer and nearer together,
they were constantly within sound of each other's voices, and
friendly conversations continually took place between soldiers
who would have destroyed each other in a moment with their
rifles, if they had come within sight.

For siege operations of this enormous extent the force of
engineers in the army was, of course, altogether inadequate.
Grant, Sherman, and McPherson multiplied themselves all
along the line. Every graduate of West Point in the army was
assigned to energetic duty, and the cleverest and most capable
collegians from the volunteer regiments were detailed, and given

an opportunity to show what their Euclid and Legendre had done for them.

While holding the enemy in front in this grip of iron Grant was equally vigilant in regard to the enemy in his rear. After his reënforcements arrived he felt strong enough to remove Sherman from his duty on the heights above Vicksburg, and to place him in command of a large army to observe Johnston. He gave him Generals Parke, Washburn, James M. Tuttle, McArthur, and Osterhaus, who massed a force of about thirty thousand men; and a strong division of McPherson's was also held in constant readiness to join him. Sherman occupied the country from Haines's Bluff on the left to a bridge over the Black River on the right, a space of eight miles. Foraging expeditions sent out previously had made a waste of the entire region between the two rivers, gathering large supplies for the Union army, and spoiling the country to the point of starvation, to prevent General Johnston from drawing provisions from it. . . .

The heads of sap had reached the enemy's lines at several points. Grant had fired one heavy mine on the Jackson road on the 25th of June, exploding almost a ton of powder. Vast masses of earth were thrown into the air, a part of the enemy's parapet was hurled bodily into the Union lines, several Confederate soldiers being thrown in, still living, with the flying mass. An attempt was made to hold the crater thus formed, but it was commanded by an inner line, and after severe loss from hand-grenades the Union troops were compelled to abandon it. Another mine was begun with the intention of firing it when the final assault was made, but the Confederate miners being hard at work very near it, it was thought injudicious to wait and, on the 1st of July, the mine was loaded and fired, again destroying a redan of the enemy, crushing his galleries, and disabling about twenty-five men. The Union troops were deterred by the experience of the 25th of June from attempting to occupy this crater. The approaches were now in several places within a few feet of the enemy's works; every advance of a single yard resulted in a hand-to-hand contest between the troops of the two armies. No further progress could be made by digging alone. The enemy's works were everywhere weakened. At as many as ten different points Grant was able to put heads of regiments under cover within from five to one hundred yards of the enemy's line. There was little more to be done. No further delay could avail. Vicksburg was a ripe fruit only waiting to be plucked, and Grant had fixed the hour of plucking three days ahead.

Within the city the state of affairs had come to a point where much longer resistance was impossible. Absolute famine had not yet made its appearance, but the stock of provisions was dwindling fast, and prices had risen portentously. They were estimated, it is true, in Confederate money, but as the people had no other measure of value, even these fictitious prices give some idea of the general distress. Flour was $1000 a barrel; meal $140 a bushel. It was difficult to get a gallon of molasses for ten dollars. The oxen killed by the shells of the bombardment were picked up by butchers and the meat sold for two and three dollars a pound. The pack-mules which, early in the siege, had been driven outside the rebel works to forage for themselves, were now enticed inside or caught by parties in the night, and furnished the subsistence of thousands of troops and citizens. The unhappy people of Vicksburg passed their nights and a great part of their days in caves excavated in the hillsides. These troglodyte habitations became an article of commerce, selling for forty or fifty dollars each. There was still a large army within the walls and they were not yet destitute of military stores.

The most serious deficiency was that which began to declare itself in the morale of the troops. The Confederates seemed to have lost confidence in their leaders and all hope of a favorable issue of the siege. Conversation between the pickets of the opposing forces became general, and was encouraged by Grant, as the advantage was all upon his side. Late in the

siege the rebel pickets communicated a rumor current in the
city, that the place was to be evacuated by night; that the
garrison was to be transferred across the Mississippi, and that
houses were being torn down all over the city for the purpose
of constructing boats to effect this passage. They also said that
there was a disposition among the troops to mutiny if they were
called on to cut their way out. Among General Pemberton's papers communications have been found, from private soldiers,
warning him of the ominous tone of discontent in his army.
Held by the relentless embrace of a host he now considered in-
vincible, and despairing at last of any relief from the outside,
Pemberton, on the 1st of July, requested his division commanders to give him their opinion, in writing, as to the ability
of their troops "to make the marches and undergo the fa-
tigues necessary to accomplish a successful evacuation." Forney, Smith, and Bowen at once replied, advising capitulation;
Stevenson's opinion was little more encouraging. Pemberton
then called them together, and the council unanimously resolved upon capitulation. General Bowen was sent with a flag
of truce to Grant, on the morning of the 3d, proposing the
appointment of commissioners to arrange terms of surrender.
As the matter was resolved upon, Pemberton thought best to
lose no time, and as he was afterwards severely blamed for
giving to the Union arms the glory of a great victory upon
the national anniversary, he replied that he had selected
that day for the surrender, hoping for better terms through
this gratification of the national pride. To Bowen's embassy
Grant replied that the only terms he would admit were those
of "unconditional surrender"; Bowen, being a friend of
Grant's and an old neighbor in Missouri, asked for a personal
interview; this Grant declined, but consented to meet Pemberton in front of the lines at three o'clock.

In the afternoon, under a tree standing alone upon the
hillside a few hundred yards from the rebel lines, the commanders of the two armies met, Pemberton being accompanied by General Bowen and Colonel L. M. Montgomery,

and Grant by Ord and McPherson, Logan and A. J. Smith. It was a picture full of vivid and exciting interest to the troops of the two armies, who swarmed upon the parapets of the opposing lines in eager expectation and perfect security, in places where their exposure a few hours before would have been certain death. A strange and almost oppressive silence, unbroken by a single shot from the earthworks or the fleet, brooded over the scene, wrapt in the warm languor of a sultry summer evening. The two generals saluted each other, and Pemberton asked what terms of capitulation he was to expect. Grant repeated what he had said in the morning. Pemberton haughtily replied, "Then the conference may as well terminate"; and in this futile manner the meeting was on the point of breaking up, when General Bowen suggested that a conference between two of the subordinates might lead to some result. Grant neither assented nor objected to this, and Smith and Bowen retired a little way, leaving Pemberton and Grant in conversation. A few minutes later the two subordinates returned, and Bowen suggested that the Confederates should march out of Vicksburg with the honors of war. Grant promptly and smilingly rejected the proposition. Without coming to any conclusion the generals separated, Grant promising to send his ultimatum before ten o'clock at night; the truce to last as long as the correspondence should be in progress. Grant returned to his camp, and sent to Pemberton the following letter:

In conformity with agreement of this afternoon, I will submit the following proposition for the surrender of the city of Vicksburg, public stores, etc. On your accepting the terms proposed, I will march in one division as a guard, and take possession at 8 A.M. to-morrow. As soon as rolls can be made out, and paroles signed by officers and men, you will be allowed to march out of our lines, the officers taking with them their side-arms and clothing, and the field, staff, and cavalry officers one horse each. The rank and file will be allowed all their clothing, but no other property. If these conditions are accepted, any amount of rations you may deem necessary can be taken from the stores you now have, and also the necessary cooking utensils for preparing them. Thirty wagons also, counting two two-horse or mule teams as one, will be allowed to transport such articles as cannot be carried along. The same conditions will be allowed to all sick and wounded officers and soldiers as fast as they become able to travel. The paroles for these latter must be signed, however, while officers are present authorized to sign the roll of prisoners.

Late at night Pemberton replied, accepting these terms in the main, "but in justice both to the honor and spirit" of his troops, manifested in the defense of Vicksburg, he proposed by way of amendment to evacuate the works in and around Vicksburg, and to surrender the city and garrison under his command, by marching out with his colors and arms, and stacking them in front of his present lines, after which Grant should take possession. He asked also that officers should retain their side-arms and personal property, and the rights and property of citizens should be respected. Shortly after midnight Grant sent his final answer, acceding only partly to Pemberton's proposed amendment.

It will be necessary to furnish every officer and man with a parole signed by himself, which, with the completion of the rolls of prisoners, will necessarily take some time. Again I can make no stipulations with regard to the treatment of citizens and their private property. While I do not propose to cause them any undue annoyance or loss, I cannot consent to leave myself under any restraint by stipulations. The property which officers will be allowed to take with them will be as stated in my proposition of last evening; that is, officers will be allowed their private baggage and side-arms, and mounted officers one horse each. If you mean by your proposition for each brigade to march to the front of the lines now occupied by it, and stack arms at ten o'clock A.M., and then return to the inside and there remain as prisoners until properly paroled, I will make no objection to it. Should no notification be received of your acceptance of my terms by 9 A.M., I shall regard them as having been rejected, and shall act accordingly. Should these terms be accepted, white flags should be displayed along your lines to prevent such of my troops as may not have been notified from firing upon your men.

These terms were accepted by Pemberton.

The last shot had been fired on the heights of Vicksburg. At ten o'clock on the morning of the 4th of July the Union soldiers, standing upon the parapets of their works, witnessed with deep emotion the army of the Confederates issuing from their sally ports, stacking their arms in front of the works which they had defended so long and so gallantly, and retiring again within their lines as prisoners of war. They were so near together that every word spoken on one side could easily be heard on the other, and it is not the least of the glories gained by the Army of the Tennessee in this wonderful campaign that not a cheer went up from the Union ranks, not a single word that could offend their beaten foes. Logan's command, which was nearest to the works, had the merited honor of marching first into Vicksburg. The soldiers of the two armies immediately began to fraternize, and the Northern boys shared the contents of their well-filled haversacks with their hungry brethren of the South. In the higher ranks this fraternization was not so prompt. General Grant was received by Pemberton and his staff, at headquarters, with sulky coldness. No one, at first, offered him a seat; when he asked for a drink of water he was told where he might find it himself; and during the interview between the two generals, which lasted half an hour, Grant remained standing while officers, girded with the swords which his magnanimity had allowed them to retain, sat sullenly about him. General Pemberton asked for supplies to feed his troops. Grant asked him how many rations would be required, and, to his amazement, Pemberton replied thirty-two thousand, for from these words the conqueror gained the first intelligence of the magnitude of his triumph. With his habit of minimizing the number of his enemy he had thought, up to this moment, that he had captured less than twenty thousand men. He rode down to the wharf and exchanged congratulations with Porter, who had rendered him such manful assistance through evil and good report during the last year, and then went back through the cheering lines of his troops to his old quarters in the camp beyond Vicksburg.

The paroling of the troops was rapidly accomplished, and they marched away on the 11th of July, Pemberton vainly imploring the assistance of Grant to keep them in their ranks; the disposition to desert was so general that he feared he could not bring his army intact to its destination. This was, of course, refused. General Grant always afterwards, in his reports and in his memoirs, showed an unwonted anxiety to defend his action in thus paroling Pemberton's army. Immediately on receiving the news of the great victory General Halleck had suggested to him that this action might be construed into an absolute release, and the men be put at once into the ranks of the enemy, such having been the action of the Confederates elsewhere. Grant's defense of this proceeding was that he saved thereby several days in the capture and left the troops and the transports ready for other service. But it must be counted, on the whole, an error of judgment; for even before Pemberton, with his unarmed host, had marched away from Vicksburg, Jefferson Davis had telegraphed to him that all the general officers had been exchanged and were released from their parole, and two months later the Confederate agent of exchange notified the United States agent that all the effective troops paroled at Vicksburg were declared exchanged and ordered to duty. In spite of the protests on the part of the National authorities this lawless proceeding was carried through, and Grant confronted, a few months later, on the heights of Chattanooga, some of the soldiers to whom he had allowed such generous terms on the bluffs of Vicksburg. The confusion arising from this lasted till the end of the war, and it was due to General Grant's belief that the Confederate authorities had acted in bad faith in this matter that he maintained so rigid an attitude in regard to the exchange of prisoners during the last year of the war. On the other hand, during the march of the paroled Confederates to Demopolis, the place where they were to await their exchange, some of the results which General Grant looked forward to became apparent. Grant having refused Pemberton the means of maintaining order among his demoralized troops, the gravest indications of a mutinous spirit appeared as soon as they left Vicksburg, and continually increased as they moved along the hot and dusty roads. They insulted their officers, and at one time loudly called upon Pemberton to "come and be hanged"; all along their route they scattered the germs of discouragement and discontent.

But the victory was too great, too important, and too beneficent for criticism. Seldom in the history of the world have results so vast been attained with equal expenditure. Grant had captured 29,491 men, 172 cannon, 60,000 muskets, generally new arms which had recently run the blockade, and which were at once adopted by the regiments of our army in exchange for their own inferior pieces, battered with use, and associated with many victories. General Pemberton's returns for March showed 61,495 actually present, and of these all that remained saved from death, wounds, or capture, on the 4th of July, were those who had escaped with Loring from Champion's Hill, and 11,000 or 12,000 more who were in the force which Sherman was chasing before him towards Jackson. The Confederate cause had lost not much less than fifty thousand supporters in this destructive campaign, and with them the control of that great artery of the West, the Mississippi River. The Confederacy was cut in two at a cost to the Union of 9362 men. There were still two years of labor, and toil, and bloodshed before the end came, but the war reached its crisis and the fate of the rebellion was no longer doubtful from that hour, in the afternoon of the 3d of July, when Grant and Pemberton sat in stern and joyless conversation beneath the oak tree on the hillside of Vicksburg, and Pickett's veterans were reeling back, baffled and broken by the guns of Meade at Gettysburg.

FOR THREE DAYS, *at the very end of 1862 and the beginning of 1863, the Army of the Cumberland under Rosecrans and the Army of Tennessee under Bragg fought the bloody but inconclusive Battle of Stone's River. For the next six months Rosecrans kept his men in camp around Murfreesboro. Late in June he began an advance toward Bragg, whose men occupied a series of fortified camps in south-central Tennessee. In a brilliant campaign of maneuver, Rosecrans forced his opponent to draw back to Chattanooga and beyond. A few miles southeast of that city the two armies collided in the Battle of Chickamauga, September 19 and 20. This time Bragg held the field. The Army of the Cumberland retreated to Chattanooga, where it was virtually besieged.*

Late in October the administration put Grant in command of all the Western armies, relieved Rosecrans, and gave Thomas his place. Grant went at once to Chattanooga, opened the supply lines, and prepared to take the offensive. Bragg's troops held what seemed to be impregnable positions on Lookout Mountain and Missionary Ridge.

Chattanooga

GRANT'S original plan had been to throw Sherman's force across the river at a point near the mouth of Chickamauga Creek, from which he should attack and carry the extremity of Missionary Ridge. Thomas was so to dispose his troops as to coöperate in this movement, and after the ridge was carried the united forces were to rush to the railroad between Cleveland and Dalton. Hooker was to attack and carry Lookout Mountain, if possible, while a demonstration was to be made on Trenton, to induce Bragg to believe that the movement of Rosecrans in September was to be repeated. He changed his mind, however, a few days later, having resolved to throw a very large force into the attack on the northwest end of Missionary Ridge. He determined to detach Howard's corps from Hooker, and to hold it in readiness to move to the support of Sherman or Thomas; but even Grant, the most masterful of all our generals, could not absolutely control the course of events, and on the very eve of battle he reverted to the former plan.

He had intended that the attack should be made on the 21st, but a furious rainstorm, which began on the 20th and continued for two days, made the movement impossible. Though Sherman pushed his troops forward with his habitual fiery zeal, they could not get into position on the day fixed. The time, however, was not lost. While Sherman, in spite of flooded roads, and bridges repeatedly broken as fast as repaired, was bringing his troops into a sheltered position behind the hills north of Chattanooga, where they were entirely concealed from the view of the enemy, Thomas brought Howard's corps in full view of Bragg's observatory on Missionary Ridge, across the river, through the town of Chattanooga, out into the open fields in front of the Union works. This move was made to induce the enemy to believe that the troops from Brown's Ferry had been brought to reënforce the Union center. While this dramatic display of a splendidly appointed corps from the Army of the Potomac passed under the watching eyes of the enemy, the serious attack upon his right wing was preparing north of the river, screened behind the hills of Chattanooga; and Hugh Ewing, having made his demonstration at Trenton, had been hurried forward to the extreme left of the National army.

Even on the 23d, the disposition of the troops was not yet completed, but Grant resolved to postpone his movement no longer. He had received a letter from Bragg, on the 20th, notifying him that prudence would dictate the early withdrawal of non-combatants from Chattanooga. This ruse was altogether too gross to be taken seriously. Grant suspected at once that Bragg was intending to retire, and this suspicion was strengthened on the night of the 22d by the report of a deserter that Confederate troops were already moving to the rear. This report, although untrue, Grant afterwards thought was made in good faith, and was founded on the fact that Bragg had sent reënforcements to Longstreet, and, with incredible fatuity, was preparing to send others. Believing that Bragg was about to retire, and not willing to allow him the privilege of withdrawing his army intact, Grant ordered Thomas to make such a demonstration in front of his line on the 23d as to determine whether the enemy was still there in force or not. This duty was assigned to General Gordon Granger, commanding the new Fourth Corps, made up principally of the remains of McCook's and Crittenden's former commands. At the most prominent salient of the Union lines stood a redoubt called Fort Wood, where twenty-two heavy guns had been placed in position. On either side of this fort two divisions of Granger's command were formed; on the left General Wood, and on the right General P. H. Sheridan, who was this day to fight for the first time under the eyes of Grant, and to enter on the career of unbroken success which was to bring him to the head of the army.

During the early part of the day the valley was filled with fog, which concealed it from the view of the enemy on the surrounding heights; but in the afternoon the veil lifted, and the Confederates on the ridge saw below them a sight full of scenic beauty. Two splendid divisions moved out in front of the Union line, drums beating and colors flying; behind them the Eleventh Corps was drawn up in mass; and on Granger's right Baird and Johnson, of Palmer's Fourteenth Corps, were held under arms in the intrenchments. So measured and precise were the movements of the troops that the Confederates imagined it was a dress parade going on in the plain, and they assisted at the show with no interest, except that of pleased spectators; but suddenly, after the troops had rested some half an hour in line, the order to advance was given. Sheridan's and Wood's divisions rushed forward upon the rebel pickets, driving them rapidly through the low-lying ground and the thin woods, reaching the grand guards almost as soon as the pickets themselves, capturing Bragg's first line of rifle-pits and several hundred men, and securing themselves in their new position before reënforcements could arrive from the main Confederate line.

The Union line was thus pushed forward in the arc of a circle about a mile in front of the position it had held the day before. An eminence called Orchard Knob was seized and hastily fortified, and although this success led immediately to no substantial result (and, indeed, it has been criticized as a needless and premature warning to the enemy), its moral effect seems to have been an ample compensation. It was a brilliant and easy success, important in the ground gained for future work, and valuable in the cheer and encouragement it gave to the troops who had been beaten at Chickamauga and so long shut up in the intrenchments at Chattanooga. They had met the enemy they had been confronting, and had gained the first round of a fight which all felt sure was to be decisive. Evening closed in with the roar of artillery from every point of the opposing lines, which seemed to the excited soldiers to express the exultation of the National troops and the defiance of the Confederates.

It was night on the 23d before Sherman's forces had been brought together opposite the mouth of the Chickamauga, and even then his rear division under Osterhaus had been cut off by the broken bridge at Brown's Ferry; but Grant determined to wait no longer. He detached Osterhaus's division to Hooker, and ordered Sherman to make his attack with the other three, assisted by J. C. Davis, who had been detached from Thomas to support him. Before midnight his pontoons were loaded; they dropped silently down to the point above the mouth of the creek; then, moving cautiously along the river, his troops captured, successively, all the Confederate pickets except one. By daylight of the 24th, eight thousand men were on the south bank of the Tennessee, safely established in their rifle trenches. As soon as it was light a pontoon bridge was built over the Tennessee and another over the creek.

"I have never," says Sherman, "beheld any work done so quietly, so well, and I doubt if the history of war can show a bridge of that extent, 1350 feet, laid so noiselessly and well in so short a time. I attribute it to the genius and intelligence of General W. F. Smith."

Sherman had carefully explained to each of his division commanders the work required of him, and shortly after noon he marched from the river in three columns, the left commanded by General M. L. Smith on Chickamauga Creek, the center under General J. E. Smith, and the right under General Ewing. A light rain fell, and the valley was shrouded in mist and fog. Reaching the foot-hills, the skirmishers of Sherman kept up the face of the hill, followed by their supports; a brigade of each division went rapidly to the top of the hill; and, though energetically opposed by the enemy, the point which Sherman had selected as the first position to be gained was reached. Here a grave disappointment awaited him. All the maps he had seen were imperfect, and represented Missionary Ridge as one continuous hill. From his observatory north of the river the vast wrinkles of the ridge were not seen, and now, on gaining the top of the hill for which he had so gallantly fought, he found that a considerable valley lay between him and the strong position of the enemy over the railroad tunnel, which had been his chief objective point. He fortified himself strongly, however, during the night, and the blaze of his campfires gave to Grant the assurance of a success greater than had really been gained.

While Sherman was attacking on the extreme left of the Union line, Hooker, thirteen miles away at Wauhatchie, was executing, with no less gallantry than good fortune, the task allotted to him. In the changes of troops which the exigencies at the eve of battle required, Howard had been taken from him, and Osterhaus's division from the Fifteenth Corps, and Cruft's from the Fourth, had been added to Geary's of the Twelfth—the only division which remained to him of the army he had brought from Virginia. Those three divisions, entirely strange to each other, were to participate in an attack upon the formidable position, equally unknown to them all, of Lookout Mountain, which was held by a strong force of the enemy. General Bragg, in his report, says that General Stevenson had six brigades at his disposal, and, upon his urgent appeal, another brigade was dispatched in the afternoon to his support. Hooker had a force not much superior in numbers, and utterly inadequate to the attack of such a position as the enemy occupied, if it had been properly defended. The enemy's pickets formed a continuous line round the right bank of Lookout Creek, with strong reserves in the coves of the hills, while his main force was encamped in a hollow half way up the slope of the mountain. The only means of access to the summit was by narrow trails, which were defended by strong pickets of the enemy; but if Hooker could succeed in rounding the northern slope of the mountain he was sure of compelling the evacuation of the place, as the only road by which the enemy could connect with their main body was one which zigzagged up the eastern slope. "Viewed from whatever point," says Hooker, "Lookout Mountain, with its high, palisaded crest and its steep, rugged, rocky, and deeply furrowed slopes, presented an imposing barrier to our advance; and when to these were added almost interminable well-planned, well-constructed defenses, held by Americans, the assault became an enterprise worthy the ambition and renown of the troops to whom it was intrusted."

Geary with his own and a part of Charles Cruft's division crossed the creek near Wauhatchie early in the morning and moved down the valley, his right resting on the rocky palisades, capturing the rebel pickets as he moved. William Grose's brigade advanced resolutely to the bridge and began under a brisk fire to repair it. The Confederates were at once seen swarming down the mountain from their camps, filling their rifle-pits and breastworks; but they were so much occupied with the men at the bridge that they paid little attention to Geary, who was moving down in a slight mist that obscured the valley, and they also neglected the passage of C. R. Woods's brigade between Geary and the bridge. At eleven o'clock both these brigades sprang across the river, connecting with Geary's left, which was in position to enfilade the Confederate works at the north end of Lookout, and the whole command rushed solidly up the mountain-side driving the Confederates rapidly before them. "The right passed directly under the muzzles of the enemy's guns on the summit, climbing over ledges and boulders up hill and down, furiously driving the enemy from his camp and from position after position."

At noon Geary's advance rounded the northern point of the mountain. They had gained such an impetus that although this was the strongest point of the enemy's position, and although it had not been Hooker's intention to attack the Confederate works at that point without a pause for preparation, fired by success the troops pressed impetuously forward with uninterrupted and irresistible progress. By two o'clock the clouds, which since morning had been hanging over the mountain, settled so thickly about the troops that their operations were arrested by the darkness; they halted and began strengthening their position, while their comrades in the field gazed with intense excitement upon the dense mass of vapor that hid this extraordinary battle from their view. Occasional flashes of musketry and glimpses of moving lines and of advancing banners were caught through the drifting clouds, and proved that all was going well with Hooker. At four o'clock he sent to Grant the welcome intelligence that he had established himself on the northern slope of Lookout in a position which he considered impregnable. Direct communication having been opened with Chattanooga, W. P. Carlin's brigade arrived late in the afternoon, after sharp fighting, and went to Hooker's right, relieving Geary's exhausted division.

By this brilliant and picturesque victory the Union line was greatly shortened and strengthened, and brought into connection, so that on the morning of the 25th, the enemy having evacuated the mountain in the night, the National troops were drawn up in perfect communication from the point where Sherman's left rested on Chickamauga Creek to the lofty summit of Lookout Mountain where the Eighth Kentucky had planted the Union flag to catch the first rays of the morning sun. It was not only the material advantages gained on this epic march which made the "battle above the clouds" memorable: moral benefits of the highest character also came from it. When Hooker first started west, Mr. Lincoln wrote to Rosecrans that the relations between Hooker and Slocum were not such as to promise good in their relative positions. He therefore earnestly requested Rosecrans to make a transposition by which Slocum and his corps might pass from under the command of Hooker, and Hooker in return receive some other equal force. Rosecrans answered that "any attempt to mingle them [the troops of his army] with Potomac troops by placing them under Potomac generals would kindle a flame of jealousy and dislike"; but here without a moment's warning, troops from the veteran Army of the Tennessee had been mingled with troops transferred from the soil of Virginia, and these, joined to soldiers of the Army of the Cumberland, had been put unexpectedly under the command of a Potomac general, and all had marched like brothers, under extraordinary circumstances, to battle and to victory, showing how incapable were the rank and file of that patriot army of the petty meanness imputed to them by their general. It was a happy augury of final success that this lofty watchtower, the possession of which had been so ardently desired for two weary years by the President, should at last be permanently occupied by the National power, through the fraternal and unselfish valor of soldiers coming from every Army and almost every State of the Union.

Sherman had been ordered to renew his attack on the left at daybreak on the 25th. He obeyed his orders with the utmost gallantry and no lack of skill, but not with the success for which Grant had hoped and planned. It had been his expectation that Hooker's demonstration on the left, and the threatening attitude of Thomas in the center, would have occupied enough of Bragg's army to enable Sherman to gain Missionary Ridge with comparative ease, and to push the National left between Longstreet and Bragg; but the Confederate general, perceiving at once in what direction his real danger lay, threw the bulk of his force against Sherman, and having obstinately barred his passage on the 24th, was prepared on the 25th also to make his principal battle against him.

Though deeply chagrined by the failure of Stevenson to hold Lookout Mountain, Bragg comprehended the situation on the night of the 24th, and ordered the withdrawal of his forces from Lookout, concentrating them all on Missionary Ridge. He relied to a great extent on the strength of his works to defend his left flank and his center, which was under the command of Breckinridge, with Stewart's, Buckner's, and Hindman's divisions, and threw to the right his heavy columns under Cleburne, Cheatham, Walker, and Stevenson, the whole under command of Hardee.

The morning broke clear and cold; the fog and mist of the previous day had passed away, and as Sherman, who had mounted his horse in the twilight before dawn, and had ridden from one end to the other of his line, began to marshal his forces for the attack, he could see from his commanding position on the left the whole field of battle, the most grandiose and picturesque of the war. The plain of Chattanooga, broken by low ridges and small watercourses, interspersed with clumps of sparsely growing trees, and cut throughout its length by the parallel intrenchments of the hostile armies; to the north, the tortuous stream of the Tennessee winding among wooded hills and lofty rocks, and still further to the north the bare and rugged heights of Walden's Ridge and the Cumberland Mountains. On the extreme right the sheer precipices of Lookout Mountain closed the view, and in front the steep slope of Missionary Ridge, crowded with the Confederate batteries and fringed by the waving battle flags of the rebellion, barred the passage of the Union arms to Atlanta and the heart of the South. But the first sight that greeted the eyes of Sherman was that the hill in front of him was held by the enemy with breastworks of logs and fresh earth, and that the high hills beyond swarmed with heavy masses of Confederates supporting formidable batteries. A great gorge lay between, where, although Sherman could not see them, his quick intelligence surmised the presence of the Confederate reserves. The sun had risen before his preparations were completed and the bugles sounded forward. General J. M. Corse led the center along the ridge; M. L. Smith commanded the left, as he had done the day before, and J. M. Loomis the right, supported by two reserve brigades of J. E. Smith. General Howard had reported to Sherman early in the day with the Eleventh Corps, and had been posted on the left. Baird also, who had been feeling Chattanooga Creek early in the morning, was ordered to report to Sherman, and hurried to the left, only to be told that he was not needed, and returned to take his place between the point where Sherman's battle was going on and the left of T. J. Wood's division, which was standing under orders in front of Missionary Ridge.

There is but little to be said of the morning's work, except that both armies fought with the greatest possible gallantry and determination, without seriously damaging either side. From early noon until three o'clock, Sherman was expecting a coöperative movement on the part of Thomas, and as often as the imperative demands of the work before him gave him an instant of leisure, he looked anxiously to his right for the opening of the battle in that direction; but "an occasional shot," he says, "from Fort Wood and Orchard Knob, and some musketry-fire and artillery over about Lookout, was all that I could detect on our side; but about 3 P.M. I noticed the white line of musketry-fire in front of Orchard Knob, extending farther and farther right and left and on.

We could only hear a faint echo of sound, but enough was seen to satisfy me that General Thomas was at last moving on the center." But night had fallen on his gallant but unavailing struggle before he heard of the exploit of the Army of the Cumberland, which will remain forever immortal in our annals.

The short afternoon was rapidly waning. Grant and his principal generals were waiting upon Orchard Knob for news of such decisive success from Sherman as to justify the coöperating movement on the part of Thomas which had been ordered, and also for tidings that Hooker had descended from the slope of Lookout, and had made his expected attack on the left flank of the enemy at Rossville. But Sherman, as we have seen, had met with unexpected obstacles; and though the greater part of the Union army was under his orders, they had not been able to make head against the heavy masses of Confederate infantry, and the formidable works which he found springing up, as if by magic, in his path; while Hooker had also been detained several hours in the passage of Chattanooga Creek. But he had at length got his forces across that stream, and was even now, by a rapid and skillful movement on each side of the gap, driving the enemy from their works (the same, by the way, which Rosecrans had thrown up to defend his retreat from Chickamauga), and was striking the heavy blows which were soon to force the Confederate left in upon the center.

This, however, was not yet known to Grant, and the absence of tidings gave him some anxiety. At last, concluding that Hooker must from the nature of the case have already made his way to Rossville, he gave orders for Thomas's advance. Baird had by this time got into position on the left of Wood, and the Union line stretched in martial array from left to right in this order: Baird, Wood, and Sheridan, each with three brigades, and Johnson far on the right, his two brigades slightly refused. They had stood there all day, like well-bred hounds straining at the leash, excited and restless at their apparent inaction, while the sound of furious battle, coming from the left, showed how their comrades were striving. At a distance varying from four to nine hundred yards in their front was the first line of the enemy's intrenchments; from there the slope of Missionary Ridge ran up nine hundred yards to the crest, bristling with batteries and protected by rifle-pits, while half way up this steep ascent was another imperfect line of works. Their orders were to take the first line of rifle-pits, there to halt and re-form. As firmly and steadily as if upon holiday drill this magnificent line of veterans passed through the intervening wood, and arriving at the open ground beyond broke into double-quick, and rushed at full speed upon the Confederate intrenchments. Sheridan, who was in advance of his division, looked back at this serried line of waving and glittering steel behind him, and felt from that moment that nothing could withstand a rush of arms so terrible and imposing.

The Confederates threw themselves flat in their trenches, and the Union troops rushed over and beyond them. A thousand prisoners were sent to the rear, crouching before the rain of metal their own batteries were flinging upon both armies from the crest. Here, according to orders, the whole force should have halted; but a spirit had been raised in that long line of brave men that no order could hold in check. The position was, in fact, untenable; the rifle-pits they had taken were commanded in every nook and corner by the blazing batteries above; to stay there was useless slaughter, to give way in the spirit that then animated the troops was impossible. One by one, without orders, the color-bearers rushed to the front and the men followed. Sheridan and others sent back for orders to take the crest; they came in such contradictory shape that a moment's confusion resulted. Wagner's brigade, with superb obedience, marched back to the rifle-pits and held their places for a little while with terrible loss; but the delay lasted only a few minutes. In the heat of valorous expectation, and a certain prescience of victory that spread over the whole line, the orders of the morning passed out of view; and the officers, from the commanders of corps to the last corporal, gave, by common consent, the word to go forward. Captain Avery came to Sheridan from Granger with permission to go to the crest, if he could do so. Sheridan asked the aide-de-camp for his flask, and raising it towards the crest of the ridge, where Bragg's headquarters were visible, he bowed and drank to his adversary with the frontier salutation, "How," and dashed forward with his men up the precipitous slope of the mountain.

This continent has never beheld a scene of such grandeur as that which followed. The whole army was swept forward by an irresistible impulse. In each brigade and regiment little attention was paid to lines of formation. The color-bearers sprang forward first, a few of the strongest men gathered immediately about them, and groups of soldiers, which a spectator describes as looking from a distance like inverted "V's," began climbing the mountain at every point. And yet so homogeneous was the spirit of daring and patriotism in every division that, taken as a whole, the entire mass went up the hill together. Several times, out of breath with the furious rush, they dropped panting upon the mountain-side for a moment's rest, and the enemy at the top of the hill thought they were repulsed; but still the blue line went up, gaining ground every moment, under the frightful fire of grape and canister from the batteries, and the incessant hail of musketry from the rifle-pits.

The commanders on Orchard Knob watched the movement with intense concern. When the troops broke away from the enemy's first line of rifle-pits, Grant turned to Thomas and said: "By whose orders is this?" Thomas, who knew his soldiers, said with his imperturbable smile: "By their own, I fancy"; but still, as the soldiers drew nearer and nearer to the summit, the anxiety increased every instant, and when at last the blue line reached the last range of rifle-pits near the crest, General W. F. Smith says that he turned away his face in the intolerable suspense, until the cheer that filled the whole valley with its echoes showed that the victory was won. The troops poured over the top of the ridge like the crest of a breaking wave, without firing a shot. They captured a large number of the rebels in the rifle-pits, driving the rest in panic across the narrow plateau, seizing the guns and turning their enfilading fire against their late owners. So sudden and so overwhelming was the rush, so ineffectual against the spirit of the Union soldiers had been the rain of fire and lead as they swept up the mountain-side, that no impulse of fight seemed to be left in the Confederates when they reached the summit. The labor of that strenuous climb up a slope of nearly one thousand yards must have exhausted the attacking force, so as to render them an easy prey to the fresh troops on the summit if they had shown any enterprise; but all accounts agree that, once up, they met with no resistance.

General Bragg himself who, by some strange hallucination the moment before, had imagined the enemy repulsed, and who was riding along the crest swinging his hat in triumph and congratulating his troops, suddenly heard that Wood's men had broken the line behind him and were crowning the ridge. Thinking this but a local misfortune, he sent General Bate to repair it, and at the same moment he heard that his left had given way at the point where Sheridan, mounting his short person upon a captured cannon, to make himself seen, in the confusion, was ordering a hot pursuit of the flying enemy. Hardee, on the extreme Confederate right, still, and for some time afterwards, held his own with energy, as well against Sheridan as with the division of Baird, which, after gaining the crest, had wheeled to the north and attacked the rebel right; but, says General Bragg himself, "all to the left . . . was entirely routed and in rapid flight, nearly all the artillery having been shamefully abandoned by its infantry support. Every effort which could be made by myself and staff and by many other mounted officers availed but little. A panic which I had never before witnessed seemed to have seized upon officers and men, and each seemed to be struggling for his personal safety regardless of his duty or his character."

Meanwhile General Hooker was advancing on the left. Osterhaus took the road to the east of the ridge, Geary that to the left, while Cruft pushed along the crest. After the first break at the gap little effective resistance was made. The three divisions pushed rapidly along, driving the huddled Confederates before them till, reaching the scene of the greater battle, they rushed into the arms of R. W. Johnson's division of the Fourteenth Corps, and large numbers were captured.

Seeing the victory won, General Grant spurred his horse from Orchard Knob and soon gained the crest intent upon pursuit; but even before his arrival the keen eye of Sheridan had marked in the valley below a crowd of fugitives with trains and artillery which excited his martial cupidity. He ordered Wagner and Harker to press the rear-guard and capture the trains if possible. They marched rapidly forward, gathering in many guns and wagons. A mile beyond the battlefield the road ran over a high and formidable ridge, upon which the enemy made a determined stand with a heavy force of infantry and several batteries. Sheridan, with Harker, Wagner, and Colonel Wood, in spite of the fatigue of his soldiers, here made another spirited attack, the men climbing and clinging to the face of the hill as they had done in the afternoon on Missionary Ridge. Holding the enemy in front, Sheridan sent a part of Harker's brigade to the right—and he pauses in his report at this point to draw an exquisite picture of a rare and beautiful scene—a nocturne in blue and silver. "But a few moments elapsed ere the Twenty-sixth Ohio and the Fifteenth Indiana carried the crest. When the head of the column reached the summit of the hill the moon rose from behind, and a medallion view of the column was disclosed as it crossed the moon's disk and attacked the enemy, who, outflanked on the left and right, fled, leaving two pieces of artillery and many wagons."

The enemy abandoned his position near the railroad tunnel in front of Sherman about midnight, and on the morning of the 26th Sherman advanced by way of Chickamauga Station, and Thomas's force under Hooker and Palmer moved out in pursuit on the Rossville road in the direction of Ringgold. At that point they found the enemy's rear-guard, under Cleburne, in a strong position, well defended by artillery, in a narrow gorge, and on the slopes of the hill on either side of it. A spirited action here took place, in which Hooker's column fought at a great disadvantage on account of his entire lack of artillery. When his guns came up, however, Hooker succeeded in dislodging Cleburne and continued in pursuit as far as Tunnel Hill, some twenty miles from Chattanooga, where Grant ordered it to cease. Howard's corps was sent forward to Red Clay to break up the railroad between Dalton and Cleveland, thus cutting off Bragg's communication with Longstreet. General Grant says it was only the imperative necessity of relieving Burnside which prevented him from pursuing the retreating enemy as long as he could find supplies in the country; but his last advice having been that Burnside could probably hold out no longer than the 3d of December, he called back his victorious columns from pursuit and ordered Sherman to take Granger's corps, and with that and his own to proceed immediately to the rescue of Knoxville.

So great a success was not to be obtained without serious loss. Only fifty-five minutes elapsed from the time the National soldiers left their positions until they poured over the crest of the ridge, but every step of the way cost valuable lives. In this charge and in the smaller engagements Sheridan lost 1346, of whom 121 were officers; Wood 1035, of whom 72 bore commissions; Johnson on the right had the easiest task, though he lost 304; and Baird, who was favored by the ground in front of him, lost 566, including 39 officers, among whom was the gallant Colonel Edward H. Phelps, commanding the brigade on the extreme left of the line, who fell in the moment of victory after the heights were gained. The Union loss in the battle of Chattanooga aggregated 753 killéd, 4722 wounded, and 349 captured or missing: a total of 5824. The enemy's loss in killed and wounded was far less, as he fought almost entirely behind intrenchments; General Bragg in his official report is prevented by his grief and disgust from entering into details. He admits a large loss of prisoners and stragglers, and of forty guns. Grant reported the capture of 6142 prisoners, 239 of whom were commissioned officers. Bragg's losses at Chattanooga were 361 killed, 2180 wounded, 4146 captured or missing: in all 6687. The disparity in numbers engaged was not so great as Bragg claims, and such as it was he had only himself, or Mr. Davis, to thank for it. Grant had about 60,000 men, and Bragg some 20,000 less; if the latter had had on Missionary Ridge the force which Longstreet took off on his wild-goose chase to Knoxville, he would have had superior numbers as well as his vast advantage of position. Grant always thought that the sudden disappearance of Sherman's army, behind the hills north of Chattanooga, deluded Bragg into the belief that Sherman had gone on to the help of Burnside and that his feeble and irresolute tactics had their rise in that impression.

Bragg, when he made his official report, five days after the battle, was still suffering an agony of rage and shame. He spoke frankly of "the panic," and "the shameful conduct" of his troops. "The position," he says, "was one which ought to have been held by a line of skirmishers against any assaulting column, and wherever resistance was made the enemy fled in disorder after suffering heavy loss. Those who reached the ridge did so in a condition of exhaustion, from the great physical exertion in climbing, which rendered them powerless, and the slightest effort would have destroyed them. . . . Had all parts of the line been maintained with equal gallantry and persistence, no enemy could ever have dislodged us." He had but one explanation to give for a "disaster and disgrace" otherwise inexplicable, and that is wholly insufficient. He says his troops "had for two days confronted the enemy, marshaling his immense forces in plain view, and exhibiting to their sight such a superiority in numbers as may have intimidated weak minds and untried soldiers; but our veterans had so often encountered similar hosts, when the strength of position was against us, and with perfect success, that not a doubt crossed my mind."

There is nothing so potent or so inexplicable as that mysterious essence called the morale of an army. The spirit which informed the Army of the Cumberland on the afternoon of the 25th of November, and which rendered it impossible for its generals to hold it back, made it irresistible. Officers and men were swept up the rugged face of the mountain as if by some divine fury of purpose. They faced the fiery rain of death as if it had been a summer shower, though the Fourth Corps was twice decimated before it reached the summit. General Bragg was too severe on his soldiers. They did all they could be asked to do; they shot one in five of their assailants in that few minutes' breathless rush. They were beaten, and they felt it instinctively; they were barely holding their own on their right against Sherman's heavy battalions; Hooker, they knew, had defeated them on the left and was even now thundering upon their flank; and when they saw Thomas's splendid army swarming upon them from the plain, and apparently caring no more for their deadliest volleys than if they were snow-flakes, it is no wonder that their hearts failed, and that they gave up the fight, when the Army of the Cumberland poured over their trenches.

Grant General-in-Chief

Immediately after the victories at Chattanooga Mr. Washburne of Illinois, the devoted friend and firm supporter of General Grant through good and evil report, introduced a bill in Congress to revive the grade of lieutenant-general in the army. The measure occasioned a good deal of discussion. This high rank had never been conferred on any citizen of the republic except Washington, who held it for a short time before his death. It was discontinued for more than half a century and then conferred by brevet only upon General Scott. There were those who feared, or affected to fear, that so high military rank was threatening to the liberties of the republic. The great majority of Congress, however, considered the liberties of the republic more robust than this fear would indicate, and the bill was finally passed on the 26th of February, and received the approval of the President on the 29th of February. It provided for the revival of the grade of lieutenant-general, and authorized the President "to appoint, by and with the advice and consent of the Senate, a lieutenant-general, to be selected from among those officers in the military service of the United States not below the grade of major-general, most distinguished for courage, skill, and ability, who, being commissioned as lieutenant-general, may be authorized, under the direction and during the pleasure of the President, to command the armies of the United States." Immediately upon signing the bill the President nominated Grant to the Senate for the office created by it.

Although the bill, of course, mentioned the name of no general, there was no pretense from the beginning that any one else was thought of in connection with the place. The Administration exercised no influence in the matter, neither help-

ing nor hindering the progress of the bill through the Houses
of Congress. It had already become clearly manifest that
General Halleck, although an officer of great learning and
ability, was not fitted by character or temperament for the assumption of such weighty responsibilities as the military situation required. The President himself said about this time:
"When it appeared that McClellan was incompetent to the
work of handling the army and we sent for Halleck to take
command, he stipulated that it should be with the full powers
and responsibilities of general-in-chief. He kept that attitude until Pope's defeat, but ever since that event he has
shrunk from responsibility whenever it was possible."   So
that in the mind of the President, as well as in the intention of Congress and the acquiescence of the public, there
was no thought of nominating any one but Grant to the chief
command of all the armies. Whether he was or was not the
ablest of all our generals is a question which can never be decided; perhaps there were legionaries in the army of Gaul as
able as Cæsar if occasion had been given them to show it. The
success and fame of generals is the joint result of merit and of
opportunity; and Grant was, beyond all comparison, the most
fortunate of American soldiers. Whatever criticism might be
made on his character, his learning, or his methods, the fact was
not to be denied that he had reaped the most substantial successes of the war; he had captured two armies and utterly defeated a third; he was justly entitled, by virtue of the *spolia
opima* with which he had presented the republic, to his triumph,
to be celebrated with all the pomp and circumstance possible.

The Senate immediately confirmed his nomination, and on
the 3d of March the Secretary of War directed him to report
in person to the War Department as early as practicable, considering the condition of his command. He started for Washington the next day, but in the midst of his hurried preparations
for departure he found time to write a letter of the most warm
and generous friendship to Sherman. He had not even yet

heard the news of his confirmation, but he took it for granted. He said:

I start in the morning to comply with the order, but I shall say very distinctly on my arrival there that I shall accept no appointment which will require me to make that city [Washington] my headquarters. . . . While I have been eminently successful in this war, in at least gaining the confidence of the public, no one feels more than I how much of this success is due to the energy, skill, and the harmonious putting forth of that energy and skill, of those whom it has been my good fortune to have occupying subordinate positions under me. There are many officers to whom these remarks are applicable to a greater or less degree, proportionate to their ability as soldiers, but what I want is to express my thanks to you and McPherson as the men to whom, above all others, I feel indebted for whatever I have had of success. How far your advice and suggestions have been of assistance you know. How far your execution of whatever has been given you to do entitles you to the reward I am receiving you cannot know as well as I do. I feel all the gratitude this letter would express, giving it the most flattering construction. the word you I use in the plural, intending it for McPherson also.

This letter was as unique as it was admirable, for Grant wrote in this strain to no one else in the world. There seemed no room in his heart for more than two such friends. When McPherson died in the flower of his young manhood, Sheridan took the vacant place in the confidence and affection of his great chief where he and Sherman remained ever after without rivals. Sherman, who received the letter on his way up the river from the Meridian raid, answered in a similar strain with even more of ardent and liberal eulogy:

You do yourself injustice and us too much honor in assigning to us so large a share of the merits which have led to your high advancement. . . . You are now Washington's legitimate successor and occupy a position of almost dangerous elevation; but if you can continue as heretofore to be yourself, simple, honest, and unpretending, you will enjoy through life the respect and love of friends, and the homage of millions of human beings who

will award to you a large share for securing to them and their
descendants a government of law and stability. I repeat you do
General McPherson and myself too much honor. At Belmont,
you manifested your traits, neither of us being near; at Donelson also you illustrated your whole character. I was not near,
and General McPherson in too subordinate a capacity to influence you. . . . I believe you are as brave, patriotic, and just as
the great prototype Washington; as unselfish, kindhearted, and
honest as a man should be; but the chief characteristic in your
nature is the simple faith in success you have always manifested, which I can liken to nothing else than the faith a Christian has in his Saviour. This faith gave you victory at Shiloh
and Vicksburg. Also, when you have completed your best preparations, you go into battle without hesitation, as at Chattanooga
—no doubts, no reserve; and I tell you that it was this that made
us act with confidence. I knew, wherever I was, that you thought
of me, and if I got in a tight place you would come, if alive. . . .
Now as to the future. Do not stay in Washington. Halleck is
better qualified than you are to stand the buffets of intrigue
and policy. Come out West; take to yourself the whole Mississippi Valley, let us make it dead-sure, and I tell you the Atlantic
slope and Pacific shores will follow its destiny, as sure as the
limbs of a tree live or die with the main trunk. We have done
much; still much remains to be done. Time and time's influences
are all with us; we could almost afford to sit still and let these
influences work. Even in the seceded States your word now
would go further than a President's proclamation or an act of
Congress. For God's sake and for your country's sake, come
out of Washington. I foretold to General Halleck before he left
Corinth the inevitable result to him, and I now exhort you to
come out West. Here lies the seat of the coming empire; and
from the West, when our task is done, we will make short work
of Charleston and Richmond, and the impoverished coast of the
Atlantic.

In both of these letters there is apparent a not very intelligent
dread of Washington and its political influences; something of
the feeling which sailors have towards lawyers. Grant assures
Sherman beforehand that he shall not accept his new grade if
he is compelled to make his headquarters in Washington, and
Sherman adjures him by all that is sacred to avoid the Atlantic
coast altogether. It evidently did not enter the minds of either

that the loftiest honors and no small degree of enjoyment awaited both of them in years to come in the city which they regarded with such superstitious apprehensions.

Grant proceeded on his way to the capital as quietly as possible, but the rumors of his coming went everywhere before him, and his train moved through a continual storm of cheering and enthusiasm from Nashville to Washington. He reached there on the evening of the 8th of March. There was to be a reception at the Executive Mansion and, as Grant's arrival was expected, the throng was very great. At about half-past nine Grant entered, and he and the President met for the first time. A certain movement and rumor in the crowd heralded the approach of the most famous guest of the evening, and when General Grant stood before Mr. Lincoln they recognized each other without formal presentation, and cordially shook hands. The thronging crowd with instinctive deference stood back for a moment, while the President and the general exchanged a few words of conversation. Lincoln then introduced Seward to Grant, and the Secretary of State took him away to present him to Mrs. Lincoln. He then went on to the East Room, where his presence excited a feeling which burst the bonds of etiquette, and cheer after cheer rose from the assembled crowd. Hot and blushing with embarrassment he was forced to mount a sofa from which he could shake hands with the eager admirers who rushed upon him from all sides of the great room.

It was an hour before he could return to the small drawing-room, where, after the departure of the crowd, the President awaited him. The President here made an appointment with him for the formal presentation next day of his commission as lieutenant-general. "I shall make a very short speech to you," said Lincoln, "to which I desire you to reply, for an object; and that you may be properly prepared to do so I have written what I shall say, only four sentences in all, which I will read from my manuscript as an example which you may follow and also read your reply—as you are perhaps not so much accustomed to public speaking as I am; and I therefore give you what

I shall say so that you may consider it. There are two points that I would like to have you make in your answer: First, to say something which shall prevent or obviate any jealousy of you from any of the other generals in the service; and second, something which shall put you on as good terms as possible with the Army of the Potomac. If you see any objection to doing this, be under no restraint whatever in expressing that objection to the Secretary of War."

General Grant and Mr. Stanton left the room together. The next day, at one o'clock, in presence of the Cabinet, General Halleck, two members of Grant's staff, and the President's private secretary, the commission of lieutenant-general was formally delivered by the President. Mr. Lincoln said: "General Grant, the nation's appreciation of what you have done, and its reliance upon you for what remains to do in the existing great struggle, are now presented, with this commission constituting you Lieutenant-General in the Army of the United States. With this high honor devolves upon you, also, a corresponding responsibility. As the country herein trusts you, so, under God, it will sustain you. I scarcely need to add that with what I here speak for the nation, goes my own hearty personal concurrence." The general had hurriedly and almost illegibly written his speech on half of a sheet of note paper in lead pencil. His embarrassment was evident and extreme; he found his own writing very difficult to read; but what he said could hardly have been improved: "Mr. President, I accept this commission with gratitude for the high honor conferred. With the aid of the noble armies that have fought on so many fields for our common country, it will be my earnest endeavor not to disappoint your expectations. I feel the full weight of the responsibilities now devolving on me; and I know that if they are met, it will be due to those armies, and above all to the favor of that Providence which leads both nations and men." It will be observed that he made no reference whatever to the subject of the President's request the night before. It is not known whether he did this after consultation with Stanton or whether, with his deep distrust of Washington politicians, he thought it wise to begin by disregarding all their suggestions.

On the same day General Halleck sent a letter to the Secretary of War, respectfully requesting that since the grade of lieutenant-general, superior to his own, had been created, and the distinguished officer promoted to that rank had received his commission and reported for duty, that orders might be issued placing him in command of the army and relieving General Halleck from that duty. "In making this request," he says, "I am influenced solely by a desire to conform to the provisions of the law which, in my opinion, impose upon a lieutenant-general the duties and responsibilities of general-in-chief of the army."

After the presentation of the commission a brief conversation took place. General Grant inquired what special service was expected of him. The President replied that the country wanted him to take Richmond; he said our generals had not been fortunate in their efforts in that direction and asked if the Lieutenant-General could do it. Grant, without hesitation, answered that he could if he had the troops. These the President assured him he should have. There was not one word said as to what route to Richmond should be chosen.

The next day Grant visited General Meade at the headquarters of the Army of the Potomac at Brandy Station. He had known General Meade slightly in the Mexican war, but had not met him since. He was a stranger to the Army of the Potomac with the exception of a few officers of the regular army whom he had known in Mexico. Meade received him not only with the courtesy and deference due to his high rank and great services, but with a generosity and magnanimity which impressed Grant most favorably. Meade said that it was possible Grant might want an officer to command the Army of the Potomac who had been with him in the West, and made especial mention of Sherman. He begged him that if that was the case not to hesitate about making the change. "He urged," says Grant, "that the work before us was of such vast importance to the whole nation that the feelings or wishes of no one person should stand in the way of selecting the right men for all positions. For himself, he would serve to the best of his ability wherever placed." Grant assured him that he had no thought of making any change; and that Sherman could not be spared from the West. He returned to Washington on the 11th.

The next day he was placed in command of all the armies by orders from the War Department; but without waiting for a single day to accept the lavish proffers of hospitality which were showered upon him, he started West again on the evening of the 11th of March. In that short time he had utterly changed his views and plans for the future conduct of the war. He had relinquished the purpose he had hitherto firmly held of leading the Western armies on the great campaign to Atlanta and the sea, and had decided to take the field with the Army of the Potomac. "When I got to Washington," he said, "and saw the situation, it was plain that here was the point for the commanding general to be. No one else could probably resist the pressure that would be brought to bear upon him to desist from his own plans and pursue others." He, therefore, hurried back to the West to make preparations for finally severing his relations with those magnificent armies which had gained him so many victories. Sherman at his request was promoted to command the Military Division of the Mississippi, McPherson succeeded to Sherman's command of the Department of the Tennessee, and Logan was promoted to the command of McPherson's corps.

EVEN IN THE MIDST *of bloody and bitter civil war there was no thought of suspending the democratic process. The presidential election would take place in 1864, as usual. (The South faced no such necessity. The Confederate Constitution gave the president a six-year term.)*

Nicolay and Hay cover the nominating convention, summoned in the name of the National Union party, a designation which Republicans hoped would attract a substantial number of War Democrats.

Lincoln Renominated

IN other chapters we have mentioned the unavailing efforts made by a few politicians to defeat the will of the people which everywhere demanded the renomination of Mr. Lincoln. These efforts were worth studying as manifestations of eccentric human nature, but they never had the least effect upon the great currents of public opinion. Death alone could have prevented the choice of Mr. Lincoln by the Union Convention. So absolute and universal was this tendency that most of the politicians made no effort to direct or guide it; they simply exerted themselves to keep in the van and not be overwhelmed. The Convention was to meet on the 7th of June, but the irregular nominations of the President began at the feast of the Epiphany. The first convention of the year was held in New Hampshire on the 6th of January—for the nomination of State officers. It had properly no concern with the National nominations. The Convention consisted in great part of the friends of Mr. Chase, and those employees of the Treasury Department whose homes were in New Hampshire had come together determined to smother any mistimed demonstration for the President; but the first mention of his name set the assembly on fire, and before the chairman knew what he was doing the Convention had declared in favor of the renomination of Lincoln.

The same day a far more important demonstration came to

the surface in Pennsylvania. The State Legislature met on the 5th of January, and the following day a paper, prepared in advance, addressed to the President, requesting him to accept a second term of the Presidency, began to be circulated among the Union members. Not one to whom it was presented declined to sign it. Within a day or two it received the signature of every Union member of the Senate and the Assembly of Pennsylvania, and Simon Cameron, transmitting it to the President on the 14th of January, could say:

"You are now fairly launched on your second voyage, and of its success I am as confident as ever I was of anything in my life. Providence has decreed your reëlection, and no combination of the wicked can prevent it."

This remarkable address began by congratulating the President upon the successes of the recent election, which were generously ascribed to the policy of his Administration. Referring to the Republican victory in their own State, the members of the Legislature said: "If the voice of Pennsylvania became thus potential in indorsing the policy of your Administration, we consider that, as the representatives of those who have so completely indorsed your official course, we are only responding to their demands when we thus publicly announce our unshaken preference for your reëlection to the Presidency in 1864." This preference was justified by them purely on public grounds.

To make a change in the Administration until its authority has been fully reëstablished in the revolted States would be to give the enemies of the Government abroad a pretext for asserting that the Government had failed at home. To change the policy in operation to crush rebellion and restore the land to peace would be to afford the traitors in arms time to gather new strength—if not for immediate victory, at least for ultimate success in their efforts permanently to dissolve the Union. . . . We do not make this communication at this time to elicit from you any expression of opinion on this subject. Having confidence in your patriotism, we believe that you will abide the decision of the friends of the Union, and yield consent to any honorable use which they may deem proper to make of your name in order to secure the greatest good to the country and the speediest success to our arms. . . . Expressing what we feel to be the language not only of our own constituents, but also of the people of all the loyal States, we claim to indulge the expectation that you will yield to the preference which has already made you the people's candidate for the Presidency in 1864.

In every gathering of the supporters of the Union the same irrepressible sentiment broke forth. The "New-York Times" on the 15th of January clearly expressed the general feeling: "The same wise policy which would forbid a man of business in troublous times to change his agent of proved efficiency, impels the loyal people of our country to continue President Lincoln in his responsible position; and against the confirmed will of the people politicians are powerless."

The sentiment was so potent in its pressure upon the politicians that they everywhere gave way and broke into premature indorsement of the nomination. The Union Central Committee of New York held a special meeting, and unanimously recommended the renomination of the President. Senator Morgan, sending this news to Mr. Lincoln, added: "It is going to be difficult to restrain the boys, and there is not much use in trying to do so."

At a local election some of the ward tickets were headed, with an irrelevancy which showed the spirit of the hour, "For President of the United States in 1864, Abraham Lincoln."

From one end to the other of the country these spontaneous nominations joyously echoed one another. Towards the close of January the Radical Legislature of Kansas, with but one dissenting voice, passed through both its houses a resolution renominating Lincoln. All through the next month these demonstrations continued. The Union members of the New Jersey Legislature united in an address to the President, saying: "Without any disparagement of the true men who surround you, and whose counsel you have shared, believing that you are the choice of the people, whose servants we are, and firmly satisfied that they desire and intend to give you four years for a policy of peace, we present your name as the man for President of the American people, in 1864."

Connecticut instructed her delegates by resolutions on the 17th of February; Maryland, Minnesota, and Colorado expressed in the same way the sentiment of their people. Wisconsin and Indiana made haste to range themselves with the other Northern States; and Ohio seized the opportunity to put a stop to the restless ambition of her favorite son by a resolution of the Republican members of the Legislature declaring that "the people of Ohio, and her soldiers in the field, demand the renomination of Abraham Lincoln to the Presidency"—the members rising to their feet and cheering with uncontrollable clamor when the resolution passed. The State of Maine, on the extreme eastern border, spoke next. Early in March the President received this dispatch, signed by a name afterwards illustrious in our political annals: "Both branches of the Maine Legislature have this day adopted resolutions cordially recommending your renomination. Every Union member voted in favor of them. Maine is a unit for you.—James G. Blaine."

Nowhere except in the State of Missouri was the name of Mr. Lincoln mentioned without overwhelming adhesion, and even in the Missouri Assembly the resolution in favor of his renomination was laid upon the table by a majority of only eight. There had been some anxiety on the part of Mr. Lincoln's friends lest the powerful secret organization called the Union League, which represented the most ardent and vehement Republican sentiment of the country, should fall into the hands of his opponents; but it was speedily seen that out of Missouri these apprehensions were groundless. The Union Leagues of New York, Illinois, and even Vicksburg, where the victory of Grant had allowed the development of a robust Union sentiment, were among the first to declare for the President. The Union League Club in Philadelphia, powerful in wealth, intelligence, and personal influence, so early as the 11th of January had resolved that to the "prudence, sagacity, comprehension,

and perseverance of Mr. Lincoln, under the guidance of a be-
nign Providence, the nation is more indebted for the grand results of the war, which Southern rebels have wickedly waged
against liberty and the Union, than to any other single instru-
mentality; and that he is justly entitled to whatever reward it is
in the power of the nation to bestow." They declared also:
"That as Mr. Lincoln has had to endure the largest share of the
labor required to suppress the Rebellion, now rapidly verging
to its close, he should also enjoy the largest share of the honors
which await those who have contended for the right. They therefore recognize with pleasure the unmistakable indications of the
popular will in all the loyal States, and heartily join with their
fellow-citizens, without any distinction of party, here and elsewhere, in presenting him as the people's candidate for the Presidency."

The current swept on irresistibly throughout the months of
spring. A few opponents of Mr. Lincoln, seeing that he would
be nominated the moment the Convention should meet, made
one last effort to postpone the meeting of the Convention until
September, knowing that their only reliance was in some possible accident of the summer. So earnest and important a
Republican as William Cullen Bryant united with a self-consti-
tuted committee of others equally earnest, but not so important, to induce the National Committee to postpone the Convention. In their opinion the country was not now in a position
to enter into a Presidential contest; it was clear to them that no
nomination could be made with any unanimity so early as June.
They thought it best to see what the result of the summer campaign would be, as the wish of the people to continue their present leaders in power would depend very much upon this. The
committee, of course, took no notice of this appeal, though it
was favored by so strong a Republican authority as the "New
York Tribune." The National Committee wisely thought that
they might with as much reason take into consideration the
request of a committee of prominent citizens to check an impending thunder-storm. All the movements in opposition to Mr.

Lincoln were marked with the same naïveté and futility. The secret circular of Senator Pomeroy, the farcical Cleveland Convention, the attempt of Mr. Bryant's committee to postpone the Baltimore Convention, were all equally feeble and nugatory in their effect.

Mr. Lincoln took no measures whatever to promote his candidacy. It is true he did not, like other candidates, assume airs of reluctance or bashfulness. While he discouraged on the part of strangers any suggestions as to his reëlection, among his friends he made no secret of his readiness to continue the work he was engaged in, if such should seem to be the general wish. In a private letter to Elihu B. Washburne, he said: "A second term would be a great honor and a great labor, which together perhaps I would not decline if tendered." To another Congressman he is reported to have said: "I do not desire a renomination, except for the reason that such action on the part of the Republican party would be the most emphatic indorsement which could be given to the policy of my Administration." We have already mentioned the equanimity with which he treated the efforts of a leading member of his Cabinet to supplant him, and he received in the same manner the frequent suggestions of apprehensive friends that he would do well to beware of Grant. His usual reply was: "If he takes Richmond, let him have it." In reality, General Grant was never at any time a competitor for the nomination. Of course, after the battle of Missionary Ridge there was no lack of such suggestions on the part of those who surrounded the victorious general; but he positively refused to put himself in the lists or to give any sanction to the use of his name.

The President constantly discouraged on the part of officeholders of the Government, civil or military, any especial eagerness in his behalf. General Schurz wrote, late in February, asking permission to take an active part in the Presidential canvass, to which Mr. Lincoln replied: "Allow me to suggest that if you wish to remain in the military service, it is very dangerous for you to get temporarily out of it; because, with a major-

general once out, it is next to impossible for even the President
to get him in again. With my appreciation of your ability and
correct principle, of course I would be very glad to have your
service for the country in the approaching political canvass; but
I fear we cannot properly have it without separating you from
the military." And in a subsequent letter addressed to the same
general, he said: "I perceive no objection to your making a political speech when you are where one is to be made; but quite
surely speaking in the North and fighting in the South at the
same time are not possible; nor could I be justified to detail
any officer to the political campaign during its continuance and
then return him to the army."

The experience of a hundred years of our politics has shown
what perils environ a Presidential candidate who makes
speeches. The temptation to flatter the immediate audience,
without regard to the ultimate effect of the words spoken, has
often proved too strong for the wariest politician to resist. Especially is a candidate in danger when confronting an audience
belonging to a special race or class. Mr. Lincoln made no mistake either in 1860 or in 1864. Even when exposed to the strongest possible temptation, the reception of an address from a
deputation of a workingmen's association, he preserved his
mental balance undisturbed. To such a committee, who approached him on the 21st of March, 1864, he replied by repeating to them the passage from his message of December, 1861,
in which the relations of labor and capital are set down with
mathematical and logical precision, illuminated by the light of
a broad humanity; and he only added to the views thus expressed the following words, than which nothing wiser or more
humane has ever been said by social economists:

None are so deeply interested to resist the present Rebellion
as the working people. Let them beware of prejudices working
disunion and hostility among themselves. The most notable
feature of a disturbance in your city last summer was the hanging of some working people by other working people. It should
never be so. The strongest bond of human sympathy, outside

of the family relation, should be one uniting all working people, of all nations and tongues and kindreds. Nor should this lead to a war upon property or the owners of property. Property is the fruit of labor, property is desirable, is a positive good in the world. That some should be rich shows that others may become rich, and hence, is just encouragement to industry and enterprise. Let not him who is houseless pull down the house of another, but let him labor diligently and build one for himself, thus by example assuring that his own shall be safe from violence when built.

The politicians who opposed Mr. Lincoln, whether from pure motives or from motives not so pure, met with one common fate: they were almost universally beaten in their own districts by men who, whatever their other incentives, were sufficiently adroit to perceive the sign in which they should conquer. It gave a man all this year a quite unfair advantage in his district to be known as a friend of the President, when his opponent was not equally outspoken; and many of the most radical politicians, seeing in which direction their advantage lay, suddenly turned upon their opponents and vanquished them in the President's name. General Lane, for example, who had been engaged in a bitter controversy with Pomeroy in regard to local interests in Kansas, saw his opportunity in the anti-Lincoln circular of his colleague; and although before this it would have been hard to say which of the two had been most free in his criticisms of the President, General Lane instantly trimmed his sails to catch the favoring breeze and elected himself and a full list of delegates to the Baltimore Convention, whom he called, in his characteristic language, "all vindictive friends of the President." Other Members of Congress, equally radical and more sincere and honest, made haste to range themselves on the side of the President against those with whom they had been more intimately associated. William D. Kelley of Philadelphia publicly proclaimed him "the wisest Radical of us all"; James M. Ashley, of Ohio, to whom one of his abolitionist constituents had objected that he wanted no more of a President who had not crushed a rebellion in four years, replied that this was unreasonable, as the Lord had not crushed the devil in a much longer time.

As the day for the meeting at Baltimore drew near, and its unanimous verdict became more and more evident, the President was besieged from every quarter of the Union with solicitations to make known his wishes in regard to the work of the Convention. To all such inquiries he returned an energetic refusal to give any word of counsel or to express any personal desire. During a few days preceding the Convention a great many delegates took the road to Washington, either to get some intimation of the President's wishes or to impress their own faces and names on his expectant mind. They were all welcomed with genial and cordial courtesy, but received not the slightest intimation of what would be agreeable to him. The most powerful politicians from New York and Pennsylvania were listened to with no more confidential consideration than the shy and awkward representatives of the rebellious States, who had elected themselves in sutlers' tents and in the shadow of department headquarters. "What is that crowd of people in the hall?" he asked one day of his secretary. "It is a delegation from South Carolina. They are a swindle." "Let them in," said Lincoln; "they will not swindle me."

When at last the Convention came together on the 7th of June, 1864, it had less to do than any other convention in our political history. The delegates were bound by a peremptory mandate. John W. Forney, the editor of the "Philadelphia Press," in an article printed the day before the meeting, put forth with unusual candor the attitude of the Convention towards its constituents. The permanent policy of the Republican party of the nation was already absolutely established by the acts of the President and accepted and ratified by Congress and the people. "For this reason," said Mr. Forney, "it is less important as a political body, as it cannot originate but will simply republish a policy. Yet for this reason it is transcendently the more imposing in its expression of the national will. Nor has the Convention a candidate to choose. Choice is forbidden it by the previous action of the people. It is a body which almost beyond parallel is directly responsible to the people, and little more than the instrument of their will. Mr. Lincoln is already renominated, and the Convention will but formally announce the decision of the people. If this absence of independence lessens the mere political interest of the Convention in one respect, the fact that it will thoroughly and unquestionably obey national instructions gives it higher importance."

These words represented the well-nigh universal sentiment among Republicans. There were, of course, those to whom such a sentiment was not agreeable. Horace Greeley found it hard to accept an opinion which ran counter to his personal views. In an article of the same date as that last quoted, although he admitted the predestined action of the Convention, he still protested vehemently against the impolicy of such action. He quoted the message sent by Mr. Lincoln to Governor Seymour in the dark winter of 1862-63, "that if he wants to be President of the United States, he must take care that there shall be a United States."

"We could wish," he said, "the Presidency utterly forgotten or ignored for the next two months, while every impulse, every effort of the loyal millions should be directed toward the overthrow of the armed hosts of the Rebellion. That effected, or its speedy accomplishment proved impossible, we should be ready to enter clear-sightedly on the Presidential canvass. Now we are not. We feel that the expected nomination, if made at this time, exposes the Union party to a dangerous 'flank movement'—possibly a successful one."

Among the Democratic newspapers a still more blind and obstinate disinclination to accept the existing facts was seen up to the hour of the meeting of the Convention. They still insisted that the nomination of Mr. Lincoln was in the highest degree doubtful; some pretended that the delegates were equally divided between Lincoln and Grant; others insisted that the nomination of Frémont at Cleveland had electrified the country and would probably carry the Convention by storm.

The Convention was opened by a brief speech from Senator Morgan of New York, who was chairman of the executive committee. It contained one significant sentence. He said the party of which they were the delegates and honored representatives would fall short of accomplishing its great mission unless among its other resolves it should declare for such amendment of the Constitution as would positively prohibit African slavery in the United States. The sentence was greeted with prolonged applause, which burst at last into three cheers, in the midst of which Governor Morgan announced the choice by the National Committee of the Rev. Dr. Robert J. Breckinridge of Kentucky as temporary chairman. The venerable Kentuckian on taking the chair made a speech which, though entirely extemporaneous, was delivered with great ease and dignity, and profoundly impressed his auditors.

Disregarding the etiquette which assumes that a convention is a deliberative assembly and that its choice cannot be foretold until it is made, he calmly took it for granted at the very beginning of his remarks that the Union candidate for the Presidency was already nominated, and as soon as the tumultuous cheers which greeted his mention of the name of Abraham Lincoln had died away he turned at once to the discussion of what he considered the real business of the day—the declaration of principles. Coming from a section of the country where the Constitution had been especially reverenced in words and vehemently assailed in action, he declared that with all the outcry about our violations of the Constitution this present living generation and this present Union party are more thoroughly devoted to that Constitution than any generation that ever lived under it; but he contended also that sacred as was the Constitution the nation was not its slave. "We ought to have it distinctly understood by friends and enemies that while we love that instrument, [while] we will maintain it, and will, with undoubted certainty, put to death friend or foe who undertakes to trample it under foot; yet, beyond a doubt, we will reserve the right to alter it to suit ourselves from time to time and from generation to generation." This speech was full of brief and powerful apothegms, some of which were startling as coming from an aged theologian of an aspect equally strong and benignant. "The only enduring, the only imperishable cement of all free institutions," he said, "has been the blood of traitors. . . . It is a fearful truth, but we had as well avow it at once; and every blow you strike, and every rebel you kill, every battle you win, dreadful as it is to do it, you are adding, it may be a year, it may be ten years, it may be a century, it may be ten centuries, to the life of the Government and the freedom of your children." Though presiding over a political convention, he declared himself absolutely detached from politics. "As a Union party I will follow you to the ends of the earth, and to the gates of death. But as an Abolition party, as a Republican party, as a Whig party, as a Democratic party, as an American party I will not follow you one foot." He echoed the brief speech in which E. D. Morgan had struck the keynote. He said: "I unite myself with those who believe it [slavery] is contrary to the brightest interests of all men and of all governments, contrary to the spirit of the Christian religion, and incompatible with the natural rights of man. I join myself with those who say, Away with it forever; and I fervently pray God that the day may come when throughout the whole land every man may be as free as you are, and as capable of enjoying regulated liberty. . . . I know very well that the sentiments which I am uttering will cause me great odium in the State in which I was born, which I love, where the bones of two generations of my ancestors and some of my children are, and where very soon I shall lay my own. . . . But we have put our faces toward the way in which we intend to go, and we will go in it to the end."

In the evening the permanent organization of the Convention was effected, William Dennison of Ohio being made chairman. He, also, in a brief and eloquent speech took for granted the unanimous nomination for the Presidency of the United States "of the wise and good man whose unselfish devotion to the country, in the administration of the Government, has secured to him not only the admiration but the warmest affection of every friend of constitutional liberty"; and also, in the tone of both the speakers who had preceded him, said that the loyal people of the country expected the Convention "to declare the cause and the support of the Rebellion to be slavery, which, as well for its treasonable offenses against the Government as for its incompatibility with the rights of humanity and the permanent peace of the country, must, with the termination of the war, and as much speedier as possible, be made to cease forever in every State and Territory of the Union."

There were in fact but three tasks before the Convention. The first was to settle the status of contesting delegations from the States and Territories; the second, to agree upon the usual platform; and the third, to nominate a candidate for the Vice-Presidency. All of these questions were handled skillfully, and with a spirit of moderation which led to the most successful result in the canvass.

There were no questions of consequence in regard to the delegations of any of the Northern States, nor did any questions arise in regard to those from Kentucky and West Virginia, Delaware and Maryland. There were two delegations from Missouri, both making special claims of loyalty and of regularity of election. The committee on credentials decided that those styling themselves the "Radical Union" delegates should be awarded the seats. As this was the only delegation which had presented itself opposed to the nomination of Lincoln, and as a large majority, not only of the Convention, but of the committee on credentials, were of the contrary opinion, their action in admitting the recalcitrant Missourians was sagacious. It quieted at once the beginnings of what might have been a dangerous schism. The question as to admitting the delegates from Tennessee also raised some discussion, but was decided in their favor by more than a two-thirds vote. The delegates from Louisiana and Arkansas were also admitted by a vote nearly as large. The delegates from Nevada, Colorado, and Nebraska were admitted with the right to vote; those from the States of Virginia and Florida, and the remaining Territories, were admitted to the privileges of the floor without the right to vote; and those from South Carolina were rejected altogether.

The same wise spirit of compromise was shown in the platform reported by Henry J. Raymond of New York. The first resolution declared it the highest duty of every citizen to maintain the integrity of the Union and to quell the Rebellion by force of arms; the second approved the determination of the Government to enter into no compromise with the rebels; the third, while approving all the acts hitherto done against slavery, declared in favor of an amendment to the Constitution, terminating and forever prohibiting the existence of slavery in the United States. This resolution was received with an outburst of spontaneous and thunderous applause. The fourth resolution gave thanks to the soldiers and sailors; the fifth applauded the practical wisdom, unselfish patriotism, and unswerving fidelity with which Abraham Lincoln had discharged, under circumstances of unparalleled difficulty, the great duties and responsibilities of the Presidential office, and it enumerated and approved the acts of his Administration. The sixth resolution was of sufficient significance to be given entire.

Resolved, That we deem it essential to the general welfare that harmony should prevail in our national councils, and we regard as worthy of public confidence and official trust those only who cordially indorse the principles proclaimed in these resolutions and which should characterize the administration of the Government.

This resolution, like the admission of the Missouri Radicals, was intended in general to win the support and heal the dissatisfaction of the so-called Radicals throughout the Union. Its specific meaning, however, was not entirely clear. There were not many of the delegates who voted for it who would have agreed upon all the details of a scheme for reorganizing the

Cabinet. If measures for ostracizing all the objectionable members of the Government had been set on foot in the hall of the Convention, it is probable that the name of every member of the Cabinet would have been found on some of the shells. It is altogether likely, however, that the name of the Postmaster-General would have occurred more frequently than that of any other minister. The controversy between his brother and the Radicals of Missouri, in which he had, in accordance with his habit and temperament, taken an energetic part, had embittered against him the feelings of the radical Republicans, not only in the West, but throughout the North, and his habit of candid and trenchant criticism had raised for him enemies in all political circles.

The seventh resolution claimed for the colored troops the full protection of the laws of war. The eighth declared that foreign immigration should be fostered and encouraged. The ninth spoke in favor of the speedy construction of a railroad to the Pacific coast. The tenth declared that the national faith pledged for the redemption of the public debt must be kept inviolate; and the eleventh declared against the efforts of any European power to establish monarchical governments sustained by foreign military forces in near proximity to the United States.

This last resolution showed the result of an adroit and sagacious compromise. The Radicals in the Convention desired to make it a censure upon the action of the President and the Secretary of State; but the friends of the Administration, while accepting to its utmost results the declaration in favor of the Monroe Doctrine, assumed that the President and his Cabinet were of the same mind, and therefore headed the resolution with the declaration, "That we approve the decision taken by the Government that the people of the United States can never regard with indifference the attempt of any European power to overthrow by force or to supplant by fraud the institutions of any Republican Government on the Western continent."

There was nothing more before the Convention but the nominations, and one of those was in fact already made. The

only delay in registering the will of the Convention occurred
as a consequence of the attempt of members to do it by irregular and summary methods. Mr. Delano of Ohio made the customary motion to proceed to the nomination; Simon Cameron
moved as a substitute the renomination of Lincoln and Hamlin
by acclamation. A long wrangle ensued on the motion to lay
this substitute on the table, which was brought to a close by a
brief speech from Henry J. Raymond, representing the cooler
heads, who were determined that whatever opposition there
might be should have the fullest opportunity of expression; and
by a motion, which was adopted, to nominate in the usual way,
by the call of States. The interminable nominating speeches of
recent years had not come into fashion: B. C. Cook, the chairman of the Illinois delegation, merely said, "The State of Illinois again presents to the loyal people of this nation, for Presi-
den of the United States, Abraham Lincoln—God bless him!"
and those who seconded the nomination were equally brief.
Every State gave its undivided voice for Lincoln, with the exception of Missouri, which cast its vote, as the chairman stated,
under positive instructions, for Grant. But before the result was
announced John F. Hume of Missouri moved that the nomination of Lincoln be declared unanimous. This could not be done
until the result of the balloting was made known—484 for Lincoln, 22 for Grant. Missouri then changed its vote, and the
secretary read the grand total of 506 for Lincoln. The announcement was greeted with a storm of cheering, which during many
minutes as often as it died away burst out anew.

The principal names mentioned for the Vice-Presidency
were, besides Hannibal Hamlin, the actual incumbent, Andrew
Johnson of Tennessee, and Daniel S. Dickinson of New York;
besides these General L. H. Rousseau had the vote of his own
State, Kentucky. The Radicals of Missouri favored General
B. F. Butler, who had a few scattered votes also from New England. But among the three principal candidates the voters were
equally enough divided to make the contest exceedingly spirited
and interesting. For several days before the Convention the

President had been besieged by inquiries as to his personal wishes in regard to his associate on the ticket. He had persistently refused to give the slightest intimation of such wish. His private secretary, Mr. Nicolay, was at Baltimore in attendance at the Convention; and although he was acquainted with this attitude of the President, at last, overborne by the solicitations of the chairman of the Illinois delegation, who had been perplexed at the advocacy of Joseph Holt by Leonard Swett, one of the President's most intimate friends, Mr. Nicolay wrote a letter to Mr. Hay, who had been left in charge of the executive office in his absence, containing among other matters this passage: "Cook wants to know confidentially whether Swett is all right; whether in urging Holt for Vice-President he reflects the President's wishes; whether the President has any preference, either personal or on the score of policy; or whether he wishes not even to interfere by a confidential intimation. . . . Please get this information for me, if possible." The letter was shown to the President, who indorsed upon it this memorandum: "Swett is unquestionably all right. Mr. Holt is a good man, but I had not heard or thought of him for V. P. Wish not to interfere about V. P. Can not interfere about platform. Convention must judge for itself."

This positive and final instruction was sent at once to Mr. Nicolay, and by him communicated to the President's most intimate friends in the Convention. It was therefore with minds absolutely untrammeled by even any knowledge of the President's wishes that the Convention went about its work of selecting his associate on the ticket.

It is altogether probable that the ticket of 1864 would have been nominated without a contest had it not been for the general impression, in and out of the Convention, that it would be advisable to select as a candidate for the Vice-Presidency a war Democrat. Mr. Dickinson, while not putting himself forward as a candidate, had sanctioned the use of his name by his friends on the especial ground that his candidacy might attract to the support of the Union party many Demo-

crats who would have been unwilling to support a ticket avowedly Republican; but these considerations weighed with still
greater force in favor of Mr. Johnson, who was not only a
Democrat, but also a citizen of a border slave-holding State,
and had rendered distinguished services to the Union cause. At
the first show of hands it was at once evident that the Tennes-
sean was stronger than the New Yorker, receiving four more
votes than Mr. Dickinson even in the New York delegation.
When the votes on the first ballot were counted it was found
that Mr. Johnson had received 200, Mr. Hamlin 150, Mr.
Dickinson 108; but before the result was announced almost
the whole Convention turned their votes to Johnson, and on
motion of Lyman Tremain of New York his nomination was
declared unanimous. The work was quickly done. Mr. Lincoln,
walking over to the War Department in the afternoon, as usual,
for military news, received the dispatch announcing the nomination of Andrew Johnson before he was informed of his own.
The telegram containing the news of his own nomination had
gone to the White House a few minutes before.

In the evening the National Grand Council of the Union
League came together. A large proportion of its members had
participated in the National Convention, and their action was
therefore a foregone conclusion. They adopted a platform similar to that of the Convention, with the exception that they declared, as the Cleveland people had done, in favor of the confiscation of the property of rebels. They heartily approved and
indorsed the nominations already made, and passed a resolution to the effect that as Lincoln and Johnson were the only
candidates who could hope to be elected as loyal men, they regarded it as the imperative duty of the Union League to do all
that lay in its power to secure their election. They also earnestly approved and indorsed the platform and principles
adopted by the Convention, and pledged themselves, as individuals and as members of the League, to do all in their power
to elect the candidates. The seal of secrecy was removed from
this action and a copy of the resolution transmitted to the

President by W. R. Erwin, the Grand Recording Secretary.

A committee, headed by Governor Dennison, came on the next day to notify the President of his nomination. "I need not say to you, sir," said Mr. Dennison, "that the Convention, in thus unanimously nominating you for reëlection, but gave utterance to the almost universal voice of the loyal people of the country. To doubt of your triumphant election would be little short of abandoning the hope of the final suppression of the Rebellion and the restoration of the authority of the Government over the insurgent States."

The President answered:

I will neither conceal my gratification nor restrain the expression of my gratitude that the Union people, through their Convention, in the continued effort to save and advance the nation, have deemed me not unworthy to remain in my present position. I know no reason to doubt that I shall accept the nomination tendered; and yet perhaps I should not declare definitely before reading and considering what is called the platform. I will say now, however, I approve the declaration in favor of so amending the Constitution as to prohibit slavery throughout the nation. When the people in revolt, with a hundred days of explicit notice that they could within those days resume their allegiance without the overthrow of their institutions, and that they could not resume it afterwards, elected to stand out, such amendment to the Constitution as is now proposed became a fitting and necessary conclusion to the final success of the Union cause. Such alone can meet and cover all cavils. Now the unconditional Union men, North and South, perceive its importance and embrace it. In the joint names of Liberty and Union, let us labor to give it legal form and practical effect.

On the same day a committee of the Union League presented themselves to inform him of the action taken the night before. The President answered them more informally, saying that he did not allow himself to suppose that either the Convention or the League had concluded that he was either the greatest or the best man in America, but rather that they had decided that it was not best "to swap horses while crossing the river." All day the throngs of shouting and congratulating delegates filled the approaches to the Executive Mansion. In a brief speech at night, in answer to a serenade from citizens of Ohio, the President said: "What we want, still more than Baltimore conventions or Presidential elections, is success under General Grant. I propose that you constantly bear in mind that the support you owe to the brave officers and soldiers in the field is of the very first importance, and we should therefore bend all our energies to that point." He then proposed three cheers for General Grant and the officers and soldiers with him, and, swinging his own hat, led off in the cheering.

The more formal notification of the Convention was made in a letter written by George William Curtis of New York, in which he paraphrased the platform and expressed the sentiment of the Convention and of the people of the country with his usual elegance and force.

"They have watched your official course . . . with unflagging attention; and amid the bitter taunts of eager friends and the fierce denunciation of enemies, now moving too fast for some, now too slowly for others, they have seen you throughout this tremendous contest patient, sagacious, faithful, just; leaning upon the heart of the great mass of the people, and satisfied to be moved by its mighty pulsations. It is for this reason that, long before the Convention met, the popular instinct had plainly indicated you as its candidate, and the Convention therefore merely recorded the popular will. Your character and career prove your unswerving fidelity to the cardinal principles of American liberty and of the American Constitution. In the name of that liberty and Constitution, sir, we earnestly request your acceptance of this nomination, reverently commending our beloved country, and you, its Chief Magistrate, with all its brave sons who, on sea and land, are faithfully defending the good old American cause of equal rights, to the blessing of Almighty God.

In accepting the nomination the President observed the same wise rule of brevity which he had followed four years before. He made but one specific reference to any subject of discussion. While he accepted the resolution in regard to the supplanting of republican government upon the Western continent, he gave the Convention and the country distinctly to understand that he stood by the action already adopted by himself and the Secretary of State. He said: "There might be misunderstanding were I not to say that the position of the Government in relation to the action of France in Mexico, as assumed through the State Department and approved and indorsed by the Convention among the measures and acts of the Executive, will be faithfully maintained so long as the state of facts shall leave that position pertinent and applicable."

THE DEMOCRATS *put off their national convention as long as possible in the hope that in some way events might work in their favor. Throughout the summer of 1864 the strategy seemed sound. When the convention met in Chicago on August 29, Grant's army was immobilized at Petersburg after a campaign in which it had suffered staggering losses, while Sherman appeared to have met a similar fate at Atlanta. Growing numbers in the North were plainly weary of the war.*

At Chicago the Democrats adopted a platform declaring the war a failure and calling for a cessation of hostilities and a convention of the states to restore peace. The delegates then nominated George B. McClellan as their candidate.

The timing, so cunningly devised, turned out to be disastrous.

Lincoln Reëlected

FROM the moment the Democratic Convention named its candidates the stars in their courses seemed to fight against them. During the very hours when the streets of Chicago were blazing with torches, and the air was filled with the perfervid rhetoric of the peace men, rejoicing over their work, Hood was preparing for the evacuation of Atlanta; and the same newspapers which laid before their readers the craven utterances of the Vallandigham platform announced the entry of Sherman into the great manufacturing metropolis of Georgia—so close together came bane and antidote. The Convention had declared the war was a failure, and demanded that the Government should sue for terms of peace. Lincoln's reply three days afterwards was a proclamation announcing "the signal success that Divine Providence has recently vouchsafed" the country at Mobile and Atlanta, and calling for "devout acknowledgment to the Supreme Being in whose hands are the destinies of nations." He also tendered, by proclamation, the national thanks to Farragut, Canby, and Granger, and to General Sherman and the gallant officers and soldiers of their respective commands, and ordered that national salutes of one hundred guns should be fired on successive days from all the arsenals and navy yards in the United States in honor of these glorious victories. Thus, amid the prayers and thanksgiving of a grateful people, and the thunder and smoke of great guns, uttering from their iron throats the general joy, the Presidential campaign began. The darkest hour had come just before the dawn, and the light broadened on the political campaign from the beginning to end.

It would of course be unjust to describe the mass of the Democratic party as lacking in patriotism and as advocates of a dishonorable peace. But parties are judged by their general tendencies and not by the virtues or vices of individuals; and the two parties in the North in 1864 were differentiated with sufficient definiteness in the public mind as the peace and war parties. In the South there was no shade of doubt as to this distinction. The hopes and prayers of the revolt were centered on McClellan's success. They deplored Confederate military disasters more for their political effect in the North than for any other reason. The "Charleston Courier" of the 7th of September contained a leader on the fall of Atlanta in which the dependence of the rebellion upon Democratic success was frankly avowed. "All of us perceive," it said, "the intimate connection existing between the armies of the Confederacy and the peace men in the United States. These constitute two immense forces that are working together for the procurement of peace. . . . Our success in battle insures the success of McClellan. Our failure will inevitably lead to his defeat." The article goes on to lament the disaster at Atlanta, which would cloud the promising prospect of the peace organization; by which the entire Democratic party was meant.

One of the earliest speeches of the autumn was made by Mr. Seward at his home in Auburn, New York. He spoke avowedly without authority from the President; yet, as well from his intimacy with Mr. Lincoln as from his commanding place in the Administration, his speech demanded and received great attention. He said: "While the rebels continue to wage war against the Government of the United States, the military measures affecting slavery, which have been adopted from necessity to bring the war to a speedy and successful end, will be continued, except so far as practical experience shall show that they can be modified advantageously, with a view to the same end. When the insurgents shall have disbanded their armies and laid down their arms the war will instantly cease; and all the war measures then existing, including those which affect slavery, will cease also; and all the moral, economical, and political questions, as well questions affecting slavery as others which shall then be existing between individuals and States and the Federal Government, whether they arose before the civil war began, or whether they grew out of it, will, by force of the Constitution, pass over to the arbitrament of courts of law and to the councils of legislation."

Referring to the Chicago declaration in favor of the immediate cessation of hostilities, and the paralyzing effect on the action of the Government which would follow the success of the Democrats upon such a platform, he asked, in that contingency, "Who can vouch for the safety of the country against the rebels during the interval which must elapse before the new Administration can constitutionally come into power?" The opposition journalists immediately seized upon this as a threat that the Administration was determined to keep itself in power whatever might be the verdict of the people, and this clamor went on until the President, as we shall show, put an effectual quietus upon it.

Mr. Lincoln himself took little part in the contest. He was forced, from time to time, to assist with his presence charitable demonstrations in favor of the sick and wounded soldiers; and being always obliged on these occasions to say a few words, he acquitted himself of these necessary tasks with dignity and discretion. He made no personal reference to his opponents, and spoke of his enemies North and South with unfailing charity and moderation. Regiments of soldiers returning to their homes after their term of service was over sometimes called upon him, and in brief and pithy speeches he thanked them for calling, and always added a word or two of wise or witty political thought. Speaking to an Ohio regiment, he defined in one phrase the essential character of our republican government with more accuracy and clearness than ever Jefferson had done: "I wish it might be more generally and universally understood what the country is now engaged in. We have, as all will agree, a free government, where every man has a right to be equal with every other man. In this great struggle this form of government, and every form of human right, is endangered if our enemies succeed. . . . There is involved in this struggle the question whether your children and my children shall enjoy the privileges we have enjoyed. . . . When you return to your homes, rise up to the height of a generation of men worthy of a free government, and we will carry out the great work we have commenced."

To another regiment he said: "I happen, temporarily, to occupy this big white house. I am a living witness that any one of your children may look to come here as my father's child has. It is in order that each one of you may have, through this free government which we have enjoyed, an open field and a fair chance for your industry, enterprise, and intelligence— that you may all have equal privileges in the race of life with all its desirable human aspirations—it is for this that the struggle should be maintained, that we may not lose our birthright. . . . The nation is worth fighting for to secure such an inestimable jewel."

Being invited to attend a Union mass meeting at Buffalo, the President at first thought of writing a letter, and we find among his papers the following fragment in his own manuscript:

Yours inviting me to attend a Union mass meeting at Buffalo is received. Much is being said about peace, and no man desires peace more ardently than I. Still I am yet unprepared to give up the Union for a peace which, so achieved, could not be of much duration. The preservation of our Union was *not* the sole avowed object for which the war was commenced. It was commenced for precisely the reverse object—*to destroy our Union.* The insurgents commenced it by firing upon the *Star of the West* and on Fort Sumter, and by other similar acts. It is true, however, that the Administration accepted the war thus commenced for the sole avowed object of preserving our Union; and it is not true that it has since been, or will be, prosecuted by this Administration for any other object. In declaring this I only declare what I can know, and do know, to be true, and what no other man can know to be false.

In taking the various steps which have led to my present position in relation to the war, the public interest and my private interest have been perfectly parallel, because in no other way could I serve myself so well as by truly serving the Union. The whole field has been open to me where to choose. No place-hunting necessity has been upon me urging me to seek a position of antagonism to some other man, irrespective of whether such position might be favorable or unfavorable to the Union.

Of course, I may err in judgment; but my present position in reference to the rebellion is the result of my best judgment, and, according to that best judgment, it is the only position upon which any executive can or could save the Union. Any substantial departure from it insures the success of the rebellion. An armistice—a cessation of hostilities—is the end of the struggle, and the insurgents would be in peaceable possession of all that has been struggled for. Any different policy in regard to the colored man deprives us of his help, and this is more than we can bear. We cannot spare the hundred and forty or fifty thousand now serving us as soldiers, seamen, and laborers. This is not a question of sentiment or taste, but one of physical force, which may be measured and estimated as horse-power and steam-power are measured and estimated. Keep it, and you can save the Union. Throw it away, and the Union goes with it. Nor is it possible for any administration to retain the service of these people with the express or implied understanding that upon the first convenient occasion they are to be reënslaved. It can not be, and it ought not to be.

After he had written thus far he seems to have changed his mind as to the good taste or the expediency of aiding even thus far in his own canvass. He therefore laid his letter aside unsigned and wrote a brief note declining to address the meeting, on the ground, first, that it would be a breach of precedent, and, secondly, that if he once began to write letters it would be difficult to discriminate between meetings having equal claims.

Although the dignity and self-control with which Mr. Lincoln held himself aloof from the work of the canvass has been generally acknowledged, there is one incident of the campaign which was the object of severe criticism at the time. Governor Johnson, in accordance with the request of the State Convention of Tennessee, had issued a proclamation specifying the manner in which the vote for Presidential electors should be taken, the qualification of voters, and the oath which they should be required to take. The Democratic candidates on the electoral ticket of that State, regarding themselves aggrieved by these requirements of the Convention and the Governor, united in a protest against this proceeding, and one of their number, John Lellyett, was sent to present the protest in person. In the account of his interview with the President, which he published in the newspapers, Mr. Lellyett said that the President told him he would manage his side of the contest in his own way, and the friends of General McClellan could manage their side in theirs. It is not impossible that, in a moment of irritation at the presentation of a petition which was in itself an insinuation that he was making a selfish and corrupt use of his power, the President may have treated Mr. Lellyett with scant courtesy; but he took the protest, nevertheless, and told him he would answer it at his convenience. There is certainly nothing of malice or of petulance in the grave and serious tone of the reply which the President sent a few days later to the McClellan electors of Tennessee. He informed them that he had had no communication whatever with Governor Johnson on the subject of his proclamation; that he had given to the subject such consideration as was in his power in the midst of so many pressing public duties. He said:

My conclusion is that I can have nothing to do with the matter, either to sustain the plan as the Convention and Governor Johnson have initiated it, or to revoke or modify it as you demand. By the Constitution and laws the President is charged with no duty in the conduct of a Presidential election in any State; nor do I, in this case, perceive any military reason for his interference in the matter.

The movement set on foot by the Convention and Governor Johnson does not, as seems to be assumed by you, emanate from the National Executive. In no proper sense can it be considered other than as an independent movement of at least a portion of the loyal people of Tennessee.

I do not perceive in the plan any menace of violence or coercion toward any one. Governor Johnson, like any other loyal citizen of Tennessee, has the right to favor any political plan he chooses, and, as military governor, it is his duty to keep the peace among and for the loyal people of the State. I cannot discern that by this plan he purposes any more.

But you object to the plan. Leaving it alone will be your perfect security against it. Do as you please on your own account, peacefully and loyally, and Governor Johnson will not molest you, but will protect you against violence so far as in his power.

I presume that the conducting of a Presidential election in Tennessee in strict accordance with the old code of the State is not now a possibility.

It is scarcely necessary to add that if any election shall be held, and any votes shall be cast in the State of Tennessee for President and Vice-President of the United States, it will belong not to the military agents, nor yet to the Executive Department, but exclusively to another department of the Government, to determine whether they are entitled to be counted in conformity with the Constitution and laws of the United States. Except it be to give protection against violence, I decline to interfere in any way with any Presidential election.

The McClellan electors thereupon withdrew from the contest; Lincoln and Johnson electors were chosen, but their votes were not counted by Congress.

The most important utterance of the President during the campaign was a speech which he made on the evening of the 19th of October, in which he referred to the construction which had been placed on the remarks of the Secretary of State at Auburn, already quoted. He thought the distorted and unjust conclusions which had been drawn from Seward's remarks had gone far enough, and that the time had come to put an end to them, and he seized, for that purpose, the occasion of a serenade from a party of loyal Marylanders who were celebrating in Washington the victory which the party of emancipation had gained in the elections in their State. He said a few words of congratulation upon that auspicious event, and then added:

A word upon another subject. Something said by the Secretary of State, in his recent speech at Auburn, has been construed by some into a threat that if I shall be beaten at the election I will, between then and the end of my constitutional term, do what I may be able to ruin the Government. Others regard the fact that the Chicago Convention adjourned, not *sine die,* but to meet again, if called to do so by a particular individual, as the intimation of a purpose that if their nominee shall be elected he will at once seize control of the Government. I hope the good people will permit themselves to suffer no uneasiness on either point.

I am struggling to maintain government, not to overthrow it. I am struggling especially to prevent others from overthrowing it. I therefore say that if I shall live I shall remain President until the 4th of next March; and that whoever shall be constitutionally elected therefor, in November, shall be duly installed as President on the 4th of March; and that, in the interval, I shall do my utmost that whoever is to hold the helm for the next voyage shall start with the best possible chance to save the ship.

This is due to the people both on principle and under the Constitution. Their will, constitutionally expressed, is the ultimate law for all. If they should deliberately resolve to have immediate peace, even at the loss of their country and their liberty, I know not the power or the right to resist them. It is their own business, and they must do as they please with their own. I believe, however, they are still resolved to preserve their country and their liberty; and in this, in office or out of it, I am resolved to stand by them.

During the progress of the campaign Mr. Lincoln was frequently called upon to assist his friends, to oppose his enemies, and to exercise his powerful influence in appeasing discord in different States and districts. He interfered as little as possible, and always in the interests of the party at large, rather than in those of individuals. He took no account of the personal attitude of candidates towards himself. In the case of those who were among his intimate friends he would go no further than to demand that Government officers should not work against them. When Isaac N. Arnold of Chicago, who had incurred the hostility of Mr. Scripps, the postmaster at that place, complained of the opposition of that official and called upon the President to put a stop to it, the President would do nothing more than to order the offending postmaster to content himself with the exercise of his own rights as a citizen and a voter and to allow his subordinates to do the same. The postmaster answered, as was natural, that this was precisely what he had been doing, and that this was the source of Mr. Arnold's complaint; that the congressman wanted his active official assistance, and would be satisfied with nothing less. Although Arnold was an intimate and valued friend of the President, he declined to exercise any further pressure upon the postmaster, and Mr. Arnold soon afterwards withdrew from the contest.

After candidates had been regularly and fairly nominated, the President had no hesitation in doing all in his power to conciliate hostilities and to unite the party in support of them. He tolerated in these cases no factious or malicious opposition on the part of his office-holders, and he laid his hands most heavily upon those injudicious friends of his own who attempted to defeat the reëlection of Republican congressmen who had not been especially friendly to him. A large number of the leading Republicans in Roscoe Conkling's district had declared their intention to oppose him. Mr. Conkling's friends appealed to the President, claiming that the Republican opposition to him had its rise and origin among friends of the Secretary of State. The President commended their complaint to the attention of Mr. Seward, and answered for himself: "I am for the regular nominee in all cases, and no one could be more satisfactory to me as the nominee in that district than Mr. [Roscoe] Conkling. I do not mean to say there [are] not others as good as he in the district, but I think I know him to be at least good enough." Being informed of some hostility on the part of the custom-house officials in New York against Frederick A. Conkling, he wrote similar admonitions to them. The postmaster of Philadelphia being accused of interference against William D. Kelley, the President sent for him, and, following his custom in grave matters, he read to him a reprimand which he had committed to paper in the following words:

Complaint is made to me that you are using your official power to defeat Judge Kelley's renomination to Congress. I am well satisfied with Judge Kelley as a Member of Congress, and I do not know that the man who might supplant him would be as satisfactory; but the correct principle, I think, is that all our friends should have absolute freedom of choice among our friends. My wish, therefore, is that you will do just as you think fit with your own suffrage in the case, and not constrain any of your subordinates to do other than as he thinks fit with his. This is precisely the rule I inculcated and adhered to on my part when a certain other nomination now recently made was being canvassed for.

The reform of the civil service had not at that time been formulated by its friends, nor even adopted in principle by the country at large, yet it would be difficult even in the light of this day to improve upon this statement of its essential principle as applied to the conduct of office-holders. The postmaster, of course, promised exact obedience; but later in the summer the President was informed, on authority that he credited, that of the two or three hundred employees in the post-office not one was openly in favor of the renomination of Judge Kelley. Upon learning this, Mr. Lincoln wrote to an influential friend in Philadelphia, stating these facts and adding:

"This, if true, is not accidental. Left to their free choice, there can be no doubt that a large number of them, probably as much or more than half, would be for Kelley. And if they are for him and are not restrained they can put it beyond question by publicly saying so. Please tell the postmaster he must find a way to relieve me from the suspicion that he is not keeping his promise to me in good faith." The postmaster felt at last the hand of iron under the velvet glove, and Kelley was renominated and reëlected, as he was ever after till his death —to the honor and advantage of his district and State.

The summer was full of brief panics and flurries among the politicians, and they were continually rushing to Mr. Lincoln to urge him to action or inaction in the interests of the canvass. We believe there is no instance in which he yielded to these solicitations. A matter of especial difficulty was the draft for half a million of men which had been issued on the 18th of July. Leading Republicans all over the country, fearing the effect of the draft upon the elections, begged the President to withdraw the call or suspend operations under it. Mr. Cameron, so late as the 19th of October, after the State elections had been secured, advised against the draft in Philadelphia. Mr. Chase, on the same day, telegraphed from Ohio, which had been carried triumphantly by the Republicans a few days before, recommending the suspension of the draft for three weeks. Judge Johnson of Ohio reports that he was with the President when a committee came from Ohio to request him to suspend the draft until after the elections, and that Mr. Lincoln quietly answered, "What is the Presidency worth to me if I have no country?" But these solicitations were not all in the same direction. General Sherman telegraphed from the field, "If the President modifies it [the draft] to the extent of one man, or wavers in its execution, he is gone forever; the army would vote against him."

The politicians and the general probably exaggerated in equal measure; the army would not have rejected him if he had seen fit to suspend the draft; and the people stood by him in his refusal to do it. He went so far in compliance with the earnest request of the Union people in Indiana as to write to Sherman expressing his sense of the importance of allowing as many of the Indiana soldiers as possible to go home to vote. Most of the other States which voted in October allowed their soldiers to vote in the field. Indiana had not passed the necessary legis-

lation for this purpose. The draft was steadily proceeding in
that State, and, in the opinion of leading men there, was endangering the success of the Union party in the elections. "Anything you can safely do," Mr. Lincoln wrote, "to let her soldiers,
or any part of them, go home and vote at the State election
will be greatly in point. They need not remain for the Presidential election, but may return to you at once."

He was careful, however, not to urge General Sherman to
any course of action which he might consider injurious. "This
is," he added, "in no sense an order, but is merely intended to
impress you with the importance, to the army itself, of your
doing all you safely can, yourself being the judge of what you
can safely do." There were also reports from Missouri that
Rosecrans was inclined to deny the soldiers the right of attend-
ing elections, on the assumed ground that they would get drunk
and make disturbance. The President, on being informed of this,
quoted to Rosecrans the following words from the letter which
he had written to Schofield; " 'At elections see that those, and
only those, are allowed to vote who are entitled to do so by
the laws of Missouri, including as of those laws the restrictions
laid by the Missouri Convention upon those who may have
participated in the rebellion.' This," said Lincoln, "I thought
right then and think right now, and I may add I do not remember that either party complained after the election of
General Schofield's action under it. Wherever the law allows
soldiers to vote, their officers must also allow it."

The opposition to Mr. Lincoln within the ranks of his own
party did not entirely die away, even after the Chicago nomination and the changed political prospect which immediately
followed it. So late as the 20th of September Thurlow Weed
wrote to Mr. Seward that "the conspiracy against Mr. Lincoln collapsed on Monday last. It was equally formidable and
vicious, embracing a larger number of leading men than I supposed possible. Knowing that I was not satisfied with the President, they came to me for coöperation; but my objection to
Mr. Lincoln is that he has done too much for those who now

seek to drive him out of the field. Their last meeting was early last week at the house of Dudley Field. It was attended by Greeley, Godwin, Wilkes, Tilton, Opdyke, Curtis Noyes, and twenty-five others of the same stripe."

He also stated that a circular had been sent to leading Republicans in other States inquiring as to the feasibility of making another nomination for President at that time; that the malcontents, finding themselves in solitude, had concluded to break up operations and try to control the regular State Convention.

This letter referred to a movement which at one time assumed a certain importance. About the middle of August a number of leading Republicans, belonging to the faction in New York opposed to Mr. Seward, who had been displeased at the unanimous nomination of Lincoln at Baltimore, and who by constant conversation among themselves had become convinced of his unpopularity, endeavored to organize a demonstration against him which should force him to withdraw from the ticket. They had the earnest support and eager instigation of Henry Winter Davis in Maryland, of the editors of the "Cincinnati Gazette" in Ohio, and what would have surprised Mr. Lincoln if he had known it, of Charles Sumner in Massachusetts. General Butler was the favorite candidate of most of this singular cabal, and he sent a representative to their conferences. Mr. Chase gave in a guarded adhesion and Daniel S. Dickinson—not having been nominated for the Vice-Presidency at Baltimore—was naturally "full of anxiety and alarm over the manifest downward tendency of things." They met with severe rebuffs from several quarters where they expected assistance; Roscoe Conkling refused bluntly to sign their call; Jacob Collamer thought it inexpedient. When the country woke up to the true significance of the Chicago platform, the successes of Sherman excited the enthusiasm of the people, and the Unionists, arousing from their midsummer languor, began to show their confidence and regard towards the Republican candidate, the hopelessness of all efforts to undermine him became apparent, and, one by one, all the men engaged in this secret movement against him fell into line and did their best to elect him.

After every semblance of open hostility had disappeared everywhere else in the country the fire of faction still kept it alive in Missouri. A singular state of things existed there. The Radical party had almost entirely absorbed the Union sentiment of the State; the Conservative party, the President's friends, had almost ceased to exist. The incumbents of the Government offices, a few of the intimate personal friends of Blair, still stood out against the Radicals; and so long as this attitude was maintained the Radicals, while working vigorously for their State and local tickets, refused to avow themselves in favor of Lincoln. So far as can be ascertained the only reason for this absurd position was that the "Claybanks," as the Conservatives were called, wished the Radicals to declare for Lincoln as a pretext by which they could join the vast majority of their party, and the Radicals spitefully refused to allow them this accommodation. Thomas C. Fletcher, the Radical candidate for governor, refused during the greater part of the campaign to make any public statement that he would vote for Lincoln. His reason for this, privately given, was that he feared such an announcement would alienate from his support a large number of the more furious anti-Lincoln Germans. At last, however, he concluded to declare for the regular Republican Presidential ticket, and a meeting was appointed for the purpose; but, to the astonishment of the moderate Union men, he went no further at this meeting than to say he would not vote for McClellan, and in explanation of this singular performance he told the President's private secretary that he had found at the hotel where his speech was made a letter of the "Claybank" committee offering their support on condition of his declaring for Lincoln, and that he would not be coerced into it.

The President sent messages to the moderate Unionists expressing his desire that the childish quarrel should come to an end, and they, to do them justice, desired nothing more. The only condition of their support which they made was that candidates should declare themselves for Lincoln, which they in turn would have been willing to do if it were not that the "Claybanks" requested it. So far as practical results went the party was united enough, Mr. Nicolay reported; "it seems to be very well understood that, with the exception of very few impracticables, the Union men will cast their votes for you, for the Radical Congressmen, for the emancipation candidates, for the State Legislature and the State Convention, so that in practice nearly everybody is right and united, while in profession everybody is wrong or at cross purposes." This was surmised while the clatter of factious fighting was going on, and was abundantly proved by the result. While the Radical candidate for governor only claimed that he would be elected by a majority of ten thousand, which claim by many of his party was considered sanguine, when the votes were counted it was found that Lincoln had carried the State by the immense majority of forty thousand.

The electoral contest began with the picket firing in Vermont and Maine in September, was continued in what might be called the grand guard fighting in October, in the great States of Pennsylvania, Ohio, and Indiana, and the final battle all along the line took place in November. Vermont and Maine were carried by good Republican majorities, the canvass in the latter State having been managed by James G. Blaine with a dash and energy which gave a presage of his subsequent career. Before the October elections came on, auguries of Republican success had become so significant and universal that there was little doubt of the result in the best-informed political circles. The President, however, was too old a politician to be sure of anything until the votes were counted, and it was not without some natural trepidation that on the evening of the 11th of October he walked over to the War Department to get from the telegraphic instruments the earliest intimations of the course of the contest. The first dispatch he received contained the welcome intelligence of the election of Rutherford

B. Hayes and his Republican colleague from the hard-fought Cincinnati districts. Next came dispatches announcing a Republican majority in Philadelphia and indicating a similar result in the State of Pennsylvania.

The news continued very much in the same strain during the evening, and the President, in the lull of dispatches, read aloud to Stanton and Dana selected chapters of the Nasby papers. As the votes of the soldiers in the different camps in the vicinity of Washington began to be reported they were found to be nearly unanimous in favor of the Republican candidate, the proportion among Western troops being generally that of ten to one: among the Eastern troops, although there was everywhere a majority, it was not so large. Carver Hospital, by which Lincoln and Stanton passed every day on their way to the country, gave the heaviest opposition vote reported—about one out of three. Lincoln turned to the Secretary and said, "That's hard on us, Stanton! They know us better than the others." The sum of the day's work was of enormous importance. Indiana indicated a gain of thirty thousand in two years. Governor Morton and the entire Republican ticket were elected by twenty thousand majority, with the gain of four Congressmen. Pennsylvania, whose Representatives in Congress had been equally divided, now changed their proportion to fifteen against nine, and made her Legislature strongly Republican in both branches, with popular majorities ranging from ten to fifteen thousand. The Unionists carried Ohio by a majority of over 54,000, and effected a complete revolution in her representation in Congress; for while in 1862 she had elected fourteen Democrats and five Republicans, she now sent to Washington seventeen Republicans and two Democrats. But the success of the day which lay nearest to the heart of the President was the adoption in Maryland of the new State constitution abolishing slavery forever on her soil. The majority was a very slender one, the vote of the soldiers in the field being necessary to save emancipation; but it served, and the next month the Union majority was greatly increased.

It would seem strange that after this decisive victory there should have been any room left for hope or confidence on the side of the opposition or for anxiety and panic among Republican politicians; but alternating fits of confidence and despondency are inseparable from all long-continued political campaigns, and even after these overwhelming successes we find the Democratic speeches and papers full of boasting, and the private correspondence of experienced Republican leaders full of tremor and apprehension. The President, however, had passed through his moment of despondency, and from this time to the end entertained no shadow of doubt of the result. Mr. Washburne wrote to him on the 17th of October from Galena: "It is no use to deceive ourselves about this State. . . . Everything is at sixes and sevens; and no head or tail to anything. There is imminent danger of our losing the State"; and more in the same strain. The President laid away the letter, writing on the envelope the single word, "Stampeded." Ten days later Washburne had recovered his spirits, and wrote, "Logan is carrying all before him in Egypt." Earlier in the campaign Mr. Washburne, desiring to do all in his power to forward the Union cause, had written to Grant asking permission to print a letter from him in favor of Lincoln. Grant replied that he had no objection to this, but he thought that "for the President to answer all the charges the opposition would bring against him would be like setting a maiden to work to prove her chastity." A friend of Mr. Seward communicated to him about the same time an astonishing mare's nest, in which he claimed to have discovered that the opposition policy for the Presidential campaign would be to abstain from voting. The Secretary submitted this letter to the President. To Mr. Lincoln, with his lifelong observation of politics, this idea of abstention from voting seemed more amusing than threatening. He returned the letter to the Secretary with this indorsement: "More likely to abstain from stopping when once they get at it."

As the time drew near for the election in November a flight of rumors of intended secessionist demonstrations in the principal States of the North covered the land. The points of danger which were most clearly indicated were the cities of Chicago and New York. We have related in another place the efficient measures taken to prevent any outbreak in Chicago, with the arrest and punishment of the conspirators. The precautionary measures in other States prevented any attempt at disorder. To preserve the public peace in the city of New York and to secure the guarantee of a fair and orderly election there, General Butler was sent with a considerable force of troops to that city. He issued an order on the 5th of November declaring that troops had been detailed for duty in that district sufficient to preserve the peace of the United States, to protect public property, to prevent disorder, and to insure calm and quiet. He referred to the charge made by the opposition that the presence of Union troops might possibly have an effect upon the free exercise of the duty of voting at the ensuing election. He hotly repudiated this accusation.

"The armies of the United States," he said, "are ministers of good and not of evil. . . . Those who fear them are accused by their own consciences. Let every citizen having the right to vote act according to the inspiration of his own judgment freely. He will be protected in that right by the whole power of the Government if it shall become necessary."

He denounced energetically the crime of fraudulent voting, but did not assume to himself the duty of separating the tares from the wheat. He simply warned the evil-intentioned that fraudulent voting would be detected and punished after the election was over. Governor Seymour had been, as usual, much exercised for fear of executive usurpation at the polls, and had issued a proclamation on the 2d of November urging the avoidance of all measures which would tend to strife or disorder. He called upon sheriffs of counties to take care that every voter should have a free ballot in the manner secured to him by the constitution and laws, and to exercise the full force of the law and call forth, if need be, the power of their districts against the interference of the military in the vicinity of the polling-places.

There was by no means a unanimous agreement among even the supporters of the Administration as to the expediency of sending General Butler to New York at this time. The action was taken by Mr. Stanton on his own responsibility. Thurlow Weed disapproved of it, and up to the day of election thought, on the whole, the proceeding was injurious, in spite of Butler's admirable general order; but Butler acted under the circumstances with remarkable judgment and discretion. He devoted the days which elapsed between his arrival and the election to making himself thoroughly acquainted with the city, with its police arrangements, and the means at his disposal to preserve order. Every hour was occupied with a careful study of maps, of police arrangements, of telegraphic communication between his headquarters and every part of the city, and in consultations with general officers, the creation of an improvised engineer department, and the planning of a system of barricades in case of widespread insurrection. But the object to which he gave special attention, and in which he most thoroughly succeeded, was the avoidance of every pretext for any charge of interference with the rights of citizens at the polls. On the morning of the 8th of November, although the city was absolutely in the hands of the disciplined military force which had been sent to guard it, not a soldier was visible to the thousands of voters who thronged the streets; but everybody knew that they were there, and the result was, as Butler telegraphed to Lincoln at noon on election day, "the quietest city ever seen."

To Mr. Lincoln this was one of the most solemn days of his life. Assured of his personal success, and devoutly confident that the day of peace and the reëstablishment of the Union was not far off, he felt no elation and no sense of triumph over his opponents. His mind seemed filled with mingled feelings of deep and humble gratitude to the vast majority of his fellow-citizens who were this day testifying to him their heartfelt confidence and affection, and of a keen and somewhat surprised regret that he should be an object in so many quarters of so bitter and vindictive an opposition. He said to one of his secretaries: "It is singular that I, who am not a vindictive man, should always, except once, have been before the people for election in canvasses marked for their bitterness. When I came to Congress it was a quiet time; but always, except that, the contests in which I have been prominent have been marked with great rancor."

In the evening he went over, as was his custom, to the War Department. The night was rainy and dark. As he entered the telegraph room he was handed a dispatch from John W. Forney claiming 10,000 Union majority in Philadelphia. The figures were so far above his estimate that he said, "Forney is a little excitable." A moment after a dispatch came from Mr. Fulton in Baltimore, "15,000 in the city, 5000 in the State. All hail, free Maryland!" A moment after there came messages from Boston announcing majorities for Samuel Hooper and A. H. Rice of something like 4000 each. The President, astonished, asked if this was not a clerical error for 400, but the larger figures were soon confirmed. Mr. Rice afterwards, in speaking of these astounding majorities in districts where there was never the least charge made of irregularity at the polls, quoted an explanation made by a constituent of his, with no irreverent intention, "The Almighty must have stuffed the ballot-boxes."

The entrance of General Thomas T. Eckert, who came in covered with mud from a fall in crossing the street, reminded the President of an incident of his defeat by Douglas. He said: "For such an awkward fellow, I am pretty sure-footed. It used to take a rather dexterous man to throw me. I remember the evening of the day in 1858 that decided the contest for the Senate between Mr. Douglas and myself was something like this—dark, raining, and gloomy. From reading the returns I had ascertained that we had lost the Legislature, and started to go home. The path had been worn hog-backed and was slippery. Both my feet slipped from under me, but I recovered myself and lit clear; and I said to myself, 'It is a slip, and not a fall.'"

Mr. Fox, the Assistant Secretary of the Navy, indulged in

some not unnatural exultation over the complete effacement of Henry Winter Davis from Maryland politics. Mr. Davis had assailed the navy with a peculiarly malicious opposition for two years for no cause that Mr. Fox could assign except that he was a brother-in-law of Montgomery Blair. The President would not agree with him. "You have more of that feeling of personal resentment than I," he said. "Perhaps I have too little of it; but I never thought it paid. A man has no time to spend half his life in quarrels. If any man ceases to attack me I never remember the past against him." All the evening the dispatches kept the same tenor of widespread success—in almost all cases above the estimates. The October States showed increased majorities, and long before midnight the indications were that the State of New York had cast her ponderous vote for Lincoln, and made the verdict of the North almost unanimous in his favor, leaving General McClellan but twenty-one electoral votes, derived from New Jersey, Delaware, and Kentucky, 212 being cast for Lincoln and Johnson.

It was two o'clock in the morning before the President left the War Department. At the door he met a party of serenaders with a brass band who saluted him with music and cheers, and, in the American fashion, demanded a speech. He made a brief response, saying that he did not pretend that those who had thought the best interests of the nation were to be subserved by the support of the present Administration embraced all the patriotism and loyalty of the country. He continued:

I do believe, and I trust without personal interest, that the welfare of the country does require that such support and indorsement should be given.

I earnestly believe that the consequences of this day's work, if it be as you assume, and as now seems probable, will be to the lasting advantage, if not to the very salvation, of the country. I cannot at this hour say what has been the result of the election. But, whatever it may be, I have no desire to modify this opinion, that all who have labored to-day in behalf of the Union have wrought for the best interests of the country and the world, not only for the present, but for all future ages.

I am thankful to God for this approval of the people; but, while deeply grateful for this mark of their confidence in me, if I know my heart, my gratitude is free from any taint of personal triumph. I do not impugn the motives of any one opposed to me. It is no pleasure to me to triumph over any one, but I give thanks to the Almighty for this evidence of the people's resolution to stand by free government and the rights of humanity.

For several days the torrent of congratulations came pouring in. General Blair wrote from Georgia, where he was leading an army corps under Sherman to the sea: "The vote in this army to-day is almost unanimous for Lincoln. Give Uncle Abe my compliments and congratulations." Grant paused for a moment in his labors in the investment of Richmond to express his sense of the vast importance and significance of the election. He thought a tremendous crisis in the history of the country had been met and triumphantly passed by the quiet and orderly conduct of the American people on the 8th of November.

The manner in which the President received these tumultuous demonstrations of good-will was so characteristic that it seems to us worthy of special attention. He was absolutely free from elation or self-congratulation. He seemed to deprecate his own triumph and to sympathize rather with the beaten than the victorious party. He received notice that on the night of the 10th of November the various Republican clubs in the District of Columbia would serenade him. Not wishing to speak extempore on an occasion where his words would receive so wide a publication, he sat down and hastily wrote a speech which, while it has not received the world-wide fame of certain other of his utterances, is one of the weightiest and wisest of all his discourses. He read it at the window which opens on the north portico of the Executive Mansion, a secretary standing beside him lighting the page with a candle. "Not very graceful," he said, "but I am growing old enough not to care much for the manner of doing things." There was certainly never an equal compliment paid to a serenading crowd. The inmost philosophy of republican governments was in the President's little speech. He said:

It has long been a grave question whether any Government not too strong for the liberties of its people can be strong enough to maintain its own existence in great emergencies. On this point the present rebellion brought our republic to a severe test, and a Presidential election occurring in regular course during the rebellion added not a little to the strain. If the loyal people united were put to the utmost of their strength by the rebellion, must they not fail when divided and partially paralyzed by a political war among themselves? But the election was a necessity. We can not have free Government without elections; and if the rebellion could force us to forego or postpone a national election, it might fairly claim to have already conquered and ruined us. The strife of the election is but human nature practically applied to the facts of the case. What has occurred in this case must ever recur in similar cases. Human nature will not change. In any future great national trial, compared with the men of this, we shall have as weak and as strong, as silly and as wise, as bad and as good. Let us, therefore, study the incidents of this, as philosophy to learn wisdom from, and none of them as wrongs to be revenged. But the election, along with its incidental and undesirable strife, has done good, too. It has demonstrated that a people's Government can sustain a national election in the midst of a great civil war. Until now, it has not been known to the world that this was a possibility. It shows, also, how sound and how strong we still are. It shows that, even among candidates of the same party, he who is most devoted to the Union and most opposed to treason can receive most of the people's votes. It shows, also, to the extent yet known, that we have more men now than we had when the war began. Gold is good in its place; but living, brave, patriotic men are better than gold.

But the rebellion continues; and, now that the election is over, may not all having a common interest reunite in a common effort to save our common country? For my own part, I have striven and shall strive to avoid placing any obstacle in the way. So long as I have been here, I have not willingly planted a thorn in any man's bosom. While I am deeply sensible to the high compliment of a reëlection, and duly grateful, as I trust, to Almighty God for having directed my countrymen to a right conclusion, as I think, for their own good, it adds nothing to my satisfaction that any other man may be disappointed or pained by the result.

May I ask those who have not differed with me to join with me in this same spirit towards those who have? And now let me close by asking three hearty cheers for our brave soldiers and seamen, and their gallant and skillful commanders.

In this lofty and magnanimous spirit he received all the addresses of congratulation that came in upon him in these days. To a delegation from Maryland who ascribed it to his rare discretion that Maryland was then a free State he replied with deep appreciation of their courtesy, and added, that those who differed from and opposed us would yet see that defeat was better for their own good than if they had been successful. He not only had no feeling of malicious triumph himself, he had no patience with it in others. When Mr. Raymond, who represented his special friends in New York, wrote a letter breathing fire and vengeance against the officials of the customhouse, who, he said, had come near defeating him in the race for Congress, the President merely observed that it was "the spirit of such letters as that which created the factious malignity of which Mr. Raymond complained." To all those who begged for a rigorous and exemplary course of punishment for political derelictions in the late canvass his favorite expression was, "I am in favor of short statutes of limitation in politics." He rejected peremptorily some suggestions of General Butler and the War Department having in view the punishment of flagrant offenders in New York: "We must not sully victory with harshness." His thoughtful and chivalrous consideration for the beaten party did not, however, prevent him from feeling the deepest gratitude for those who had labored on his side. He felt that the humblest citizen who had done his duty had claims upon him. Hearing that Deacon John Phillips of Sturbridge, Massachusetts, a man who had already completed his 104th year, and had voted at every Presidential election since the foundation of the Government, had taken the pains to go to the polls to vote for him, the President wrote him a grateful letter of thanks. "The example," he said, "of such devotion to civic duties in one whose days have already been extended an average lifetime beyond the Psalmist's limit cannot but be valuable and fruitful. It is not for myself only, but for the country which you have in your sphere served so long and so well, that I thank you."

The venerable man, who had attained his majority in the midst of the war of the Revolution, and who had arrived at middle age before this century opened, answered in a note which greatly pleased and moved the President, as coming from one of the oldest men living on the earth. He said:

I feel that I have no desire to live but to see the conclusion of this wicked rebellion and the power of God displayed in the conversion of the nations. I believe, by the help of God, you will finish the first, and also be the means of establishing universal freedom and restoring peace to the Union. That the God of mercy will bless you in this great work, and through life, is the prayer of your unworthy servant,   JOHN PHILLIPS.

There is one phrase of the President's speech of the 10th of November which we have quoted which is singularly illustrative, not only of the quick apprehension with which he seized upon facts of importance, but also of the accuracy and method with which he ascertained and established them. Within a few hours after the voting had closed he was able to say that the election had shown that "we have more men now than we had when the war began." A great bundle of papers which lies before us as we write, filled with telegrams from every quarter annotated in his own neat handwriting, with a mass of figures which would have dismayed an ordinary accountant, shows the importance which he attached to this fact and the industry with which he investigated it. In his message to Congress a few weeks later he elaborated this statement with the utmost care. He showed from the comparative votes in 1860 and in 1864 a net increase of votes during the three years and a half of war of 145,551. The accomplished statisticians of the "Tribune" almanac in the following month, after the closest study of the official returns, expressed their surprise "at the singular accuracy of the President's figures."

An extract from his annual message to Congress gives the best summing up of the results of the election that has ever been written.

The purpose of the people within the loyal States to maintain the integrity of the Union was never more firm nor more nearly unanimous than now. The extraordinary calmness and good order with which the millions of voters met and mingled at the polls give strong assurance of this. Not only all those who supported the Union ticket so called, but a great majority of the opposing party also, may be fairly claimed to entertain and to be actuated by the same purpose. It is an unanswerable argument to this effect, that no candidate for any office whatever, high or low, has ventured to seek votes on the avowal that he was for giving up the Union. There have been much impugning of motives, and much heated controversy as to the proper means and best mode of advancing the Union cause; but on the distinct issue of Union or no Union the politicians have shown their instinctive knowledge that there is no diversity among the people. In affording the people the fair opportunity of showing one to another and to the world this firmness and unanimity of purpose, the election has been of vast value to the national cause.

On the day of election General McClellan resigned his commission in the army, and the place thus made vacant was filled by the appointment of General Philip H. Sheridan, a fit type and illustration of the turn in the tide of affairs, which was to sweep from that time rapidly onward to the great and decisive national triumph.

NICOLAY AND HAY *describe the narrow failure of the Union Army to cap Grant's campaign against Richmond with victory. Petersburg, the key to success, lies twenty-five miles south of the Confederate capital.*

Petersburg

MEANTIME General Grant had executed the most important of all his turning movements with notable ability and success. His object was now to get south of Richmond and to destroy the lines of supply on that side of the Confederate army. After the destruction of the Virginia Central road, the capture of Petersburg would leave but one railroad in their hands, the Richmond and Danville; this would be ultimately severed, and Richmond must fall. He chose, as his place of crossing the James, a guarded and sheltered spot near Wilcox's landing; far enough from Richmond to give an opportunity for attacking Lee out of his intrenchments if he should attempt to interrupt the passage. All Grant's dispositions for the great movement were skillful and judicious. Warren, with the Fifth Corps, preceded by Wilson's cavalry, crossed the Chickahominy before daylight on the 13th, and took positions on roads leading to Richmond, creating the impression in General Lee's mind that an advance upon that city was in progress. The rest of the army was then withdrawn from its works, and moved by long and rapid marches to Wilcox's landing, where the battalion of engineers constructed, between four in the afternoon and midnight, a bridge which was one of the most notable triumphs of military engineering in our times. The river was 2100 feet wide, 15 fathoms deep in midchannel, and there was a strong tidal current with a rise and fall of four feet. One hundred and one pontoons were required; they were anchored to vessels moored above and below.

The Fifth Corps and Wilson's cavalry having accomplished their mission with perfect success withdrew from their menac-

ing attitude, and the whole army with all its artillery and trains
was south of the James by midnight of the 16th, General Wright
covering the movement and crossing last. General Lee was still
holding his force north of the river to protect Richmond from
the attack he thought imminent from that quarter. The whole
movement was so far brilliantly successful. Grant announced
his action to the Government at Washington. The President
received the news with joy and gratitude. In spite of all asser-
tions to the contrary, he had no apprehensions for the safety of
Washington while Lee was kept busy somewhere else. He telegraphed to Grant on the 15th, "I have just received your dispatch of 1 P.M. yesterday. I begin to see it. You will succeed.
God bless you all."

The first great object of the movement was the seizure of
Petersburg. It was a place of the utmost importance, nothing
less than an outlying bastion of Richmond, whose possession by
the National troops made the tenure of the rebel capital impossible. An important expedition to effect this momentous capture had been confided to General W. F. Smith. With some
16,000 men he started on the morning of the 15th, under verbal
orders from General Butler, to "attack Petersburg as soon as
possible." The work had been represented to him at Butler's
headquarters as very easy; he was told that "he could ride over
the fortifications on horseback"; that from the heights on the
Appomattox his sharp-shooters could clear out the Confederate
garrison, which consisted only of a few militia. On arriving
before the place, however, which he did about noon, after sharp
skirmishing on the road, he found the works so much stronger
than he had been led to expect and the artillery fire from them
so well sustained that he came to the erroneous conclusion that
they must also be fully supported by infantry. He therefore
proceeded with the greatest caution and deliberation. Having
no engineer on his staff he thought himself compelled to re-
connoitre the enemy's position in person, and, not willing to
risk an assault in column under such a heavy fire from the guns,
he concluded to open with his own artillery and then try to

carry the works with a strong skirmish line. But at this juncture he found his chief of artillery had without authority taken the horses to the rear to water them, and an hour of inestimable value was thus lost.

It was seven o'clock and the sun was setting when his attack was made. His skirmishers sprang gallantly forward to their work and captured the intrenchments, which were immediately occupied by the lines of battle. A mile and a half of the rebel works, with sixteen guns, were in his hands at nine o'clock; the city of Petersburg, defended only by a force of about 2500 Confederates, seemed at his mercy. An hour more of daylight might have hastened the capture of Richmond by six months. Even as it was, General Smith was severely blamed by General Grant for not having pushed forward in the darkness and possessed himself of the town. But he felt that the risk of a night march forward over unknown obstacles, in the presence of an enemy, was too great; he preferred to hold what he had gained rather than incur the danger of a disaster by groping in the dark about the enemy's inner line of works. He had heard that Lee was crossing at Drewry's Bluff and he did not know what force might be confronting him. He knew that Hancock's corps was on its way to support him, and when, late at night, it arrived, he asked Hancock to relieve his own troops in the captured works, and feeling that he had done a good day's work, waited for morning. It was not Hancock's fault that he was not on the ground earlier. He had been delayed several hours in the morning waiting for rations, and at last was compelled to march without them. He says he was not informed until between five and six o'clock on the afternoon of the 15th that Petersburg was to be attacked that day; and Meade relieved him of all censure by saying, "Had General Hancock and myself been apprised in time of the contemplated movement against Petersburg and the necessity of his coöperation . . . he could have been pushed much earlier to the scene of operations."

In the night the golden opportunity passed away. Beauregard had acted with the greatest energy and promptness. He saw,

far more plainly than General Lee, the point of danger; he un-
hesitatingly stripped the Bermuda Hundred lines and begged
for troops to defend Petersburg, while Lee was holding all his
forces in hand to fight Grant on the roads to Richmond between the Chickahominy and the James. Lee sent him, however,
Hoke's division, which arrived during the night, and in the
morning Smith and Hancock saw in front of them a new line
of intrenchments, manned by veteran Confederate infantry;
though Lee, still incredulous, so late as ten o'clock on the morning of the 16th telegraphed Beauregard that he did not know
where Grant was, and could not strip the north bank. Butler's
force at daylight had taken the intrenchments in front of Bermuda Hundred disgarnished by Beauregard, and captured
much of the small force left to guard them; but in the evening
of the same day Pickett's division, crossing from the north side,
retook the works. So that nothing was lost to the Confederates
by Beauregard's bold and judicious action, and Petersburg was
saved to them; for on the morning of the 16th he had some fourteen thousand effective infantry supporting the powerful artillery of his intrenchments, and two days later the bulk of Lee's
army was there.

Now that the last chance of an easy victory was gone, Meade
acted with all possible energy and spirit. Hancock was placed
in command of all the troops on the ground, and the Second
Corps, supported by portions of the Ninth and the Eighteenth
to left and right, assaulted the intrenchments, carrying three
redans with their connecting lines.

At dawn on the 17th R. B. Potter's division of the Ninth
Corps, forming in silence in a deep ravine, obeying a whispered
word of command, and without firing a shot, carried another
succession of redans and connecting lines, with many guns and
prisoners. There was heavy fighting all this day, resulting in
constant encroachments by the National troops on the Confederate lines; and in the night Beauregard withdrew 500 or
1000 yards in rear of the line so hotly disputed, and intrenched
himself in the new one with that rapidity and skill which both

armies had attained. In the morning he was heavily reënforced by the Army of Northern Virginia, with General Lee in person at its head.

Meade, not knowing the full extent of the Confederate reën-forcements, and being fully impressed with the immense importance of the capture of Petersburg, ordered another vigorous assault on the Confederate works to take place at noon on the 18th. This was made with the utmost spirit and gallantry: Hancock's corps, under Birney, their old commander having been disabled by the opening of his Gettysburg wounds; the Fifth, under the immediate command of Warren; the Ninth, under General Parke's personal direction, attacked again and again with high but fruitless valor; Barlow, Potter, Willcox, Griffin, and J. L. Chamberlain did all that could have been asked of them. The works were too powerful to be carried by assault, though ground was gained; the positions carried close to the enemy were everywhere intrenched, and the National lines were established substantially as they remained until the war ended. Grant, at the close of the day, saw that all which was possible had been done, and he commanded that the fighting should cease; that the troops should be put under cover, and take the rest which had become indispensable. In the four days' struggle about ten thousand men had been lost on the Union side; there is no official statement of the Confederate losses—they were, of course, less, as they fought behind intrenchments, but were still not inconsiderable.

The Army of the Potomac was exhausted by its incessant and protracted exertions. Its long and arduous marches; its daily assaults upon an intrenched enemy, defended by entanglements in front and guarded by powerful artillery; its heavy losses in brave and experienced officers and veteran soldiers, unrelieved by any decided success, had begun to have their effect not only on the strength but the spirit of even that brave and patient army. It was time to put them also behind intrenchments, to give them some rest and protection. General Grant determined to invest Petersburg by a line of intrench-

ments, which might be held by a part of his troops, leaving the
rest free for whatever movements might be required. General
Butler, with the Army of the James, was assigned to the care
of Bermuda Hundred and Deep Bottom on either side of the
river, the two positions being connected by a pontoon bridge.
About Petersburg the Army of the Potomac was disposed in
this order from right to left: Burnside with the Ninth Corps,
Warren with the Fifth, Birney with the Second, Wright with
the Sixth; the last corps holding the extreme left and being
refused to the west and south.

Grant's first attempt at seizing the Weldon and South Side
railroads was unsuccessful. The Second and Sixth Corps were
moved to the left with that purpose on the 22d of June; but,
not being well closed up, A. P. Hill's corps was thrust between
them, and inflicted considerable damage, taking a large number of prisoners and some guns. A little ground was, however,
gained and held, and the armies remained quiescent for several
weeks, the Union army being busily engaged in intrenching and
fortifying their lines. The position on the Jerusalem plank road,
midway between the Norfolk and Weldon railroads, was made
impregnable by two strong redoubts by the middle of July.

The cavalry in both armies was kept busy in constant raids.
While Sheridan was away on his raid to Trevilian's, Wilson was
sent with two divisions to destroy, if possible, all three of the
railroads connecting Richmond with the South. He started on
the 22d of June, breaking the Weldon road at Reams's Station,
destroying thirty miles of the Lynchburg road and as much of
the Danville road, where the two lines crossed at Burkesville
Junction. He did not effect this without some keen fighting
with the Confederate cavalry, and when, the object of his expedition being accomplished, he started to return, a heavy con-
centration of the enemy's cavalry was effected against him. A
severe engagement took place at Stony Creek on the Weldon
road, with indecisive results; and at Reams's Station, Wilson
found himself confronted by a strong force of Confederate infantry and artillery which he was unable to dislodge. He was

here compelled to retire and make the best of his way back to Petersburg, with a heavy loss in guns and wagons. His loss in killed and wounded was only 240, but 1261 were reported missing. Brilliant as these cavalry raids were, General Grant in his "Memoirs" intimates that they cost more than they were worth. Both sides were very expert in repairing railroads after they seemed utterly destroyed; the Confederates, especially, were disheartened at the facility with which Sherman would run his trains a few hours after they had raided his tracks; so that it came to be a saying among them that Sherman carried duplicate tunnels in his baggage.

At this point General Humphreys, in his admirable history of this campaign, pauses to estimate the losses in the Union Army from the crossing of the Rapidan to the 1st of July. The Army of the Potomac lost in killed and wounded about 50,000, and including the missing 61,400; the Army of the James about 7000. A large number of regiments were mustered out; great numbers of sick were sent home. The constant policy of the Confederate authorities was to conceal their losses; there are even at this day no trustworthy estimates of them. The steadfast heart of the President sickened at the slaughter. In a dispatch to Sherman, on the 16th of July, Grant announced his intention to "make a desperate effort to get a position here which will hold the enemy without the necessity of so many men." The President, referring to this, telegraphed to Grant in these words: "Pressed as we are by lapse of time I am glad to hear you say this; and yet I do hope you may find a way that the effort shall not be desperate in the sense of great loss of life."

The dull, dry midsummer passed away with little accomplished by the Army of the Potomac. No rain fell for forty-six days together; the troops suffered greatly from thirst; the dust lay thick on the roads and the barren fields. The slightest movement of troops filled the air with suffocating clouds. There was no water in the springs or the ponds; the soldiers everywhere were forced to dig wells for themselves. But even amid these hardships they throve and soon recovered their spirits. General

Lee, foreseeing the inevitable end if the siege of Petersburg was to endure indefinitely, and yet unwilling to risk a conflict in the open field, was anxious for Grant to attack him in his works. The hope that threatening Washington with a strong detachment might induce Grant to do this was one of the motives which led Lee to send Early down the Valley in the latter part of June. On the 20th he wrote to Jefferson Davis, "I still think it is our policy to draw the attention of the enemy to his own territory. It may force Grant to attack me, or to weaken his force." The movement was made with results which are more particularly mentioned in another place. Neither the Administration at Washington nor General Grant were especially disturbed. The Sixth Corps was sent north to meet Early and drive him south, and General Lee reporting the movement of troops on the river expresses his 'fear that they are on the way to Washington," and his deep disappointment at such action. "It is so repugnant to Grant's principles and practice to send troops from him, that I had hoped before resorting to it he would have preferred attacking me." Four days later he wrote again to Mr. Davis; his dissatisfaction with Grant's conduct is confirmed. "I had hoped that General Grant rather than weaken his army would have attempted to drive us from our position. I fear I shall not be able to attack him to advantage." The menace upon Washington failed of its purpose; the siege of Petersburg continued without relaxation. The siege train was on the ground in the latter days of June; on the 9th of July Meade issued orders regulating the approaches of the Army of the Potomac in front of Burnside's and Warren's corps; days and nights were filled with the clamor of guns and the labors of the spade.

The most noteworthy incident of the summer—though it led to no significant result—was that of the mine in front of Burnside. Near the end of June Lieutenant-Colonel Henry Pleasants of the Forty-eighth Pennsylvania, a regiment composed chiefly of coal-miners, proposed to run a mine under that part of the Confederate works called Elliott's salient. The only advantage of the position was that the entrance to the gallery was in a sheltered ravine, which was concealed from the view of the enemy; and even this advantage proved illusory, as Beauregard soon became aware of the work which was going on, and promptly threw up intrenchments at the gorge of the salient, and planted batteries to give him a front and flank fire on the point of assault. The work was completed towards the end of July; it was a vast gallery, 511 feet long, with lateral branches of 38 feet each; eight magazines were charged each with 1000 pounds of powder. While the excavation was going on Burnside had been drilling Edward Ferrero's colored division to make the charge when the mine should be exploded; but this arrangement being reported to General Meade on the 26th of July, and by him referred to General Grant, it did not meet their approval. This division having never been in action, General Meade was not sure of its steadiness; in case of disaster coming to it he would naturally apprehend severe criticism from Republican sources, on the charge that he was sacrificing the colored troops. Burnside seeing his judgment overruled in this respect then took the deplorable resolution of leaving the decision between his three white divisions to lot; and an evil chance, passing by the able and energetic commanders, Potter and O. B. Willcox, selected General J. H. Ledlie for a work to which he was totally inadequate.

On the night of the 26th of July, General Grant sent the Second Corps with a heavy force of cavalry to the north side of the James River, to join with Butler's forces in an attack upon the enemy's positions on that side. His object was twofold; first, to cut, if possible, the railroads between Richmond and the Anna River and disturb the enemy's operations in the Shenandoah; and, second, to cause the withdrawal of a large body of troops from Petersburg at the time of the explosion of the mine. The first purpose failed entirely; though a large body of the Confederates was moved north of the river it availed Grant nothing in the end. Some ground, it is true, was gained on the 27th; but the enemy reënforced so heavily on the 28th that no advantage resulted to the Union troops from the fighting on that day, and Grant at once resolved to withdraw the Second

Corps to the lines of Petersburg, to support the meditated assault. This was effected on the nights of the 28th and 29th.

On the morning of the 30th the mine was exploded at a quarter before five o'clock. The whole salient rose in the air, a vast
mass of earth; and as the smoke and dust cleared away a crater
200 feet long, 50 feet wide, and 25 feet deep was disclosed where
the rebel fort had been. Colonel Pleasants stood on the Union
breastworks and watched the effect; his task, at least, had been
well done. The enemy were for the moment stupefied by the
catastrophe. They ran in horror from the crater on both sides;
the breach was virtually four hundred yards in extent. Now was
the moment for Burnside to pour his men through the gap and
gain the crest of Cemetery Hill, which commanded the town
of Petersburg. But the advance was languid. General Ledlie was
suffering from sickness; he spent the morning in a bomb-proof.
Burnside had neglected to level his parapets and remove the
abatis in his front, and his leading division made their way
slowly out of the works by the flank instead of in extended
front. They pushed on, however, to the crater, and crowding
into that narrow hole, stayed there, and no efforts could induce
them to leave it. In the course of half an hour the enemy recovered from their surprise and began a furious fire from front
and both flanks. Potter's division was sent in on the right, Willcox on the left. Each of them made some progress, but the
frightful chaos and confusion of the center division in the crater
continued, and neither of them could hold what they had
gained; and when at last Ferrero's colored division was sent
forward without their commander, who considered it his duty
to remain in the rear, they rushed to the front with great spirit,
but under conditions which made disaster certain. Being badly
led, they poured over the edge of the crater in great numbers,
and although they did their best to get through to the other
side they emerged with their formation shattered. Advancing
towards the enemy they encountered a heavy fire of infantry
and artillery, and were soon stampeded and driven back in great
confusion.

General John W. Turner had by this time managed to get

a division of Ord's corps forward through the disorder and charged with one brigade upon the enemy's works to the right of the crater, taking possession of about one hundred yards of their line; he was just giving the order to another brigade to go forward, when the retrograde rush of the stampeded troops swept his whole command backward to the Union lines. Warren on the left saw no opportunity to advance; the enemy in his front kept their works strongly manned, and the confusion in and about the crater was such that the troops already there were more than could be handled, and any addition to their numbers would only have increased the disaster. Grant saw early in the day that the affair was not prospering. He rode forward as far as he could go on horseback, and then went through to the front on foot. He soon convinced himself that the evil was beyond remedy; the impulse of the assault was gone; the enemy had recovered from the shock of the surprise and were sweeping the edges of the crater and its approaches with a hot and destructive fire.

The Confederate infantry now advanced and assaulted the position, and although some good fighting was still done by Potter's command and part of Ord's, the huddled mass, in the intense heat, was unable to move, recover its formation, or its spirit. At half-past nine Meade in a dispatch to Burnside assumed that his attack had resulted in a repulse, and ordered "if, in his judgment, nothing further could be effected that he withdraw to his own lines, taking every precaution to get the men back safely." Burnside on receiving this order hurried to Meade's headquarters to protest against it. He thought he had not fought long enough; that there was still hope of carrying the crest; but Meade repeated the order in a peremptory manner—leaving, however, the time and manner of retiring to Burnside's discretion—and Burnside sent it to the crater at noon. The lamentable inefficiency which had marked every operation of the day still continued, and even the orders to retire were so languidly executed that a heavy loss in prisoners occurred at the crater and between the lines.

This unhappy day closed Burnside's military career. Meade, whose stern and fiery temper often got control of him on the battlefield, had sent some stinging dispatches in the course of the fight, to which Burnside had returned a resentful and contumacious reply; and after his troops had been driven from the crater he preserved a sullen silence, making no reply to Meade's anxious and angry questions. It was possibly this insubordinate attitude, as much as the failure of the attack, that induced Meade to prefer charges against Burnside. Grant also was eager for some process of censure. Two days after the fight he wrote to Meade speaking of "the miserable failure of Saturday. I think there will have to be an investigation of the matter. So fair an opportunity will probably never occur again for carrying fortifications; preparations were good, orders ample, and everything, so far as I could see, subsequent to the explosion of the mine shows that almost without loss the crest beyond the mine could have been carried; this would have given us Petersburg with all its artillery and a large part of the garrison."

Burnside was relieved from command a few days after this battle. A court of inquiry ordered by the President, at the request of General Meade, over which General Hancock presided, censured General Burnside for the neglect of such preparations as would have insured success, Generals Ledlie and Ferrero and Colonel Z. R. Bliss, for inefficiency and positive misbehavior in action, and General Willcox for a lack of energy in pushing his division forward towards the crest; the court also, by implication, blamed Grant and Meade for not having put all the troops intended to coöperate under one command. Meade preferred charges against Burnside which were never acted upon. The Committee on the Conduct of the War investigated the same matter, and came to a far different conclusion. The political orthodoxy of Burnside outweighed in their minds the purely military judgment of Grant and Meade; the change made by these generals in the plan of attack, substituting white for colored soldiers, was decided to be "the first and great cause of disaster." Their report justified Burnside in every particular, and censured Meade for everything that went wrong. But it was too late to restore Burnside to command. The war was ending by the time the committee reported, and his resignation, tendered on the very day of Lincoln's assassination was accepted by President Johnson among his first official acts. Burnside returned to civil life, and entered at once upon a career of unbroken and eminent popularity and success.

After this disastrous failure the engineers, under General Grant's orders, went on perfecting the redoubts and the lines connecting them so that at the proper time the works might be held by a small force and the rest of the army be free to move upon the enemy's communications. But the summer wore away without the accomplishment of this purpose, though several more or less serious attempts in that direction were made. During the summer and autumn the attention of both Grant and Lee was constantly diverted to the operations in the Shenandoah to the neglect of important movements about Petersburg. Sheridan was assigned to that field of duty in which he was to win imperishable laurels; two divisions of cavalry under Wilson and Torbert were given him, and Lee sent one of his best divisions under Kershaw to reënforce Early. Grant himself made two visits to that part of his command; one early in August, at the time he placed Sheridan in command, and one in September, when he gave him the order to begin his glorious campaign in the Valley, which resulted in the victory of Winchester. The Army of the Potomac during this period was by no means idle; besides their engineering work, several partial movements to right and left were made, with the result of extending the Union lines, and forcing the Confederates to give a corresponding extension to theirs; the effect of which was in all cases to weaken the inferior force. But even in those movements, Grant's mind was occupied rather with Sheridan and Early than with Lee.

Near the middle of August Grant was led to believe that Lee had made a detachment of three divisions of infantry and some cavalry from his army to reënforce Early, and he at once resolved to make a heavy demonstration north of the James to prevent the dispatch of any further forces to the Valley, and, if possible, to draw back those already sent. Hancock, who had resumed command of the Second Corps, and Birney, with a part of the Tenth, crossed the river and marched, on the 14th, along the three principal roads between the Chickahominy and the James, in the direction of Richmond. But they met the enemy everywhere in full force, under Field, Wilcox, and Mahone, and gained no special advantage, except in learning that no such force as Grant had apprehended had gone to Early, and in detaining a large body of troops in that neighborhood. Hancock was kept, however, for several days north of the James, maintaining a menacing attitude and skirmishing constantly, but forbidden to attack the Confederate works, as an assault, under existing circumstances, offered no probable chance of success.

While this energetic demonstration was going on, General Warren was withdrawn from the lines before Petersburg (the Ninth Corps being stretched over the space vacated by the Fifth) and ordered to seize the Weldon road at the Globe Tavern, a point about four miles due south from Petersburg, and destroy it from that point as far south as possible. In this movement, also, Grant's constant preoccupation in regard to Sheridan is seen. "I want," he said, "to make such demonstrations as will force Lee to withdraw a portion of his troops from the Valley, so that Sheridan can strike a blow against the balance." He was under some temptation to go in person with a large detachment to Sheridan's assistance, but wisely concluded to stay where he was. This determination the President heartily approved and applauded. On the 17th he sent to Grant this terse and vehement dispatch, which indicates in a singular manner the close moral sympathy between the two men: "I have seen your dispatch expressing your unwillingness to break your hold where you are. Neither am I willing. Hold on with a bulldog grip, and chew and choke as much as possible.— A. Lincoln, President."

Warren moved out at dawn on the 18th, seized the Weldon road at the place directed, and immediately began the work of destruction. A force sent by Beauregard under General Heth attacked him about two o'clock, and a sharp action ensued, resulting in the loss of about a thousand men on each side, the Unionists finally holding the field. The next day, both sides having been strongly reënforced, an impetuous attack by the Confederates, now under the command of A. P. Hill, produced for a time some confusion on the right of Warren's force; but Warren speedily reformed his troops and drove the Confederates back to their intrenchments. On the 20th, Warren, feeling sure that Lee would not willingly acquiesce in the loss of the Weldon road, and that he would have to fight further to retain the advantage he had gained, took up a stronger position a mile in rear, and awaited the attack of the enemy. This came on the 21st; Hill opening with a severe artillery fire and assaulting at two o'clock with great energy. He was, however, completely repulsed, leaving his dead and wounded and several hundred prisoners in Warren's hands. No further attempt was made on his position. The Weldon road, thus boldly clutched and bravely held, remained in the hands of the Union army till the war ended.

The mere possession of a point on the road was not all that General Grant desired. By destroying the road to Rowanty Creek, some thirteen miles beyond Warren's left, he could force the Confederates to haul their supplies a distance of thirty miles. General Hancock, with two divisions of infantry and Gregg's cavalry, was sent to accomplish this work, and did it so expeditiously that by the night of the 24th the destruction of the road was complete to a cross road three miles south of Reams's Station, leaving only five miles of the work undone. But General Lee could not afford to allow this work of destruction to go on undisturbed, and therefore sent A. P. Hill with a large force of infantry, cavalry, and artillery to prevent it. He attacked Hancock on the 25th, and in spite of admirable conduct of the Union general and his subordinates, Miles and

Gibbon, they were driven from their position with considerable loss. Night coming on, Hill made no effort to pursue his advantage and both parties returned to their respective intrenchments near Petersburg.

In this battle, as in nearly every engagement since Cold Harbor, there was apparent a certain loss of morale in the army. In the operations of the week before, north of the James, the utmost efforts of such intrepid soldiers as Barlow and Gibbon could not get the requisite work out of their troops, and in this affair, the splendid personal conduct of Hancock and Miles was not enough to inspire their commands. The causes of this laxity were not difficult to discover. The weather was hot and enervating; the constant marching and lack of repose had wearied the soldiers; they were composed in great numbers of raw recruits not inured to such warfare; and, worse than all, the terrible loss in competent and experienced officers, which had been suffered on the dozen sanguinary fields of May, June, and July, had for the moment rendered the Army of the Potomac no longer the elastic and perfect tempered weapon it had been in other days, and which it became once more after a few months of discipline and drill.

After Sheridan's victory in the Shenandoah, and his hot pursuit of Early, the President was anxious lest Lee should detach a large force to reënforce Early; and Grant, to prevent this, and hold Lee in position, made another movement against the Confederate lines north of the James. He sent Ord and Birney, with the Eighteenth and Tenth Army Corps, on the 28th of September, to threaten Richmond from that direction and to take advantage of any favorable opening they might be able to find, or make, in the enemy's lines. By daylight the next day the whole force was over the river and moving swiftly upon the Confederate skirmishers. At first all went prosperously with Ord's column. George J. Stannard's division captured Fort Harrison, an important Confederate work, with sixteen guns and some prisoners, after a gallant fight in which General Hiram Burnham was killed. But in the attempt to push his success by capturing a redan by the riverside, General Ord was severely wounded; and his troops, under General C. A. Heckman, met with a serious repulse in the effort to carry Fort Gilmer by storm.

Birney on the right carried the skirmish line on the New Market road, and then at the order of General Grant, who had arrived at Fort Harrison, assaulted Fort Gilmer with Adelbert Ames's division and William Birney's brigade of colored troops. The attack was made with the greatest energy; the colored soldiers rushing to the ditch with splendid gallantry and climbing to the parapet on each other's shoulders, only to be killed when they reached it. General Ewell commanded the Confederate troops, under the eye of Lee, who was present on the field. Though all efforts to take Fort Gilmer proved fruitless, the National troops established themselves firmly in the captured Fort Harrison and with astonishing celerity converted it under the enemy's fire into an inclosed work. A heavy force was concentrated by Lee to retake it, and on the afternoon of the 30th General Anderson, commanding Longstreet's Corps, assaulted the work, supported by a heavy fire of Confederate artillery. Stannard, in the fort, reserved his musketry until the rebel columns emerged from the underbrush, and then delivered a deadly volley which swept them from the ground. Three times the attack was made and as often repulsed, though the resolute Stannard lost his arm in the second assault. The losses in the two days were about even, some 2000 on the Confederate side and 2272 among the Union troops. The fort was never retaken.

During these operations General Meade was directed to make such demonstrations to his left as should prevent any considerable force from being sent to the other side of the river, and on the 30th a strong reconnaissance was made under command of Warren, which captured the Confederate intrenchments at the junction of the Squirrel Level and Poplar Spring roads. Pushing on from that position in the direction of the Boydton Plank road and the South Side Railroad, the National troops under Parke and Potter met with a severe repulse from a force commanded by Heth and C. M. Wilcox, which General A. P. Hill, who had succeeded Beauregard in command at Petersburg, had thrown out to meet them. The next day, however, General Parke advanced again, with sharp skirmishing, and established a line about a mile from the enemy's, which was at once firmly connected with the works on the Weldon road and was not thereafter disturbed.

The principal event of October was the campaign of Early against Sheridan, which ended in the crushing defeat of the Confederates at Cedar Creek. Grant's anxiety about the Valley prevented any important operations during the early part of this month. The Confederates under C. W. Field and Hoke made a violent assault upon Kautz on the 6th of October, driving him from his position on the Darby road and capturing his guns; but venturing to attack the intrenched infantry lines they were severely repulsed. A week later, General Butler in his turn assaulted the Confederate works on the north of the James and was defeated with considerable loss.

On the 27th, the Army of the Potomac made one last effort to get possession of the South Side Railroad. A sufficient force was left in the redoubts to hold them; all the available infantry, amounting to some 35,000, with a due proportion of artillery and about 3000 horse, under Gregg, on the 27th moved to the left under the command of Hancock and Warren. The morning was dark and rainy; there were unavoidable delays in the start. The movement was not a surprise and the enemy was encountered everywhere in force. The different commands met with some partial success during the morning, and at two o'clock the leading corps was still six miles from the railroad. The movement had failed, and Grant ordered the troops back to their lines. But they were not even to accomplish this order without serious disturbance. The roads were difficult; the topography unknown to the National commanders. There was a considerable gap between the forces of Hancock and those of Warren, and through this, late in the afternoon, the Confederates under William Mahone rushed and made a vigorous attack on Hancock's right and rear. Hancock pulled his force together with wonderful readiness and address, and, assisted by T. W. Egan, Gershom Mott, and Gregg, turned upon Mahone and drove him from the field. By this time it was dark, and the next day the troops were withdrawn to their lines. This action is called the battle of Hatcher's Run.

In support of this movement General Butler made a demonstration on the same day on the north side of the James which was unsuccessful. His forces under Weitzel were met by the local defenses under Longstreet, who had recovered from his wounds and been assigned to command a week before, and were roughly handled. The Union loss was over a thousand men; that of the Confederates much less. This ended the active operations of the year so far as concerned any grand movement by the Army of the Potomac. They were still employed in defending and strengthening their lines and in occasional demonstrations against the enemy's communications; so that by the 7th of February, 1865, the Union lines reached to Hatcher's Run, and the Weldon road was destroyed to Hicks's Ford. But the hard fighting ended with the close of October. The troops had reached a dangerous condition of weariness. The frightful losses in competent officers and veteran soldiers could not be compensated by any number of raw recruits. Warren said that at the time of the affair at Hatcher's Run 3913 of his men had never fired a musket and that 1649 of them were ignorant of the manual. Hancock gives the same significant testimony. General Parke in his report of the movement of September 30 says: "The large amount of raw material in the ranks has diminished greatly the efficiency of the corps." The composition of the army was so changed by the inferior material obtained by drafting and the heavy bounties, that a rigid system of instruction and discipline was necessary to make the new men homogeneous. It was no longer the old historic Army of the Potomac. But the work of the winter wrought a rapid transformation, and when, in the early spring, the order "Forward" was given the troops sprang to the summons and finished the war.

Sherman's troops marched into Atlanta on September 2, 1864. For the next two months the Confederate commander, John B. Hood, operating around the city, menaced the Union supply lines. Despite several engagements and considerable maneuvering, Sherman never succeeded in inflicting a sharp defeat upon his opponent. Finally Sherman decided to ignore Hood and embark on the audacious venture on which he had set his heart: a march through Georgia to Savannah, and from there northward to join Grant before Richmond.

Nicolay and Hay take up the story.

The March to the Sea

ON THE 3d of November Sherman reported to Halleck the situation of affairs announcing his settled intention to move forward as soon as he could send back all rubbish to the rear and get forward the necessary supplies with which to start; advised coöperative movements from Thomas's and Canby's front which, he said, would completely bewilder Beauregard and make him "burst with French despair." On the 6th he issued orders to all commanding officers of forts directing preparations to go forward with as much speed as possible, but intimated that time would be allowed in present camps for the complete payment of all troops, the sending home of the soldiers' money, and the voting of the soldiers in their camp for President. He found time on the same day to write a long letter to Grant explaining and justifying his conduct in the October movement, expressing his confidence that with Stanley and Schofield Thomas would be able to take care of Hood, and enlarging upon the vast moral benefit to be derived from the contemplated march. "If we can march a well-appointed army right through his territory it is a demonstration to the world, foreign and domestic, that we have a power which Davis cannot resist. . . . There are thousands of people abroad and in the South who will reason thus: If the North can march an army right through the South it is proof positive that the North can prevail in this contest. . . . Mr. Lincoln's election, which is assured, coupled with the conclusion thus reached, makes a complete logical whole." He then discusses the three routes open to him, decides in favor of that having its terminus at Charleston or Savannah, but leaves himself open to adopt either alternative.

All preparations being completed he caused the foundries, mills, and shops of every kind in Rome to be destroyed on the 10th of November. The next day he telegraphed to Halleck, "All appearances still indicate that Beauregard has got back to his old hole at Corinth and I hope he will enjoy it. My army prefers to enjoy the fresh sweet-potato fields of the Ocmulgee." He started on the 12th with his full staff from Kingston to Atlanta. Resting at noon, his telegraphic operator, with a small pocket instrument which he held in his lap, called the Chattanooga office, and received this last message from General Thomas. The "Rock of Chickamauga" had not been especially pleased with his assignment to defend Tennessee, but he accepted it as he did every duty ever confided him with modest confidence and devotion. "I have no fears," he said, "that Beauregard can do us any harm now, and if he attempts to follow you I will follow him as far as possible. If he does not follow you, I will then thoroughly organize my troops and, I believe, shall have men enough to ruin him unless he gets out of the way very rapidly . . . I am now convinced that the greater part of Beauregard's army is near Florence and Tuscumbia and that you will at least have a clear road before you for several days, and that your success will fully equal your expectations." Sherman began to reply, "Dispatch received. All right," and at that instant the wires were cut and communications ceased. As Sherman rode towards Atlanta that night he met railroad trains going to the rear with furious speed. He was profoundly impressed with the strange aspect of affairs: two hostile armies marching in opposite directions, each in the full belief that it was achieving a final and conclusive result in the great war. "I was strongly inspired," he writes, "with a feeling that the movement on our part was a direct attack upon the rebel army and the rebel capital at Richmond, though a full thousand miles of hostile country intervened; and that for better or worse it would end the war." The result was a magnificent vindication of this soldierly intuition.

His army consisted in round numbers of sixty thousand men, the most perfect in strength, health, and intelligence that ever went to war. He had thoroughly purged it of all inefficient material, sending to the rear all organizations and even all individuals that he thought would be a drag upon his celerity or strength. His right wing, under Howard, consisted of the Fifteenth Corps, commanded by Osterhaus, in the absence of John A. Logan; and the Seventeenth Corps, commanded by Frank P. Blair, Jr. The left wing, commanded by Slocum, comprised the Fourteenth Corps under Jeff. C. Davis, and the Twentieth Corps under A. S. Williams. In his general orders he had not intimated to the army the object of their march. "It is sufficient for you to know," he said, "that it involves a departure from our present base and a long, difficult march to a new one." His special field orders are a model of clearness and conciseness.

The habitual order of march was to be, wherever practicable, by four roads as nearly parallel as possible, and converging at points to be indicated from time to time. There was to be no general train of supplies; behind each regiment should follow one wagon and one ambulance; a due proportion of wagons for ammunition and provision behind each brigade; the separate columns were to start at seven in the morning and make about fifteen miles a day. The army was to subsist liberally on the country; forage parties, under the command of discreet officers, were to gather near the routes traveled whatever was needed by the command, aiming to keep in the wagons a reserve of at least ten days' provisions; soldiers were strictly forbidden to enter dwellings of inhabitants or commit trespasses; the power to destroy mills, houses, cotton gins, etc., was intrusted to corps commanders alone. No destruction of property was to be permitted in districts where the army was unmolested; but relent-less devastation was ordered in case of the manifestation of local hostility by the shooting of soldiers or the burning of bridges. The cavalry were ordered to appropriate, freely, horses, mules, and wagons from the country passed through. It was strictly enjoined that the negroes should not be encouraged to follow the army, and that none but a certain proportion of able-bodied young men, whose services were needed, should be allowed to follow.

Precisely at seven o'clock on the morning of the 16th of November the great army started on its march. A band struck up the anthem of "John Brown's body lies a-moldering in the grave"; the soldiers caught up the refrain, and, to the swelling chorus of "Glory, Hallelujah," the great march was begun. The month that followed will always remain to those sixty thousand men the most romantic and inspiring memory of their lives. The weather was favorable all the way; to veterans the marches were of reasonable length; the work of destroying the Southern railroads was so easy to their experienced hands that it hardly delayed the day's march. With the exception of the affair on the 22d of November, when P. J. Phillips with a di-vision of Smith's Georgia troops attacked C. C. Walcutt's Brigade, which was marching as the rear-guard of the right wing at Griswoldville, and met with a severe repulse, and a series of cavalry fights between Wheeler and Kilpatrick near Waynesboro', there was no fighting to do between Atlanta and Savannah. A swarm of militia and irregular cavalry hung, it is true, about the front and flank of the marching army, but were hardly a source of more annoyance than so many mosqui-toes would have been. The foragers brought in every evening their heterogeneous supplies from the outlying plantations, and although they had to defend themselves every day from scat-tered forces of the enemy, the casualties which they reported each evening were insignificant. The utmost efforts of Sherman and his officers to induce the negroes to remain quietly at home were not entirely successful. The promise of freedom which was to come to them from the victory of the Union cause was too vague and indefinite to content them. When they saw this vast army moving by before their cabins, with flaunting banners, which were to them the visible sign and symbol of emancipation, in spite of every effort made to drive them away, the simple-hearted freedmen gathered in an ever-increasing cloud in rear of the army; and when the campaign was over they peopled the sea-islands of Georgia and furnished, after the war, the principal employment of the Freedmen's Commission.

The march produced an extraordinary effervescence throughout the Confederacy. If words could avail anything against heavy battalions, Sherman would have been annihilated in his first day's march. Beauregard fulminated his proclamations, filled with lurid Creole rhetoric, to the people of Georgia, calling them to rally around their "patriotic Governor"—an adjective which hardly agreed with Jefferson Davis's recent characterization of Governor Brown. He called on them to obstruct and destroy all the roads in Sherman's front, flank, and rear, promising that his army should soon starve in their midst. From Richmond the same vehement proclamations were rained upon Georgia. The people were assured that President Davis and the Secretary of War had done and were still doing all that could be done to meet the emergency. "Let every man fly to arms!" shouted the Georgia members of Congress. "Remove your negroes, horses, cattle, and provisions from Sherman's army, and burn what you cannot carry. . . . Assail the invader in front, flank, and rear, by night and by day. Let him have no rest."

As Sherman drew near to Milledgeville on the 23d of November the Georgia Legislature passed an act to levy the population *en masse;* but this act of desperate legislation had no effect in checking the march of the "Yankees," and the Governor, State officers, and Legislature fled in the utmost confusion as Sherman entered the place. The Union general occupied the Executive Mansion for a day; some of the soldiers went to the State House, organized themselves into a constituent assembly, and after a spirited mock-serious debate, repealed the ordinance

of secession. Sherman took the greatest possible pains to prevent
any damage to the city and marched out on the 24th on the way
to Millen. He ordered his force of cavalry in the direction of
Augusta, but pushed steadily forward with his main body, and
on the 3d of December entered Millen with Blair's corps and
paused there a day to bring the army together. Finding it impossible to stop him, the Georgia State troops by sharp marching had made their way directly to the vicinity of Savannah,
where Sherman himself arrived and invested the city from
the Savannah to the little Ogeechee River, on the 10th of
December.

General Hardee had found it impossible to hold his outer line
of works. He destroyed the Charleston and Savannah Railroad
bridge over the Savannah River and withdrew to his inner line.
He had had in the last days of November a piece of singular
good fortune. The Georgia militia under General G. W. Smith
had arrived at Grahamsville on the Charleston Railroad exactly
at the proper time to repulse an attack of a division of National
troops under General John P. Hatch, which had been sent by
General J. G. Foster to occupy that important road in the rear
of Hardee. Several spirited assaults were made by Hatch's
troops, but they were all unsuccessful; so that this inestimable
route of retreat by way of the Union causeway and the Charleston road, was saved to Hardee. He had no confidence in his
ability to hold Savannah permanently against Sherman. He
and Richard Taylor, who had hurried across the Confederacy
from the west to join him, agreed that Hardee ought to be ready
to abandon Savannah before it could be thoroughly invested.
It was of the utmost importance that his army and the garrison of Charleston should be saved and united to oppose the
northward march of Sherman after Savannah should be taken,
and the repulse of Hatch made this most desirable consummation entirely practicable. The Union causeway was so protected by inundated rice fields that it was impossible, or at
least exceedingly difficult, for Sherman to close this avenue of
retreat without making a large detachment from his army and
a long detour to the north.

But the first necessity of the situation to Sherman was to establish his communications with the sea. Howard had sent an intelligent scout, Captain William Duncan, down the Ogeechee in a canoe, but had heard no report as to his success in communicating with the fleet. The way to the sea was barred by a formidable work called Fort McAllister, on the south side of the Ogeechee River. Sherman determined to reduce this work by assault, and assigned for the purpose his own favorite division of the Fifteenth Corps, the same which he had commanded at Shiloh and Vicksburg. His engineers, to whom nothing now seemed difficult, speedily built a bridge over the river, and at sunrise Hazen's division passed over with orders to march rapidly down the right bank of the Ogeechee and to assault and carry the fort by storm. Sherman reasoned that the strongest side of the work would be that which was constructed to resist an attack by sea, and that the gorge would be comparatively weak. Hazen, however, found so many and such formidable obstacles in his way, that it was five o'clock in the afternoon before he was ready for the assault. Sherman waited with intense anxiety, on a signal station, in full sight of the work; finally he received from Hazen a signal message that he was ready, and at that moment a small steamer approached from the sea whose officers inquired by signal whether Fort McAllister was taken. Sherman answered, "Not yet; but it will be in a minute." Never was a promise more promptly and perfectly kept. "At that instant," as Sherman says, "we saw Hazen's troops come out of the dark fringe of woods that encompassed the fort, the lines dressed as on parade, with colors flying, and moving forward with a quick, steady pace. Fort McAllister was then all alive, its big guns belching forth dense clouds of smoke, which soon enveloped our assaulting lines. One color went down, but was up in a moment. On the lines advanced, faintly seen in the white, sulphurous smoke; there was a pause, a cessation of fire; the smoke cleared away, and the parapets were blue with our men, who fired their muskets in the air, and shouted so that we actually heard them, or felt that we did. Fort McAllister was taken."

Sherman, without losing a moment's time, took a boat and pushed out to sea to visit General Foster, who, on account of the breaking out of an old wound, was unable to visit him. He also visited Admiral Dahlgren on his flagship, the *Harvest Moon*, and having arranged with these officers for assistance and supplies, he returned to Fort McAllister. The capture of this important work had placed his right wing upon impregnable ground, and assured permanently and perfectly his communications with the fleet.

At this moment, when all his energies and all his resources should have been free for operations on his left against Savannah, he was thrown into great perplexity by dispatches from General Grant. An aide-de-camp arrived on the 14th with a letter from the Lieutenant-General, somewhat indefinite in terms; but it was followed, on the next day, by one written on the 6th, saying: "I have concluded that the most important operation toward closing out the rebellion will be to close out Lee and his army." He therefore suggested that Sherman should establish a base on the seacoast, leaving there all his artillery and cavalry, and with the rest of his army come north by water, with all dispatch. "The contents of these letters," says Sherman, "gave me great uneasiness, for I had set my heart on the capture of Savannah, which I believed to be practicable and to be near; for me to embark for Virginia by sea was so complete a change from what I had supposed would be the course of events that I was very much concerned." Slocum had already occupied Argyle Island and the upper end of Hutchison Island, and had a brigade on the South Carolina shore opposite, and was urging that he might be permitted to pass one of his corps to the north side of the Savannah to operate against Hardee's communications with South Carolina.

But Sherman, feeling hampered by Grant's orders, supposing that a fleet of vessels would soon be pouring in ready to convey his army to Virginia, instead of acting at once with his usual energy against Hardee, set about preparing the ground around Fort McAllister for the fortified camp which Grant had directed him to establish. Betaking himself to his pen, which he handled with as much ease and alacrity as his sword, he wrote, on the 17th of December, a summons to Hardee for the surrender of Savannah. He assured him that he had sufficient means for the reduction of Savannah, that he had guns that could cast heavy and destructive shot to the heart of the city; that he held and controlled every avenue by which Savannah could be supplied, and was, therefore, justified in demanding its surrender. Had his note ended there, it would have been liable to no criticism, except ineffectiveness; but he closed by the threat, that if forced to assault, he should feel justified in resorting to the harshest measures, and should make little effort to restrain his army. He inclosed, as a final blunder, a copy of Hood's demand for the surrender of Resaca, in which, it will be remembered, that indiscreet warrior had threatened to put the garrison to the sword, and on his demand being refused had marched away from the place; Sherman thus suggesting a historical parallel which he should have avoided at any cost.

Hardee answered with great calmness and propriety, denying all General Sherman's premises, and refusing to surrender the town. In reply to the menace of Sherman, Hardee said: "I have hitherto conducted the military operations intrusted to my direction in strict accordance with the rules of civilized warfare, and I should deeply regret the adoption of any course by you that may force me to deviate from them in the future." Sherman now resolved, in consideration of the short time allowed him by his understanding of Grant's orders, to assault the place; but, in view of the difficulty of the ground, the only avenues of approach being narrow causeways, running across inundated rice fields, he determined to make a final effort to invest the city completely, so that in case of success Hardee's entire army might be captured. The only avenue by which Hardee remained in communication with South Carolina was the Union causeway, connecting his pontoon bridge with the outlying works at Grahamsville, which had been thus far held successfully against Foster by the Georgia militia.

Sherman visited Foster again to request him to move Hatch's division down to Bluffton, a point from which it might reach the Union causeway, fortify, and hold it. Foster at once engaged to perform this work, and Sherman returned, after a tedious trip, so delayed by contrary winds and low tides that it was evening on the 21st of December before he arrived at his camp. The startling news that awaited him was that Hardee had successfully evacuated Savannah. During the night of the 20th and the morning of the 21st, he had marched his garrison over the pontoon bridge and northward along the Union causeway, undisturbed by Foster's troops. He had carried away his men and his light artillery, but had destroyed his ironclads and the navy yard, leaving, however, Savannah, a rich prize in itself, and made still richer in spoil of every kind. So quietly was the change in the government of the city effected, that a blockade runner, which had eluded the fleet outside, steamed up to the wharf unconscious of danger, and its captain did not learn he had lost his vessel until he presented his papers at the Custom-House.

Though somewhat disappointed at Hardee's escape, whatever chagrin Sherman may have felt speedily passed away in view of the enormous importance of the acquisition he had made. Riding into Savannah he sent a brief dispatch to the President in these words: "I beg to present to you as a Christmas gift the city of Savannah, with 150 heavy guns and plenty of ammunition; also about 25,000 bales of cotton." His gratification was increased by the receipt a few days later of letters from Grant and Halleck, full of generous and unqualified praise for his great campaign, and what was still more grateful to his feelings, an absolute revocation of the orders to proceed North by sea. General Halleck said: "General Grant's wishes . . . are that this whole matter of your future actions should be left entirely to your own discretion." Grant said, "If you capture the garrison of Savannah it certainly will compel Lee to detach from Richmond or give us nearly the whole South. My own opinion is that Lee is averse to going out of Virginia;

and if the cause of the South is lost he wants Richmond to be the last place surrendered. If he has such views, it may be well to indulge him until we get everything else in our hands." He closed by congratulating Sherman upon the splendid results of his campaign, "the like of which is not read of in past history." To crown the year's work with the most transcendent gratification possible to a soldier, came also letters detailing the check inflicted upon Hood at Franklin, and the glorious victory at Nashville, where Thomas had utterly broken in pieces the last invading army of the Confederates in the West. This was to Sherman the final vindication of his great campaign, proving, as he held, that "his army had been properly divided, and that each part was duly proportioned to its work."

Congress passed at once a joint resolution tendering the thanks of the nation "to Major-General William T. Sherman, and through him to the officers and men under his command for their gallantry and good conduct in their late campaign from Chattanooga to Atlanta, and the triumphal march thence through Georgia to Savannah terminating in the capture and occupation of that city." But no expression of appreciation and of gratitude equaled in the mind of Sherman the letter with which the President acknowledged the receipt, on Christmas Eve, of his dispatch from Savannah, for Mr. Lincoln in this remarkable letter gave to Sherman, as he had given to Grant after Vicksburg, the inestimable assurance that the credit of the victory was exclusively his own; that the Government claimed no part in it.

MY DEAR GENERAL SHERMAN: Many, many thanks for your Christmas gift, the capture of Savannah. When you were about leaving Atlanta for the Atlantic coast I was anxious, if not fearful; but feeling that you were the better judge, and remembering that "nothing risked, nothing gained," I did not interfere. Now, the undertaking being a success, the honor is all yours, for I believe none of us went farther than to acquiesce. And taking the work of General Thomas into the count, as it should be taken, it is, indeed, a great success. Not only does it afford the obvious and immediate military advantages, but in showing to the world that your army could be divided, putting the stronger part to an important new service, and yet leaving enough to vanquish the old opposing force of the whole—Hood's army—it brings those who sat in darkness to see a great light. But what next? I suppose it will be safe if I leave General Grant and yourself to decide. Please make my grateful acknowledgments to your whole army, officers and men.

Upon this letter General Sherman may safely rest his claim to the glory of the march to the sea. It would be a fruitless toil to examine and refute the claims which are made by the friends of other generals that Sherman only adopted and executed the original thought of somebody else. It is not to be questioned that many other people had thought of marching through the center of the Confederacy. Hunter had proposed to march a column westward from Hilton Head; Burnside, while at Knoxville, had suggested to Halleck that he should be allowed to move by Bragg's flank to Atlanta, "destroy the enemy's communications, . . . and thence move to such a place on the coast, where cover can be obtained, as shall be agreed upon with you. It is proposed to take no trains, but live upon the country. . . ." But it is idle to multiply these quotations from the men who imagined such a march. There were men before Columbus who dreamed of sailing west to find India. The glory and honor belong of right to the man who translates the vague thought into substantial achievement. General Sherman has the right to have his own account of the ripening of this plan in his mind implicitly accepted. He says: "As soon as Hood had shifted across from Lovejoy's to Palmetto, I saw the move in my 'mind's eye,' and after Jeff. Davis's speech at Palmetto of September 26, I was more positive in my conviction, but was in doubt as to the time and manner. When General Hood first struck our railroad above Marietta we were not ready, and I was forced to watch his movements further till he had 'carromed' off to the west of Decatur. Then I was perfectly convinced, and had no longer a shadow of doubt. The only possible question was as to Thomas's strength and ability to meet Hood in the open field. I did not suppose that General Hood, though rash, would venture to attack fortified places like Allatoona, Resaca, Decatur, and Nashville; but he did so, and in so doing he played into our hands perfectly."

IF SHERMAN'S PLAN *were to succeed, the Federal forces must maintain their hold on Tessessee and Kentucky. To secure these states he left George H. Thomas in command of the Department of the Cumberland and sent him north with twenty-two thousand effective infantry and some seventy-five hundred cavalry, soon to be supplemented by thousands of recruits and some veteran troops. Thomas garrisoned posts along the southern border of Tennessee and waited.*

Hood had a plan as bold as Sherman's. Hood would move north, defeat Thomas, and thousands of sympathizers in Tennessee and Kentucky would join the Confederate ranks. He could menace Cincinnati, and Sherman would be forced to abandon his own invasion and come to the defense of the Union territory north of the Ohio River.

When Hood began his campaign Thomas, well informed of his opponent's movements, started to draw his own scattered troops to Nashville. On November 29 Hood caught Schofield at Spring Hill, Tennessee, but the Federal commander escaped the trap and withdrew his command to Franklin, eighteen miles south of Nashville. There, on November 30, a decisive battle took place.

Franklin and Nashville

BUT while these operations were going on it became necessary to provide for receiving Hood's attack on the other side of the village. The Twenty-third Corps was posted on both sides of the main road, upon which Hood's army was expected. The village of Franklin stands in a bend of the Harpeth River, so that Cox, who commanded the lines, had his left on the stream, and extended across the Columbia pike to the Carter's Creek pike, but could not reach to the bend of the river on the other side. Kimball's division was, therefore, given the duty of closing the line on that flank. The instant the men were assigned their

positions they went to work with instinctive alacrity to build
such slight breastworks as the means at hand afforded. The
roadway was left open to enable a double line of wagons and
artillery to pass, and this opening was protected by a retrenchment a few rods further back.

Wagner's division, which had held the lines at Spring Hill
all the day before, and which had brought up the rear in a long
night march, came in about noon. Colonel Opdycke's brigade,
which had formed the rear guard, and upon which had fallen
the double duty of beating back Hood's advance, and driving
forward the weary and limping recruits of Schofield's army,
now came inside the lines, and was posted as a reserve in rear
of the center. Wagner's other two brigades were left outside the
principal line, about half a mile forward on the Columbia pike,
with instructions to observe the enemy, and to retire as soon as
the Confederates showed a disposition to advance in force.
The weary soldiers threw themselves down for a little repose
behind their breastworks; neither Schofield nor his corps commanders imagined that a great battle was to burst upon them
in a few moments. The artillery and trains were nearly all across
the river by the middle of the afternoon, and Schofield had
issued orders for the troops to pass over at six o'clock. But there
was a state of things in the Confederate army which made any
moderate or prudent measures impossible to Hood. His failure
to destroy Schofield at Spring Hill had so embittered and exasperated him that he was ready for any enterprise, however
desperate. The irritation had communicated itself to his principal officers; his reproaches had stung them beyond endurance;
and, therefore, on arriving in sight of Schofield's army, in position on the south bank of the Harpeth, there was no thought
of anything among the Confederate commanders but immediate
and furious attack. All the Confederate accounts agree in describing this spirit in Hood's army on the morning of the 30th
of November, though Hood and his generals entirely disagree
as to the cause of it. Generals Cheatham and John C. Brown,
and, according to their account, General Cleburne also, ascribed

it to to Hood's unreasonable and angry censures of their conduct the day before, while Hood attributes the new spirit
of the army to mortification for the great opportunity lost
and a renewed access of admiration and confidence towards
himself.

The assault was made at about four o'clock. The Confederates never rushed forward to battle with more furious impetus,
and by a strange accident it seemed for a moment as if this desperate assault of Hood was to succeed, and he was to gain the
glory he so ardently longed for of a success like Stonewall Jackson's best. Wagner's two brigades, that had been left outside the
line with instructions to retire before becoming actually engaged with the enemy, stayed too long. The wide and heavy
lines of Cheatham and Stewart had enveloped them on both
flanks and the bayonets of Hood's center were almost touching
them when they turned and ran for the Union lines. They
rushed over the parapets on either side of the pike, the Confederates following immediately after them, overwhelming and
carrying to the rear the troops who were defending the breastworks. A gap of about one thousand feet was instantly made in
the Union lines; Hood's battalions were rapidly converging to
this point. If the damage were not immediately repaired, it
would be irreparable; with a superior force wedged into the
Union center, short work would have been made of the two
wings, and nothing but annihilation would have been left for
Schofield's army.

General D. S. Stanley, the commander of the Fourth Corps,
seeing from the north side of the river the Confederate advance,
started at the instant for his line. He reached it just as the
breach was made and the confused mass of fugitives and Confederates came pouring to the rear. The only force available
at the instant to meet them was Opdycke's brigade, which had
fought all the day before at Spring Hill and afterwards had
marched all night; but even while Stanley was galloping to
order Opdycke to lead his men to the charge he saw that gallant commander taking position himself on the right of his line;

seeing that no orders were necessary he gave none, but placed himself at the left of this heroic brigade. A shout rose among the veteran soldiers about him, "We can go where the general can"; and the brigade, supported on the right and left by Cox's men, who instantly rallied to the rescue, rushed forward and regained the lines. Opdycke's magnificent courage met its adequate reward. He fought on horseback till his revolver was empty, then dealt about him with the butt of his pistol, and descending from his horse seized the musket of a fallen soldier, and fought like a private until the intrenchments were regained. Although four regimental commanders fell in this furious charge, Opdycke was unhurt. Stanley did not fare so well; his horse was killed under him and he received a serious wound in the neck and was carried to the rear.

The battle did not cease with this fierce onset and repulse. All along the line the Confederates made attack after attack. Hood sitting on horseback, a little way behind his lines, sent them forward again and again with furious orders "to drive the Yankees into the river." To show with what desperate gallantry the Confederates were led, it need only be said that six generals were killed on or near the parapets, six were wounded, and one captured. Cleburne closed his brilliant career in front of the Union breastworks. John Adams charged his horse over the ditch, leaped it, and horse and rider were killed upon the parapet. General O. F. Strahl fought with his men in the ditch until evening came; he was struck down; he turned over the command to Colonel F. E. P. Stafford, but while his men were carrying him to the rear he was struck twice more and killed. Stafford took up his fallen sword and carried on the fight with a courage which will form the theme of fable and legend in time to come. An eye witness says that his men were piled about him in such numbers that when at last he was shot dead he could not fall, but was found the next morning, partially upright, as if still commanding the gallant dead who surrounded him. Along the whole line the attack and defense were carried on, until nothing but the flashes of the muskets could be seen in the darkness, with the same furious gallantry on the one side and the same immovable determination on the other.

Few battles so frightfully destructive are recorded in the wars of modern times. In the terrible fight at Ezra Church, a Union picket shouted across the lines to a Confederate with that friendly chaff common to both armies, "I say, Johnny, how many of you are there left?" To which the undaunted Confederate replied, "About enough for another killing." On this terrible afternoon at Franklin, Hood's army suffered the last killing it was able to endure. He admitted in his dispatch to Richmond a loss of "about 4500"; but Thomas in his careful report foots the Confederate loss at 6252, of which all but 700 were killed and wounded. Schofield's loss was very much less, amounting to 2326 in all, of which Wagner's unfortunate division lost 1200. Had it not been for the mistake made in those two advanced brigades, Schofield's army would have slaughtered Hood's at its leisure. Thomas, in his grave and sober manner, thus sums up the result of this signal victory: "It not only seriously checked the enemy's advance and gave General Schofield time to move his troops and all his property to Nashville, but it also caused deep depression among the men of Hood's army, making them doubly cautious in their subsequent movements."

Schofield reported the day's work to Thomas and by his advice and direction fell back during the night to Nashville. His retreat was entirely unmolested; for Wilson, while the battle was going on at Franklin, had met and checked Forrest, holding him at the river and driving some of his detachments back. Schofield's army, on arriving at Nashville, occupied a position selected for it in advance by General Thomas. General Schofield held the left extending to the Nolensville pike; the Fourth Corps, under the command of General Wood, held the center, and the Sixteenth Corps under General A. J. Smith, who had just arrived in time to assist in the defense of Tennessee, occupied the right, his flank resting on the Cumberland River below the city. Wilson, with his cavalry, was stationed first at Schofield's left, but Steedman's provisional command having arrived at Nashville on the evening of the 1st of December Wilson was moved to the north side of the river and Steedman occupied the space from Schofield's left to the Cumberland.

Hood, as if driven by his evil genius, followed rapidly after Schofield and sat down before Nashville. He was aware, he said, of the reënforcements which had reached Thomas, and had brought the strength of the National army above his own, but he was in the position of a desperate gamester who has so little to lose that he feels it better policy to stake all than to leave the game. He knew that Mr. Davis was urgent in his orders for the reënforcement of the Army of Tennessee from Texas; he hoped that with this expected accession he might still realize the roseate dreams with which he had started out on this ill-starred campaign. He trusted to the chapter of accidents to give him some dazzling successes which would draw the Tennesseeans and Kentuckians to his standard.

He formed his line of battle in front of Nashville on the 2d of December. Lee's corps took the center, astride the Franklin pike, Stewart occupied the left, and Cheatham the right, their flanks widely extending towards the Cumberland River, and Forrest's cavalry filling the gap. But no sooner had he established himself there than, as if determined to give himself no chance in the impending battle, he detached Forrest on the 5th with W. B. Bate's division of infantry to invest and capture, if possible, the garrison of Murfreesboro', commanded by General Rousseau. This expedition totally failed. A sally was made on the 7th by some of Rousseau's troops under General Milroy, who won that day a merited consolation for his disaster at Winchester, and inflicted a sharp defeat upon Bate's infantry, which was thereupon recalled to Nashville; while Forrest, in this useless adventure, remained away from Hood too far to be recalled when he was most needed.

While General Hood was strengthening his intrenchments and waiting in vain for good news from Forrest, and the arrival of reënforcements from across the Mississippi, which were never to come, Thomas upon his side was completing in his unhurried and patient manner his preparations for a crushing blow. He would have been ready to strike in about a week after Hood's arrival. Nothing exhibits more vividly the tension of spirit which had come with four years of terrible war, than the fact that the Administration at Washington, which had patiently allowed McClellan to sit motionless in front of Johnston from July to February, began to urge Thomas to move against Hood within twenty-four hours of the victory at Franklin. General Grant felt and exhibited this impatience in a much stronger degree. He not only sent out daily messages urging immediate action, but betrayed an irritation which reads strangely in the light of Thomas's career. He carried this feeling much further than the civil authorities at Washington, though it is true that Mr. Stanton, in a strain of whimsical exaggeration, wrote to Grant on the 7th of December, "If he [Thomas] waits for Wilson to get ready, Gabriel will be blowing his last horn." Grant the next day telegraphed to Halleck, "If Thomas has not struck yet he ought to be ordered to hand over his command to Schofield." Halleck replied, showing that the Government at Washington, impatient as they felt for immediate action, cherished a higher regard for Thomas than that felt by the General-in-Chief. "If you wish General Thomas relieved," he said, "give the order. No one here will, I think, interfere. The responsibility, however, will be yours, as no one here, so far as I am informed, wishes General Thomas removed."

This dispatch saved General Thomas his command for a few days longer; but Grant refused to be placated. Thomas telegraphed him on the 8th in extenuation of his not having attacked Hood that he could not concentrate his troops and get their transportation in order in shorter time than it had been done. Halleck answered, expressing the deep dissatisfaction of Grant at Thomas's delay, and Grant, on the 9th, with growing indignation, requested Halleck to telegraph orders relieving Thomas at once and placing Schofield in command. These orders were immediately written out, but before they were transmitted to Nashville Thomas reported in his usual manly and reasonable style, "I regret that General Grant should feel dissatisfaction at my delay in attacking the enemy. I feel conscious that I have done everything in my power to prepare, and that the troops could not have been gotten ready before this. And if he should order me to be relieved I will submit without a murmur. A terrible storm of freezing rain has come on since daylight, which will render an attack impossible till it breaks." On the receipt of this dispatch the authorities took the responsibility of delaying the order for Thomas's relief until Grant could be consulted, and he, the same evening, suspended the order until, as he said, "it is seen whether he will do anything."

The spell of bad weather announced by Thomas in this dispatch continued for six days. It made any movement of either army impracticable. The rain froze as it fell, covering road and field with a thick coating of ice, upon which it was impossible for men to march, and on which every effort to move cavalry resulted in serious casualties to men and horses. General Grant knew this; but his fear that Hood might elude Thomas and lead him in a race to the Ohio River became so overpowering that it clouded his better judgment, and his dispatches of censure and vehement command came raining in day by day upon Thomas, causing that most subordinate and conscientious of soldiers exquisite pain, but never for an instant disturbing the calm equipoise of his mind. He replied from day to day, acknowledging the receipt of orders, and promising to execute them at the earliest moment possible. "The whole country," he said, on the 11th, "is covered with a perfect sheet of ice and sleet, and it is with difficulty that troops are able to move about on level ground." On the 12th it was no better. He again described in a dispatch the utter impossibility of moving men or horses, and his belief that an attack at this time would only result in a useless sacrifice of life.

It is hard to believe, and painful to write, that after the receipt of this truthful and loyal statement, General Grant dispatched General John A. Logan, who was then visiting him at

City Point, to relieve General Thomas at Nashville. He directed him, however, not to deliver the order or publish it until he reached his destination, and then, if Thomas had moved, not to deliver it at all. Even after Logan had started, Grant's uneasiness at the situation so gained upon him that he himself started for Nashville, and was met at Washington by news which electrified the country, saved General Thomas his command, and established him immutably in the respect and affection of his country. Thomas nowhere appears to greater advantage, not even on the hills of Chickamauga opposing his indomitable spirit to the surging tide of disaster and defeat, than he does during this week, opposing his sense of duty to the will of his omnipotent superior, and refusing to move one hour before he thought the interests of the country permitted it, even under the threat of removal and disgrace. In answer to Halleck's last peremptory dispatch, he replied on the evening of the 14th of December: "The ice having melted away to-day, the enemy will be attacked to-morrow morning"; and the next night he sent this laconic dispatch, "Attacked enemy's left this morning; drove it from the river below city very nearly to Franklin pike —distance about eight miles."

The frightful storms of rain and sleet which had held Thomas as if spell-bound had interfered equally with the mobility of Hood. Neither one nor the other could stir. Still, without the slightest trepidation, the Confederate chief waited for Thomas's attack, feeling sure, as he says in his report, "that I could defeat him and thus gain possession of Nashville with abundant supplies for the army. This would give me possession of Tennessee." So late as the 11th of December he wrote in a most encouraging strain to the Confederate Secretary of War, making suggestions as to his spring campaign, and saying with unconscious humor, "I think the position of this army is now such as to force the enemy to take the initiative."

On the morning of the 15th of December, in the midst of a heavy fog which masked the movements of Thomas's army, he threw it forward to the long desired attack. It was the sort of

weather which from time immemorial had been held as a justification for absolute inaction. The warm rains had changed the
sleety roads and fields to a sea of mire, through which the
troops floundered painfully. To divert Hood's attention from
his real purpose, Thomas had ordered Steedman to demon-
strate heavily with his command against the Confederate right,
east of the Nolensville pike, orders which that energetic commander carried out with such tumultuous zeal as to draw
Hood's attention almost entirely to that side of the field. Wilson's cavalry and Smith's infantry corps then moved out along
the Hardin pike and commenced the grand movement of the
day, by wheeling to the left, and advancing against the left
flank of Hood's position. Wilson first struck the enemy along
Richland Creek, which bounds the city on the west, and drove
him rapidly, making numerous captures, until he came upon a
detached redoubt, intended as a protection to Hood's left flank,
which was carried in splendid style by a portion of Edward
Hatch's dismounted troopers; another work and some hundreds
of prisoners were immediately after captured by the combined
assault of Smith's and Wilson's men.

But finding that Smith had not gone as far to the right as he
had hoped, Thomas directed Schofield to move the Twenty-
third Corps to the right of General Smith, by this means ena-
bling the cavalry to act freely upon Hood's left flank and rear.
Schofield's two divisions, admirably commanded by Generals Couch and Cox, marched with great spirit and swiftness to
the position assigned them and gained ground rapidly all the
afternoon. The Fourth Corps, under General T. J. Wood, which
held the center of the Union line, assaulted about one o'clock
Hood's advanced position at Montgomery Hill, a gallant feat
of arms executed by the brigade of Colonel P. Sidney Post.
From this point a rapid advance was made, the whole line
working steadily forward until Hood was driven everywhere
from his position, and forced back to a new line having its
right and left flank respectively on the Overton and the Brentwood Hills, his left occupying a commanding range of hills on

the east of the Franklin pike; his center stretched across from that road to another a mile to the west called the Granny White turnpike; both flanks were refused and strongly intrenched to the east and west and to the south, while the main line fronted northward. The Union lines closed rapidly about him, and in this position both sides waited for the morning.

The events of the day had filled the Union army with confidence and enthusiasm, and at early dawn on the morning of the 16th Thomas sent his whole line forward. Wood pressed the Confederate skirmishers across the Franklin pike, and swinging a little to the right, advanced due south, driving the enemy before him, until he came upon his new main line of works, constructed during the night on Overton's Hill. Steedman marched out on the Nolensville pike and formed on the left of Wood, the latter general taking command of both corps. Smith connected with Wood's right, his corps facing southward, while Schofield began the morning's work in the position where night had overtaken him, his line running almost due southward and perpendicular to that of Wood. Thomas now rode along the entire line surveying every inch of the field, and at last gave orders that the movement should continue against the Confederate left. His entire line was closely crowding that of Hood, there being only a space of 600 yards between them.

At about three o'clock, Post's brigade, which had on the day before so gallantly carried Montgomery Hill, was ordered by General Wood to assault the works on the Overton Heights. C. R. Thompson's brigade of colored troops of Steedman's command joined in this desperate enterprise. "Our men," says Thomas, "moved steadily onward up the hill until near the crest, when the reserve of the enemy rose and poured into the assaulting column a most destructive fire, causing the men first to waver and then to fall back, leaving their dead and wounded, black and white indiscriminately mingled, lying amidst the abatis, the gallant Colonel Post among the wounded." This was the only Confederate success of the day; but it was enough to excite the wildest hopes in the always sanguine breast of General Hood. Sitting on his horse and observing the repulse of Post's storming party, he says, "I had matured the movement for the next morning. The enemy's right flank, by this hour, stood in air some six miles from Nashville, and I had determined to withdraw my entire force during the night and attack this exposed flank in rear"; still intent on his reverent imitation of Stonewall Jackson. But even at the moment he was maturing this strategic scheme, his line, he says, "broke at all points," and he "beheld for the first and only time a Confederate army abandon the field in confusion."

Immediately after Post's assault had failed, the commands of Smith and Schofield advanced to the work assigned them, and with marvelous celerity and success they burst over the enemy's works in every direction, "carrying all before them, irreparably breaking his lines in a dozen places and capturing all his artillery and thousands of prisoners." The result was so sudden and so overwhelming that neither side was quite prepared for it.

Wilson had been making rapid progress with his cavalry on the extreme right, and had come to report his success to Thomas, who stood with Schofield directing operations; he saw the rush for the Confederate position and galloped back to his command to share in the final struggle; but as Cox says, "Before he could get half way there the whole Confederate left was crushed in like an egg-shell; . . . the arch was broken, there were no reserves to restore it, and from right and left the Confederate troops peeled away from the works in wild confusion." With the exception of the casualties in the gallant rush made by Post's and Thompson's brigades Thomas's entire loss was but slight. The Confederates abandoned their artillery, rushed across the Granny White road to the Franklin pike, and poured in a disorganized mass down the only avenue to the South which was left open to them. No rout during the war was ever more complete. Thomas captured in the two days 4462 prisoners, including 287 officers of all grades from that of major-general, fifty-three pieces of artillery, and thousands of small arms.

One or two of the brigades that still retained their organization formed as a rear guard on the Franklin pike, under command of S. D. Lee, and during the first hours of the night efficiently maintained a certain show of resistance to the pursuing cavalry. Night quickly closed in, and a drenching rain came down which made pursuit extremely difficult. General Grant was never satisfied with the swiftness and efficiency of Thomas's pursuit of Hood's beaten army; yet with the exception of that historic chase which began at Petersburg and ended at Appomattox there was no other pursuit of a beaten army during the war so energetic, so prolonged, and so fruitful. The cavalry column came up with the enemy's rear guard four miles north of Franklin. They charged it in front and flank, capturing 413 prisoners and three colors. They drove the Confederates through Franklin, capturing 2000 wounded in the hospitals there, and liberated some hundreds of Union prisoners. The cavalry pressed on, followed by the infantry, who moved with such expedition as was possible over the frightful roads, incumbered by all the débris of two armies.

On the 18th, the enemy crossed Harpeth River, destroying the bridges behind them. The profuse rains of the month now began to show their effects in the swollen water-courses. At Rutherford's Creek they found the stream, which was usually a rivulet, a foaming torrent. It took two days to get the command across; material for a bridge over Duck River was hastily pushed forward to that point so that Wood crossed late on the 22d, and got into position on the Pulaski road. Hood's army, though still retreating at the top of their speed, had by this time gained the powerful assistance of Forrest, who had joined them at Columbia; and Hood had formed a strong rear guard of four thousand infantry, under E. C. Walthall,—Lee having been wounded on the 17th,—and all his available cavalry. "With the exception of his rear guard," says Thomas, "his army had become a disheartened and disorganized rabble of half-armed and barefooted men, who sought every opportunity to fall out by the wayside and desert their cause to put an end to their sufferings." On Christmas morning Thomas, still continuing the pursuit, drove the enemy out of Pulaski, and chased him towards Lamb's Ferry over roads which had become almost impassable "and through a country devoid of sustenance for man and beast." The Confederates were, however, more fleet than their pursuers; the swollen rivers and other accidents everywhere favored them, and during the 26th and 27th Hood crossed the Tennessee River.

Even here he did not feel in safety, but continued his headlong retreat to Tupelo, Mississippi. From there, on the 13th of January, he sent a dispatch to the Confederate War Department requesting to be relieved from the command of the army. After consultation with General Beauregard, he issued furloughs to most of his Tennessee troops; his army, what there was of it, rapidly melted away. Four thousand of them went to join Maury at Mobile. It is hard to say what became of the rest. After the pressure of public opinion had forced the Richmond authorities to the bitter necessity of reappointing General Johnston to the command of that spectral army which was expected to oppose the triumphal march of Sherman to the North, the three corps of Hood's army which reported to him consisted of 2000 men under C. L. Stevenson,—S. D. Lee's successor,— 2000 under Cheatham, and 1000 under Stewart; in addition to these there were, he says, little parties who gradually made their way into North Carolina, as groups and individuals, and were brought to him at last by General S. D. Lee. The pursuit of Hood's retreating army was not continued longer by Thomas. On the 29th of December, a small force of cavalry of only 600 men, under command of Col. W. J. Palmer, of the Fifteenth Pennsylvania, went roving through North Alabama and Mississippi striking the enemy here and there, destroying one day his pontoon trains, on another day a large supply train, sabering and shooting his mules, attacking the Confederate general W. W. Russell near Thorn Hill, routing him, capturing some prisoners, burning some wagons, and then proceeding at his leisure back to camp at Decatur, after a march of over 250 miles, reporting a loss of one killed and two wounded.

Mr. Davis promptly complied with Hood's request for relief, and he bade farewell on the 23d of January, 1865, to what was left of the army of 50,000 men which Johnston had led with such unfailing prudence and wisdom from Tunnel Hill to Atlanta, and which Hood had dashed to pieces against the National breastworks on every field from Atlanta to Nashville. Hood then visited Virginia, was kindly received by Jefferson Davis, with whom he always remained a favorite, even amid the impending ruin of the Confederacy, and was on his way to Texas with instructions to bring a new army from that remote but gallant State to the rescue of the falling cause, when he heard of Lee's surrender. He tried for many days to cross the Mississippi, several times, as he says, "hotly chased by Federal cavalry through the wood and cane-brakes"; but, at last, making a virtue of necessity, he surrendered to General John W. Davidson, at Natchez, on the 31st of May.

The Thirteenth Amendment

WE have enumerated with some detail the series of radical antislavery measures enacted at the second session of the Thirty-seventh Congress, which ended July 17, 1862—the abolition of slavery in the District of Columbia; the prohibition of slavery in the National Territories; the practical repeal of the fugitive-slave law; and the sweeping measures of confiscation which in different forms decreed forfeiture of slave property for the crimes of treason and rebellion. When this wholesale legislation was supplemented by the President's preliminary Emancipation Proclamation of September 22, 1862, and his final Edict of Freedom of January 1, 1863, the institution had clearly received its *coup de grâce* in all except the loyal border States. Consequently the third session of the Thirty-seventh Congress, ending March 4, 1863, occupied itself with this phase of the slavery question only to the extent of an effort to put into operation the President's plan of compensated abolishment. That effort took practical shape in a bill to give the State of Missouri fifteen millions on condition that she would emancipate her slaves; but the proposition failed, largely through the opposition of a few conservative Members from Missouri, and the session adjourned without having by its legislation advanced the destruction of slavery.

When Congress met again in December, 1863, and organized by the election of Schuyler Colfax of Indiana as Speaker, the whole situation had undergone further change. The Union arms had been triumphant—Gettysburg had been won and Vicksburg had capitulated; Lincoln's Edict of Freedom had become an accepted fact; fifty regiments of negro soldiers carried bayonets in the Union armies; Vallandigham had been beaten for governor in Ohio by a hundred thousand majority;

the draft had been successfully enforced in every district of every loyal State in the Union. Under these brightening prospects, military and political, the more progressive spirits in Congress took up anew the suspended battle with slavery which the institution had itself invited by its unprovoked assault on the life of the Government.

The President's reference to the subject in his annual message was very brief: "The movements by State action for emancipation in several of the States not included in the Emancipation Proclamation are matters of profound gratulation. And while I do not repeat in detail what I have heretofore so earnestly urged upon this subject, my general views and feelings remain unchanged; and I trust that Congress will omit no fair opportunity of aiding these important steps to a great consummation." His language had reference to Maryland, where during the autumn of 1863 the question of emancipation had been actively discussed by political parties, and where at the election of November 4, 1863, a legislature had been chosen containing a considerable majority pledged to emancipation.

More especially did it refer to Missouri, where, notwithstanding the failure of the fifteen-million compensation bill at the previous session, a State Convention had actually passed an ordinance of emancipation, though with such limitations as rendered it unacceptable to the more advanced public opinion of the State. Prudence was the very essence of Mr. Lincoln's statesmanship, and he doubtless felt it was not safe for the Executive to venture farther at that time. "We are like whalers," he said to Governor Morgan one day, "who have been long on a chase: we have at last got the harpoon into the monster, but we must now look how we steer, or with one 'flop' of his tail he will send us all into eternity."

Senators and Members of the House, especially those representing antislavery States or districts, did not need to be so circumspect. It was doubtless with this consciousness that J. M.

Ashley, a Republican Representative from Ohio, and James F. Wilson, a Republican Representative from Iowa, on the 14th of December, 1863,—that being the earliest opportunity after the House was organized,—introduced the former a bill and the latter a joint resolution to propose to the several States an amendment of the Constitution prohibiting slavery throughout the United States. Both the propositions were referred to the committee on the judiciary, of which Mr. Wilson was chairman; but before he made any report on the subject it had been brought before the Senate, where its discussion attracted marked public attention.

Senator John B. Henderson, who with rare courage and skill had, as a progressive Conservative, made himself one of the leading champions of Missouri emancipation, on the 11th of January, 1864, introduced into the Senate a Joint Resolution proposing an amendment to the Constitution that slavery shall not exist in the United States. It is not probable that either he or the Senate saw any near hope of success in such a measure. The resolution went to the committee on the judiciary, apparently without being treated as a matter of pressing importance. Nearly a month had elapsed when Mr. Sumner also introduced a Joint Resolution, proposing an amendment that "everywhere within the limits of the United States, and of each State or Territory thereof, all persons are equal before the law, so that no person can hold another as a slave." He asked its reference to the select committee on slavery, of which he was chairman; but several Senators argued that such an amendment properly belonged to the committee on the judiciary, and in this reference Mr. Sumner finally acquiesced. It is possible that this slight and courteously worded rivalry between the two committees induced earlier action than would otherwise have happened, for two days later Lyman Trumbull, chairman of the judiciary committee, reported back a substitute in the following language, differing from the phraseology of both Mr. Sumner and Mr. Henderson:

ARTICLE XIII.

SECTION 1. Neither slavery nor involuntary servitude, except as a punishment for crime, whereof the party shall have been duly convicted, shall exist within the United States, or any place subject to their jurisdiction.

SECTION 2. Congress shall have power to enforce this article by appropriate legislation.

Even after the committee on the judiciary by this report had adopted the measure, it was evidently thought to be merely in an experimental stage, for more than six weeks elapsed before the Senate again took it up for action. On the 28th of March, however, Mr. Trumbull formally opened debate upon it in an elaborate speech. The discussion was continued from time to time until the 8th of April. As the Republicans had almost unanimous control of the Senate, their speeches, though able and eloquent, seemed perfunctory and devoted to a foregone conclusion. Those which attracted most attention were the arguments of Reverdy Johnson of Maryland and Mr. Henderson of Missouri,—Senators representing slave States,—advocating the amendment. Senator Sumner, whose pride of erudition amounted almost to vanity, pleaded earnestly for his phrase, "All persons are equal before the law," copied from the Constitution of revolutionary France. But Jacob M. Howard of Michigan, one of the soundest lawyers and clearest thinkers of the Senate, pointed out the inapplicability of the words, and declared it safer to follow the Ordinance of 1787, with its historical associations and its well adjudicated meaning.

There was, of course, from the first no doubt whatever that the Senate would pass the constitutional amendment, the political classification of that body being thirty-six Republicans, five Conditional Unionists, and nine Democrats. Not only was the whole Republican strength, thirty-six votes, cast in its favor, but two Democrats,—Reverdy Johnson of Maryland and James W. Nesmith of Oregon,—with a political wisdom far in advance of their party, also voted for it, giving more than the two-thirds required by the Constitution.

When, however, the Joint Resolution went to the House of Representatives there was such a formidable party strength arrayed against it as to foreshadow its failure. The party classification of the House stood one hundred and two Republicans, seventy-five Democrats, and nine from the border States, leaving but little chance of obtaining the required two-thirds vote in favor of the measure. Nevertheless there was sufficient Republican strength to secure its discussion; and when it came up on the 31st of May the first vote showed seventy-six to fifty-five against rejecting the Joint Resolution.

We may infer that the conviction of the present hopelessness of the measure greatly shortened the debate upon it. The question occupied the House only on three different days—the 31st of May, when it was taken up, and the 14th and 15th of June. The speeches in opposition all came from Democrats; the speeches in its favor all came from Republicans, except one. From its adoption the former predicted the direst evils to the Constitution and the Republic; the latter the most beneficial results in the restoration of the country to peace and the fulfillment of the high destiny intended for it by its founders. Upon the final question of its passage the vote stood: yeas, ninety-three; nays, sixty-five; absent or not voting, twenty-three. Of those voting in favor of the Resolution eighty-seven were Republicans and four were Democrats. Those voting against it were all Democrats. The resolution, not having secured a two-thirds vote, was thus lost; seeing which Mr. Ashley, Republican, who had the measure in charge, changed his vote so that he might, if occasion arose, move its reconsideration.

The ever-vigilant public opinion of the loyal States, intensified by the burdens and anxieties of the war, took up this far-reaching question of abolishing slavery by constitutional amendment with an interest fully as deep as that manifested by Congress. Before the Joint Resolution had failed in the House of Representatives the issue was already transferred to discussion and prospective decision in a new forum.

When on the 7th of June, 1864, the National Republican

Convention met in Baltimore, the two most vital thoughts which animated its members were the renomination of Mr. Lincoln and the success of the constitutional amendment. The first was recognized as a popular decision needing only the formality of an announcement by the Convention; and the full emphasis of speech and resolution was therefore centered on the latter, as the dominant and aggressive reform upon which the party would stake its political fortunes in the coming campaign.

It is not among the least of the evidences of President Lincoln's political sagacity and political courage that it was he himself who supplied the spark that fired this train of popular action. The editor of the "New York Independent," who attended the Convention, and who with others visited Mr. Lincoln immediately after the nomination, printed the following in his paper of June 16, 1864: "When one of us mentioned the great enthusiasm at the Convention, after Senator E. D. Morgan's proposition to amend the Constitution, abolishing slavery, Mr. Lincoln instantly said, 'It was I who suggested to Mr. Morgan that he should put that idea into his opening speech.'"

The declaration of Morgan, who was chairman of the National Republican Committee, and as such called the Convention to order, immediately found an echo in the speech of the temporary chairman, the Rev. Dr. Robert J. Breckinridge. The indorsement of the principle by the eminent Kentucky divine, not on the ground of party but on the high philosophy of true universal government and of genuine Christian religion, gave the announcement an interest and significance accorded to few planks in party platforms. The permanent chairman, William Dennison, reaffirmed the doctrine of Morgan and Breckinridge, and the thunderous applause of the whole Convention greeted the formal proclamation of the new dogma of political faith in the third resolution of the platform:

Resolved, That as slavery was the cause and now constitutes the strength of this rebellion, and as it must be always and everywhere hostile to the principles of republican government, justice and the National safety demand its utter and complete extirpation from the soil of the Republic; and that while we uphold and maintain the acts and proclamations by which the Government in its own defense has aimed a death blow at this gigantic evil, we are in favor, furthermore, of such an amendment to the Constitution, to be made by the people, in conformity with its provisions, as shall terminate and forever prohibit the existence of slavery within the limits or the jurisdiction of the United States.

We have related elsewhere how upon this and the other declarations of the platform the Republican party went to battle and gained an overwhelming victory—a popular majority of 411,281, an electoral majority of 191, and a House of Representatives of 138 Unionists to 35 Democrats. In view of this result the President was able to take up the question with confidence among his official recommendations; and in the annual message which he transmitted to Congress on the 6th of December, 1864, he urged upon the Members whose terms were about to expire the propriety of at once carrying into effect the clearly expressed popular will. Said he:

At the last session of Congress a proposed amendment of the Constitution, abolishing slavery throughout the United States, passed the Senate, but failed, for lack of the requisite two-thirds vote, in the House of Representatives. Although the present is the same Congress, and nearly the same members, and without questioning the wisdom or patriotism of those who stood in opposition, I venture to recommend the reconsideration and passage of the measure at the present session. Of course the abstract question is not changed, but an intervening election shows, almost certainly, that the next Congress will pass the measure if this does not. Hence there is only a question of *time* as to when the proposed amendment will go to the States for their action. And as it is to so go at all events, may we not agree that the sooner the better? It is not claimed that the election has imposed a duty on Members to change their views or their votes any further than, as an additional element to be considered, their judgment may be affected by it. It is the voice of the people, now for the first time heard upon the question. In a great National crisis like ours unanimity of action among those seeking a common end is very desirable—almost indispensable. And yet no approach to such unanimity is attainable unless some deference shall be paid to the will of the majority, simply because it is the will of the majority. In this case the common end is the maintenance of the Union; and among the means to secure that end, such will, through the election, is most clearly declared in favor of such constitutional amendment.

On the 15th of December Mr. Ashley gave notice that he would, on the 6th of January, 1865, call up the constitutional amendment for reconsideration; and accordingly, on the day appointed, he opened the new debate upon it in an earnest speech. General discussion followed from time to time, occupying perhaps half the days of the month of January. As at the previous session, the Republicans all favored, while the Democrats mainly opposed it; but the important exceptions among the latter showed what immense gains the proposition had made in popular opinion and in Congressional willingness to recognize and embody it. The logic of events had become more powerful than party creed or strategy. For fifteen years the Democratic party had stood as sentinel and bulwark to slavery; and yet, despite its alliance and championship, the peculiar institution was being consumed like dry leaves in the fire of war. For a whole decade it had been defeated in every great contest of Congressional debate and legislation. It had withered in popular elections, been paralyzed by confiscation laws, crushed by executive decrees, trampled upon by marching Union armies. More notable than all, the agony of dissolution had come upon it in its final stronghold—the constitutions of the slave States. Local public opinion had throttled it in West Virginia, in Missouri, in Arkansas, in Louisiana, in Maryland; and the same spirit of change was upon Tennessee, and even showing itself in Kentucky.

Here was a great revolution of ideas, a mighty sweep of sentiment, which could not be explained away by the stale charge of sectional fanaticism, or by alleging technical irregularities of political procedure. Here was a mighty flood of public opinion, overleaping old barriers and rushing into new channels.

The Democratic party did not and could not shut its eyes to the accomplished facts. "In my judgment," said William S. Holman of Indiana, "the fate of slavery is sealed. It dies by the rebellious hand of its votaries, untouched by the law. Its fate is determined by the war; by the measures of the war; by the results of the war. These, sir, must determine it, even if the Constitution were amended." He opposed the amendment, he declared, simply because it was unnecessary. Though few other Democrats were so frank, all their speeches were weighed down by the same consciousness of a losing fight, a hopeless cause. The Democratic leader of the House, and lately defeated Democratic candidate for Vice-President, George H. Pendleton, opposed the amendment, as he had done at the previous session, by asserting that three-fourths of the States did not possess constitutional power to pass it, this being—if the paradox be excused—at the same time the weakest and the strongest argument: weakest, because the Constitution in terms contradicted the assertion; strongest, because under the circumstances nothing less than unconstitutionality could justify opposition.

But while the Democrats as a party thus persisted in a false attitude, more progressive Members had the courage to take independent and wiser action. Not only did the four Democrats —Moses F. Odell and John A. Griswold of New York, Joseph Baily of Pennsylvania, and Ezra Wheeler of Wisconsin—who supported the amendment at the first session again record their votes in its favor, but they were now joined by thirteen others of their party associates, namely: Augustus C. Baldwin of Michigan; Alexander H. Coffroth and Archibald McAllister of Pennsylvania; James E. English of Connecticut; John Ganson, Anson Herrick, Homer A. Nelson, William Radford, and John B. Steele of New York; Wells A. Hutchins of Ohio; Austin A. King and James S. Rollins of Missouri; and George H. Yeaman of Kentucky; and by their help the favorable two-thirds vote was secured. But special credit for the result must not be accorded to these alone. Even more than of Northern Democrats must be recognized the courage and progressive liberality of Members from the border slave States—one from Delaware, four from Maryland, three from West Virginia, four from Kentucky, and seven from Missouri, whose speeches and votes aided the consummation of the great act; and finally, something is due to those Democrats, eight in number, who were absent without pairs, and thus, perhaps not altogether by accident, reduced somewhat the two-thirds vote necessary to the passage of the Joint Resolution.

Mingled with these influences of a public and moral nature it is not unlikely that others of more selfish interest, operating both for and against the amendment, were not entirely wanting. One, who was a member of the House, writes: "The success of the measure had been considered very doubtful, and depended upon certain negotiations the result of which was not fully assured, and the particulars of which never reached the public." So also one of the President's secretaries wrote on the 18th of January:

I went to the President this afternoon at the request of Mr. Ashley, on a matter connecting itself with the pending amendment of the Constitution. The Camden and Amboy Railroad interest promised Mr. Ashley that if he would help postpone the Raritan railroad bill over this session they would in return make the New Jersey Democrats help about the amendment, either by their votes or absence. Sumner being the Senate champion of the Raritan bill, Ashley went to him to ask him to drop it for this session. Sumner, however, showed reluctance to adopt Mr. Ashley's suggestion, saying that he hoped the amendment would pass anyhow, etc. Ashley thought he discerned in Sumner's manner two reasons: (1) That if the present Senate resolution were not adopted by the House, the Senate would send them another in which they would most likely adopt Sumner's own phraseology and thereby gratify his ambition; and (2) that Sumner thinks the defeat of the Camden and Amboy monopoly would establish a principle by legislative enactment which would effectually crush out the last lingering relics of the States rights dogma. Ashley therefore desired the President to send for Sumner, and urge him to be practical and secure the passage of the amendment in the manner suggested by Mr. Ashley. I stated these points to the President, who replied at once: "I can do nothing with Mr. Sumner in these matters. While Mr. Sumner is very cordial with me, he is making his history in an issue with me on this very point. He hopes to succeed in beating the President so as to change this Government from its original form and make it a strong centralized power." Then calling Mr. Ashley into the room, the President said to him, "I think I understand Mr. Sumner; and I think he would be all the more resolute in his persistence on the points which Mr. Nicolay has mentioned to me if he supposed I were at all watching his course on this matter."

The issue was decided in the afternoon of the 31st of January, 1865. The scene was one of unusual interest. The galleries were filled to overflowing; the Members watched the proceedings with unconcealed solicitude. "Up to noon," said a contemporaneous formal report, "the pro-slavery party are said to have been confident of defeating the amendment, and, after that time had passed, one of the most earnest advocates of the measure said, ' 'T is the toss of a copper.' " There were the usual pleas for postponement and for permission to offer amendments or substitutes, but at four o'clock the House came to a final vote, and the roll-call showed, yeas, 119; nays, 56; not voting, 8. Scattering murmurs of applause had followed the announcement of affirmative votes from several of the Democratic Members. This was renewed when by direction of the Speaker the clerk called his name and he voted aye. But when the Speaker finally announced, "The constitutional majority of two-thirds having voted in the affirmative, the Joint Resolution is passed," "the announcement"—so continues the official report printed in the "Globe"—"was received by the House and by the spectators with an outburst of enthusiasm. The Members on the Republican side of the House instantly sprung to their feet, and, regardless of parliamentary rules, applauded with cheers and clapping of hands. The example was followed by the male spectators in the galleries, which were crowded to excess, who waved their hats and cheered loud and long, while the ladies, hundreds of whom were present, rose in their seats and waved their handkerchiefs, participating in and adding to the general excitement and intense interest of the scene. This lasted for several minutes." "In honor of this immortal and sublime event," cried Ebon C. Ingersoll of Illinois, "I move that the House do now adjourn," and against the objection of a Maryland Democrat the motion was carried by a yea and nay vote.

A salute of one hundred guns soon made the occasion the subject of comment and congratulation throughout the city. On the following night a considerable procession marched with music to the Executive Mansion to carry popular greetings to the President. In response to their calls, Mr. Lincoln appeared at a window and made a brief speech, of which only an abstract report was preserved, but which is nevertheless important as showing the searching analysis of cause and effect which this question had undergone in his mind, the deep interest he felt in, and the far-reaching consequences he attached to the measure and its success.

He supposed the passage through Congress of the constitutional amendment for the abolishment of slavery throughout the United States was the occasion to which he was indebted for the honor of this call. The occasion was one of congratulation to the country and to the whole world. But there is a task yet before us—to go forward and have consummated by the votes of the States that which Congress had so nobly begun yesterday. He had the honor to inform those present that Illinois had already to-day done the work. Maryland was about half through, but he felt proud that Illinois was a little ahead. He thought this measure was a very fitting if not an indispensable adjunct to the winding up of the great difficulty. He wished the reunion of all the States perfected, and so effected as to remove all causes of disturbance in the future; and to attain this end it was necessary that the original disturbing cause should, if possible, be rooted out. He thought all would bear him witness that he had never shrunk from doing all that he could to eradicate slavery, by issuing an Emancipation Proclamation. But that proclamation falls far short of what the amendment will be when fully consummated. A question might be raised whether the proclamation was legally valid. It might be urged that it only aided those that came into our lines, and that it was inoperative as to those who did not give themselves up; or that it would have no effect upon the children of slaves born hereafter; in fact, it would be urged that it did not meet the evil. But this amendment is a king's cure-all for all the evils. It winds the whole thing up. He would repeat that it was the fitting, if not the indispensable, adjunct to the consummation of the great game we are playing. He could not but congratulate all present—himself, the country, and the whole world—upon this great moral victory.

Widely divergent views were expressed by able constitutional lawyers in both branches of Congress as to what, in the anomalous condition of the country, would constitute a valid ratification of the Thirteenth Amendment; some contending that ratification by three-fourths of the loyal States would be sufficient, others that three-fourths of all the States, whether loyal or insurrectionary, would be necessary. We have seen that Mr. Lincoln, in his speech on Louisiana reconstruction, while expressing no opinion against the first proposition, nevertheless declared, with great argumentative force, that the latter "would be unquestioned and unquestionable"; and this view appears to have governed the action of his successor.

As Mr. Lincoln mentioned with just pride in his address, Illinois was the first state to ratify the amendment, taking her action on February 1, the day after the Joint Resolution was passed by the House of Representatives; and ratification by other States continued in the following order: Rhode Island, February 2, 1865; Michigan, February 2, 1865; Maryland, February 3, 1865; New York, February 3, 1865; West Virginia, February 3, 1865; Maine, February 7, 1865; Kansas, February 7, 1865; Massachusetts, February 8, 1865; Pennsylvania, February 8, 1865; Virginia, February 9, 1865; Ohio, February 10, 1865; Missouri, February 10, 1865; Indiana, February 16, 1865; Nevada, February 16, 1865; Louisiana, February 17, 1865; Minnesota, February 23, 1865; Wisconsin, March 1, 1865; Vermont, March 9, 1865; Tennessee, April 7, 1865; Arkansas, April 20, 1865; Connecticut, May 5, 1865; New Hampshire, July 1, 1865; South Carolina, November 13, 1865; Alabama, December 2, 1865; North Carolina, December 4, 1865; Georgia, December

9, 1865; Oregon, December 11, 1865; California, December 20, 1865; Florida, December 28, 1865; New Jersey, January 23, 1866; Iowa, January 24, 1866; Texas, February 18, 1870.

Without waiting for the ratification by the last six of these States, Mr. Seward, who remained as Secretary of State in the Cabinet of President Johnson, made official proclamation on December 18, 1865, that the Legislatures of twenty-seven States, constituting three-fourths of the thirty-six States of the Union, had ratified the amendment, and that it had become valid as a part of the Constitution of the United States. It needs to be noted that four of the States constituting this number of twenty-seven were Virginia, Louisiana, Tennessee, and Arkansas, whose reconstruction had been effected under the direction and by the authority of President Lincoln.

The profound political transformation which the American Republic had undergone can perhaps best be measured by contrasting for an instant the two constitutional amendments which Congress made it the duty of the Lincoln Administration to submit officially to the several States. The first was that offered by Thomas Corwin, chairman of the Committee of Thirty-three, in February, 1861, and passed by the House of Representatives, yeas, 133; nays, 65; and by the Senate, yeas, 24; nays, 12. It was signed by President Buchanan as one of his last official acts, and accepted and indorsed by Lincoln in his inaugural address. The language of that amendment was:

"No amendment shall be made to the Constitution which will authorize or give to Congress the power to abolish or interfere within any State with the domestic institutions thereof, including that of persons held to labor or service by the laws of said State."

Between Lincoln's inauguration and the outbreak of war, the Department of State, under Seward, transmitted this amendment of 1861 to the several States for their action; and had the South shown a willingness to desist from secession and accept it as a peace offering, there is little doubt that the required three-fourths of the States would have made it a part of the Constitution. But the South refused to halt in her rebellion, and the thunder of Beauregard's guns against Fort Sumter drove away all further thought or possibility of such a ratification; and within four years Congress framed and the same Lincoln Administration sent forth the amendment of 1865, sweeping out of existence by one sentence the institution to which it had in its first proposal offered a virtual claim to perpetual recognition and tolerance. The "new birth of freedom," which Lincoln invoked for the nation in his Gettysburg address, was accomplished.

WITH THE COMING *of spring, 1865, Grant embarked on the campaign that would end the war. Except at Richmond, Confederate military power had been nearly used up. Sheridan had scorched the rich Shenandoah Valley, long a source of food and forage for Lee; Sherman had devastated much of Georgia, taken Savannah, and invaded the Carolinas. On March 19-21 he fought his last battle—a victory—at Bentonville, North Carolina. Thomas, at Nashville, had smashed Hood's army so thoroughly that it was never again an effective fighting force. In January a combined land and sea force took Fort Fisher at the mouth of the Cape Fear River and closed Wilmington, North Carolina, the South's last important port, to blockade runners. But Jefferson Davis would fight on as long as the Army of Northern Virginia remained unconquered.*

Lee, aware that as soon as the roads dried Grant would move to the west of Petersburg to cut the last remaining Confederate supply line, tried on March 25 to break the Federal hold by an attack on Fort Stedman but was soundly defeated. On March 29 Grant sent Sheridan and others to turn the Confederate right and cut the Southside Railroad. Lee dispatched Pickett to counter the move. The opposing forces met at Five Forks, seventeen miles west and south of Petersburg. In two days of fighting, Pickett lost half of his ten thousand men.

Grant immediately followed up Sheridan's victory by ordering an assault on April 2 all along the Petersburg line, and the outer defenses were pierced at several points. Nicolay and Hay relate the remainder of the last campaign.

Appomattox

BEFORE the advance of the National army had been reported to Lee or A. P. Hill, they saw squads of men in blue scattered about the Boydton road, and it was in riding forward to ascertain what the strange apparition meant that General Hill lost

Vol. X, Chap. IX, pp. 180-98.

his life. General Lee, in full uniform, with his dress sword, which he seldom wore, but which he had put on that morning in honor of the momentous day he saw coming,—being determined with that chivalrous spirit of his to receive adversity splendidly,—watched from the lawn in front of his headquarters the formidable advance of the National troops before whom his weakened lines were breaking into spray, and then, mounting his iron-gray charger, slowly rode back to his inner line. There his ragged troops received him with shouts and cheers, which showed there was plenty of fight left in them; and there he spent the day in making preparations for the evacuation which was now the only resort left him. He sent a dispatch to Richmond, carrying in brief and simple words the message of despair to the Confederate authorities: "I see no prospect of doing more than holding our position here till night. I am not certain I can do that." He succinctly stated the disaster that had befallen him, announced his purpose of concentrating on the Danville road, and advised that all preparations be made for leaving Richmond that night.

Some Confederate writers express surprise that General Grant did not attack and destroy Lee's army on the afternoon of the 2d of April; but this is a view, after the fact, easy to express. Wright's and Humphreys's troops on the Union left had been on foot for eighteen hours; they had fought an important battle, marched and countermarched many miles, and were now confronted by Longstreet's fresh corps, behind formidable works, led by the best of Lee's generals; while the attitude of the force under Gordon, on the south side of the town, was such as to require the close attention of Parke. Grant, anticipating an early retirement of Lee from his citadel, wisely resolved to avoid the waste and bloodshed of an immediate assault on the inner lines at Petersburg. He ordered Sheridan to get upon Lee's line of retreat, sent Humphreys to strengthen him; then, directing a general bombardment for five o'clock the next morning, and an assault at six, he gave himself and his soldiers a little of the rest they had so richly earned, and which they so seriously needed, as a restorative after the labors past and a preparation for the labors to come.

He had telegraphed during the day to President Lincoln, who was at City Point, the great day's news as it developed hour by hour. He was particularly happy at the large captures. "How many prisoners?" was always the first question as an aide-de-camp came galloping in with news of success. Prisoners he regarded as so much net gain: he was weary of slaughter; he wanted the war ended with the least bloodshed possible. It was with the greatest delight that he was able to telegraph on this Sunday afternoon, "The whole captures since the army started out gunning will not amount to less than twelve thousand men and probably fifty pieces of artillery."

General Lee, after the first shock of the breaking of his lines, soon recovered his usual *sang froid*, and bent all his energies to saving his army and leading it out of its untenable position on the James to a point from which he could effect a junction with Johnston in North Carolina. The place selected for this purpose was Burkeville, at the crossing of the South Side and Danville roads, fifty miles from Richmond, whence a short distance would bring him to Danville, where the desired junction might be made. Even in this ruin of the Confederacy, when the organized revolt which he had sustained so long with the bayonets of his soldiers was crashing about his ears, he was able still to cradle himself in the illusion that it was only a campaign that had failed; that he might withdraw his troops, form a junction with Johnston, and continue the war indefinitely in another field. Whatever we may think of his judgment, it is impossible not to admire the coolness of a general who, in the midst of irremediable disaster such as encompassed Lee on the afternoon of the 2d of April, could write such a letter as he wrote to Jefferson Davis under date of three o'clock. He began it by a quiet and calm discussion of the question of negro recruitment; promised to give his attention to the business of finding suitable officers

for the black regiments; hoped the appeal Mr. Davis had made
to the governors would have a good effect; and, altogether, wrote
as if years of struggle and effort were before him and his chief.
He then went on to narrate the story of the day's catastrophe
and to give his plans for the future. He closed by apologizing
for writing "such a hurried letter to your Excellency," on the
ground that he was "in the presence of the enemy, endeavoring
to resist his advance."

At nightfall all his preparations were completed. He mounted
his horse, and riding out of the town dismounted at the mouth
of the road leading to Amelia Court House, the first point of
rendezvous, where he had directed supplies to be sent, and
standing beside his horse, the bridle reins in his hand, he
watched his troops file noiselessly by in the darkness. At three
o'clock the town, which had been so long and so stoutly defended, was abandoned; only a thin line of skirmishers was left
in front of Parke, and before daybreak he pierced the line in
several places, gathering in the few pickets that were left. The
town was formally surrendered to Colonel Ralph Ely at half-
past four, anticipating the capitulation which some one else
offered to General Wright a few minutes later. Meade reported
the news to Grant, and received the order to march his army
immediately up the Appomattox by the river road; Grant,
divining the intentions of Lee, dispatched an officer to Sheridan,
directing him to push with all speed to the Danville road with
Humphreys and Griffin and all the cavalry.

Thus the flight and the pursuit began almost at the same
moment. The swift-footed Army of Northern Virginia was now
racing for its life; and Grant, inspired with more than his
habitual tenacity and energy, and thoroughly aroused to the
tremendous task of ending the war at once, not only pressed
his enemy in the rear, but hung upon his flank, and strained
every nerve to get in his front. It is characteristic of him that
he did not even allow himself the pleasure of entering Richmond, which, deserted by those who had so often promised to

protect it, and wrapped in flames lighted by the reckless hands of Confederate officials, surrendered to Weitzel early on the morning of the 3d.

All that day Lee pushed forward towards Amelia Court House. He seemed in higher spirits than usual. As one who has long been dreading bankruptcy feels a great load taken from his mind when his assignment is made, so the Virginian chief, when he drew out from the ruin and conflagration in which the Confederate dream of independent power was passing away, and marched with his men into the vernal fields and woods of his native State, was filled with a new sense of encouragement and cheer. "I have got my army safe out of its breastworks," he said, "and in order to follow me the enemy must abandon his lines, and can derive no further benefit from his railroads or James River." But he was now dealing with the man who, in Mississippi, had boldly swung loose from his base of supplies in an enemy's country, in face of an army equal to his own, and had won a victory a day without a wagon train.

There was little fighting the first day except among the cavalry. Custer attacked the Confederates at Namozine Church, and later in the day Merritt's cavalry had a sharp contest with Fitzhugh Lee at Deep Creek. On the 4th, Sheridan, who was aware of Lee's intention to concentrate at Amelia Court House, brought his cavalry with great speed to Jetersville, about eight miles southwest of the Court House, where Lee's army was resting. Sheridan intrenched, and sent tidings of his own and the enemy's position to Grant, and on the afternoon of the next day the Second and Sixth Corps came up. A terrible disappointment awaited General Lee on his arrival at Amelia Court House. He had ordered, he says, supplies to be forwarded there; but when his half-starved troops arrived on the 4th of April they found that no food had been sent to meet them, and nearly twenty-four hours were lost in collecting subsistence for men and horses. "This delay was fatal and could not be retrieved." The whole pursuing force was south and stretching out to the west of him, when he started on the night of the 5th of April to make one more effort to reach a place of temporary safety. Burkeville, the junction of the Lynchburg and Danville roads, was in Grant's possession; the way to Danville was barred, and the supply of provisions from the south cut off. Lee was compelled to change his route to the west; and he now started for Lynchburg, which he was destined never to reach.

It had been Meade's intention to attack Lee at Amelia Court House on the morning of the 6th of April, but before he reached that place he discovered that Lee's westward march had already begun, and that the Confederates were well beyond the Union left. Meade quickly faced his army about and started in pursuit. A running fight ensued for fourteen miles; the enemy, with remarkable quickness and dexterity, halting and partly intrenching themselves from time to time, and the National forces driving them out of every position, moving so swiftly that lines of battle followed closely on the skirmish line. At several points the cavalry, on this and the preceding day, harassed the moving left flank of the Confederates and worked havoc on the trains, on one occasion causing a grievous loss to history by burning Lee's headquarters baggage with all its wealth of returns and reports. Sheridan and Meade pressed so closely at last that Ewell's corps was brought to bay at Sailor's Creek, a rivulet running northward into the Appomattox. Here an important battle, or rather series of battles, took place, with fatal results to Lee's fast-vanishing army. The Fifth Corps held the extreme right and was not engaged. Humphreys, coming to where the roads divided, took the right fork and drove Gordon down towards the mouth of the creek. A sharp battle was fought about dark, which resulted in the total defeat of the Confederates, Humphreys capturing 1700 prisoners, 13 flags, 4 guns, and a large part of the main trains; Gordon making his escape in the night to High Bridge with what was left of his command. Wright, on the left-hand road, had also a keen fight, and won a most valuable victory. With Wheaton's and Seymour's divisions he attacked Ewell's corps, in position on the banks of the creek, enveloping him with the utmost swiftness and vehemence; Sheridan, whose cavalry had intercepted the Confederates, ordered Crook and Merritt to attack on the left, which was done with such vigor—Davies's horsemen riding over the enemy's breastworks at a single rush—that, smitten in front and flank, unable either to stand or to get away, Ewell's whole force was captured on the field. The day's loss was deadly to Lee, not less than eight thousand in all; among them such famous generals as Ewell, Kershaw, G. W. Custis Lee, M. D. Corse, and others were prisoners.

In the mean time Ord, under Sheridan's orders, had moved rapidly along the Lynchburg road to Rice's Station, where he found Longstreet's corps intrenched, and night came on before he could get into position to attack. General Theodore Read, Ord's chief-of-staff, had gone still farther forward with eighty horsemen and five hundred infantry to burn High Bridge, if possible. In the attempt to execute this intention he fell in, in the neighborhood of Farmville, with two divisions of Confederate cavalry under Rosser and T. T. Munford. One of the most gallant and pathetic battles of the war took place. General Read, Colonel Francis Washburn, and all the cavalry officers with Read were killed and the rest captured; the Confederate loss was also heavy. Read's generous self-sacrifice halted the Confederate army for several hours. Longstreet lost the day at Rice's Station waiting for Anderson, Ewell, and Gordon to unite with him. They were engaged in a fruitless attempt to save their trains, which resulted, as we have seen, in the almost total loss of the trains, in the capture of Ewell's entire force, and in the routing and shattering of the other commands. The day's work was of incalculable value to the National arms. Sheridan's unerring eye appreciated the full importance of it; his hasty report ended with the words, "If the thing is pressed, I think that Lee will surrender." Grant sent the dispatch to President Lincoln, who instantly replied, "Let the thing be pressed."

In fact, after nightfall of the 6th Lee's army could only flutter like a wounded bird with one wing shattered; there was no longer any possibility of escape. Yet General Lee found it hard to relinquish the illusions of years, and his valiant heart still dreamed of evading the gathering toils and forming somewhere a junction with Johnston and indefinitely prolonging the war. As soon as night had come down on the disastrous field of Sailor's Creek, he again took up his weary march westward. Longstreet marched for Farmville, crossed to the north bank of the Appomattox, and on the 7th moved out on the road which ran through Appomattox Court House to Lynchburg. His famishing troops had found provisions at Farmville, and with this refreshment marched with such celerity that Grant and Sheridan, with all the energy they could breathe into their subordinates, could not head them off, or bring them to decisive battle that day. Nevertheless the advance of the Union army hung close upon the heels of the Confederates. The rear corps under Gordon had burned the railroad bridge near Farmville behind them; but General Barlow, sending his men forward at double-quick, saved the wagon bridge, and the Second Corps crossed over without delay and continued the chase, Humphreys taking the northern road, and sending Barlow by the railroad bed along the river. Barlow overtook Gordon's rear, working great destruction among his trains. Humphreys came up with the main body shortly after noon, and pressing them closely held them till evening, expecting Barlow to join him, and Wright and Crook to cross the river and attack from the south, a movement which the swollen water and the destruction of the bridge prevented. General Irvin Gregg's brigade had indeed succeeded in getting over, but was attacked by an overwhelming force of Confederate cavalry,—three divisions,—Gregg being captured, and his brigade driven back. This trivial success in the midst of unspeakable disaster delighted General Lee. He said to his son, W. H. F. Lee, "Keep your command together and in good spirits, General; do not let it think of surrender. I will get you out of this."

But his inveterate optimism was not shared by his subordinates. A number of his principal officers, selecting General William N. Pendleton as their spokesman, made known to him on the 7th their belief that further resistance was useless, and advised surrender. General Lee replied: "I trust it has not come to that. . . . We have yet too many bold men to think of laying down our arms." Besides, he feared that if he made the first overtures for capitulation Grant would regard it as a confession of weakness, and demand unconditional surrender. But General Grant did not wish to drive a gallant antagonist to such extremes. On this same day, seeing how desperate was Lee's condition, and anxious to have an end of the now useless strife, he sent him this courteous and generous summons:

The results of the last week must convince you of the hopelessness of further resistance, on the part of the Army of Northern Virginia, in this struggle. I feel that it is so, and regard it as my duty to shift from myself the responsibility of any further effusion of blood, by asking of you the surrender of that portion of the Confederate States army known as the Army of Northern Virginia.

This letter was sent at night through Humphreys's lines to Lee, who at once answered: "Though not entertaining the opinion you express on the hopelessness of further resistance on the part of the Army of Northern Virginia, I reciprocate your desire to avoid useless effusion of blood, and therefore, before considering your proposition, ask the terms you will offer on condition of its surrender."

The forlorn remnant of the Confederate army stole away in the night, on the desperate chance of finding food at Appomattox and a way of escape to Lynchburg, and at daybreak the hot pursuit was resumed by the Second and Sixth Corps. All this day the flight and chase continued, through a portion of Virginia never as yet wasted by the passage of hostile armies. The air was sweet and pure, scented by opening buds and the breath of spring; the early peach trees were in flower; the sylvan bypaths were slightly shaded by the pale-green foliage of leafing trees. Through these quiet solitudes the diminishing army of Lee plodded on, in the apathetic obedience which is all there is left to brave men when hope is gone, and behind them came the victorious legions of Grant, inspired to the forgetfulness of pain and fatigue by the stimulus of a prodigious success. Sheridan, on the extreme left, by unheard-of exertions, at last accomplished the important task of placing himself squarely on Lee's line of retreat. His advance, under George A. Custer, captured, about sunset on the evening of the 8th, Appomattox Station with four trains of provisions, then attacked the rebel force advancing from Farmville, and drove it towards the Court House, taking twenty-five guns and many prisoners. A reconnaissance revealed the startling fact that Lee's whole army was coming up the road. Though he had nothing but cavalry, Sheridan, with undaunted courage, resolved to hold the inestimable advantage he had gained, sending a request to Grant to hurry up the required infantry support, saying that if Gibbon and Griffin could get to him that night, they might "perhaps finish the job in the morning." He added, with singular prescience, referring to the negotiations which had been opened, "I do not think Lee means to surrender until compelled to do so."

This was strictly true. When Grant received Lee's first letter he replied on the morning of the 8th, saying: "Peace being my great desire, there is but one condition I would insist upon, namely, that the men and officers surrendered shall be disqualified from taking up arms again against the Government of the United States until properly exchanged. I will meet you, or will designate officers to meet any officers you may name for the same purpose, at any point agreeable to you, for the purpose of arranging definitely the terms upon which the surrender of the Army of Northern Virginia will be received." But in the course of the day a last hope seemed to have come to Lee that he might yet reach Appomattox in safety and thence make his way to Lynchburg—a hope utterly fallacious, for Stoneman was now on the railroad near Lynchburg. He therefore, while giving orders to his subordinates to press with the utmost energy westward, answered General Grant's letter in a tone more ingenious than candid, reserving, while negotiations were going on, the chance of breaking away. He said:

I received at a late hour your note of to-day. In mine of yesterday I did not intend to propose the surrender of the Army of Northern Virginia, but to ask the terms of your proposition. To be frank, I do not think the emergency has arisen to call for the surrender of this army; but as the restoration of peace should be the sole object of all, I desired to know whether your proposals would lead to that end. I cannot, therefore, meet you with a view to surrender the Army of Northern Virginia; but as far as your proposal may affect the Confederate States forces under my command, and tend to the restoration of peace, I should be pleased to meet you at 10 A.M. to-morrow, on the old stage road to Richmond between the picket lines of the two armies.

Grant was not to be entrapped into a futile negotiation for the restoration of peace. He doubtless had in view the President's peremptory instructions of the 3d of March, forbidding him to engage in any political discussion or conference, or to entertain any proposition except for the surrender of armies. He therefore answered General Lee on the morning of the 9th of April with perfect courtesy, but with unmistakable frankness, saying: "I have no authority to treat on the subject of peace. The meeting proposed for 10 A.M. to-day could lead to no good. I will state, however, General, that I am equally anxious for peace with yourself, and the whole North entertains the same feeling. The terms upon which peace can be had are well understood. By the South laying down their arms they will hasten that most desirable event, save thousands of human lives and hundreds of millions of property not yet destroyed. Seriously hoping that all our difficulties may be settled without the loss of another life, I subscribe myself, etc." He dispatched this letter to Lee and then set off to the left, where Sheridan was barring Lee's last avenue of escape.

It appears from General Lee's report, made three days after the surrender, that he had no intention on the night of the 8th of giving up the fight. He ordered Fitz Lee, supported by Gor-

don, in the morning "to drive the enemy from his front, wheel
to the left and cover the passage of trains, while Longstreet
. . . should close up and hold the position." He expected to find
only cavalry on the ground, and thought even his remnant of
infantry could break through Sheridan's horse while he himself was amusing Grant with platonic discussions in the rear.
But he received, on arriving at the rendezvous he had suggested,
not only Grant's stern refusal to enter into a political negotiation, but other intelligence which was to him the trump of doom.
Ord and Griffin had made an almost incredible march of about
thirty miles during the preceding day and night, and had come
up at daylight to the post assigned them in support of Sheridan;
and when Fitzhugh Lee and Gordon made their advance in the
morning and the National cavalry fell slowly back, in obedience
to their orders, there suddenly appeared before the amazed
Confederates a formidable force of infantry filling the road,
covering the adjacent hills and valley, and barring as with
an adamantine wall the further progress of the army of the
revolt. The marching of the Confederate army was over forever.

The appalling tidings were instantly carried to Lee. He at
once sent orders to cease hostilities, and, suddenly brought to
a sense of his real situation, sent a note to Grant, asking an interview in accordance with the offer contained in Grant's letter
of the 8th for the surrender of his army. Grant had created the
emergency calling for such action. As Sheridan was about to
charge on the huddled mass of astonished horse and foot in
front of him a flag of truce was displayed, and the war was at an
end. The Army of Northern Virginia was already captured.
"I've got 'em, like that!" cried Sheridan, doubling up his fist,
fearful of some ruse or evasion in the white flag. The Army of
the Potomac on the north and east, Sheridan and Ord on the
south and west, completely encircled the demoralized and
crumbled army of Lee. There was not another day's fighting in
them. That morning at three o'clock Gordon had sent word to
Lee that he had fought his corps "to a frazzle," and could do
nothing more unless heavily supported by Longstreet. Lee and

his army were prisoners of war before he and Grant met at Appomattox.

The meeting took place at the house of Wilmer McLean, in the edge of the village. Lee met Grant at the threshold, and ushered him into a small and barely furnished parlor, where were soon assembled the leading officers of the National army. General Lee was accompanied only by his secretary, Colonel Charles Marshall. A short conversation led up to a request from Lee for the terms on which the surrender of his army would be received. Grant briefly stated the terms which would be accorded. Lee acceded to them, and Grant wrote the following letter:

In accordance with the substance of my letter to you of the 8th inst., I propose to receive the surrender of the Army of Northern Virginia on the following terms, to wit: Rolls of all the officers and men to be made in duplicate; one copy to be given to an officer designated by me, the other to be retained by such officer or officers as you may designate. The officers to give their individual paroles not to take up arms against the Government of the United States until properly exchanged; and each company or regimental commander sign a like parole for the men of their commands. The arms, artillery, and public property to be parked and stacked, and turned over to the officer appointed by me to receive them. This will not embrace the side-arms of the officers, nor their private horses or baggage. This done, each officer and man will be allowed to return to their homes, not to be disturbed by United States authority so long as they observe their parole and the laws in force where they may reside.

General Grant says in his "Memoirs" that up to the moment when he put pen to paper he had not thought of a word that he should write. The terms he had verbally proposed, and which Lee had accepted, were soon put in writing, and there he might have stopped. But as he wrote, a feeling of sympathy for his gallant antagonist gradually came over him, and he added the extremely liberal terms with which his letter closed. The sight of Lee's sword, an especially fine one, suggested the paragraph allowing officers to retain their side-arms; and he ended with a phrase which he had evidently not thought of, and for which he had no authority, which practically pardoned and amnestied every man in Lee's army—a thing he had refused to consider the day before, and which had been expressly forbidden him in President Lincoln's order of the 3d of March. Yet so great was the joy over the crowning victory, so deep was the gratitude of the Government and the people to Grant and his heroic army, that his terms were accepted as he wrote them, and his exercise of the Executive prerogative of pardon entirely overlooked. It must be noticed here, however, as a few days later it led the greatest of Grant's generals into a serious error.

Lee must have read the memorandum of terms with as much surprise as gratification. He said the permission for officers to retain their side-arms would have a happy effect. He then suggested and gained another important concession — that those of the cavalry and artillery who owned their own horses should be allowed to take them home to put in their crops. Lee wrote a brief reply accepting the terms. He then remarked that his army was in a starving condition, and asked Grant to provide them with subsistence and forage, to which he at once assented, and asked for how many men the rations would be wanted. Lee answered, "About twenty-five thousand," and orders were at once given to issue them. The number surrendered turned out to be even larger than this. The paroles signed amounted to 28,231. If we add to this the captures at Five Forks, Petersburg, and Sailor's Creek, the thousands who deserted the failing cause at every by-road leading to their homes, and filled every wood and thicket between Richmond and Lynchburg, we can see how considerable an army Lee commanded when Grant "started out gunning." Yet every Confederate writer, speaker, and singer who refers to the surrender says, and will say forever, that Lee surrendered only seven thousand muskets.

With these brief and simple formalities one of the most momentous transactions of modern times was concluded. The news soon transpired, and the Union gunners prepared to fire a National salute; but Grant would not permit it. He forbade any rejoicing over a fallen enemy, who he hoped would hereafter be an enemy no longer. The next day he rode to the Confederate lines to make a visit of farewell to General Lee. Sitting on horseback between the lines, the two heroes of the war held a friendly conversation. Lee considered the war at an end, slavery dead, the National authority restored; Johnston must now surrender—the sooner the better. Grant urged him to make a public appeal to hasten the return of peace; but Lee, true to his ideas of subordination to a government which had ceased to exist, said he could not do this without consulting the Confederate President. They parted with courteous good wishes, and Grant, without pausing to look at the city he had taken or the enormous system of works which had so long held him at bay, intent only upon reaping the peaceful results of his colossal victory, and putting an end to the waste and the burden of war, hurried away to Washington to do what he could for this practical and beneficent purpose. He had done an inestimable service to the Republic; he had won immortal honor for himself; but neither then nor at any subsequent period of his life was there any sign in his words or his bearing of the least touch of vainglory. The day after Appomattox he was as simple, modest, and unassuming a citizen as he was the day before Sumter.

FIVE DAYS *after Appomattox, as all the world knows,
John Wilkes Booth shot Abraham Lincoln. On April
17, the day news of the tragedy reached North Carolina, Sherman and Johnston met to bring their part
of the war to an end. Sherman extended terms so
generous, and so far beyond his authority, that the
War Department summarily rejected them. The two
men met again, and on April 26 Johnston surrendered
on practically the same terms Lee had accepted for
the Army of Northern Virginia. On May 10 Jefferson Davis, who still wanted to prolong the war, was
captured in Georgia.*

But the end came raggedly.

The End of Rebellion

IN the early years of the war, after every considerable success
of the national arms, the newspapers were in the habit of announcing that "the back of the rebellion was broken." But at
last the time came when the phrase was true; after Appomattox,
the rebellion fell to pieces all at once, Lee surrendered less
than one-sixth of the Confederates in arms on the 9th of April;
the armies that still remained to them, though inconsiderable
when compared with the mighty host under the national colors,
were yet infinitely larger than any Washington had commanded, and were capable of strenuous resistance and of incalculable mischief. Leading minds on both sides thought the war
might be indefinitely prolonged. We have seen that Jefferson
Davis, after Richmond fell, issued his swelling manifesto, saying the Confederates had "now entered upon a new phase of
the struggle," and that he would "never consent to abandon
to the enemy one foot of the soil of any of the States of the
Confederacy." General Sherman, so late as the 25th of April,
said, "I now apprehend that the rebel armies will disperse;
and instead of dealing with six or seven States, we will have to
deal with numberless bands of desperadoes." Neither side comprehended fully the intense weariness of war that had taken

possession of the South; and peace came more swiftly and completely than any one had ever dared to hope.

The march of Sherman from Atlanta to the sea and his northward progress through the Carolinas had predisposed the great interior region to make an end of strife, a tendency which was greatly promoted by Wilson's energetic and masterly raid. The rough usage received by Taylor and by Forrest at his hands, and the blow their dignity suffered in the chase of their fugitive President, made their surrender more practicable. An officer of Taylor's staff came to Canby's headquarters on the 19th of April to make arrangements for the surrender of all the Confederate forces east of the Mississippi not already paroled by Sherman and by Wilson—embracing some 42,000 men. On the 4th of May the terms were agreed upon and signed at the village of Citronelle in Alabama. General Taylor gives a picturesque incident of his meeting with General Canby. The Union officers invited the Confederates to a luncheon, and while the latter were enjoying a menu to which they had long been unaccustomed, the military band in attendance began playing "Hail, Columbia." Canby—with a courtesy, Taylor says, equal to anything recorded by Froissart—excused himself, and walked to the door; the music ceased for a moment, and then the air of "Dixie" was heard. The Confederates, not to be left in arrears of good-breeding, then demanded the national air, and the flag of the reunited country was toasted by both sides. The terms agreed upon were those accorded by Grant to Lee, with slight changes of detail, the United States Government furnishing transportation and subsistence on the way home to the men lately engaged in the effort to destroy it. The Confederates willingly testify to the cordial generosity with which they were treated. "Public property," says General Taylor, "was turned over and receipted for, and this as orderly and quickly as in time of peace between officers of the same service." At the same time and place the Confederate commodore Ebenezer Farrand surrendered to Rear-Admiral Henry K. Thatcher all the naval forces of the Confederacy in the neighborhood of Mobile—a dozen vessels and some hundreds of officers.

General E. Kirby Smith commanded all the insurgent forces west of the Mississippi. On him the desperate hopes of Mr. Davis and his flying Cabinet were fixed, after the successive surrenders of Lee and Johnston had left them no prospect in the East. They imagined they could move westward, gathering up stragglers as they fled, and, crossing the river, could join Smith's forces, and "form an army, which in that portion of the country, abounding in supplies and deficient in rivers and railroads, could have continued the war . . ." "To this hope," adds Mr. Davis, "I persistently clung." Smith, on the 21st of April, called upon his soldiers to continue the fight. "You possess the means of long resisting invasion. You have hopes of succor from abroad . . . The great resources of this department, its vast extent, the numbers, the discipline, and the efficiency of the army, will secure to our country terms that a proud people can with honor accept, and may, under the providence of God, be the means of checking the triumph of our enemy and securing the final success of our cause."

The attitude of Smith seemed so threatening that Sheridan was sent from Washington to bring him to reason. But he did not long hold his position of solitary defiance. One more needless skirmish took place near Brazos, and then Smith followed the example of Taylor, and surrendered his entire force, some eighteen thousand, to General Canby, on the 26th of May. The same generous terms were accorded him that had been given to Taylor—the Government fed his troops and carried them to their homes.

Meanwhile, General Wilson had been paroling many thousands of prisoners, who wandered in straggling parties within the limits of his command. One hundred and seventy-five thousand men in all were surrendered by the different Confederate commanders, and there were, in addition to these, about 99,000 prisoners in national custody during the year; one-third of these were exchanged and two-thirds released. This was done as rapidly as possible, by successive orders of the War Department, beginning on the 9th of May and continuing through the summer.

The first object of the Government was to stop the waste of war. Recruiting ceased immediately after Lee's surrender; the purchase of arms and supplies was curtailed, and measures were taken to reduce as promptly as possible the vast military establishment. It had grown during the last few months to portentous dimensions. The impression that a great and final victory was near at hand, the stimulus of the national hope, the prospect of a brief and prosperous campaign, had brought the army up to the magnificent complement of a million men. The reduction of this vast armament, the retrenchment of the enormous expenses incident to it, were immediately undertaken with a method and despatch which were the result of four years' thorough and practical training, and which would have been impossible under any other circumstances. Every chief of bureau was ordered, on the 28th of April, to proceed at once to the reduction of expenses in his department to a peace footing, and this before Taylor or Smith had surrendered, and while Jefferson Davis was still at large. The transportation department gave up the railroads of the South to their owners, mainly in better condition than that in which they had been received. They began without delay to sell the immense accumulation of draught animals; eight million dollars were realized from that source within the year. The other departments also disposed of their surplus stores. The stupendous difference which the close of the war at once caused in the finances of the country may be seen in the fact that the appropriations for the army in the fiscal year succeeding the war were $33,-814,461 as against $516,240,131 for the preceding year. The army of a million men was brought down, with incredible ease and celerity, to one of twenty-five thousand.

Before the great army melted away into the greater body of citizens the soldiers enjoyed one final triumph, a march through the capital, undisturbed by death or danger, under the eyes of their highest commanders, military and civilian, and the representatives of the people whose nationality they had saved. The Army of the Potomac and the army of Sherman—such corps of them as were stationed within reach, waiting their discharge—were ordered to pass in review before General Grant and President Johnson, in front of the Executive Mansion, on the 23d and 24th of May. Those who witnessed this solemn yet joyous pageant will never forget it, and will pray that their children may never witness anything like it. For two whole days this formidable host, eight times the number of the entire peace establishment, marched the long stretch of Pennsylvania Avenue, starting from the shadow of the dome of the Capitol, and filling that wide thoroughfare to Georgetown with their serried mass, moving with the easy, yet rapid pace of veterans in cadence step. On a platform in front of the White House stood the President and all the first officers of the state, the judges of the highest court, the most eminent generals and admirals of the army and the navy. The weather, on both days, was the finest a Washington May could afford; the trees of Lafayette Square were leafing out in their strong and delicate verdure.

The Army of the Potomac, which for four years had been the living bulwark of the capital, was rightly given the precedence. Meade himself rode at the head of his column, then came the cavalry headed by Merritt—Sheridan having already started for his new command in the Southwest. Custer, commanding the Third Division, had an opportunity of displaying his splendid horsemanship, as his charger, excited beyond control by the pomp and martial music, bolted near the Treasury, and dashed with the speed of the wind past the reviewing stand, but was soon mastered by the young general, who was greeted with stormy applause as he rode gravely by the second time, covered with garlands of flowers, the gifts of friends on the pavement. The same graceful guerdon was given all the leading commanders; even subalterns and hundreds of private soldiers marched decked with these fragrant offerings. The three infantry corps, the Ninth under Parke, the Fifth,

under Griffin,—though Warren was on the stand, hailed with
tumultuous cheers by his soldiers,—and the Second, under
Humphreys, moved swiftly forward. Wright, with the Sixth,
was too far away to join in the day's parade. The memory of
hundreds of hard-fought battles, of saddening defeats and
glorious victories, of the dead and maimed comrades who had
fallen forever out of the thinned ranks, was present to every one
who saw the veteran divisions marching by under the charge
of generals who had served with them in every vicissitude of
battle and siege—trained officers like Crook and Ayres, and
young and brilliant soldiers who had risen like rockets from
among the volunteers, such as Barlow and Miles. Every brigade
had its days of immortal prowess to boast, every tattered guidon
had its history.

On the 24th Sherman's army marched in review. The general
rode in person at the head of his troops, and was received by
the dense multitude that thronged the avenue with a tumult of
rapturous plaudits which might have assured him of the peculiar place he was to hold thereafter in the hearts of his fellow-
citizens. He and his horse were loaded with flowers; and his
principal commanders were not neglected. Howard had just
been appointed chief of the Freedmen's Bureau, and therefore
Logan commanded the right wing of the Army of the Tennessee,
the place he had hoped for, and, his friends insist, deserved,
when McPherson fell; Hazen had succeeded to the Fifteenth
Corps, and Frank Blair, a chivalrous and martial figure, rode
at the head of the Seventeenth. Slocum led the left wing,—
the Army of Georgia,—consisting of the Twentieth Corps under
Mower, and the Fourteenth under J. C. Davis. The armies of
Meade and Sherman were not exclusively from the East and
West respectively; for Sherman had the contingent which
Hooker and Howard had brought to Chattanooga from the
East; and there were regiments from as far West as Wisconsin
and Minnesota in the Army of the Potomac. But Sherman's
troops were to all intents and purposes Western men, and they
were scanned with keen and hospitable interest by the vast

crowd of spectators, who were mainly from the East. There
was little to choose between the two armies; a trifle more neat-
ness and discipline, perhaps, among the veterans of Meade;
a slight preponderance in physique and in swinging vigor of
march among the Westerners; but the trivial differences were
lost in the immense and evident likeness, as of brothers in one
family. There was a touch of the grotesque in the march of
Sherman's legions which was absent from the well-ordered
corps of Meade. A small squad of bummers followed each brigade, in their characteristic garb and accessories; small don-
keys loaded with queer spoils; goats and game cocks, regimental pets, sitting gravely on the backs of mules; and picka-
ninnies, the adopted children of companies, showed their black
faces between the ranks, their eyes and teeth gleaming with
delight.

As a mere spectacle, this march of the mightiest host the
continent has ever seen gathered together was grand and imposing, but it was not as a spectacle alone that it affected the
beholder most deeply. It was not a mere holiday parade; it
was an army of citizens on their way home after a long and
terrible war. Their clothes were worn with toilsome marches
and pierced with bullets; their banners had been torn with
shot and shell and lashed in the winds of a thousand battles;
the very drums and fifes that played the ruffles as each battalion
passed the President had called out the troops to numberless
night alarms, had sounded the onset at Vicksburg and Antietam, had inspired the wasted valor of Kenesaw and Fredericksburg, had throbbed with the electric pulse of victory at Chattanooga and Five Forks. The whole country claimed these
heroes as a part of themselves, an infinite gratification forever
to the national self-love; and the thoughtful diplomatists who
looked on the scene from the reviewing stand could not help
seeing that there was a conservative force in an intelligent
democracy which the world had never before known.

With all the shouting and the laughter and the joy of this
unprecedented ceremony there was one sad and dominant

thought which could not be driven from the minds of those who saw it—that of the men who were absent, and who had, nevertheless, richly earned the right to be there. The soldiers, in their shrunken companies, were conscious of the ever-present memories of the brave comrades who had fallen by the way; and in the whole army there was the passionate and unavailing regret that their wise, gentle, and powerful friend, Abraham Lincoln, was gone forever from the house by the avenue, where their loyal votes, supporting their loyal bayonets, had contributed so much to place him.

The world has had many lessons to learn from this great war: the naval fight in Hampton Roads opened a new era in maritime warfare; the marches of Sherman disturbed all previous axioms of logistics; the system of instantaneous intrenchments, adopted by the soldiers of both sides in the latter part of the war, changed the whole character of modern field tactics. But the greatest of all the lessons afforded to humanity by the Titanic struggle in which the American Republic saved its life is the manner in which its armies were levied, and, when the occasion for their employment was over, were dismissed. Though there were periods when recruiting was slow and expensive, yet there were others, when some crying necessity for troops was apparent, that showed almost incredible speed and efficiency in the supply of men. Mr. Stanton, in his report for 1865, says: "After the disasters on the Peninsula, in 1862, over 80,000 troops were enlisted, organized, armed, equipped, and sent into the field in less than a month. Sixty thousand troops have repeatedly gone to the field within four weeks; and 90,000 infantry were sent to the armies from the five States of Ohio, Indiana, Illinois, Iowa, and Wisconsin within twenty days."

This certainly shows a wealth of resources nothing less than imperial, and a power of commanding the physical and moral forces of the nation which has rarely been paralleled. Even more important, by way of instruction and example, was the lesson given the nations by the quick and noiseless dispersion of the enormous host when the war was done. The best friends of the Republic in Europe feared for it in this crisis, and those who disbelieved in the conservative power of democracy were loud in their prophecies of the trouble which would arise on the attempt to disband the army. A million men, with arms in their hands, flushed with intoxicating victory, led by officers schooled in battle, loved and trusted—were they not ready for any adventure? Was it reasonable to believe that they would consent to disband and go to work again at the bidding of a few men in black coats at Washington? Especially after Lincoln was dead, could the tailor from Tennessee direct these myriads of warriors to lay down their arms and melt away into the everyday life of citizens? In America there was no anxiety on this score among the friends of the Union. Without giving the subject a thought they knew there was no danger. The war had been made to execute the laws and to save the national existence, and when those objects were attained there was no thought among the soldiers, from the general to the humblest file-closer, but to wait for the expected orders from the civil authorities for their disbandment.

The orders came as a mere matter of course, and were executed with a thoroughness and rapidity which then seemed also a matter of course, but which will appear more and more wonderful to succeeding generations. The muster-out began on the 29th of April, before Lincoln was borne to his grave, before Davis was caught, before the rebels of the trans-Mississippi had ceased uttering their boasts of eternal defiance. First the new recruits, next the veterans whose terms were nearly expired, next those expensive corps the cavalry and artillery, and so on in regular order. Sherman's laurel-crowned army was the first to complete its muster-out, and the heroic Army of the Potomac was not far behind it. These veterans of hundreds of battlefields were soon found mingled in all the pursuits of civic activity. By the 7th of August 641,000 troops had become citizens; by the middle of November over 800,000 had been mustered out—without a fancy in any mind that there was anything else to do.

The Navy Department had not waited for the return of peace to begin the reduction of expenses. As soon as Fort Fisher fell the retrenchment began, and before Grant started on his last campaign considerable progress had been made in that direction. By the 1st of May the squadrons were reduced one-half, and in July but thirty steamers comprised the entire blockading squadron on the Atlantic and the Gulf. The Potomac and Mississippi flotillas were wholly discontinued in another month. When Mr. Welles made his annual report, in December, he could say: "There were in the several blockading squadrons in January last, exclusive of other duty, 471 vessels and 2455 guns. There are now but 29 vessels remaining on the coast, carrying 210 guns, exclusive of howitzers." Superfluous vessels were sold by hundreds and the money covered into the Treasury; thousands of the officers and sailors who had patriotically left the merchant service to fight under the national flag went back to the pursuits of peace.

For the purposes of pacification and the reëstablishment of the national authority the country was divided into five grand divisions—that of the Atlantic, commanded by Meade; the Mississippi, by Sherman; the Gulf, by Sheridan; the Tennessee, by Thomas; and the Pacific, by Halleck. These again were subdivided into nineteen departments, and we print here the names of the generals commanding them for the last time, as a roll of the men who survived the war, most favored by fortune and their own merits: Hooker, Hancock, Augur, Ord, Stoneman, Palmer (J. M.), Pope, Terry, Schofield, Sickles, Steedman, Foster (J. G.), Wood (T. J.), Wood (R. C.), Canby, Wright, Reynolds (J. J.), Steele, McDowell. The success or failure of these soldiers in administering the trust confided to them, their relations to the people among whom they were stationed, and to the President who succeeded to the vacant chair of Lincoln, form no part of the story we have attempted to tell.

On the 13th of June the President proclaimed the insurrection at an end in the State of Tennessee; it was not until the second day of April, 1866, that he proclaimed a state of peace. as existing in the rest of the United States, and then he excepted the State of Texas; on the 20th of August, in the same year, he made his final proclamation, announcing the reëstablishment of the national authority in Texas, and thereupon he concluded, "I do further proclaim that the said insurrection is at an end, and that peace, order, tranquillity, and civil authority now exist in and throughout the whole of the United States of America."

Thus the war ended. The carnage and the waste of it had surpassed the darkest forebodings, the most reckless prophecies. On the Union side 2,200,000 men had enlisted; on the Confederate, about 1,000,000. Of these 110,000 Union soldiers were killed or mortally wounded in battle; a quarter of a million died of other causes. The total of deaths by the war on the Northern side amounted to 360,282. The number of the Confederate dead cannot be accurately ascertained; it ranges between 250,-000 and 300,000. The expense of the war to the Union, over and above the ordinary expenses of the government, was about $3,250,000,000; to the Confederacy less than half that amount, about $1,500,000,000.

It seems a disheartening paradox to the lovers of peace that all this homicide and spoil gave only a new impulse to the growth and the wealth of the nation. We have seen how the quick eye of Lincoln recognized the fact, on the very night of election, that the voting strength of the country was greater in 1864 than it had been in 1860, and the census of 1870 showed a prodigious advance in prosperity and population. The 31,443,-321 of 1860 had in the ten troubled years of war and reconstruction increased to 38,558,371; and the wealth of the country had waxed in an astonishing proportion, from $16,159,616,068 to $30,068,518,507. Even the reconquered States shared in this enormous progress.

APPROPRIATELY, *Nicolay and Hay concluded their massive work with an appraisal of Lincoln's place in history.*

Lincoln's Fame

IT WAS among the common people of the entire civilized world that the most genuine and spontaneous manifestations of sorrow and appreciation were produced, and to this fact we attribute the sudden and solid foundation of Lincoln's fame. It requires years, perhaps centuries, to build the structure of a reputation which rests upon the opinion of those distinguished for learning or intelligence; the progress of opinion from the few to the many is slow and painful. But in the case of Lincoln the many imposed their opinion all at once; he was canonized, as he lay on his bier, by the irresistible decree of countless millions. The greater part of the aristocracy of England thought little of him, but the burst of grief from the English people silenced in an instant every discordant voice. It would have been as imprudent to speak slightingly of him in London as it was in New York. Especially among the Dissenters was honor and reverence shown to his name. The humbler people instinctively felt that their order had lost its wisest champion.

Not only among those of Saxon blood was this outburst of emotion seen. In France a national manifestation took place which the Government disliked, but did not think it wise to suppress. The students of Paris marched in a body to the American Legation to express their sympathy. A two-cent subscription was started to strike a massive gold medal; the money was soon raised, but the committee was forced to have the work done in Switzerland. A committee of French Liberals brought the medal to the American minister, to be sent to Mrs. Lincoln. "Tell her," said Eugène Pelletan, "the heart of France is in that little box." The inscription had a double sense; while honoring the dead Republican, it struck at the Empire. "Lincoln—the Honest Man; abolished slavery, reëstablished the Union; Saved the Republic, without veiling the Statue of Liberty." Everywhere on the Continent the same swift apotheosis of the people's hero was seen. An Austrian deputy said to the writer, "Among my people his memory has already assumed superhuman proportions; he has become a myth, a type of ideal democracy." Almost before the earth closed over him he began to be the subject of fable. The Freemasons of Europe generally regard him as one of them—his portrait in Masonic garb is often displayed; yet he was not one of that brotherhood. The Spiritualists claim him as their most illustrious adept, but he was not a Spiritualist; and there is hardly a sect in the Western world, from the Calvinist to the atheist, but affects to believe he was of their opinion.

A collection of the expressions of sympathy and condolence which came to Washington from foreign governments, associations, and public bodies of all sorts was made by the State Department, and afterwards published by order of Congress. It forms a large quarto of a thousand pages, and embraces the utterances of grief and regret from every country under the sun, in almost every language spoken by man.

But admired and venerated as he was in Europe, he was best understood and appreciated at home. It is not to be denied that in his case, as in that of all heroic personages who occupy a great place in history, a certain element of legend mingles with his righteous fame. He was a man, in fact, especially liable to legend. We have been told by farmers in Central Illinois that the brown thrush did not sing for a year after he died. He was gentle and merciful, and therefore he seems in a certain class of annals to have passed all his time in soothing misfortune and pardoning crime. He had more than his share of the shrewd native humor, and therefore the loose jest-books of two centuries have been ransacked for anecdotes to be attributed to him. He was a great and powerful lover of mankind, especially of those not favored by fortune. One night he had a dream, which he repeated the next morning to the writer of these lines, which

quaintly illustrates his unpretending and kindly democracy.
He was in some great assembly; the people made a lane to
let him pass. "He is a common-looking fellow," some one said.
Lincoln in his dream turned to his critic and replied, in his
Quaker phrase, "Friend, the Lord prefers common-looking
people: that is why he made so many of them." He that abases
himself shall be exalted. Because Lincoln kept himself in such
constant sympathy with the common people, whom he respected too highly to flatter or mislead, he was rewarded by
a reverence and a love hardly ever given to a human being.
Among the humble working people of the South whom he had
made free, this veneration and affection easily passed into
the supernatural. At a religious meeting among the negroes
of the Sea Islands a young man expressed the wish that he might
see Lincoln. A gray-headed negro rebuked the rash aspiration:
"No man see Linkum. Linkum walk as Jesus walk—no man see
Linkum."

But leaving aside these fables, which are a natural enough
expression of a popular awe and love, it seems to us no more
just estimate of Lincoln's relation to his time has ever been
made—nor perhaps ever will be—than that uttered by one of
the wisest and most American of thinkers, Ralph Waldo Emerson, a few days after the assassination. We cannot forbear
quoting a few words of this remarkable discourse, which shows
how Lincoln seemed to the greatest of his contemporaries:

A plain man of the people, an extraordinary fortune attended him. Lord Bacon says, "Manifest virtues procure reputation; occult ones fortune." . . . His occupying the chair of
state was a triumph of the good sense of mankind and of the
public conscience. . . . He grew according to the need; his mind
mastered the problem of the day; and as the problem grew,
so did his comprehension of it. Rarely was a man so fitted to
the event. . . . It cannot be said that there is any exaggeration
of his worth. If ever a man was fairly tested, he was. There
was no lack of resistance, nor of slander, nor of ridicule. . . .
Then what an occasion was the whirlwind of the war! Here
was no place for holiday magistrate, nor fair-weather sailor;

the new pilot was hurried to the helm in a tornado. In four years—four years of battle-days—his endurance, his fertility of resources, his magnanimity, were sorely tried and never found wanting. There by his courage, his justice, his even temper, his fertile counsel, his humanity, he stood a heroic figure in the center of a heroic epoch. He is the true history of the American people in his time; the true representative of this continent—father of his country, the pulse of twenty millions throbbing in his heart, the thought of their minds articulated by his tongue.

The quick instinct by which the world recognized him, even at the moment of his death, as one of the greatest men, was not deceived. It has been confirmed by the sober thought of a quarter of a century. The writers of each nation compare him with their first popular hero. The French find points of resemblance in him to Henry IV.; the Dutch liken him to William of Orange; the cruel stroke of murder and treason by which all three perished in the height of their power naturally suggests the comparison, which is strangely justified in both cases, though the two princes were so widely different in character. Lincoln had the wit, the bonhomie, the keen, practical insight into affairs of the Béarnais; and the tyrannous moral sense, the wide comprehension, the heroic patience of the Dutch patriot, whose motto might have served equally well for the American President—*Sævis tranquillus in undis.* European historians speak of him in words reserved for the most illustrious names. Merle d'Aubigné says, "The name of Lincoln will remain one of the greatest that history has to inscribe on its annals." Henri Martin predicts nothing less than a universal apotheosis: "This man will stand out in the traditions of his country and the world as an incarnation of the people, and of modern democracy itself." Emilio Castelar, in an oration against slavery in the Spanish Cortes, called him "humblest of the humble before his conscience, greatest of the great before history."

In this country, where millions still live who were his contemporaries, and thousands who knew him personally, where the envies and jealousies which dog the footsteps of success still linger in the hearts of a few, where journals still exist that loaded his name for four years with daily calumny, and writers of memoirs vainly try to make themselves important by belittling him, his fame has become as universal as the air, as deeply rooted as the hills. The faint discords are not heard in the wide chorus that hails him second to none and equaled by Washington alone. The eulogies of him form a special literature. Preachers, poets, soldiers, and statesmen employ the same phrases of unconditional love and reverence. Men speaking with the authority of fame use unqualified superlatives. Lowell, in an immortal ode, calls him "New birth of our new soil, the first American." General Sherman says, "Of all the men I ever met, he seemed to possess more of the elements of greatness, combined with goodness, than any other." General Grant, after having met the rulers of almost every civilized country on earth, said Lincoln impressed him as the greatest intellectual force with which he had ever come in contact.

He is spoken of, with scarcely less of enthusiasm, by the more generous and liberal spirits among those who revolted against his election and were vanquished by his power. General Longstreet calls him "the greatest man of rebellion times, the one matchless among forty millions for the peculiar difficulties of the period." An eminent Southern orator, referring to our mixed Northern and Southern ancestry, says: "From the union of those colonists, from the straightening of their purposes and the crossing of their blood, slowly perfecting through a century, came he who stands as the first typical American, the first who comprehended within himself all the strength and gentleness, all the majesty and grace of this republic—Abraham Lincoln."

It is not difficult to perceive the basis of this sudden and world-wide fame, nor rash to predict its indefinite duration. There are two classes of men whose names are more enduring than any monument—the great writers; and the men of great achievement, the founders of states, the conquerors. Lincoln has the singular fortune to belong to both these categories; upon these broad and stable foundations his renown is securely built. Nothing would have more amazed him while he lived than to hear himself called a man of letters; but this age has produced few greater writers. We are only recording here the judgment of his peers. Emerson ranks him with Æsop and Pilpay in his lighter moods, and says: "The weight and penetration of many passages in his letters, messages, and speeches, hidden now by the very closeness of their application to the moment, are destined to a wide fame. What pregnant definitions, what unerring common-sense, what foresight, and on great occasions what lofty, and more than national, what human tone! His brief speech at Gettysburg will not easily be surpassed by words on any recorded occasion."

His style extorted the high praise of French Academicians; Montalembert commended it as a model for the imitation of princes. Many of his phrases form part of the common speech of mankind. It is true that in his writings the range of subjects is not great; he is concerned chiefly with the political problems of the time, and the moral considerations involved in them. But the range of treatment is remarkably wide; it runs from the wit, the gay humor, the florid eloquence of his stump speeches to the marvelous sententiousness and brevity of the letter to Greeley and the address at Gettysburg, and the sustained and lofty grandeur of the Second Inaugural.

The more his writings are studied in connection with the important transactions of his age the higher will his reputation stand in the opinion of the lettered class. But the men of study and research are never numerous; and it is principally as a man of action that the world at large will regard him. It is the story of his objective life that will forever touch and hold the heart of mankind. His birthright was privation and ignorance—not peculiar to his family, but the universal environment of his place and time; he burst through those enchaining conditions by the force of native genius and will; vice had no temptation for him; his course was as naturally upward as the skylark's;

he won, against all conceivable obstacles, a high place in an exacting profession and an honorable position in public and private life; he became the foremost representative of a party founded on an uprising of the national conscience against a secular wrong, and thus came to the awful responsibilities of power in a time of terror and gloom. He met them with incomparable strength and virtue. Caring for nothing but the public good, free from envy or jealous fears, he surrounded himself with the leading men of his party, his most formidable rivals in public esteem, and through four years of stupendous difficulties he was head and shoulders above them all in the vital qualities of wisdom, foresight, knowledge of men, and thorough comprehension of measures. Personally opposed, as the radicals claim, by more than half of his own party in Congress, and bitterly denounced and maligned by his open adversaries, he yet bore himself with such extraordinary discretion and skill, that he obtained for the Government all the legislation it required, and so impressed himself upon the national mind that without personal effort or solicitation he became the only possible candidate of his party for reëlection, and was chosen by almost unanimous vote of the Electoral Colleges.

His qualities would have rendered his administration illustrious even in time of peace; but when we consider that in addition to the ordinary work of the executive office he was forced to assume the duties of Commander-in-Chief of the National forces engaged in the most complex and difficult war of modern times, the greatness of spirit as well as the intellectual strength he evinced in that capacity is nothing short of prodigious. After times will wonder, not at the few and unimportant mistakes he may have committed, but at the intuitive knowledge of his business that he displayed. We would not presume to express a personal opinion in this matter. We use the testimony only of the most authoritative names. General W. T. Sherman has repeatedly expressed the admiration and surprise with which he has read Mr. Lincoln's correspondence with his generals, and his opinion of the remarkable correctness of his military views. General W. F. Smith says: "I have long held to the opinion that at the close of the war Mr. Lincoln was the superior of his generals in his comprehension of the effect of strategic movements and the proper method of following up victories to their legitimate conclusions." General J. H. Wilson holds the same opinion; and Colonel Robert N. Scott, in whose lamented death the army lost one of its most vigorous and best-trained intellects, frequently called Mr. Lincoln "the ablest strategist of the war."

To these qualifications of high literary excellence, and easy practical mastery of affairs of transcendent importance, we must add, as an explanation of his immediate and world-wide fame, his possession of certain moral qualities rarely combined, in such high degree, in one individual. His heart was so tender that he would dismount from his horse in a forest to replace in their nest young birds which had fallen by the roadside; he could not sleep at night if he knew that a soldier-boy was under sentence of death; he could not, even at the bidding of duty or policy, refuse the prayer of age or helplessness in distress. Children instinctively loved him; they never found his rugged features ugly; his sympathies were quick and seemingly unlimited. He was absolutely without prejudice of class or condition. Frederick Douglass says he was the only man of distinction he ever met who never reminded him by word or manner of his color; he was as just and generous to the rich and well born as to the poor and humble—a thing rare among politicians. He was tolerant even of evil: though no man can ever have lived with a loftier scorn of meanness and selfishness, he yet recognized their existence and counted with them. He said one day, with a flash of cynical wisdom worthy of La Rochefoucauld, that honest statesmanship was the employment of individual meannesses for the public good. He never asked perfection of any one; he did not even insist, for others, upon the high standards he set up for himself. At a time before the word was invented he was the first of opportunists. With the fire of a reformer and a martyr in his heart he yet proceeded by the ways of cautious and practical statecraft. He always worked with things as they were, while never relinquishing the desire and effort to make them better. To a hope which saw the Delectable Mountains of absolute justice and peace in the future, to a faith that God in his own time would give to all men the things convenient to them, he added a charity which embraced in its deep bosom all the good and the bad, all the virtues and the infirmities of men, and a patience like that of nature, which in its vast and fruitful activity knows neither haste nor rest.

A character like this is among the precious heirlooms of the Republic; and by a special good fortune every part of the country has an equal claim and pride in it. Lincoln's blood came from the veins of New England emigrants, of Middle State Quakers, of Virginia planters, of Kentucky pioneers; he himself was one of the men who grew up with the earliest growth of the Great West. Every jewel of his mind or his conduct sheds radiance on each portion of the nation. The marvelous symmetry and balance of his intellect and character may have owed something to this varied environment of his race, and they may fitly typify the variety and solidity of the Republic. It may not be unreasonable to hope that his name and his renown may be forever a bond of union to the country which he loved with an affection so impartial, and served, in life and in death, with such entire devotion.

Bibliographical Note

Abraham Lincoln: A History was published in book form by the Century Company in 1890. It was reprinted at various times since that date, but always from the original plates. The work is no longer in print.

Index

Abolitionists; *see* Free-soil party

Aiken, William, 25

Alton, Illinois, 68–69

Amelia Court House, 355–57

Anderson, Robert, 32, 48

Antietam, Maryland: McClellan's forces at, 152, 157; effect of the battle of, 163, 173

Anti-Nebraska; *see* Free-soil party

Appomattox: attacked by W. F. Smith, 291; Confederate movements at, 359–60; provisions at, 359–60; meeting of Grant and Lee at, 364

Arkansas: sympathies of, 47; regiments from, 48, 82; admission to Confederacy, 83; and Thirteenth Amendment, 344, 349

Ashley, James M.; *see* Joint Resolution

Atlanta, 309–20, 336

Baltimore: rebel recruiting in, 50; riot in, 59, 63, 75; National Republican Convention in, 342

Banks, Nathaniel P., 25

Banks's Ford, Virginia, 176–77, 179

Bates, Edward, 70

Beauregard, G. T.: at Fort Sumter, 49, 351; at Manassas Junction, 87–88, 90; at Corinth, 115–16, 120; at Pittsburg Landing, 123–24; at Savannah, 309–10, 313

Bell, John, 28

Blackburn's Ford, Virginia, 86, 88

Blair, Francis Preston, Sr., 54–55

Blair, Montgomery, 54

Bonham, Milledge L., 36, 38

Boonsboro', 154–55

Booth, John Wilkes, 367

Bragg, Braxton: at Pittsburgh Landing, 116; and Battle of Stone's River, 217; at Chattanooga, 218–22; at Lookout Mountain, 225, 230, 232–34

Breckinridge, John Cabell, 28, 29

Brentwood Hill, Tennessee, 331

Buchanan, James, 32–40

Buckner, Simon B., 71

Buell, D. C., 115–16, 121, 123–25

Bull Run: Battle of, 85–98; Second Battle of, 152

Bunker Hill, W. Virginia, 86–87

Burnside, Ambrose E.: and McClellan, 139, 151; at Antietam, 159, 161; and Army of the Potomac, 163, 176, 188, 302; at Petersburg, 297; tactics of, 320

Butler, Benjamin F.: as administrator, 127–36, 281–82; and woman order, 132–33; as politician, 276

Cairo, Illinois, 63–67, 69–71

Calhoun, John C., 29

Cameron, Simon: and Letcher, 49; on Lee, 54; and defense of capital, 59; on emancipation, 165; and Lincoln's reëlection, 244, 258, 274

Campbell, John A., 81

Camp Dennison, Ohio, 70

Canby, E. R. S., 368, 369

Carter's Creek, Tennessee, 322

Cemetery Ridge, Pennsylvania, 194, 196–97, 299
Centreville: Confederate forces at, 85; Union forces at, 87, 90, 94, 152; Beauregard's attack on, 89
Chancellorsville, 178, 184–86
Charleston, 31–32, 39–43
Chase, Salmon Portland: and Nebraska bill, 23; and red tape, 78; and *Merrimac*, 106; and McClellan, 139; and emancipation, 168; and draft, 274; and presidential election, 276
Chattanooga, 217–33
Chicago, 64, 264–66
Chicahominy River, 290, 293, 303
Chickamauga, Battle of, 217–32
Clay, Cassius M., 60
Claybanks, 277–78
Cleburne, Patrick R., 323–25
Cobb, Howell, 81
Congress, 103–6
Connecticut, 24, 74, 349
Corinth, Mississippi, 115–17, 125, 148
Crump's Landing, Tennessee, 118, 122, 125
Cumberland, 103–4
Cumberland, Army of the; *see* Rosecrans, William Starke
Cumberland River, 326–27
Cushing, Caleb, 39–41

Dahlgren, John A., 160
Danville Road, 353–57
Davis, Henry Winter, 51, 276, 284
Davis, Jefferson: and letters of marque and reprisal, 47; and secession, 81–84; at Manassas Junction, 90; and Butler, 128–30, 133; at end of war, 352, 367–70, 375
Delaware, 50, 346
Democrats: and Missouri Compromise, 20, 25; on anti-slavery, 26; and McClellan's politics, 144; and convention of 1864, 264–67; and Thirteenth Amendment, 340–47
Dickinson, Daniel S., 258–60, 276
District of Columbia, 50
Dix, John A., 139, 141
Dixon, Archibald, 21

Douglas, Stephen A.: and Nebraska bill, 18, 23–24; as Democratic leader, 19; and senatorial election, 26; and presidential election, 28; and Scott's resignation, 58

Eads, James B., 70–71
Ellis, John W., 48
Ericsson, John, 100
Evansville, Indiana, 70

Farragut, David G.: at New Orleans, 127–30; at Fort Jackson, 137
Fayetteville arsenal, 82
Five Forks, Virginia, 352, 365
Foote, Andrew Hull, 99
Fort Donelson, 65, 99, 115
Fort Fisher, 352, 376
Fort Henry, 99
Fort Jackson, 127, 137
Fort McAllister, 315–16
Fort McComb, 127
Fort Monroe: secured for Union, 49, 52–53; and *Merrimac* reports, 99, 101–14; as path to Richmond, 102, 114, 137, 139
Fort Moultrie, 31, 37, 44
Fort Pickens, 81
Fort Pike, 127
Fort St. Philip, 127, 137
Fort Stedman, 352
Fort Sumter: Governor Pickens' request for, 33–35; attacks upon, 44, 48, 56, 351
Fort Wood, 219, 226
Fox, Gustavus V., 102, 283–84
Fox's Gap, Maryland, 156
Franklin, W. B.: strategy of, 147, 149; at Antietam, 156
Franklin, Tennessee, 322–36
Franklin Pike, Tennessee, 332
Frederick, Maryland, 153–55
Fredericksburg: attacks upon, 173, 186, 190; fords across river to, 176; roads to, 178, 185
Free-soil party, 18–22, 26
Frémont, John C., 99, 141, 253

Gaines's Mill, 137
Gainesville, Virginia, 87

Geary, John White, 221–23, 321
Gettysburg, 190–202, 203
Giddings, Joshua Reed, 23
Gist, William H., 26–29, 36
Gosport Navy Yard, 52–53, 99, 113
Granny White turnpike, Tennessee, 332–33
Grant, Ulysses Simpson: at Fort Donelson, 99, 115; at Pittsburg Landing, 115, 121–23, 125–26; at Vicksburg, 203–16; and armies of the United States, 235–42; and presidential election, 248; at Petersburg, 290–92, 295–308; and Sherman, 316–17; at Appomattox, 352, 353–66; and peace negotiations with Lee, 362; discusses Lincoln, 382
Greene, S. D., 108–9

Halleck, Henry Wagner: promotion of, 99, 148–51, 236; orders to McClellan, 140; as presidential voice, 200, 309–20; and Thomas, 328; at end of war, 376
Hampton Roads, 103, 106–14, 374
Hancock, Winfield Scott: at Chancellorsville, 179; and Richmond, 292–308
Hardee, William J.: at Shiloh, 116; at Savannah, 314, 316–18
Harney, William S., 67–68
Harper's Ferry: Confederates at, 49, 82, 153–54; Union defense of, 52–53, 95, 156
Harpeth River, 322–23
Harris, Isham G., 48, 66–67
Harrison's Landing, 137–39, 145–46
Heintzelman, Samuel P., 88–89, 147
Henderson, John B., *see* Joint Resolution
Hicks, Thomas H., 50–52, 60
Hill, Ambrose P.: at Antietam, 159, at Richmond, 304; at Appomattox, 352
Hill, Daniel H., 156
Hood, John B.: evacuates Atlanta, 264; in Tennessee, 322–36
Hooker, Joseph: under McClellan, 150, 158; at Antietam, 158, 161; and Army of the Potomac, 173–

89; at Chancellorsville, 177–89; and Lee, 190; at Lookout Mountain, 217, 220–26, 231, 234; at Atlanta, 309; and Sherman, 320–31; at Nashville, 326–35, 352
Hunter, David, 60, 88–89
Hurlbut, S. A., 117, 119, 122, 125

Illinois: enlistments in, 45; as military frontier, 64, 70–74; in presidential election, 246; and Thirteenth Amendment, 349
Indiana: enlistments in, 45, as military frontier, 70, 72, 74; in presidential election, 246; and Thirteenth Amendment, 349
Iowa, 45, 350

Jackson, T. J. (Stonewall): at Bull Run, 89; at Antietam, 156–57; attacks Hooker, 180–81; death of, 182–84
Jackson, Mississippi, 203, 205
Jackson, Tennessee, 115–16
James River: as route to Norfolk, 49; battles on, 103, 303, 305, 308; as route to Richmond, 137, 175, 290, 298; Union forces at, 139, 147–48, 354, 256
Jefferson, Thomas, 22
Johnston, Albert Sidney, 116, 119
Johnston, Joseph Eggleston: in politics, 53; in Shenandoah Valley, 86–91; 98; and Vicksburg, 204, 207; joins Lee, 354, 359; and Sherman, 367, 369
Joint Resolution, 339–47

Kansas, 18
Kentucky: troops from, 48, 82–83; as neutral, 63–64, 70–71
Know-Nothings, 21–22, 25

Lane, Henry S., 29
Lane, James H., 60–61
Lee, Robert E.: joins Confederates, 53–58; provisions for, 65; in Richmond, 137, 146, 290–97, 353; in Maryland, 153, 155, 157–60; at Chancellorsville, 182–88; at Gettysburg, 190–202; at Appomattox, 352–66; surrender of, 365–67

Leesburg, Virginia, 153

Letcher, John: as secessionist leader, 48–49; and secession ordinance, 57, 59, 81

Lincoln, Abraham: as sectional candidate, 28; calls for volunteers, 64; on seizure complaints, 66–67; on emancipation, 165–68; 171–72; analyzed by Europeans, 378–81, 383; analyzed by his generals, 382–85

Longstreet, James, 353, 358, 382

Lookout Mountain, Tennessee, 217–27

Lynchburg: seizure of powder at, 49; as rendezvous for Confederates, 82; Lee at, 357, 361, 365; Ord at, 358; Longstreet at, 359

Lyon, Nathaniel, 67–68

McClellan, George Brinton: at Cairo, 70–71; at Washington, 93–94, 105; and Richmond campaign, 137–51; and Army of the Potomac, 142, 152, 162, 173, 236; at Antietam, 157–62; nomination of, 264–65, 284, 289

McClernand, John A.: at Pittsburg Landing, 117, 119, 122, 125; at Vicksburg, 204–6

McDowell, Irvin: at Bull Run, 85–98; at Richmond, 140–41

McPherson, James B.: at Jackson, Mississippi, 203–8; Grant's letter about, 237–38; and Department of the Tennessee, 242

McQueen, John, 36, 38

Magoffin, Beriah, 48

Manassas Junction, 86–87, 89–90

Marshall, John, 43

Maryland: on secession, 50–52, 56; for defense of the capital, 60; as Confederate state, 82

Mason, James M., 59

Meade, George Gordon: and Army of the Potomac, 190–202, 371–72, 375; at Gettysburg, 190–92, 196, 198–202; at Petersburg, 294, 355; at end of war, 376

Meigs, Montgomery, 106, 149

Merrimac, 99–114

Minnesota, 103, 105–7, 111

Missionary Ridge, Tennessee, 217–33

Missouri: on secession, 48; regiments to Confederates, 82–83

Missouri Compromise, 18–22, 24

Missouri Radicals, 256–57

Monitor, 100–114

Morgan, E. D.; *see* Joint Resolution

Morton, Oliver P., 69, 70

Mumford, William B., 129–30

Nebraska bill, 18–22

Nelson, William, 124–25

New Jersey, 74

New Orleans, 127–36

Newport News, 102–3

New York Times, 78, 245

Norfolk, capture of, 49, 84; naval vessels at, 105, 109

North Carolina, 48, 82–83

Northern Virginia, Army of, 173, 190, 363–67

October States, 284

Ohio, 45, 70–72

Ohio River, 63–71, 329

Opdycke, Emerson, 324–25

Orchard Knob, Tennessee, 220, 226–31

Ord, Edward O., 206, 212, 358, 363

Ordinance of 1784, 22

Ordinance of 1787; *see* Joint Resolution

Overton's Hill, Tennessee, 331–32

Owl Creek, 116–17, 122

Patterson, Robert, 86, 91, 95, 98

Pemberton, John C., 207, 211–16

Peninsular Campaign, 101, 109, 148

Petersburg, 148, 290–94, 297–99

Pickens, F. W.: election of, 32; and President Buchanan, 33–34, 36–43; requests provisions, 65

Pickett, George Edward, 192, 195–97, 352

Pierce, Franklin, 19, 25

Pittsburg Landing, Tennessee, 117–18, 120–22, 125

Polk, James K., 19

Polk, Leonidas, 72, 116

Pope, John, 148–51, 152

Porter, David D., 127, 147, 203

Potomac, Army of the: at Battle of Bull Run, 85–98; under Mc-Clellan, 99, 138–51; 152–62; under Burnside, 173–89; as decoy at Chattanooga, 218–33; under Grant, 239–42, 290–308, 352–63; parades in Washington, 371–72; muster out of, 375–76

Prentiss, Benjamin M.: at Springfield, 46; at Cairo, 65–66; at Shiloh Church, 117–22

Rapidan River, 176

Rappahannock River, 175–77, 186–87

Republican party; *see* Free-soil party

Rice's Station, Virginia, 358

Richardson, William A., 25, 96–97

Roanoke, 103, 105

Rosecrans, William Starke: and Army of the Cumberland, 217; at Chickamauga, 227; and elections, 275

Richmond: advance upon, 99, 106, 137; McClellan's letters about, 138, 145–48; route to, 175; 291–92

Richmond and Danville railroad, 180, 290

Rock Island, Illinois, 80

St. Lawrence, 103, 105

St. Louis, 67

Salem Church, Virginia, 186

Savage's Station, Virginia, 137, 145

Savannah, 309–20

Schofield, John McAllister; and elections, 275; at Franklin, 322–29, 331, 333

Scott, Winfield: presidential nomination of, 20–21; daily reports of, 52–53; on secession, 57–59, 68; at Washington, 75, 86; strategy of, 91–97; retirement of, 99

Sedgewick, John, 177, 185

Seminary Ridge, Pennsylvania, 192–93, 198

Sewall's Point, Virginia, 105

Seward, William Henry; and ammunition, 78; and letter of intent, 80–81; and Edict of Freedom, 163, 265–66, 270–71; and Thirteenth Amendment, 350

Sharpsburg, 156–61

Sheridan, Philip Henry: at Chattanooga, 219, 228–29; promotions of, 289; at end of war, 353, 363, 376; at Amelia Court House, 356–58

Sherman, William Tecumseh: at Shiloh, 117–19, 122, 135; and McClellan, 146; at Vicksburg, 204–8; at Chattanooga, 217–18, 220–27; and Grant, 236–38; at Atlanta, 309–20; at end of war, 367, 372, 376; on Lincoln, 382, 384–85

Shiloh, Battle of, 115–26

South Carolina, 27–31, 32–43

Stanton, Edwin McMasters, 140, 240, 282, 374

Star of the West, 82

Stuart, David, 117, 120

Sudley Ford, Virginia, 87–89

Sumner, Charles, 23, 276; *see also* Joint Resolution

Swift (General), 65

Tennessee, 47–48, 82–83, 115; *see also* Bragg, Braxton

Tennessee River, 115, 120

Thomas, George Henry: at Missionary Ridge, 217; and Hood, 309, 322, 326–36, 352; at end of war, 376

Trescott, W. H., 34, 36–39

Trumbull, Lyman, 26; *see also* Joint Resolution

Turner's Gap, Maryland, 156, 162

United States Mine Ford, Virginia, 176–77

Vicksburg, 199, 203–16

Virginia: admitted to Confederacy, 64, 83; Army of, 152; on secession, 48–50, 56–62

Wagner, George D., 323–26

Walker, Leroy P., 65–66

Wallace, Lew, 118, 122, 125

Wallace, W. H. L., 118, 119, 120, 125

Warrentown turnpike, Virginia, 87–89
Whigs, 20–22, 25–26
Wilson, James F.; *see* Joint Resolution
Wilson, James H., 290
Wise, Henry A., 26, 59

Wood, Thomas J., 219–31
Woods, C. R., 309
Wool, John E., 75, 140–41
Worden, John L., 107–8

Yates, Richard, 65–68
Yorktown, 137–144